God's Word to Women

One Hundred Bible Studies
on
Woman's Place in the Church and Home

BY
KATHARINE C. BUSHNELL

"Hear the Word of the Lord, O ye women, and let your ear receive the Word of His Mouth."

"Rise up, ye women that are at ease; hear My voice, ye careless daughters. Give ear unto My speech."

Christians for Biblical Equality
122 West Franklin Ave., Ste. 218
Minneapolis, MN 55404-2451
Ph: 612-872-6898 Fax: 612-872-6891
Web site: www.cbeinternational.org
E-mail: books@cbeinternational.org

To

WOMEN OF GOD

Who, loving the praise of God more than the praise of men,

will hasten

THE COMING OF THE LORD,

by grasping His promise, and entering upon the fulfilment

of His prophecy: "In the last days, saith God,

'I will pour out of My Spirit upon all flesh, ...

Your daughters shall prophesy ... And on My handmaidens

I will pour out in those days of My Spirit, and

THEY SHALL PROPHESY.' "

———————————————

God's Word to Women:
One Hundred Bible Studies on Woman's Place in the Church and Home

Published in 2003 by Christians for Biblical Equality

ISBN 0-9743031-0-0

COVER DESIGN BY SUSIE LARSON

FOREWORD

In reading this reprint of "God's Word to Women" it will be valuable to consider seriously the "Author's Note" of introduction in which she draws attention to the undeniable inconsistencies existing between what theologians *think* Paul taught and what close examination of the original Greek (as used in his letters) reveals. Undeniably, Paul both *taught* and *acted* contrary to their interpretation of his message in regard to the female sex.

Bushnell was a scholar of both Hebrew and Greek, and when God called her to be a missionary preacher, she told God that if He would prove to her that St. Paul was not against women preaching, she would obey. The revelations of divine truth revealed in this book are the result of God anointing her "*Language Scholarship Potential*" and using it "to the praise of the glory of his grace" (Eph. 1:6). Although she was not on a man-ordained translation committee, the Lord commissioned her to reveal the glorious truth of His planned role for woman's participation in this "so great salvation" (Heb. 2:3); and this book is a "Tell It Like It Is" of God's unchanged plan for the role of the female sex in the rescue of the fallen race of the first Adam. The shameful reflections that have been cast upon the inspired ministry of St. Paul about women's ministry are clearly seen by noting the following facts:
1. The Old Testament Scriptures were all that Jesus and the early Christians had for literary authority for their message and they referred to these Scriptures many times in their teaching and preaching as is recorded many times in the four Gospels and the Epistles. In Romans 16:25, 26, Paul refers to "the Scriptures of the prophets" as the basic authority for the truth commanded of God to be preached to all nations for the obedience of faith. First Peter 1:10-12 teaches the same thing. Now notice a few things that are *attributed to Paul* teaching others: First Corinthians 14:34, 35, "Let your women keep silence in the churches: for it is not permitted unto them to speak; but they are commanded to be under obedience, as also saith the law. And if they will learn any thing, let them ask their husbands at home: for it is a shame for women to speak in the church." Also 1 Timothy 2:11, 12 is interpreted as Paul forbidding women to teach men. With the

many new translations into more modern language now being published, many of these inconsistencies are being streamlined into the *accepted traditional interpretation*, thereby strengthening error and further falsifying truth. Jeremiah 8:8 states, "How do ye say, We are wise, and the law of the Lord is with us? Lo, certainly in vain made he it." A marginal note in the King James Version states, "The false pen of the scribes hath made [of it] falsehood. Also "When Scribes with their lying pens have falsified it?" *(NEB)*. With this also note Romans 1:25 and 2 Peter 3:16.

Now let us note where *Paul's ministry contradicts this false interpretation* of both his teaching and conduct. His evangelistic ministry produced the assembly at Galatia to the extent that the miracle working power of God operated among them (Gal. 3:5). But after he left, Judaizing teachers come in and "perverted" them back into Old Testament ordinances. Paul wrote and rebuked them for their "bewitched condition" in departing from the truth (Gal. 3:1), and for his authority he quoted Genesis 21:10 which were the inspired words of Sarah (recorded in Holy Writ) to her husband, Abraham, instructing him in *what he must do to set their house in order* (and God honored her instructions and He ordered Abraham *to obey her*). Also Paul calls Phoebe deacon of the church at Cenchrea and orders the church at Rome to "*assist her* [men and all] in whatsoever business she hath need of you" (Rom. 16:2). Paul was no Scripture ignoramus, for when he was correcting the Galatians, he knew that he was quoting the words of Sarah to her husband, Abraham, as his authority to prove to them he was teaching them sound doctrine. Also he knew that there *is not one instance* recorded in the Old Testament where inspired women were divinely ordered to refrain from speaking as 1 Corinthians 14:34 would infer and as if it was a command of Paul authorized by "as also saith the law," which it was not. But it was a *requote by him* of what he had received in the letter from the spiritually reliable "House of Chloe" regarding what the Judaizing teachers were feeding the assembly at Corinth. And after he quotes it, he *immediately rebukes it*, as he remonstrates, "What? Came the word of God out from you? or came it unto you only? If any man think himself to be a prophet, or spiritual, let him acknowledge that the things that I write unto you are the commandments of the Lord (1 Cor. 14:37, 38). Satan could not cause that Judaizing teaching to succeed in Paul's day, but now he giggles as he has blinded ministers to try and silence God's ministry through the female sex of the body of Christ by changing God's truth into a lie (Rom. 1:25) and *in representing Paul as teaching* this false doctrine of the Judaizers. And as you read this book you will find that this is *only one* of the several such "sleight of men, and cunning craftiness, whereby they [ministers] lie in wait to deceive" (Eph. 4:14) in regard to God's ministry through women.

I know that Sister Bushnell at times conveys thoughts that stray from the woman ministry subject in which she expresses things that can be misleading, especially where she suggests that the first five books of the Bible could have been produced by oral history repeated down through successive generations by the overlapping lives of contemporaries of each generation and culminating in Moses writing the historical account excepting the account of his own cessation of earth ministry. Also where she suggests that the flood might have covered only the known world in Noah's day. But the Scriptures teach that God can put his Spirit upon persons and cause them to write accurately *both past and future* events as He did to the worldly ignorant Chinese children recorded in *Visions Beyond the Veil*, by H. A. Baker. Both Scripture and scientific geographical research evidence proves that a tremendous violence of water covered the *whole* world (see *The Three Worlds*, by H. A. Baker, Osterhus Publishing Company, Minneapolis, Minn.).

Nevertheless, I feel the reprint of her book is fully justified by the many important things she has clarified in respect to the misleading impression conveyed in reading the present Scripture translation of God's role for women which at the present time is being ardently discussed pro and con by Christendom, forcing Christians to decide what is really God's inspired truth about it. There is only one instance where I have deleted from the author's text, in a part of one paragraph, where I felt it could pose a problem of misunderstanding in the minds of some, but it does not in any way cancel any of the truth for which the book was written.

I want to acknowledge my indebtedness to the body of Christ for the reprinting of this book. 1. To the Lord Jesus Christ (the Head) who planned and supervised it all. 2. To the late Harry Austin of South Dayton, New York, who furnished information that led me to discover that such a book had once appeared in print (last edition was published in 1923). 3. To the prayer warriors who interceded to the throne of grace for its successful publication. 4. To those who financed the first reprinting.

May this book serve God's purpose in the lives of all whom it contacts. "The Lord giveth the word, [the women] . . . that publish the tidings are a great host" (Psa. 68:11, KJV, margin note, Oxford University Press).

Ray B. Munson

Note:
The deleted paragraph on page 243 & 244 mentioned in Ray Munson forward has been replaced in the edition.

AUTHOR'S NOTE.

"Dost thou desire to study to advantage? Consult God more than books, and ask Him humbly to make thee understand what thou readest. Go from time to time to be refreshed at the feet of Christ, under His Cross. Some moments of repose there give fresh vigour and new light: interrupt thy study by short but fervent supplications."

This is a Study Book, yet it has been our hope to make the book equally interesting for mere reading.

Having been planned as a Study Book, paragraphs are to be paid attention to, not pages; it is indexed at the back on this plan. Those who do not know Hebrew and Greek, and yet wish to test its every point, will find much help in doing this in Young's "Analytical Concordance to the Bible," especially in editions from the seventh onward, because of the valuable Index-Lexicons at the end of the volume, informing the student of the number of times any certain Greek or Hebrew word occurs in the Bible and of all its various translations.

Some years ago, Mrs. Alexander Whyte, wife of the late Principal Whyte of New College, Edinburgh, Scotland, became interested in the Lessons, and appealed to Dr. Rendel Harris for an opinion of them from his point of scholarship, or of some other able critic. Dr. Harris referred Mrs. Whyte to Dr. A. Mingana, Professor of Arabic at Manchester University, England, and Curator of Oriental Manuscripts in the John Rylands Library, which contains a wealth of such matter.

Dr. Mingana has read carefully through the Lessons of the book, and given me the benefit of his criticisms, which, for the most part, are very encouraging. In issuing this second edition, it has seemed well to add in footnotes the substance of his comments. I have not a personal acquaintance with this most obliging and helpful gentleman, but I hope that he will, as well as Mrs. Whyte, accept this acknowledgment of valuable help as the best return I am able at present to make. I understand that Dr. Mingana's name is one that stands high in rank among philologists and Orientalists. He is a voluminous writer for theological and other journals, and the author of a *Syriac Grammar;* of two volumes on *Syriac Sources;* a volume on *The Ancient Koran;* two volumes on *The Odes and Psalms of Solomon;* a work on *Early Judaeo-Christian Documents in the John Rylands Library,* and of several other books.

While we in no wise question the authority and inviolability of the original text of the Bible, we hold that the present English translation of Genesis 3:16, *"Thy desire shall be to thy husband,"* is erroneous, and *proved incorrect* by the ancient versions. Therefore the interpretation of St. Paul's rules regarding the conduct and treatment of women, since based on the erroneous translation, is incorrect.

A few persons will, of course, resign a measure of faith unless the traditional interpretation is left undisturbed. This cannot be helped. We must continually improve in our understanding of God's will, and this necessitates a continual improvement in our interpretation of God's Word. So the question is,—Shall the Church change its present treatment of women, or its interpretation of St. Paul? Its present course of inconsistency, in teaching Paul one way, and treating women in a more honouring way, is mischievous:

(1) The Church itself, thereby, sets an example of defiance of the authority of the Bible.

(2) To explain Paul by apologizing for Paul's faulty rabbinical logic involves the expositor in an attack on the inspiration of the Bible (see Lesson 46).

(3) If women must suffer domestic, legislative and ecclesiastical disabilities because Eve sinned, then must the Church harbour the appalling doctrine that Christ did *not* atone for *all* sin, because so long as the Church maintains these disabilities, the inevitable conclusion in the average mind will be the same as Tertullian's,—"God's verdict on the sex still holds good, and the sex's guilt must still hold also."

(4) At no point is faith in the entire Bible being so viciously and successfully attacked today as at the point of the "woman question," and the Church so far attempts no defence here of her children. It assumes that the interests of merely a few ambitious women are involved, whereas the very fundamentals of our faith are at stake.

TABLE OF CONTENTS

God's Word to Women

FUNDAMENTAL.

1. The *object* of these Lessons is at least three-fold:
(1) To point out to women the fallacies in the "Scriptural" argument for the supremacy of the male sex.
(2) To show the true position of women in the economy of God. (3) To show women their need of knowing the Bible in its original tongues, in order the better to equip themselves to confute these fallacies, and also to show that such a knowledge of the Bible would have great influence for good on the progress of the Church and womanhood.

2. Our argument assumes that the Bible is all that it claims for itself. It is (1) Inspired, 2 Tim. 3:16;* (2) Infallible, Isa. 40:8, and (3) Inviolable, John 10:35. Indeed, no other basis of procedure is available for us. However freely certain male scholars of the present day manipulate the text, no confidence would be placed in the results thus obtained by a woman,—at once, she would be faced with the charge that she had manipulated the text to suit her argument. But a manipulation of the text is unnecessary, even if we thought it lawful under any circumstances.

3. The assumption that the text needs amending, to any great extent, is very erroneous. A candid acceptance of the testimony as to its history proves that the original text has been preserved in manuscripts with scarcely an important change. It is known that the Scribes wrote out their copy with *immense care*, as to the Hebrew Old Testament. They copied even supposed errors, calling attention to seeming irregularities by slight marks, but not venturing to correct. They have left records to show that when copying they counted each consonant and vowel-letter in each line, and kept records of the same, in order to verify their finished work. Superstition alone was

---

* We shall use the Authorised Version of the Bible throughout these Lessons, unless we indicate the Revised by "R. V." In this place (2. Tim. 3:16) the R. V₁ is both incorrect and misleading.

1

enough to cause the Jews to preserve their Scripture text inviolable; they prized the letter beyond the spirit of the Word. The Apostle Paul speaks in indirect testimony of their faithful preservation of the Hebrew text, since had it been otherwise, the Jews would have had no "advantage" over the Gentiles, but have been less in favor with God, Rom. 3:1, 2. Jesus Christ strongly denounced the misinterpretation of the Scriptures by the "traditions" of the Jews, Mark 7:9-13, etc., but He never accused the Jews of corrupting the text of their Scriptures.

4. The Lord Jesus said, *"Till heaven and earth pass, one jot or one tittle shall in no wise pass from the law, till all be fulfilled."* The "jot" (letter j), is nearly like our single quotation mark (') , in form and size; the "tittle" is not a letter, but the distinguishing point of difference between one Hebrew letter and another much like it. For instance, the Jewish rabbis, who taught also the infallibility of the text, in a treatise called *Vayikra Rabba* (s. 19) declare:

1. "Should anyone, in Deut. 6:4, change   ד (d) to   ר (r). he would ruin the world."*

2. "Should anyone, in Ex. 34:14, change   ר (r) to   ד (d). he would ruin the world."

3. "Should anyone, in Lev. 22:32, change   ח (ch) to   ה (h). he would ruin the world."

4. "Should anyone, in Psa. 150:6, change   ה (h) to   ח (ch). he would ruin the world."

5. "Should anyone in Jer. 5:12, change   ב (b) to   כ (k). he would ruin the world."

6. "Should anyone, in 1 Sam. 2:2, change   כ (k) to   ב (b). he would ruin the world."

Because these passages would then mean respectively,—

1. "Hear, O Israel; the Lord is a *false* Lord."
2. "Thou shalt *not* worship the one true God."
3. "Neither shall ye *praise* [for "profane"] My holy name."
4. "Let every thing that hath breath *profane* [for "praise"] the Lord."
5. "They have *lied like* [for "belied"] the Lord."
6. "There is *no holiness* in [for "none holy as"] the Lord."*

---

* We select out and for convenience tabulate these statements from among others. See Dr. Adam Clarke's comments on Matt. 5:18.

5. But when we speak of the Bible as inspired, infallible and inviolable, we do not refer to our English version, or any mere version, but to the original text. Prof. Deissman has well said, *"All translation implies some, if only a slight, alteration of the sense of the original."* Now we must explain more precisely what "the original text" really implies, and how much it includes. The original Hebrew of the Old Testament was written without any spaces between words in totally different looking letters from those we call "Hebrew" at the present time; and the language as first written contained no vowels,—as though the English of Gen. 1:1 were written:

NTHBGNGGDCRTDTHHVNSNDTHRTH

No distinction existed between small and capital letters, and doubled letters were often written only once,—as we have indicated in the word, "beginning."

6. Hebrew ceased to be spoken by the common people during the Babylonian captivity. It was practically a "dead language" as early as B. C. 250. In the absence of expressed vowels, its pronunciation was likely to become lost. So the Scribes took four consonants, "a h w and j," and inserted them into the text to indicate the vowel sounds. While this device helped to some extent, in the end it led to confusion, often raising the question: "Is this letter a *consonant*, belonging to the original, or is it a *vowel-letter*, added by the Scribes?" Moreover the insertion of these vowel-letters did not prove sufficient; then, as late as 600-800 A. D., a whole system of vowel-*signs* was added, most elaborately indicating the vowels of each word as tradition had preserved it. These *vowel-signs* were interlinear, and therefore did not confuse the text, as did the vowel-letters. With vowel-signs we might indicate the pronunciation of Gen. 1:1, as given above, something like this (separating the words):

-N TH B!GNNG GD CR!TD TH HVNS -ND TH' -RTH.*

7. We understand, now, that the Hebrew text may have mistakes which we are free (with due respect for the scholarship which has given to it its present form, and due reverence for God's Word), to amend, *so far as the vowel-*

---

* The dash (-) before three words takes the place of a needed consonant,— since no word in the Hebrew begins with a vowel. The ẽ sound is always indicated by the "jot," additionally,—so we introduce this "jot" three times.

3

letters and the vowel-signs are concerned, for no one claims that the Scribes who made these additions to the text in comparatively recent times did "inspired" work, as did the original authors.

8.   And then, women must never forget that all this addition to the text was not only the work of men exclusively, but of men who, in their day, were, as Jews, bitter opponents of the teachings and of the spirit of Christianity. Furthermore, if we may judge from the spirit of the teachings of the Talmud on the "woman question" (for the Talmud was then in the ascendency, and the sayings of the rabbis considered more authoritative than Scripture itself), these amenders of the original text, as a class, held women in utter contempt.   Dr. Paul Isaac Hershon (to quote one of the many witnesses to this statement) says: "The rabbis, over and over again, teach the utter inferiority of woman: they put a definite seal as it were on the degraded life of the female sex which for ages has been lived by women in the East as in the West."   A certain Rabbi Yochanan, we are told, quotes the Mishnic (the Mishna is the most ancient and important part of the Talmud)ᶦ rabbis as teaching that a man may do as he pleases with his wife: "It is like a piece of meat brought from the shambles, which one may eat, salt, roast, partially or wholly cooked."   A woman once complained before Rav (a great rabbi) of bad treatment from her husband.   He replied: "What is the difference between thee and a fish, which one may eat either broiled or cooked?"   But Jews alone did not hold women in contempt at that time in human history.   It was an unfortunate time, as regards women, for fixing the sense of the Holy Scriptures.

LESSON 2.

TEXTUAL CRITICISM.

9.   We repeat: The Hebrew text of the Old Testament, to which Jewish scholars have added both the vowel-letters "a h w j," and vowel signs, may have mistakes, *as regards these vowels,* but must not be called into question any further.   But there are destructive critics who go much farther than this.   They manipulate the consonants. We will illustrate, in a crude manner—it cannot be critical —their method, taking an English sentence for the purpose.   First we rob it of its vowels, and then we have the following:

4

GDSLVDTHWRLDTHTHGVHSNLBGTTNSNTHT
WHSVRBLVTHNHMSHLDNTPRSH.

10. Now let us decipher, remembering that according to
Hebrew usage "the" is often lacking where we would
use it, and therefore we may supply it; and sometimes
we can read a consonant double, sometimes single. Beginning by supplying a "the," and inserting vowels in small
letters, at the same time spacing the words, we read:
"The aGeD SLaVe DoTH WeaRiLy Do THaT Hay. i
GaVe His [double the S] SoN LieBiG* To iNSiNuaTe
[HTW we alter to WTH WiTH] HiS VeRy BeLoVeD
[we insert a D here, on the supposition that the text is
incomplete] Tea [double the T] THeN He SHouLD
NoT PeRiSH." There is an M before the word "should."
but we drop it out.

11. In this long sentence we have not supposed many
correction necessary; and some of the corrections are lawful from the standpoint and practice of all who interpret
the original text. But aside from these lawful ones, is
this sort of manipulation of the consonants of the original
text lawful work, with the Word of God? NO! The
work of these destructive higher critics in clearing up
obscure passages in the Old Testament is both tempting
and fascinating, and in their works they give praise to
those who have made "brilliant guesses" as to the meaning of certain sentences. The method is tempting because
by its looseness almost any passage would permit of *some*
sense being read into it, whereas, otherwise many passages will lie in more or less obscurity for centuries, before their precise meaning will be discovered. Yet,
recalling the fact that though cut glass *looks* prettier than
uncut diamond, it is worthless in comparison, we choose
the consonants unaltered, even if the sense is obscure, to a
pretty setting forth of mere sentiment.

12. Having made our choice, then, let us think again of
the English sentence, as though it were, in very truth, an
obscure Hebrew passage. It is, in point of fact, a verse
from the Bible. If we cannot read it at once, we will
keep it at hand and pray over it. If it be indeed a very
word from God, it is worth years, or even centuries of
patient waiting for God to reveal its meaning. We will
assume that after a while you pass through a new spiritual experience, and all the Bible takes on fresh meaning

---

* i. e., beef extract.

5

to you,—for this result always follows a nearer approach to God. Your soul is full of love to God, and a deeper love of His Word. Fresh messages of love shine forth from every page of His Book. God is now first in all your thoughts, and turning to this sentence once more, for light, it seems to you that the opening consonants, GD, must mean "God," not "aGeD." Yes, and the next four consonants naturally suggest "So LoVeD." Ah! now you have it! Not "aged slave," but "God so loved." We are on the right track. How beautifully it all unravels, without the loss or change of a single consonant! The printed Word tells you half the story, and your heart's experience the other half, and the meaning of the sentence which so long may have baffled you is, *"God so loved the world that He gave His only begotten Son that whosoever believeth on Him should not perish."*

13. Now *scholarship alone* did not reveal the meaning to you, nor did *experience alone,* but a combination of the two. We are mistaken when we think we can get along on a slovenly and incomplete knowledge of the Bible. No amount of spiritual experience, or even the Spirit's help and instruction, will take the place of the *study* God requires us to put upon His Word. The world, the Church and women are suffering sadly from woman's lack of ability to read the Word of God in its original languages. There are truths therein that speak to the deepest needs of a woman's heart, and that give light upon problems that women alone are called upon to solve. Without knowledge of the original, on the part of a sufficient number of women to influence the translation of the Bible in accordance with their perception of the meaning of these truths, these needed passages will remain uninterpreted, or misinterpreted.

14. Such truths man is not equipped to understand, much less to set forth to the understanding of women, for, as the very learned Canon Payne-Smith has said: "Men never do understand anything [he refers to Bible translation] unless already in their minds they have some kindred ideas." And such truths as are messages to women, women without knowledge of the original languages, even if having the spiritual experience, cannot discover. They find such a message often an inexplicable mystery, or even distorted into meaning something painful.

15. To return to the sentence to which we supplied the vowels: We purposely took a verse from the New Testa-

6

ment, and the greatest promise in the whole Bible. (Of course it does not stand in the original text in Hebrew, but in Greek)!. We wished to demonstrate that the most precious thing in the Word might be changed into insipid nonsense, perhaps, by the manipulation of two or three consonants of a vowelless language. They are like strong talons holding tenaciously to the *only* correct sense that can be legitimately made of the sentence. Bear in mind, further, a point which is passed over lightly by the destructive critics of the present time: With each consonant that is changed in Hebrew textual criticism, there is involved a change, or several changes, of the unexpressed vowels. The alteration of a consonant is not a trivial one at all, when it invades a consonantal language.

16. Twice, since the opening of the Christian Era, Christians have so neglected the Hebrew Bible as to have lost the language, and they have turned to the Jews to acquire it again. They lost it first, Dr. Wall tells us, "for somewhat more than 100 years immediately preceding the time when Origen flourished [born A. D. 185] : and again, in the dark ages for a long series of centuries, terminated by the revival of learning in Europe." The rabbis who taught the Christians each time would naturally teach them, not towards, but away from Christian ideals, and towards Talmudic ideals. Because of this fact, some things in the Old Testament, relating to women especially, demand a very careful, critical investigation, as to their precise meaning, since we know that the Talmudic view as regards women was not a just, unprejudiced view, by any means.

17. So much, as to the Hebrew Old Testament. As to the Greek New Testament, we shall not be faced with the same difficulties, and in our Lessons are not likely to call its text, as it now stands, into serious question. The Greek has always expressed its vowels, as well as its consonants, and hence no question arises at this point. The *punctuation* of the Greek, for the most part, is of recent invention, and at some points seriously to be questioned. But as to the interpretation of its words and their usage, there is an extensive Greek literature, independent of the New Testament, to give light, whereas, practically all that exists of ancient Hebrew literature is in the Bible. Modern Hebrew, as spoken by Jews, is merely the use of Bible words in their *traditional* meanings, which may be correct, but are sometimes doubtful, or even demonstrably incorrect.

7

LESSON 3.

FACTS AND FABLES.

18. In the study of God's messages to women, I wish you to approach His Book as though, like a pagan, you had never seen it before, and knew nothing about it. Will you endeavor to cultivate this spirit of fresh inquiry? When we have heard, over and over again, with unquestioning credulity an explanation of a thing, even though the explanation be grotesque, it comes back to us with all the force of natural fact. The mention of the thing recalls to the imagination that explanation, and no other seems right. If there be an error in the explanation, we arrive at a point where we can detect it only by a real effort; the false view comes to mind first, and hinders acceptance of the true. The rabbis told their Jewish scholars that there were many fish in the sea hundreds of miles long; and that Adam was so tall, before he fell, that his head touched the firmament. After hearing such tales, oft repeated as assured facts, it is not likely that the Jewish youth could hear the story of Jonah without imagining a fish such as never existed; nor could he hear the name "Adam" without thinking of a great giant; and he would probably *suppose* that the Bible said these things. They *seemed* natural conclusions from the Scripture, but they were wildest fables. Let us get false pictures out of mind, by weighing the evidence.

19. Therefore, we will accept no views as authoritative simply because that book, so valued among the Jews, the Talmud, teaches them,—not even because Christian tradition teaches them. We will test matters by the general trend of Bible teaching itself. The famous Earl of Chatham said, once, in a great speech in the House of Commons, "I confess that I am apt to distrust the refinements of learning, because I have seen the ablest and most learned men equally liable to deceive themselves, and to mislead others." Let us maintain this attitude of mind.

20. Savonarola wrought a revolution in the morals and manners of Florence, and he did it by adhering, and teaching the people to adhere, to two underlying principles upon which he based the chapters of his remarkable book, *The Triumph of the Cross.* These were, *"Nothing has been learnt from any man,"* and, *"We accept no authority save our own experience and reason."* Dr. Campbell Morgan has recently voiced the same spirit in his words,

"Do interpret your Bible by what the Bible says, and not by what men say that it says." We will take these as our basic principles in Bible study.

21. But does not Savonarola's use of the word "reason" savour of scepticism? Yes, as to the worth of "traditions of men;" and it savours also of the "glorious liberty of the children of God," to study the Bible for themselves, under the immediate tuition of the Holy Spirit. Savonarola further explains himself: "Not that faith, the spontaneous gift of God, can be acquired through reason, but because reason is a useful weapon with which to combat unbelievers, or open to them the way of salvation, to arouse the lukewarm, and give strength to the faithful" (1 Peter 3:15).* But while not bowing to any human authority *as final,* yet we will glean what information we can from writers; we will quote them to corroborate our statements, especially if we might have expected the one quoted to have taken an opposite view, had it been tenable at all; and make use of their works in any manner useful to our purpose: But always remembering that we bow to no authority as final but the Word of God, as illuminated by the Spirit. We will endeavor to "interpret the Bible by what the Bible says, not by what men say that it says."

22. Some will say that it is not worth our while to expend any time on the early chapters of Genesis, but that we should treat them as mere "folk-lore." We are convinced that they are history, and to women very valuable history. But even if we did not believe this, yet women could not afford to ignore them, for the sufferings of women from a false interpretation of their teachings, have been no unreality, and that false interpretation must be resisted.

23. Please read Gen. 1:26-28, and with it, Gen. 5:2. We find that at the first the name "Adam" belonged equally to male and female. God said: *"Let US make man* [or "Adam,"—it is the same word] *in our likeness;"* and the story proceeds,—*"In the image of God made HE HIM, male and female made HE THEM."* Please note that in the second clause, man is spoken of as both singular and plural. What does this mean?

24. The theory has been held among the Jews, at least as far back as the days of Jesus Christ, as shown by the writings of Philo, that man was, at the beginning. male

---

* "I oppose not rational to spiritual, for spiritual is most rational,"—Whichcote.

9

and female in one person. This belief will also be found among other people besides the Jews. Next, after the *androgynous* state, it is supposed that human beings were born in pairs, male and female twins. Then there would have existed a male and female Cain; a male and female Abel, etc.; and thus Cain secured his wife. If this be correct, it lends force to the Lord's words in Matt. 19:4 (R. V.)', concerning the sanctity of marriage,—and we must remember He was speaking to men who were doubtless familiar with the theory: *"Have ye not read, that He Who made* [no "them" in the original] *from the beginning made them male and female."* The rabbis did not seem to recognize an "and" in the expression in Genesis, *"male and female,"* but read *"male-female."* Dr. Hershon, in his book, *Talmudic Miscellany,* says: "There is a notion among the rabbis that Adam was possessed originally of a bi-sexual organism, and this conclusion they draw from Gen. 1:27, where it is said, 'God created man in His own image; male-female created He them.'" This view is *not* unscientific, but the reverse, as those know who are acquainted with such books as *The Evolution of Sex* by Geddes and Thomson. We will presently continue this topic.

25. Five blessings were pronounced on them by God. Gen. 1:28. (1), *"Be fruitful."* (2), *"Multiply ye."* (3), *"Replenish the earth."* (4), *"Subdue it."* (5), *"Have dominion over . . fish . . fowl . . and every living thing that moveth upon the earth."* Dr. Harper in his *Hebrew Method and Manual* renders this literally, bringing out the plural form of each verb, so we will reproduce his translation: "Be ye fruitful and multiply ye, and fill ye the earth, and subdue ye her [the word for earth is feminine]; and have ye dominion," etc. The plural is clearly expressed in each form. As the Word distinctly says that these blessings were pronounced upon male and female, we observe the perfect equality of the sexes by God's original creation.

26. Finally, note that when God had finished all His creation, including male and female man, He pronounced all *"very good."*

Additional Notes on Paragraph 24.

The word *androgynous* means the same as the adjective *hermaphrodite,* though it applies properly to the human species. Hermaphroditism is defined by Webster as "the union of the two sexes in the same individual." The following quotations from Geddes and Thomson may be useful to those who have not seen this work,

10

or similar ones: "Some observations by Laulaine as to the embryonic organs are of interest. . . . He distinguishes in birds and mammals three stages in the individual development of the reproductive organs: (1) Germiparity, (2) Hermaphroditism, (3) Differentiated Unisexuality" (p. 35). "One view of the matter is that hermaphroditism was the primitive state among multicelular animals" (p. 84). "Minot in his *Theory of Genoblasts,* or sexual elements, ventures little further than regarding male and female as derivitives of primitive hermaphroditism in two opposite directions" (p. 127).

The following is from Darwin, whose Darwinian theory we do not believe; but that theory could never have gained acceptance anywhere had he not based it upon well-founded facts: "It has long been known that in the vertebrate kingdom one sex bears rudiments of various accessory parts, appertaining to the reproductive system, which properly belongs to the opposite sex; and it has now been ascertained that at a very early embryonic period both sexes possess true male and female glands." It is well to note, as we proceed, how the Scriptures in no way contradict scientific facts such as these, discovered only thousands of years afterwards by human research. However, in all this which we have said regarding the *physical,* or animal, form of mankind, as having resemblance to God, whose image man bears, we need to remember that God Himself is *pure Spirit.*

LESSON 4.

THE BEGINNING OF EVIL.

27. It has been fashionable of late to believe that Genesis, second chapter, along with others, was written by a different author from the one who wrote chapter first, and that they are contradictory accounts of creation. The proof is supposed to lie principally in the fact that "God" alone is mentioned in the first chapter, "the Lord God" (Jehovah God) in the second. It is not for us to wander far afield in textual and higher criticism. But it is useful to know that recent highly valuable investigations of the original state of the Hebrew text, by Mr. Harold Wiener, M. A., LL. B., (a Jewish barrister-at-law, of Lincoln's Inn, London), seem to conclusively show that our "received text" is at fault, at this point.

28. While our New Testament translation rests upon the comparison, one with another, of many ancient Greek manuscripts, heretofore the translators of the *Old* Testament have contented themselves by the use, almost wholly, of what is known as the Massoretic text of the Hebrew Old Testament. Mr. Wiener brings other authorities to the front, as to the state of the original Hebrew, and shows, among other things, that the name of God did not always stand as it does in the Massoretic text. He holds

that the scribes often made a mere sign for the name of "Jehovah," and then later scribes wrote the name in full * The copying scribe of chapter one wrote "God;" of chapter two, "Lord God." Therefore the difference may be due not to different authors, but to different *scribes*. No Higher Critic has been able, as yet, to meet or refute Wiener's challenge of their theory; and his works are making a profound impression.

29. But, did Moses write the Pentateuch? Why not? If it be true that the antediluvians lived to the great age that the Bible asserts (sin having not, as yet, wrought its havoc in shortening the length of life), then the claim is easily sustained. Adam and Methuselah were contemporary 243 years, and thus Methuselah could, according to primitive custom, be well drilled in oral, traditional history by Adam, or Eve. Methuselah and Shem were contemporary during a full century; thus Shem could learn the story. Shem and Isaac were contemporary for about 48 years; thus Isaac learns the story. Isaac and Levi were contemporary for about 33 years; thus Levi learns it. The daughter of Levi, Jochebed, was both great-aunt and mother of Moses (Num. 26:59); but long before Moses was born,—indeed, before Isaac's time,—writing had come into use. Moses could certainly have easily composed the Pentateuch, excepting the account of his own death, in Deut. ch. 34.

30. We return to the story in Genesis. We conclude that the first chapter of Genesis describes the original creation of "Adam,"—mankind. (We must bear in mind the fact that the word "Adam" is applied sometimes to mankind, and sometimes to the individual being who was husband of Eve). The second chapter describes the elaboration of the first Adam into two sexes. The second chapter nowhere uses the word "create," of Adam, but a totally different word,—"formed." Please look up this same word, "formed," in Isa. 44:2, 24 and 49:5, and convince yourself that it is used there *exclusively of* all idea of creation. Then turn to Isa. 43:1, 7; 45:18, and see how it is used of a process *additional to* creation. This is what St. Paul refers to, where he says, "*Adam was first formed then Eve,*"—I Tim. 2:13. He is speaking of development, not of original creation. Adam and Eve (so far as their primal state is concerned) were created simultaneously; but Adam was "formed," elaborated, first.

* This was because the name "Jehovah" is held by Jews as too sacred for utterance.

12

31.   After Adam was created, Gen. 1:31 tells us, *"God saw everything that He had made, and, behold, it was very good."* Therefore Adam was very good; but this condition did not last. 2:18 tells us that presently God says: *"It is not good that the man* [or "Adam"], *should be alone."* The "very good" state of humanity becomes "not good." What had wrought signs of this change? We are not told, but the following points should be weighed: (1) Adam was offered "freely" the tree of life (2:16), but did not eat of it (3:22); (2) was made keeper, as well as dresser of the Garden, (2:15), but Satan later enters it,—read pars. 36, 37. (3) Had God simply meant by the words "not good" that *one* person *alone* was not a desirable thing, the Hebrew expression for "one alone" in Josh. 22:20, Isai. 51:2, etc., would seem more appropriate. This expression means, "in-his-separation,"—and from whom was Adam "in separation" but from God?

32.   Attention to some of these matters has been called by more than one theologian, only to be ignored by the generality of Bible expositors. For instance, William Law, a learned theologian and one of the most accomplished writers of his day, declares: "Adam had lost much of his first perfection before his Eve was taken out of him; which was done to prevent worse effects of his fall, and to prepare a means of his recovery when his fall should become total, as it afterwards was, upon eating of the earthly tree of the knowledge of good and evil. *'It is not good that man should be alone,'* saith the Scripture. This shows that Adam had altered his first state, had brought some *beginning* of evil into it, and had made that *not* to be good, which God saw to be good, when He created him."

33.   The late Dr. Alexander Whyte, of Edinburgh, in his book, *Bible Characters,* set forth some of the views of William Law, and also of an earlier writer, Jacob Behman, the great German philosopher (whose writings Wesley, in his days, required all his preachers to study). Whyte quotes Behman as teaching,—
    "There must have been something of the nature of a stumble, if not an actual fall, in Adam while yet alone in Eden . . Eve was created [he should say, "elaborated"] to 'help' Adam to recover himself, and to establish himself in Paradise, and in the favor, fellowship and service of his Maker."

13

34. As to Adam's need, God said, '*I will make a help meet for him.*" This word for "help" does not imply an inferior, but a superior help, in O. T. usage. It occurs 21 times in the O. T. Here it is used twice of Eve. In Isa. 30:5, Eze. 12:14 and Dan. 11:34 of human help; but in every other use made of the word, it refers to Divine help, as, for instance, Psa. 121:2, "*My help cometh from the Lord.*" Please notice, further, that the expression is not "helpmeet," or helpmate, as is often quoted. The word "meet" is a preposition, and Gesenius, the greatest authority as to the meaning of Hebrew words, defines this preposition as often implying, "As things which are before us, and in the sight of which we delight, are objects of our care and affections, hence Isa. 49:16, '*Thy walls are before me,*' they have a place in my care and affections." With this preposition "before," or "over against," is coupled the adverb "as,"—the whole meaning "as before him,"—see Margin.

35. By the elaboration of Eve, and her separation from Adam, God intended the development of the social virtues, as an aid for Adam. Again William Law says, "Could anything be more punctually [pointedly] related in Scriptures than the gradual fall of Adam? Do you not see that he was first created with both natures [male and female] in him? Is it not expressly told you, that Eve was not taken out of him, till such a time as it was not good for him to be as he then was?

LESSON 5.

THE FABLE OF THE "RIB."

36. We do not know certainly how the decline in Adam began, but we should not overlook one fact: The man (the woman side of humanity being as yet undeveloped), was placed in the garden "*to dress and keep it*" (2:15). Two duties, not one, were laid upon Adam. This second word is the same as used in 3:24, where the "Cherubim, and a flaming sword" are placed, "to *keep* the way of the tree of life." Lange's Commentary says, "Adam must watch and protect it [the Garden]. This is, in fact, a very significant addition, and seems to give a strong indication of danger as threatening man and Paradise from the side of an already existing power of evil."

37. That "power of evil" manifests itself a little later in the form of Satan. Did not Adam let him enter the gar-

14

den? Verse 17 goes on to warn Adam as regards *"the tree of the knowledge of good and evil,"* and it seems legitimate to infer that he was not only to refrain from eating of this tree, but also to protect this tree from being tampered with by others, as it was, later, when Satan induced Eve to partake of it, and then the youthful Eve gave of the fruit of it to Adam, who ate also.

38.   Overlooking some interesting points for the present, we pass on to Gen. 2:21.   The last clause of this verse is literally translated by Dr. Harper, in his *Method and Manual,* as follows: "He took one from his sides, and closed the flesh instead of it," and the learned author of Genesis in Ellicott's Commentaries, Canon Payne-Smith, speaks of the woman as coming from the flank of man, "so curiously from ancient times rendered 'rib.'"

39.   On the same point, Archdeacon Wilberforce has written interestingly to the following effect: "I do not profess to manipulate the Hebrew a single step in advance of the possibilities of any student who may possess the *Englishman's Hebrew Concordance,* [The same can be said of *Young Analytical Concordance*],* but the 'rib' seems to be a mistranslation.   The Hebrew word translated 'rib' in both the Authorised and Revised versions, occurs forty-two times in the O. T., and in this instance alone is it translated 'rib.'   In the majority of cases it is translated 'side' or 'sides,' in other places 'corners' or 'chambers,' but never 'rib' or 'ribs,' except in these two verses describing the separation of Eve from Adam.   In the Septuagint version, which was the Scripture quoted by our Lord, the word is *pleura,* which in Homer, Hesiod and Herodotus is used for 'side,' not 'rib,' and in the Greek of the N. T. is invariably translated 'side.'   There is a word in the O. T. the true translation of which is 'rib' and nothing else, and it occurs in Dan. 7:5, but this is a totally different word from the word translated 'rib' in the passage before us."   We could have said all this, in fewer words, not quoting Wilberforce, and others, but then, we might have been accused of straining a point, because of sex bias.   Had God taken only a rib from Adam, the latter would not have exclaimed, "she is flesh of my flesh," but merely, "she is bone of my bone."   Let us never forget, when we hear a rationalist ridiculing the "rib" story

---

* Words enclosed in square brackets are invariably by the author of the Lessons.

of "creation," that he is not in reality ridiculing the Bible, though he may think he is. He is holding up to contempt a stupid mistranslation.

40. The separation of Eve from Adam was, then, an exceptional instance within the human race of what is well known to take place in lower orders of life. Professor Agassiz, the naturalist, in describing *gemmiparous* or *fissiparous* reproduction, says: "A cleft or fission, at some part of the body, takes place, very slight at first, but constantly increasing in depth, so as to become a deep furrow. . . At the same time the contained organs are divided and become double, and thus two individuals are formed of one, so similar to each other that it is impossible to say which is the parent and which is the offspring." Each human body retains still abundant traces of a dual nature, in almost every organ and part.

41. The Bible is not a treatise on science, but wherever rightly translated it is found not to contradict science. Nothing could be more unscientific than the representation that Eve was made from a single bone taken from Adam's body. We have already (par. 24, and Additional Notes thereon), commented on the possible original bisexual nature of the human being,—the *androgynous*, or *hermaphrodite* state, which persists, imperfectly, to the present time within the human family.

42. The idea that Eve was made out of one of Adam's ribs has its origin in rabbinical lore. One story says that "Eve was made out of a tail which originally belonged to Adam." Rav. the great head of the Babylonian rabbinical school, declared, "Eve was formed out of a second face, which originally belonged to Adam," and another rabbi declares, "Instead of a rib taken from Adam, a slave was given him to wait upon him." But Rabbi Joshua, in his commentary, has given the fable which has most pleased Christian commentators on the Bible. It is quite general for them to quote it in part, or give some of its many variations.

43. Rabbi Joshua says: "God deliberated from what member He would create woman, and He reasoned with Himself thus: I must not create her from Adam's head, for she would be a proud person, and hold her head high. If I create her from the eye, then she will wish to pry into all things; if from the ear, she will wish to hear all things; if from the mouth, she will talk much; if from the heart, she will envy people; if from the hand, she will

desire to take all things; if from the feet, she will be a gadabout. Therefore I will create her from the member which is hid, that is, the rib, which is not even seen when man is naked." And this is the inane fable which lies at the basis of the idea that Eve must have been made out of Adam's rib, whereas the Bible says God took one of Adam's sides (or one part of Adam's being), out of which He "builded" her.

44. We pass on to Gen. 2:24. Here is something most interesting. God seems to interrupt the ancient history, as given by Moses, and steps forth, as it were, in His own person, to address humanity directly and impressively in the words, *"Therefore shall a man leave his father and his mother and cleave unto his wife"* Some have attributed these words to Adam, who was speaking in the previous verse, or to Moses, but Jesus Christ speaks of them as God's own language, in Matt. 19:4, 5, saying *"Have ye not read, that He which made* [no "them" in the original] *at the beginning, made them male and female, and said, For this cause shall a man leave his father and mother, and cleave to his wife."* Many commandments are promulgated in masculine terms, though meant equally for both sexes, but in this instance the case is different: One man and one woman stand before the Almighty, on the very occasion of their differentiation into two sexes, and God enunciates a law as lying between those two just formed, which indicates for all time the duty of husband to wife, not of wife to husband. And then, in the Hebrew original expression, "for this cause ought *the man,*" the word for "man" is not the generic term meaning "mankind," it is *ish,* "husband," corresponding to *isha,* "wife," in the expression "his wife" of this verse. When man and woman marry, there must be created a line of cleavage, on the part of one or both, between parent, or parents, and children. This Scriptural marriage law declares that the line of cleavage shall separate the husband from his parents rather than the wife from her parents. We will continue this subject in our next Lesson.

LESSON 6.
GOD'S LAW OF MARRIAGE.
"Therefore shall a man [husband] leave his father and his mother, and cleave unto his wife."

45. Obedience to this fundamental marriage law of Gen. 2:24 would have saved women from ever becoming mere

chattels, and thus have kept the entire race on a higher level. Imagine, please, what could be accomplished even now, for the elevation of pagan races, if missionaries would require their converts to observe the Scriptural law of marriage. The factors that would operate to relieve the oppression of Oriental women would be as follows: (1), The husband, as a *bread-winner*, would have a pecuniary value in the home of his wife; whereas, as it now is, the wife, as a producer of more children to be fed, is subject to abuse, more particularly when she brings forth a female child. (2), Man, not handicapped by unborn children, nurslings, or a helpless little brood, could not be reduced to slavery in an alien home, because he would forsake it, and leave his helpless wife and children for those who abused him to support. But the hampering effects of motherhood, and the strength of mother-love, leave the mother a victim of those who would enslave her. (3), Man is not so constituted that he can be robbed, by force, of his virtue, or his person be made a matter of trade and gain for an alien household; but these calamities are so frequently the lot of a widow left in the alien home of her deceased husband, that in some Oriental countries, notably India, the very word "widow" is disreputable. (4), Before gestation and parturition a mother would generally be tenderly cared for, if with her own mother, under her father's roof, or near by. But in an alien home she is often shamefully neglected at such times; and this weakens the entire race, in course of time. (5), The practice of keeping the daughter at home, after marriage, and sending the son out of the home, after marriage, would put a tremendous check upon child-marriage, since parents would be in no great haste to part with wealth-producing members of the family.

46. All women should know that the Word of God started the world right, in this regard, and put such a tremendous bar to her degradation as this marriage law, in the very forefront of human history,—it being, in fact, the first social moral law enunciated for human guidance. Moreover, the testimony is increasing daily, that in the earliest ages of human history this law was not a dead letter, as it is at the present time, with few exceptions. It was customary for the husband either to go and live under the roof of his wife's parents, or to make frequent visits to her there,—she never leaving the protection of her par-

ents. The *parents* were the "natural protectors" of their married daughters,—not the husband who not infrequently has proved unworthy of his trust. The early custom was, to eye him with a certain amount of wholesome suspicion, as an alien, until he had actually demonstrated his ability to care for a wife in a proper manner.

47. Above all things, the greatest advantage of a woman remaining with, or near, her own kin, after marriage, (her family being her "natural protectors"), is, that it would conserve social morality. Some years ago, a physician in one of our largest cities was given police aid to make a very thorough investigation into the "social evil" of the city; and he published the sifted testimony of hundreds of women and girls in the disreputable ranks of life. I have not his book at hand to quote from, but his conclusion was, as I remember, that *marriage to wicked men* was a prolific cause of prostitution. Young girls married those who made love to them, without much thought or knowledge of the character of the men; and after that, marriage placed them in such a disadvantageous position, in relation to their husbands, that they could be driven, or worried, into the street, to earn money by their vice. Perhaps, in the first place, the husband may not have married with the object of compelling his wife to earn her living after such a manner; but having no proper sense of decency himself, when hard times came on, he could appreciate no reason why his wife should not help to earn the living by vice. Now it is precisely against such emergencies, that a woman's own kindred ought to have the right to interfere, if any such danger threatens. The marriage law should allow them to keep in close touch with their daughter or sister. But as it now is, such a husband can carry his wife off to the ends of the earth, if he wish, and no one can hinder his doing so.

48. With what results, one only has to visit a large Oriental city to learn. We shall not soon forget, to instance one such investigation only, a visit, after dark, to a notorious street in one of these great Oriental cities. Among the many unfortunate girls that we saw, we were told that a large number were young wives who had thought themselves married to gentlemen of large affairs in Oriental business houses. Slave-hunters had found these girls in the villages of Europe, England and America, they had made love to them, and gone through a regular marriage ceremony with them, and then

brought them to the Oriental slave-market. Regularly, every evening, their "husbands" would go the rounds of the houses they owned, and see that everything was in order for the night. Then they would go to their near-by Club House (which we went and saw, in their absence). feast themselves on the food and drink their slaves had earned, and return, at two or three o'clock in the morning, after an abundant carousing, and take away from their slave- wives every penny that they had earned in the meantime. Often they flogged them if the amount of money fell below the usual amount expected. The White Slave Trade will never receive its death-blow until we have marriage laws which will allow of an adequate protection of women as against wicked husbands; and such protection will not be adequate until a wife's own kindred, if respectable, are recognized by law as her "natural protectors,"—laws which will not permit a husband to take his wife away to a strange country, even if the over-trustful wife is willing to go, if the removal is against the judgment of her family,—that is, unless he can show adequate reason for doing so, before the courts.

49   Precisely this same abuse of the marriage relation can be seen among the Japanese (and to a painful extent), on the Pacific Coast of the United States. There is in Japan a secret marriage agency, constantly on the lookout for Japanese girls who will go to America to be married. Also, men of this agency return to Japan, over and over, to marry girls and bring them to America. Often these Japanese men belong to good families, but they themselves have become corrupted by residence in foreign parts. Knowing they are of good families, the parents of girls trust them to bring their daughters away, after they have married them. So these girls are entrapped; and every night, in America, they are driven out upon the street, and to Japanese lodging houses, to earn money for these "husbands," to whom they were honorably married. This is no imaginary picture. We have it on the testimony of Christian Japanese gentlemen, Christian mission workers, Japanese consuls, and such persons.

What lessons God's marriage law teaches us, as to God's fatherly care and protection for His daughters! Away back at the beginning, His first uttered commandment shows that He had their rights and dignity on His heart.

LESSON 7.

GOD'S LAW OF MARRIAGE,—Continued.

50.   God meant that human marriage should be a type of Christ's union with the Church, or "New Jerusalem," His bride.   Christ laid aside all His glory with His Father, and came to this earth to unite Himself to us.   But marriage was not meant merely to typify Christ's first coming, but to include the thought of His second coming as well; only in both these events does the type fully represent the antitype. Every Christian marriage should celebrate these two events.   The husband's renunciation of ties of kinship should offset the wife's renunciation of self-love by taking up the risks of child-bearing and child-rearing.   This is what Paul teaches, in Ephesians 5:31, 32, where he quotes the obligation that the husband should forsake his kindred for his wife, and adds, "*I speak concerning Christ and the Church.*"   Adam and Eve were created at the same time, and were together, and then they were separated during a "deep sleep," which came upon Adam.   So Christ was with us, and then separated from us by the "deep sleep" of death, while we came, as it were, from His riven side, by faith in His shed blood.   Adam was separated, that he might be re-united to Eve, in greater joy than ever,—such joy that poetry burst from his lips, in celebration of the event, which Dr. R. F. Horton renders:

> *"She, she is bone of my bone,*
> *And flesh of my flesh is she;*
> *'Woman' her name, which has grown*
> *Out of man,—out of me."*

51.   And one day Christ will come again, "to our joy,"— for it was "expedient" for Him to go, and return again, He told us.   And one day we shall recognise, as we do not now, that Christ is our very "other self," as Adam did of Eve; "*for we are members of His body,*" and "*joined to the Lord,*" we are "*one spirit,*" also.   Mary Magdalene seems to have first discovered this, in experience,—for she exclaimed to the supposed gardener: "*Tell me where thou hast laid Him, and I will take Him away,*"—an unconscious claiming of His body as *her very own property,* in a love of sexless chastity.   No wonder that He could but manifest Himself to such l o v e!   (John 20:11-18).

52.   The custom was, when Christ was on earth, for the wedding procession of the bridegroom and his male

friends to go and fetch the bride from her father's house to his own father's home. But Christ's parable of the Ten Virgins (Matt. 25:1-13), presents no such picture of the violation of God's law. The virgins wait *at the home of the bride,* and at the cry that the bridegroom is coming, go forth to meet him, and fetch him and his train to a feast at the bride's home. "Ordinarily the bride was fetched by the bridegroom and his friends; but here it is the office of the virgins to fetch the bridegroom, and the wedding seems to take place in the house of the bride, as in Judg. 14:10." (De Wette, quoted by Lange). So will it be when Christ comes again. Those who are waiting, and prepared for His coming, at the cry of His coming, will go forth to *"meet the Lord in the air,"* and return to the earth, the Bride's home, for the marriage feast, where they will live and reign with Him a thousand years (see 1 Thess. 4:17. Rev. 20:6).

We have not been merely speculating as to the advantages God's marriage law would secure to women. God's marriage law *was obeyed* in the earliest ages of humanity. This fact archæologists are now bringing to light; and we will give a short sketch (all we now have room for) of their discoveries.

53. The first, in modern times, to write on this subject, was Bachofen, a Swiss jurist, in 1861. Mr. J. F. McLennan became his exponent in English, as well as publishing his own investigations of the subject. Many others, as Tylor, Westermarck, Fraser, Lord Avebury (Sir John Lubbock), and Robertson Smith have followed. In fact, no modern history of an early people is considered complete unless it begins with the days when there were *matriarchs,* as well as patriarchs. In the 36th chapter of Genesis, we discover that some of the "dukes of Edom" were women.

54. Three leading features are characteristic of this early civilisation: (1), The parents of a wife, together with her own kin, remain her "natural protectors" throughout life: (2), the household property is held by the women; (3), kinship is reckoned through the women, not the men, because when men marry they are detached from their kin; the children are known by the mother's family name. This form of civilisation is often called by the name, "female kinship," because the 3rd point mentioned is the cause of all the rest. For instance, McLennan, in speaking of the decline in dignity of Grecian

women, says: "We see that *no causes* could have produced it, so long as relationships through women preserved their old importance. On the other hand, we can discern a sufficient cause f o r degeneration in the gradually increasing preponderance of male kinship, and in the changes in the marriage system . . which made that preponderance."

55. We may ask, what brought about this change from female to male kinship. Modern evolutionists who will not admit a Divine revelation say that, first of all universal promiscuity prevailed; and as no man knew his own children, in consequence, therefore, female kinship alone was recognized. But the foremost evolutionists, Darwin and Spencer, say that such promiscuity never prevailed; and that is very strong evidence against the theory, for they were the chief evolutionists. And besides, the Bible reveals the truth to us, and we need not stay to consider the evolutionists' theory. God's marriage law established female kinship, in the beginning; and why should such a hateful character as Lamech ever have been delineated in the Bible, excepting to record the violation of this marriage law, and the beginning of polygamy? A little further on, in the opening verses of the 6th chapter of Genesis, we read of the wholesale appropriation of women: *"and the earth was filled with violence,"* the record says. Lamech's son "whetted cutting instruments," as we read, in chapter four; and the first use of weapons of warfare was for the capture of women. As these captive wives were torn from their kindred, they became identified with their husband's kin, as well as their children; and so male kinship came to pass. The flood did not exterminate the habit of capturing women, for we read, in Judges, of Deborah waging war with Sisera, for his crimes against women; and Sisera's mother is represented as watching for her son's return with the spoils of war,—*"to every warrior a damsel or two."*

56. Dr. A. C. Dixon, in an article in the *London Christian* (Nov. 16, 1911) says: "Turn to this civilisation which God Himself founded, and you will hear Him say: *'A man shall leave his father and his mother, and shall cleave unto his wife; and they shall be one flesh.'* Woman is given the pre-eminence. It is not the woman leaving the father and the mother, and cleaving unto her husband; but it is the man leaving his mother and father, and cleaving unto his wife." At one point we disagree with Dr.

Dixon. Civilisation founded on this marriage law of God did *not* make the wife her husband's superior; but it prevented her becoming his subordinate. In this connection the story of Jacob and his wives, Leah and Rachel, is instructive. When he wishes to leave his father-in-law, he humbly asks his wives to accompany him. And they do not say: "It is our duty to follow our husband," but, "We are warranted in going for two reasons: Our father has given us no inheritance; and he has kept for himself Jacob's wages, and they should have been paid over to us, and our children" (Gen. 31:14-16). It is evident, from this, that men did not *sell* their daughters in marriage, where these women lived, nor did wives feel bound, by marriage, to follow their husbands to the ends of the earth. Scholars of note tell us that Abraham said to Abimelech, Gen. 20:13, concerning Sarah, *"When God caused her to wander with me,"* not simply, *"when God caused me to wander."* The difference in the meaning is this: It was not expected, in those days, that a wife would follow her husband in his wanderings, but quite the contrary. God wished Sarah and Abraham both to come out of idolatrous surroundings; therefore He gives a revelation of His will to Sarah, lest she should follow the usual custom and remain with her kin.

LESSON 8.
THE EARLY DIGNITY OF WOMAN.

57. Says Prof. Robertson Smith of Cambridge: "In Genesis, marriage is defined as implying that a man leaves his father and mother and cleaves to his wife and they become one flesh. . This is quite in accordance with what we find in other parts of the patriarchal story. Mr. McLennan has cited the marriages of Jacob, in which Laban plainly has the law on his side in saying that Jacob had no right to carry off his wives and their children; and also the fact that when Abraham seeks a wife for Isaac, his servant thinks that the condition will probably be that Isaac shall come and settle with her people." [In this case, Abraham would not consent, because God had expressly called him away from their idolatry]. . . "Joseph's children by his Egyptian wife became Israelites only by adoption: and so in Judges 15, Samson's Philistine wife remains with her people and he visits her there. All these things illustrate what is presented in Gen. 2:24 as the primitive type of mar-

riage." And we might ask, what does that primitive form of language mean,—"cleave to his wife; and they shall become one flesh," but that he shall become of the same kin as his wife? The same writer says: "Mother kinship is the type of kinship, common motherhood the type of kindred unity, which dominates all Semitic speech." J. P. Peters, D. D., writing of this same passage in Genesis says: "In the relation which man is here represented as holding towards woman, we have, apparently, another of those incidental evidences of the great antiquity of this story. It is not the woman who leaves father and mother, and cleaves to the man, but the man who leaves father and mother, and cleaves to his wife. It would seem as though we had a survival of the old matriarchate, that relation of marriage of which we have an example in the Samson story, where the woman remains with her tribe, or clan, or family, and is visited by the man. The offspring in such a case belongs to the woman's family, not the man's." (*Early Hebrew Story, p. 223*).

58. Prof. Flinders Petrie, the great archæologist, has also written interestingly on this topic, and we linger to quote rather lengthily from him,—our object in giving these quotations being to show that we are not straining a point. He says: "We have become so accustomed to the idea that women were always dependent in the East—as they are now under Mohammedanism—that we need to open our eyes to a very different system which is shown us in the early history of the patriarchal age. Broadly, it may be said that our present system is the entire mixture of men and women in society, while men retain all the rights and property. The early ideal in the East was separate worlds of men and women, while women retained their own rights and all the property."

59. To continue: "The first woman [aside from Eve] that appears as a personality in the O. T.* is Sarah, the 'chieftainess,' as her name implies. *Sar* is the regular old terms for a chief, still kept up in the East. . . . Her independent position is seen by her living in the palace of Pharaoh, or in the court of Abimelech, quite irrespective of Abraham. The attempt at explaining this

* Because of the length of the words, "Old Testament and New Testament," hereafter throughout these Lessons O. T. will stand for the first, and N. T. for the second expression, while the capital letter M will refer the student to the marginal reading of a verse in either.

away by later writers will not at all account for this independence, which was ignored in after ages.

"Sarah had her independent residence at Mamre, and lived there, while Abraham lived at Beersheba; and it is said that he came to mourn for her and to bury her. Her position, therefore, during her wanderings and in later life was not by any means that of secluded dependence, but rather that of an independent head of the tribe, or 'tribal mother.'

60. "As Sarah had no daughter it was needful to get one of the family to head the tribe, and Rebekah was brought over from the old home. Sarah's state tent was removed by Isaac three or four days' journey from Mamre down to Beer-lahai-roi, and as soon as Rebekah came, she was installed in the tent. Then, after that, Isaac married her; and she appears quite as independent as Sarah. Rebekah having no daughter to succeed her, Jacob needed to marry Leah, the eldest in succession, and could not have Rachel until Leah's position was thus assured.

61. "On coming to the descent into Egypt, there is only one daughter named along with eleven sons, and that is Dinah, 'the female judge,' [as the meaning is], daughter of the chieftainess Leah. On her marrying a Hivite* her brothers were furious, because she would thus subject her judgeship to another race; and only the incorporation of the Hivites with the Israelite race by circumcision could remedy the position (Gen. 34:1-24). Still later we can trace this descent in the name of the only woman of the next generation that is named, Serah (Gen. 46:17), a form of Sarah, 'the chieftainess.' As Dinah seems to have no children, the next thing was to take a descendant of Zilpah, Leah's handmaid. So Asher, over whom Leah has specially rejoiced, supplied the next chieftainess in his daughter Serah."

62. Something of this early dignity of woman can be traced throughout the Scripture story, notably in the "queen mother," next in power to the king, who is spoken of as late as the time of Jer. 13:18 (here the word is wrongly translated "queen"), 600 B. C. These matters will be considered again later.

---

*Hamor's treatment of Dinah, among those primitive Hivites really meant marriage.
That Jacob had other daughters, we know from Gen. 46:7.

Before Hebrew, were the Akkadian and Sumerian languages; and Prof. Sayce tells us that the translators of ancient Sumerian hymns into the Semitic, changed "female and male," to "male and female," and introduced other such changes, to give the male pre-eminence. Sumeria, Akkadia, Babylonia, Arabia, Phœnicia and Egypt,—all these most ancient civilizations were characterized by features of the matriarchy. Sir Wm. Ramsay tells us the same as to Asia Minor. Female kinship can also be traced in early Greece,—the Spartan woman being the last to lose her dignity. As late as B. C. 450, Herodotus wrote, of the Lycians: "If anyone asks his neighbor who he is, he will declare himself born cf such a mother, and will reckon up the ancestors of his mother." It was formerly supposed that this was due to the father having more than one wife; but it is now strongly asserted that such is not the proper explanation. The very word "brother" in Greek (*adelphos*) defines a relation through the mother, not through the father.

63. We have got so far away from God's law, that to-day, in British law, the mother is not a parent. During the reign of Edward VI, the civil and ecclesiastical courts united in declaring that the Duchess of Suffolk was no kin to the son she had borne. The English Church is severe against divorce. Yet, read the Lord's ruling as to divorce, in Matt. 19, and we discover that the conclusion, *"Therefore what God hath joined together, let not man put asunder,"* rests upon the premises, *"A man shall leave his father and mother, and shall cleave to his wife, and they twain shall become* [R. V.] *one flesh."* The Church will never effectually enforce the conclusion of that statute, while it defies the premises upon which it rests.

64. Our Hebrew grammars and lexicons call attention to the fact that nearly all collective nouns referring to peoples, and the names of cities and towns, are *feminine* in form. How did this come about, for it is simply impossible to think of men coining a word of feminine gender to describe such a crowd as Christ fed, in His day? The account states that He fed *"four thousand men, besides women and children."* And on another occasion He fed *"five thousand men, besides women and children."* Again, Peter, Stephen, and Paul on sundry occasions, all address crowds, in The Acts, as *"Men brethren,"* not even mentioning women at all. When

the male holds the first place almost exclusively, his sex alone is specified in a crowd. But we can readily see that when a nation of one blood, or a community of one blood was mentioned, in the days when blood was reckoned through women, then nations, cities, communities and crowds would acquire appellations in the feminine gender. These collective words for cities, towns, etc. came to be feminine because such places were composed of clusters of *dwellings owned by women,* and from which those women seldom removed. The very word for towns in Num. 21:25, Josh. 15:45, etc. is "daughters." For the same reason "inhabitant of Zion" stands in the original *"inhabitress* of Zion" in Isa. 12:6, and similar instances are very frequent in the O. T.

LESSON 9.

EVE'S CHOICE, AND ADAM'S.

65. In a helpful course of lectures on "The Spiritual Criticism of the Bible," Dr. A. T. Pierson said: "In the intellectual sphere man believes a thing because it is true; in the spiritual, a man knows a thing to be true because he believes it." If, having the Spirit with you to convict you of the truth, you believe what is said in our Lesson today, then *accept the truth* and live by it, and teach it to others, though it may completely overturn previous instruction which you have received, and preconceptions which you may have imbibed.

66. Let us repudiate, once for all, in our Lessons, any desire to discuss, "Which is the greater in the kingdom of heaven, man or woman?" as an unworthy question to raise. But, as women, we are interested, and should be, in woman's destiny. It was fixed in the Garden of Eden. What is it?

67. Please read Gen. 2:17, 18. Just previous to the separation of the sexes, when Adam had reached maturity, and was accountable for his conduct, God forbade him to eat of the *"tree of the knowledge of good and evil."* Eve had not been "builded" yet, as shown by verse 18; the command was given in the second person singular. Precisely what this "tree" was, we are not told. It is allowable to think the expression "good and evil" is practically equivalent to "pain and pleasure," as it is in such passages as 2 Sam. 19:35, Job 2:10, Isa. 7:15, 16, Jer. 42:6, etc. The result of Adam's disobe-

dience of such a law would be, first, the discovering of a marked contrast between "pain" and "pleasure;" and, second, a strong temptation, as to the future, to seek pleasure, and to avoid even wholesome "pain." Perhaps God wished to fix Adam's attention on higher motives and principles of conduct than mere "pain and pleasure." This prohibition, if we so interpret it, had peculiar significance, as just preceding God's providing Adam with a wife. Above all things, the avoidance of the pains of responsibility in the relation of the sexes is to be discountenanced. It means the deterioration of the individual, and eventual deterioration of the race; and it must inevitably entail suffering and undue burden-bearing, on the part of the mother-sex.

68. Eve was not "builded" until after this prohibition was uttered, and we are not informed whether she heard it afterwards from the Almighty, or merely heard of it through Adam. So far as the testimony goes, it is to the effect that she had only heard of it through Adam, when Satan beguiled her into disobeying the commandment; for in repeating the story she elaborates the language, making the statement of the law stronger at one point and weaker at another,—and these are the characteristics of a repeated story, not a first-hand account. Eventually they both ate of the tree, and God came in the cool of the evening to deal with them. He asked Adam: *"Hast thou eaten of the tree?"* and the reply was, *"The woman whom THOU gavest to be with me, SHE gave me of the tree, and I did eat."* God then questioned the woman, and she replied: *"The SERPENT beguiled me, and I did eat."* Please note the words we have put in capital letters.

69. I think we are warranted in drawing a contrast between these two answers, for in them we find a clue to what follows. Both confess, *"I did eat,"* and both tell truthfully the *immediate* influence that led to the eating. So far they are equal. But Adam is led on to say more. There was a remote cause for his downfall, through Eve, —Satan. But Adam does not, like Eve, mention Satan; and yet he does not remain silent as to a remote cause; he accuses God to His face of being Himself that remote cause,—in giving the woman to be with him. And the worst feature of the case consists in the fact that Satan was present, or near by, at the interview, and could not have been overlooked, excepting wilfully, if a remote

cause was to be mentioned at all. Satan must have rejoiced as much in Adam's attitude towards God in charging Him with folly, as in Adam's attitude towards himself, the tempter, in shielding him from blame. Is it not this scene, this conduct on the part of Adam, to which Job refers (31, 33) when he complains, *"If, like Adam, I covered my transgressions by hiding mine iniquity in my bosom"?* Dr. Lange says (see par. 36), "Adam must watch and protect" the garden from an "existing power of evil." Is not this the reason why Adam does not mention Satan, who has been let inside?

70. Destiny is an awful word. One's fate may become fixed for a life-time by the choice of a moment, and that choice, unless Divine interference be invoked, may become the natural bent of one's progeny, through succeeding generations. This is the lesson of the Israelites and Edomites of Scripture. Esau's life seemed more creditable than Jacob's up to a certain advanced point in Jacob's history. But when Esau stood at the parting of two ways, he chose physical refreshment at the cost of his birthright (Gen. 25:29-34). Much later, Jacob came to the parting of two ways, and at the risk of a murderous attack from his brother finding him alone and unprepared, he wrestled all night for the Divine blessing (Gen. 32:24-32), and secured it. God saw, even before the birth of these two, the sort of choices they would make, and made His "selection" according to this foreknowledge. God is now about to make a "selection," the same one as when, later in history, He chose Jacob as the progenitor of the coming Messiah,—this time on the basis of the choices of Adam and Eve.

71. Adam made an evil choice. Adam advanced to the side of the serpent, in becoming a false accuser of God. But Eve, by her exposure of the character of Satan before his very face, created an enmity between herself and him. What followed was the natural outcome of Eve's better choice. God proposed to draw the woman yet farther away from Satan. He said to Satan, *"I will put enmity between thee and the woman* (3:15). In effect, he said: "She has chosen to make the breach; I will widen it."

Much is made of the glorious promise which follows, but let us pause and consider this one, in which the expositors, for the most part, find no more depth of meaning than that there will be always a natural

animosity between men and the lower animal, the snake!
72. We must not forget that at this time God put enmity between Satan and the woman. This will account largely for a whole train of evils prophesied in the following verse (3:16)¦, which tradition says is the result of Eve's having introduced sin into the world by eating the forbidden fruit, and giving of it to her husband. Satan's *enmity* is the cause of woman's sufferings. More light on this point follows later in the Lessons.

73. *"And between thy seed and her seed,"* God adds, in these words addressed to Satan, and concerning woman. Despite the popular cry regarding the "universal Fatherhood of God, and the universal brotherhood of man," which is in part true, we who accept the Scriptures as authority must not forget that Satan, as well as God, has his children—moral and spiritual delinquents —among men. *"The good seed are the children of the kingdom; but the tares are the children of the wicked one."* John 6:70 reads, *"Have I not chosen you twelve and one of you is a devil?"* When the Jews declared, *"We have one Father, even God,"* Jesus replied, *"If God were your Father, ye would love Me . . . Ye are of your father the devil"* (John 8:41-43). Even the Apostle of love, John, will not admit that all men are children of God, but warns: *"Little children, let no man deceive you; he that doeth righteousness is righteous, even as He is righteous. He that committeth sin is of the devil. . . In this the children of God are manifest, and the children of the devil."* (I Jno. 3:7, 8, 10). God does not receive, or acknowledge as His, the unregenerated "bastard" children (Heb. 12:8) of a fallen Church.

74. *"It* [woman's seed] *shall bruise thy head, and thou shall bruise his heel."* The "shall," in both places, here should have been rendered "will," for the sake of clearness. They are future tenses, not imperatives. God does not command Satan to bruise the heel of the woman's seed; He only prophesies that these things will come to pass. The prophecy has special reference to the great enemy of Satan, Jesus Christ, born of the virgin Mary; but it also refers to all believers, for St. Paul says, *"The God of peace shall bruise Satan under your feet shortly,"* in his letter to the Romans (16:20). We will continue this subject in our next Lesson.

31

LESSON 10.

EVE BECOMES A BELIEVER.

75. The New Testament, in several passages, carries forward the thought of all believers being, in some special sense, the seed of the woman. At present we will call attention to one instance only, explaining first, however, that the fact is not emphasized (but clearly implied, nevertheless),—for God knew from the first the tendency of the church toward Mariolatry. John 1:12, 13 declares: *"As many as received Him, to them gave He power to become the sons of God, even to them that believe on His name; which were born, not of blood, nor of the will of the flesh, nor of the will of man, but of God."* That word "born" might, perhaps, with greater propriety, have been here translated "begotten," since the two words are identical in the original. "Sons" of God, here, of course, mean children of either sex. Now fix your thoughts for a moment on the last part of the quotation. The "not" and the "nor" are distinctly eliminative, and the word "man" in the phrase, *"nor of the will of man,"* is not the title of the race,—mankind, but the specific term used of the adult male or husband; in other words, it is *aner,* not *anthropos.* Most commentators pass this fact by unnoticed, or declare one word is used where the other is meant, but this is very doubtful. The scholarly Bengel says: "The will of man is contained in 'the will of the flesh,' and yet it is mentioned separately, as if it were the greater, and in some measure the more guilty part of it. For Christ had a mother, but one who knew not man." See par. 83.

76. Let us analyse these words in John's Gospel:
  1. In the birth of the sons of God, natural descent (*"blood"*) is counted out.
  2. Natural appetite (*"the will of the flesh"*) is counted out.
  3. The *"will of man"* (the husband), is likewise counted out.
  4. But, in that it is not mentioned, the will of the female is not counted out. This prophecy concerning womanhood, made in Eve's day, fulfilled in its first stages in Mary's day, will have its complete fulfilment only in the regeneration of every human being who becomes a child of God. Mary had a wonderful character which Protestants do n o t enough appreciate. She

reached that high pinnacle of purity and self-renunciation from which she could regard dishonor with scorn, and allying her will with the will of her God, in the conception of the Head of a new race (when she said: *"Be it unto me according to Thy word"*), she became, in her own person, the one to realize the promise that the Seed of the woman should bruise the serpent's head. Modern rationalism, which talks of "the divinity of man" (not meaning likewise "the divinity of woman"), and the "natural conception of Jesus," robs woman of her crown, and will quickly reduce her, in public esteem, to the level of the woman of paganism.

77. The Bible, from its opening chapters, pictures woman as allied with God, in the eventual salvation of the world; paganism represents her as allied with the devil, for the ruin of man; this is one great mark of distinction between the true and false religions.

God spoke to Satan of a coming Victor over him. Satan heard, and Eve, too. They both believed; and Satan began to persecute the woman who was to bring forth a conqueror, while she began to expect deliverance. We know of this expectation from Gen. 4:1. On the birth of her first-born she exclaims (and oh, the pathos of it!), *"I have gotten a man,—even The Coming One!"* Neither the translation committee of the A. V. nor of the R. V. could content themselves to leave this as in the original, without the supply of additional words. Such an exclamation on the part of Eve did not comport with the traditional representation of her character. In such cases it is not necessary for us to imply that there was any intention to mislead,—for it is impossible to lead into truth which one cannot at all apprehend, unless it be indeed the work of inspiration.

78. The earliest Hebrew often employs "v" (or "w", which is the same letter), where later Hebrew employs "j". The future form of the verb "to be" is *jhjh*,* "he will be", but in earlier times it might stand *jhvh*, which is the name for "Jehovah", "Jahve", or "Jahwe," as the name is variously spelled in English. Higher Criticism holds that the name "Jahve", can be traced back to some inconspicuous tribal god, and Wellhausen, one of the chief higher critics, blasphemously asserts: "Whatever Jahve's real nature may have been—the god of thunder

* The final "h" in these Hebrew words is merely a vowel-letter—see par. 6.

or whatever he was—it retreated more and more into the background as something secret and transcendant, and no questions were asked concerning it" . . . "Jahva had incalculable moods; he caused his face to shine, and he was wroth, it was not known why; he created good and evil, punished sin and tempted to sin. *Satan had not then robbed him of some of his attributes.*" Those who choose such instruction we leave to themselves; we consider it too polluting to the sense of all reverence for God to deserve respect. We return to the earlier teaching as to the name and character of Jehovah.

79. Payne-Smith gives the true explanation: "Jehovah" means literally "He will come", that is, "The Coming One". He says: "The name is really man's answer to and acceptance of the promise made in Gen. 3:15, and why should not Eve, to whom the promise was given, be the first to profess faith in it? . . . She, ... did not know the meaning of the words she uttered, but she had believed the promise, and for her faith's sake the spirit of prophecy rested upon her, and she gave Him on whom her hopes were fixed the title which was to grow and swell onward till all inspired truth gathered round it, and into it, and at length Elohim, the Almighty, set to it His seal by calling Himself (to Moses, Ex. 3:14), 'I shall be that I shall be.' " Eve was constituted the progenitor of Jesus Christ, and of all believers, because she was the first believer on Him,—the first redeemed through faith in His name.

80. Test the truth of this assertion, not by the witness of man, but by your own spiritual experiences. Had *you* sinned, and confessed, and been comforted by God with the assurance that there was One who would conquer your enemy for you; and had you accepted that One by faith, what would that have meant to you but the witness of sin forgiven?

And next, we are told that having been so assured of coming victory through Another, God turned upon Eve and pronounced a solemn curse—having binding force for all time upon all her female descendants—upon her head. Monstrous! What a slander upon God's mercy!

81. The Hebrew word "Jehovah", we learn from O. T. quotations in the N. T., and from the Septuagint Greek version, can be identified with the N. T. name "Lord." The Hebrew word "Anointed," that is "Messiah," is

identical with Christ. The name "Jesus" of the N. T., is identical with "Joshua" in the O. T.,—the name of the One who leads into the Promised Land of rest from all our enemies (see Luke 1:74). He who was born of woman, having no human father, was fittingly named by woman. Eve bestowed upon Him the title "Lord;" Hannah first called Him "The Anointed," that is, "Christ" (I Sam. 2:10), and the Virgin Mary was instructed to name Him, before He was born, "Jesus" (Luke 1:31). That name which is above every name, THE LORD JESUS CHRIST, at which *"every knee shall bow, of things in heaven, and things in earth, and things under the earth,"* was bestowed upon Him by three holy women of old, prophetesses of God,—Eve, Hannah, Mary.

May women never cease to honor that name, most holy, most exalted, world without end!

Note on Paragraphs 75 and 76.

Dean Alford comments on the proper translation of verse 18 of this same first chapter of John, as follows: "It would be well for the student to bear in mind as a general rule, that *no word or expression is ever 'put for' another:* . . . and where an unusual contraction is found, it points to some reason in the mind of the writer for using it, which reason is lost in the ordinary shallow method of accounting for it by saying that it is 'put for' some other word." It seems amazing, therefore, that he should nevertheless assume that *aner* ("husband") is put for *anthropos* ("mankind") in verse 13. There is yet a stronger reason than Dean Alford's for never assuming this, as to Holy Scripture,—*"Every word of God is tried,"*—Prov. 30:5, R. V.

LESSON 11

EVE AND HER TRADUCERS.

82. Did space permit, we might add interesting comments by others besides Dean Payne-Smith as to Eve's belief that Cain was the Coming One, the Messiah. Particularly valuable are the comments of Dr. Peter Lange, of Bonn University, and his editor and translator, Dr. Tayler Lewis. The latter says: "The greatness of Eve's mistake in applying the expression to one who was the type of Antichrist rather than of the Redeemer, should not so shock us as to affect the interpretation of the passage, now that the Covenant God is revealed to us as a being so transcendingly different. The limitation of Eve's knowledge, and perhaps her want of due distinction between the Divine and the human, only sets in a stronger light the intensity of her hope, and the sub-

jective truthfulness of her language. Had her reported words, at such a time, contained no reference to the promised seed of the woman, the rationalist would doubtless have used it as a proof that she could have known nothing of such a prediction, and that, therefore, Gen. 3:15 and Gen. 4:1 must have been written by different authors, ignoring or contradicting each other."

83. It is not Adam, but the Word of God itself, that says Eve was *"the mother of all living."* Delitzsch remarks here, "The promise purports truly a seed of the woman. In the very face, therefore, of the death with which he is threatened, the wife is for Adam the security for both, as well for the continuance, as for the victory of the race." On the point as to all believers being "the seed of the woman," Dr. Monroe Gibson asks, "Who are her seed?" and replies, "Many superficial readers think it is all mankind. In a certain sense, of course, all mankind are 'the seed of the woman'; but suppose you include all mankind, where do the seed of the serpent come in [with whom her seed are at enmity]? Is it not quite obvious that 'the seed of the woman' cannot mean all mankind,—but simply those who are not only literally, but spiritually the 'seed of the woman,' those who are found on the side of good, the side of God and righteousness? Those who are of an opposite spirit are the seed of the serpent, 'the children of the devil.' In the same way, when . . we are told that *'Adam called his wife's name Eve, because she was the mother of all living'* [3:20], most readers take it in the sense that she was the mother of all mankind. But why give her a name to indicate a thing so obvious? On the other hand, when you take the 'living' in the spiritual as well as the literal sense as those 'alive unto God', those who are to have the 'life' which God gives through His Son, how beautifully all the references correspond! 'The seed of the woman,' 'the mother of the living,' 'the generation of Adam.' There is, properly speaking, no present tense in Hebrew—only the past and future. So when the future is used, it may denote the present, running on into the future. So here, it is not only *'I will put enmity,'* but I am putting, and will put enmity between thee and the woman. The work is begun. . . . She is the first type and representative of all the separated ones who constitute the Church of God." (*The Ages before Moses, page 122*).

84. Now let us compare four passages, out of many that might be chosen. God tells Abraham, Gen. 22:16-18, *"By Myself have I sworn . . . in thy seed shall all the nations of the earth be blessed; because thou hast obeyed My voice."* To Isaac He says, *"In thy seed shall all the nations of the earth be blessed; because that Abraham obeyed My voice"* (Gen. 26:4, 5). To Jacob He said the same (Gen. 28:14). To David He says, *"I will raise up thy seed after thee . . and I will establish his throne forever"* (I Chron. 17:11, 12). Then, Gal. 3:29, *"If ye be Christ's, then are ye Abraham's seed, and heirs according to the promise,"* Was it a special honor to Abraham, Isaac, Jacob and David to be mentioned as in this stream of blessing which was to descend to humanity? Then it is well for us to remember that the *source* of this blessing, on the human side, is Eve, of whom God said, to Satan, *"I will put enmity between thee and the woman; . . . her seed . . . shall bruise thy head."* The promise honors Eve quite as much as Abraham, Isaac and Jacob, and the honor could not have been conferred upon her but for the same reason as upon them,—namely, because of excellence found in her.

85. In our next Lesson we will show that the N. T. teaches that Adam, rather than Eve, was the one who brought sin into the world, and death through sin. But how, then, can we account for this slandering of Eve's character? Where did it take its source? We think the answer to these questions is simple enough. Historically speaking, the earliest definite accusation against woman as the source of all evil is the pagan Greek myth of Pandora. According to Hesiod, who lived about 800 B. C., Jupiter was angry because Prometheus ("Forethought") had stolen fire from heaven, and in revenge ordered Vulcan to make a beautiful woman. Minerva adorned her with all gifts, and she was named Pandora ("All-gifted"),—but Mercury gave her a deceitful mind. She was brought to Epimetheus ("Afterthought"), who received her, contrary to warnings, in the absence of Prometheus. When admitted among men, Pandora opened a casket and allowed to escape all the evils of mankind, excepting delusive hope. There are many variations of this myth, but they all teach the one view, —that woman is the source of human ills.

86. The time between the O. T. and the N. T. story has been called in Jewish history "the days of mingling," because of the effort, on the part of the Jews, to reconcile the teachings of the O. T., and the customs of the Jews, with Greek paganism. Archdeacon Farrar* tells us that at this time, "Palestine was surrounded by a cordon of Greek cities in which many Jews mingled freely with the heathen population. In Jerusalem itself we witness the growth of a wealthy and powerful party, in close alliance, alternately, with the Greek kings of Syria and of Egypt. Fascinated by the attractions of Greek life and literature, they wished to adopt Hellenistic ideals, and to obliterate the most essential distinctions of Jewish life and religion. This semi-faithless epoch was described as 'the days of mingling'."

87. It is nothing strange, then, that during this time the attempt should have been made to reconcile the story of Pandora and the account of Eve in Genesis; and the most ancient extant reference to Eve as the source of evil is to be found in that book of the Apocrypha which is known as *Ecclesiasticus,* or *The Wisdom of Ben Sira.* This, a Palestinian production of uncertain date, was originally written in Hebrew, probably about 250 B. C., but early translated into Greek, in Egypt, and it contains these words: "From woman a beginning of sin; and because of her all die" (25:24). Tennant tells us that "Ben Sira was the precursor of the Talmudic teaching as to the Fall."† We shall presently show what some of that Talmudic teaching was as regards Eve,—so please do not forget this point.

Other Jewish writers, of later date, enlarge upon this culpability of Eve. At Alexandria, particularly, was the effort carried forward of reconciling the Scriptures with Greek pagan teachings. Unfortunately for Christian theology, after the Greek version of the O. T. was made at Alexandria (B. C. 285 saw its beginning), these Jewish, uninspired writings, called *The Apocrypha,* all written in Greek, not Hebrew, were incorporated with that version, which was used, to the exclusion of the Hebrew Scriptures by the Church; and many of the church fathers quoted the Apocrypha as authoritative; and all were influenced by its teachings. Thus it easily happens that the character of the mythological Pandora is as-

---

*The Herods, p. 15

†The Talmud contains "not less than forty" citations from Ben Sira,—Lange's Commentaries, Apocrypha, p. 276.

38

cribed to Eve. No saying that reflects upon Eve's character can be traced further back than "the days of mingling."

88. Irenaeus, Bishop of Lyons in 177 A. D., following the teaching of Ben Sira and other Jews, says of Eve: "Having become disobedient, she was made the cause of death, both to herself and to the entire human race." But Tertullian of Carthage, a few years later, is particularly severe, and visits Eve's sin on all Christian women, in the following language: "Do you not know that you are an Eve? God's verdict on the sex still holds good, and the sex's guilt must still hold also. YOU ARE THE DEVIL'S GATEWAY, you are the avenue to the forbidden tree. You are the first deserter from the law divine. It was you who persuaded him [Adam] whom the devil himself had not strength to assail. So lightly did you esteem God's image. For your deceit, for death, the very Son of God had to perish." But, except for woman, would humanity have ever afforded any entrance of the Son of God into the world, to perish, or for men to preach?

89. Many of the theological views of the present day show the shaping of Tertullian's hand upon them, for, to use the concise statement of Lippincott's Biographical Dictionary, "He acquired great influence among the Christians of his time." Not a few of his literary works remain to this day. With such a view of woman, to start with (shut out by perpetual "guilt" from participation in the merits of Christ's atonement), it is small wonder that the next Scripture verse that we shall consider (Gen. 3:16), has been construed, in accordance with the teaching of the Talmud and Tertullian, as God's perpetual curse upon the entire female sex.

LESSON 12

BIBLE INSTRUCTION AS TO ADAM'S AND EVE'S CONDUCT.

90. After the fourth chapter of Genesis, Eve is never referred to again in the O. T., and Adam is mentioned only twice,—in Job 31:33, *"If I, like Adam, covered my transgression, by hiding my iniquity in my bosom,"* and Hos. 6:7, (R. V.), *"They, like Adam, transgressed the covenant."* But when we come to the N. T., there is a

striking contrast between the estimate put upon Adam's and Eve's conduct. Of Adam it is plainly said that his conduct brought sin into the world., Theologians *infer* disastrous results to the world from Eve's conduct, but there are no clear statements to that effect in the Bible. We presently discuss the lawfulness of these inferences.

91. We will place all passages referring plainly to Adam and Eve in the N. T. in parallel columns:

ADAM.

1. *"Adam was not deceived,"*
   —1 Tim. 2:14.
2. *"In Adam all die,"*
   —1 Cor. 15:22.
3. *"By one man [person] sin entered into the world,"*
   —Rom. 5:12.
4. *"Through the offence of one many be dead,"* —Rom. 5:15.
5. *"—it was by one that sinned,"*
   —Rom. 5:16.
6. *"The judgment was by one to condemnation,"*—Rom 5:16
7. *"By one man's offence death reigned,—"*
8. [death reigned] *"by one,"*
   —Rom. 5:17.
9. *"By the offence of one judgment came upon all men to condemnation,"* —Rom. 5:18.
10. *"By one man's disobedience—"* —Rom. 5:19.
11. *"Death reigned from Adam to Moses, even over them that had not sinned after the similitude of Adam's transgression, who is the figure of Him that was to come."*
    —Rom. 5:14.

EVE.

1. *"The woman being* [thoroughly] *deceived was* [literally, "became"] *in the transgression."* Weymouth renders this, more accurately, *"was thoroughly deceived, and so became involved"*—
   1 Tim. 2:14.
2.—*"the serpent beguiled* [literally, "thoroughly deceived"] *Eve through his subtilty."*
   2 Cor. 11:3.

Both these passages employ the same verb in the Greek original,—"to deceive," with a prefix meaning "thoroughly." The verb itself is the same one which is used of Adam in our first quotation regarding him, excepting that in Adam's case there is no prefix, as in Eve's case We give the sole references to Eve in the Bible, after the Genesis story. Nor is Eve even remotely referred to elsewhere in the Bible.

Eight times over, Paul declares "one person" alone was accountable for the Fall, and twice mentions that person as "Adam."

92. Some one may claim that "Adam" and the "one" spoken of in the Roman passages means "mankind." But *anthropos*, not "Adam" is the Greek, or the N. T., equivalent for "mankind." Besides, Paul's argument is this: "What *one* did of mischief, another *One* [Christ] is well able to undo;" and if we conceive, that, after all, Paul means "two," we reduce Paul's forceful statement to inanity. The Bible here teaches that "one person," whom it explicitly states to be Adam, caused the Fall, or else no meaning can be found for its words. All the

teaching of the N. T., in which Adam and Eve are mentioned, is to the effect that Adam was the chief offender, as the one "not deceived," when the forbidden tree was partaken of. The greater culpability of Eve as causing the Fall *is taught by tradition only.*

93. But remember, we are now discussing the conduct of Adam and Eve *at one point*—in one incident only—of their lives. But that incident is the sin which has been held to have produced the Fall of the entire world of human beings. We again assert: The Bible nowhere holds Eve accountable for this particular deed; and it does, in the plain, definite language we have just quoted from the N. T., hold Adam accountable for that deed.

94. It is not by one single verse, such as Gen. 3:16 (the correct translation and interpretation of which is doubtful,—see future lessons), that Eve's greater culpability can be established, *in spite of clear statements to the contrary,* and many other incidental Scriptural proofs. For instance, God asked Adam, *"Hast thou eaten of the tree whereof I commanded thee that thou shouldst not eat?"* and He lays no such charge of express disobedience at the door of Eve. And also note that whereas the Almighty told the Serpent that his creeping gait, dust for his food, and his final mortal injury were to be *"Because thou hast done this;"* and whereas the Almighty told Adam that his drudgery, his fight with thorns and thistles, and his final return to the dust out of which he was made, were to be "because" Adam has done thus and so, God nowhere says that Eve's sorrowful and oppressed part is "because" she has done anything. Rather, from the highly honoring words regarding Eve the Almighty has just addressed to the Serpent we have sufficient reasons for concluding that all this might result to Eve because God has elevated her to the honorable position of an enemy of Satan and progenitor of the coming Messiah. William Law says that Adam's sin, which brought ruin to the world, "is not to be considered as that single act of eating," but "his express open, voluntary act and deed" of "refusing to be that which God created him to be." On Rom. 5:14, where *"Adam's transgression"* is spoken of as causing death to the entire human race, that high authority, *Bengel's Gnomen* says, "Chrysostom on this passage shows exceedingly well, what Paul intended to prove by his argument, 'that it was not the very sin of the trans-

gression of the law [Eve transgressed it, under deception], but that of the *disobedience of ADAM,* this was what brought universal destruction.'" (The capitals are ours).

95. The rest of the story (excepting Gen. 3:16, which we next explain), on the very face of it, bears evidence of Eve's favor with God, through her confession and faith. After the eating, God assigns to Adam his particular vocation (Gen. 3:19). Adam was to earn his bread by tilling the soil, *"till thou return unto the ground, for out of it thou wast taken."* Eve was not taken out of the ground, in the same sense as Adam; when she became an identity apart from Adam, it was by God's taking her out of Adam (Gen. 2:21). Now please rub your eyes carefully, search the latter end of chapter three of Genesis, and point me the place where the Bible teaches that Eve was *expelled* from Eden. I cannot find such teaching. I find that the one whose duty it was to *"till the ground,"* was expelled; the one who was *"taken out of the ground"* was expelled; but I find no account of the sex which was to bear children *"in sorrow,"* in the story of the expulsion; and I choose to believe that something of the odors of Eden have enveloped motherhood ever since creation. Yet Eve must soon have abandoned Eden to follow Adam (see pars. 122, 123, 137).

96. We are taught, in Rev. 22:14, that those who *"wash their robes"* (the R. V. is the correct reading here), *"have right to the tree of life."* If this be true for deliberate sinners, much more is it true for a wholly deceived person. We have shown that Eve was a believer. We see no reason why Eve should have found a "flaming sword" between herself and the tree of life. Adam was thrust out of Eden, with a flaming sword between himself and the tree of life, *"lest he put forth his hand and take of the tree of life, and eat, and live forever."* But if Eve was already "living" spiritually, the same motive could not have existed for cutting off her access to the tree of life; she already had eternal life.

97. It was not *physical death* which was to follow, if Adam ate of the forbidden "tree of the knowledge of good and evil." God said: *"In the day that thou eatest thereof thou shalt surely die"* (Gen. 2:17). Yet when Adam ate he did not on that very day fall to the ground

and expire. But he did die, *spiritually*, on that very day, though he lived, physically, for many years. "Death" and "life" are employed of spiritual states, all through the Bible. And since "death" is used here for the first time in the Bible we discover that its *primary* Scriptural sense is the spiritual one. Then we may lawfully infer the same of the word "life,"—at least as regards human beings, into whom God breathed His Own *"breath of life"* (Gen. 2:7). Therefore, when Adam faced his doom, to return, eventually to the ground out of which he was made, he understood this to mean spiritual death; and it is but natural to read, as the very next incident, that, marking a contrast between himself and Eve, Adam called his wife "Eve,"—*"Living,"*—*spiritually living*.

LESSON 13

DID GOD CURSE WOMAN?

98. Can anything be accomplished by clearing the reputation of one so remote in history as Eve? Much, in many ways. The false teaching that God is in some way punishing women for the sin of Eve, at certain times of anguish, has robbed women of much sympathy, and also furnished a cloak for sensuality, and for much unnecessary cruelty to women, throughout past ages, and up to the present hour. The teaching that God punishes Christian women for the sin of Eve is a wicked and cruel superstition, and unworthy the intelligence of Christians. But in addition to this, the doctrine has laid a blighting hand upon woman's self-respect, self-confidence and spiritual activity, from which causes the entire Church of Jesus Christ suffers moral and spiritual loss, and therefore we offer no apology for expending much time and thought in a thorough examination of Genesis, third chapter.

99. Woman had been constituted by God, in words addressed to Satan: (1) The progenitor of the coming destroyer of Satan and his power; (2) and *in her own person also* an enemy of Satan. This latter is a point of much importance to women, and generally passed over very lightly. With such an appointment as this to fulfill in life (and none could be nobler), what would Satan, who knew it, wish done to woman, his enemy? It is not difficult to conjecture; he would have her so crippled she could not contend with him successfully. How better could he cripple her than to incite her

husband,—the one livng closest to her who has strength to do it—to hamper her activities as much as possible? And then, knowing of a Seed whose coming would be his doom, Satan would aim his sorest blows *at her function of motherhood,* and torture her by every means that could be devised, in her child-bearing. How he would hate her every time she was about to become a mother!

100. Now all this, which common sense tells us Satan would *most certainly* wish to do, most Bible expositors (as we are about to show), tell us GOD DID. For once then, *if* God did so, God and Satan would be found working on the same side, for the same result. Can we imagine such a thing as this? God and Satan working harmoniously together in the treatment of women, after the same fashion, from the Fall in Eden as long as this world lasts?

101. Although Eve had given the evidences we have mentioned of having become one of the Household of Faith; although God had exalted her to a relation with believers equal to Abraham's; although God had put enmity between her and Satan, so that she was no longer associated with God's great enemy, yet the Bible commentary represents that God now turned and pronounced a curse, or several curses upon her. *We are sure that if anyone would..curse her under such conditions, it would not be God, but Satan, her enemy.* Surely God and Satan would not unite to curse.

102. It is not necessary to translate the language addressed to Eve by the Almighty on this occasion, as our English Bible translates it. Let us hold Savonarola's banners high today: *"Nothing has been learnt from any man;" "We accept no authority save our own experience and reason."* This teaching that God cursed Eve, and through Eve all women, comes over into theology from the Babylonian Talmud. Scripture nowhere says Eve was cursed, or women either. We do not accept as an authority that book of fables, the Talmud. Jesus Christ trampled the "traditions" of the Jews under His feet, and Paul warned solemnly against them, more than once. Our own spiritual experience as women, and the witness of the Spirit in our hearts, testify: *"Christ hath redeemed us from the curse of the law, being made a curse for us."* As Christian women, we refuse to address ourselves to the task of working out Eve's "curse"

for sin, if indeed she ever had one. We will not deny the faith; we will not discount the sufficiency of the atonement. Since theology points no other way for women through this chapter in Genesis but into a "curse", we must do some sappers' and miners' work, and hew a hermeneutical and exegetical road for ourselves.

103. But first, as to what theology teaches: The comments of Dean Alford—not the harshest by any means—quite fairly represent the line of theological teaching here, "I will greatly multiply the pain of thy pregnancy," is his translation and he adds: "And yet, though this shall be so, the woman, as a second curse, shall desire again the occasion of this pain; and thirdly, [that is, note his words, in accordancec with a third curse], "though the subject of all the suffering which accompanies the propagation of the race, she shall be subordinate, and ruled over by man."

104. But what does all this mean if not that Adam, or man, is to be wonderfully rewarded for his part in that Garden fruit-eating? He is to be *elevated* to government over women; and to be allowed to dictate, by his own whims, how much or how little physical suffering she is to endure, as the price of his fleshly indulgence! And has God so honored man for all time as to give him this, which often amounts to the power of life and death over a fellow creature, forsooth because Adam accused God of unwisdom and sheltered Satan from blame? We know very well who, if anyone, will reward man thus, if only we will exercise common sense,—the one whom Adam favored, Satan. If God and Satan both award man thus, here again we find for a third time these, two working together for the same result. We said a moment ago if anyone caused Eve to suffer, or cursed Eve it was her enemy, Satan; if anyone rewarded Adam for shielding Satan, it was Satan again.

105. Notice that Dean Alford names at least *three curses* from which, he says, woman is to suffer. But why did he not set forth all ten of them,—especially that one that declares that man was also to be awarded the privilege of practicing polygamy because of Eve's sin? Christian theology *dares not* set forth the whole of the Talmudic teaching as to the "curses" of woman, in these enlightened days. It only ventures as far as the subor-

dination of woman to the sensuality of man. To set forth the whole ten curses would effectually secure the condenmation of the whole, including the parts theology would keep. The "ten curses of Eve" will be found on p. 137 of Dr. Hershon's *"Genesis with a Talmudic Commentary"* (Bagster, London), found in most of our large libraries. We will not soil our pages with all its filthy details, but one would have thought that any portion of such a document would have been considered so debased by corrupt association as to unfit it for incorporation into Bible instruction. We number them:

106. "TEN CURSES WERE UTTERED AGAINST EVE.

1. 'Greatly multiply' refers to catamenia, etc.;
2. 'thy sorrow' in rearing children;
3. 'thy conception';
4. 'in sorrow shalt thou bring forth children';
5. 'thy desire shall be unto thy husband'; [followed by language too coarse for reproduction. leaving no doubt of the rabbinical interpretation of "desire"];
6. 'He shall rule over thee' [more, and fouler language];
7. she is wrapped up like a mourner, i. e.
8. dares not appear in public with her head uncovered;
9. is restricted to one husband, while he may have many wives;
10. and is confined to the house as to a prison."

The teaching of the Babylonian Talmud, in the "ten curses of Eve," and in parts of it unfit for quotation, has since 1528 been allowed to settle the meaning of an obscure word in Genesis 3:16, as "desire"—and that against all the testimony of the most ancient versions of Scripture. We will bring out this point clearly in forthcoming lessons. The teaching of the seventh and eighth curses has also been allowed to cast a shadow forward into the New Testament, and to pervert the meaning of St. Paul's words about veiling in worship, in the 11th chapter of 1st Corinthians.

LESSON 14.
THE FALSE INTERPRETATION.

107. But the need of a different translation and interpretation of Genesis 3:16 will scarcely be realised by

those not familiar with the usual teachings to be found in our Bible commentaries, which defy principles of morality and justice, as well as outrage the sense of the original words, as can be proved by the ancient versions. This latter statement we will make good.

Excepting that it seems necessary to the proof of our point, and to secure revision, we could not bring ourselves to reproduce samples of what is being taught along this line by scholars highly esteemed as Biblical expositors by the Church. Dean Alford's teaching, in par. 103 should be re-read: Browne says, "Desire here expresses that reverential longing with which the weaker [woman] looks up, to the stronger." Addis says "Woman is to desire man's society, notwithstanding the pain and subjection which are the result."

108. The assumption is more or less general that morbidly intense sensuality, when it displays itself in the female character, is of Divine manufacture. Knobel interprets God as saying, "Thou shalt be possessed by passionate desire for him." Keil and Delitzsch, "She was punished with a desire bordering upon disease." Dillmann comments on the passage: "The special punishment of the woman consists in the evils by which she is oppressed in her sexual vocation, in the position she occupies in her relation to man," and yet, doubtless he would scarcely hesitate to pronounce such a relation "Holy Matrimony!" Driver declares "She shall desire his cohabitation, thereby at the same time increasing her liability to the pain of childbearing." If this sensuality were the state of woman's mind in general it would not be necessary to starve women out of industrial lines, and put a check upon their mental development, lest they be disinclined to marry if capable of self support; yet these are the methods which have been used in order to maintain the "domestic" desires of women. Calvin says, "This form of speech is . . . as if He [God] said, 'Thou shalt desire nothing but what thy husband wishes'. She had, indeed, previously been subject to her husband, but that was a liberal and gentle subjection; now, however, she is cast into servitude." In other words, Calvin would have us believe God first ordained marriage, but afterwards substituted "servitude." Patrick, Lowth, etc., in their commentary declare of the husband that he shall have the power "to control thy desires," but we have never known of a husband who could do more than con-

trol the outward acts of his wife. Poole elaborates this decree into, "Thy desires shall be referred to thy husband's will and pleasure, to grant or deny them as he sees fit." Dr. Adam Clarke says: "It is a part of her punishment, and a part from which even God's mercy will not exempt her . . . Thou shalt not be able to shun the great pain and peril of child-bearing, 'thy desire shall be to thy husband.' . . . Subjection to the will of her husband is one part of her curse; and so very capricious is this will often, that a sorer punishment no human being can well have."

109. But the astounding part of this teaching is, that these men fail to see that, if a wife must be under a "curse" because she is under a husband who exercises the cruelties that constitute that curse, this is equivalent to saying that God has ordained that man and marriage shall be a curse to woman. Such teaching relieves a husband of the duty to observe nearly the entire decalogue, if only the person he practices his transgressions upon happens to be the one he has vowed, before the marriage altar, that he willl "love and cherish."

110. But does this teaching accord with the general tenor of Scriptural morals? Not at all. Abraham, once upon a time, desired to maintain a polygamous household, and Sarah objected. Did God speak to her about the matter, and say: "Remember Eve, and the penalty: Thy desire shall be thy husband?" He spoke to Abraham, saying: *"In all that Sarah saith unto thee, obey her voice"* (Gen. 21:12). The word rendered, in English, "hearken unto," in this passage means obey, and it is translated "obey" in very many other passages,—such as Gen. 22:18. When Hannah centered all her "desire" upon a hoped-for son, her husband exhorted her to center it, rather, upon himself, saying,*"Am I not better to thee than ten sons?"* Hannah did not obey the expositor's teaching as to Gen. 3:16, and God blessed her in this sort of "disobedience" to her husband, by sending the son. So we might go on illustrating the fact that God has shown no zeal in enforcing this supposed "law" of His. But one quotation is sufficient to entirely destroy the fallacious interpretation of Gen. 3:16, and that is the well-known Golden Rule, uttered by Jesus Christ: *"Whatsoever ye would that men should do unto you, do ye even so unto them."* We have never yet found the man who longed to be ruled by the will of his wife. All

48

men led by the Spirit of Christ obey this Golden Rule, which sets at defiance the so-called "law" of Gen. 3:16, as interpreted by these expositors.

111. But three passages speak to us against the specific sense that has been put upon that word "desire," by most of the commentators. Lev. 20:18 is a law which punishes the wife, with the husband, if she should yield her will to his under improper conditions. This law necessitates the view that God holds woman as a free agent in the marriage relation. Further, the Apostle Paul, 1. Cor. 7:4, makes the authority of the wife precisely equal to the husband's in the marriage relation, saying. *"The husband hath not authority over his own body, but the wife."* We are quite aware that this verse has been reduced to a mere sophism by Bible commentaries. But "authority" does not mean "authority" at all, unless it comprehends the idea of being able to act with perfect independence either one way or in the precisely opposite way. Later, we have a lesson on this passage in Corinthians. The third passage is found in three of the Gospels (Matt. 24:19, Mark 13:17, Luke 21:23). It is the "Woe" of the Lord pronounced upon mothers (not fathers), found "with child," or with sucklings at the time of the Great Tribulation, yet to come,—for, as Fronmüller has said (referring to these with other passages), woe is "an utterance . . . of frequent occurrence in the speeches of our Lord, expressive of pain and indignation, and conveying the threat of punishment." It can by no means be given an exceptional meaning here.

112. It must, then, impress reasoning minds that the interpretation of Gen. 3:16 has had a history something like this: Men of old found a phrase here that seemed to have to do with woman's relation to her husband, but it was beyond their comprehension. Unconsciously these men of olden time have consulted their own ideas of what a wife *should be,* in her relation to her husband, and inserted those ideas into their interpretation. The interpretation has been accepted by other men, without challenge, because it conformed to their unsanctified wishes, and handed on from generation to generation, until it became weighty through "tradition." No effort, scarcely, has been put forth to reconcile such teachings with the spirit of Jesus Christ. A letter, relating to the passage, has come to me, during the preparation of these Lessons, from an eminent Bible scholar, to whom I suggested the

need of a better interpretation. He replies: "I should hardly have thought a correction of the text was either called for or probable." Of course, our proposal had never been to amend the text, as he well knew, but the interpretation and translation. Prejudice blinds men, even in their treatment of the Word of God, if a faulty rendering coincides with their preconceptions.

113. The Bible nowhere uses such an expression as "the curse" regarding women. We get the teaching about the woman's "curse" wholly through tradition. Pain is invariably an outcry of God's natural law against abuse; and pain must be contrary to God's will. This is as true regarding the pain of childbirth as it is regarding any other sort of pain. If this were a lesson in Physiology, we could abundantly account for such suffering as some women endure periodically and in childbirth, quite apart from the fiction that God Himself inflicts such pain upon women. Woman suffers in childbirth more than any other female animal, because other female animals protect themselves (by the only proper means, of course), from all possibility of becoming mothers excepting at suitable seasons; they will not brook tyranny in such a matter.

LESSON 15.

SATAN'S LYING IN WAIT.

114. A clock needs a most careful fitting of all its parts. It is quite conceivable that a typewriter wheel might be used for other purposes, but it could never be fitted into a clock, to take the place of a broken clock wheel. It would be too heavy or too light; the rim too thick or too thin; the hub too big or too little, and the cogs too many or too few. It would prove to be a misfit all around; the clock would not keep proper time. So it is with Scripture: *"Every word of God is tried,"* and if we attempt to insinuate a false interpretation into it, it proves, on close inspection, a misfit all around. We shall demonstrate, by the misfit all around, that the usual interpretation of Gen. 3:16 is not correct. It bears a *resemblance* to the correct interpretation as a typewriter wheel may resemble a clock wheel, but it does not fit accurately anywhere.

115. As introductory, we go back to verse 15, *"It shall bruise thy head, and thou shalt bruise his heel."* "Bruise"

is an obscure word; to quote Dr. Tayler Lewis, "The general sense of this passage is plain, but there is great difficulty in fixing the precise action intended by the Hebrew word *shuph,* in consequence of its occurrence but three times in the Bible." The two other places are Job 9:17, "breaking," and Psa. 139:11, "cover." Now what word, could imply, according to its context, either bite, crush, break, or cover? That is the question,—for our verse certainly means that the serpent will bite the heel, and the "seed" of woman crush its head.

116. The sense "bruise," so unsuitable for the figure of a biting serpent, has been fixed upon on account of St. Paul's words, Rom. 16:20, *"The God of peace shall bruise Satan under your feet shortly."* But we have no proof that Paul meant to translate the word *shuph;* he may have meant merely to give the general sense of the phrase, as it relates to man's part, which is clear to us all, whatever *shuph* means.

Some of the ancient versions translate, here, "lying in wait," or a kindred idea; and on the strength of this the R. V. gives us this as an alternative meaning in the margin. But this leaves the thought incomplete—to say merely that the "seed" will "lie in wait for his head." In that case, the seed of woman might in the end be defeated, while the real force of the prophecy is one of victory. No, *shuph* means something else, but we must leave the matter unsettled.

117. But why was the thought of "lying in wait" ever brought in here? This is an interesting point to raise. We hold that verse 16 should have been rendered, *"Unto the woman He said. A snare hath increased thy sorrow,"* —the word "snare" being, literally rendered, "a lying-in-wait." Instead, it is rendered, *"I will greatly multiply thy sorrow."* The difference between the two in Hebrew lies wholly in the interlinear vowel-signs (see par. 6), of comparatively recent invention.* This would explain why the idea of "lying in wait" still clings to the passage, though it can scarcely be the meaning of the word *shuph.*

---

* The difference is, between HaRBeh. AaRBeh, "multiplying I will multiply," and HiRBah AoReB, "hath-caused-to-multiply," (or "made great"), a lying-in-wait."—the verb, as usual preceding its nominative. The capital letters, alike in both phrases, alone constitute the original text. This participial form, ARB, occurs fourteen times in Joshua and Judges. It is translated "ambush," and "liers-in-wait," or "in ambush." It is possible that we should read, here, "A lyer-in-wait (the subtil serpent) hath increased thy sorrow."

51

The thought was obliterated from the opening expression of verse 16, by the words being construed as "multiplying I will multiply" (literal for *"I will greatly multiply"*), and then it was reflected backwards as a possible sense for the obscure word *shuph*. In this connection we must recall that originally Hebrew had no divisions into verses, or even words.

118. We have said, and shown, that the idea of God's passing a punitive sentence upon Eve, after the wonderful prophecy regarding her in verse 15, is inconsistent. But the rendering which we give is perfectly consistent with the context. We know that the Serpent was pronounced "subtil," and Eve was said to have been "beguiled," or deceived. Here, then, is a perfect fit in place of a misfit. This, as we believe, the correct rendering, became lost to us in the "days of mingling" (see par. 86), when the first version—the Greek—was made; when, as we have shown, the natural tendency would be, and was, to conform the story of Eve to the story of Pandora. A philologist of high repute, while doubting the general acceptance of my rendering, writes me, "I agree to the possibility of your translation."

119. I have written to another gentleman, a high authority in the Hebrew language, and enquired if he could find fault, grammatical or rhetorical, with my translation. His reply simply states: "The translation proposed in your letter would seem to me quite unnatural, or, at any rate, unduly forced, where the usual rendering is natural, and to my mind perfectly correct." On this point we differ. What could be more unnatural than for God to first repose that greatest promise of all the Bible in a person, and then in the next breath pronounce a terrible punishment upon her? But to first give a great and wonderful promise, but at the same time reveal that with that high and holy calling the enemy of souls would be at war, and much suffering must attend and eventuate from it, as was the case with the Virgin Mary, (Luke 1:28 and 2:35) and St. Paul (Acts 8:15, 16),—this view is both logically and theologically sound, and we imagine that many thoughtful people will think our reading *more natural* and less forced than the traditional translation and interpretation.

120. We must now consider another portion of Eve's so-called "sentence,—*and thy conception;*" especially that last word. When our Lord was on earth He prom-

ised us that, *"Till heaven and earth pass, one jot or one tittle shall in no wise pass from the law, till all be fulfilled."* Some have supposed this promise to cover all the scope that it would if spoken concerning such a language as the English. But those who have studied our Lessons 1 and 2 will be prepared to see the case in its true light. The *consonants* of such a language as Hebrew must remain unchangeable or else we can have no hope of preserving the original sense of its words. But even as to English, our law courts every day present cases where the most tremendous decisions turn upon the exact reading of human laws. Our laws must be drafted by experts, with utmost care. We can easily imagine a case in which the fate of life or death might be determined by the precise reading of the law, or even upon its punctuation. Imagine, then, what would be the outcome if we, in the end, at the great Judgment seat, were to be tried by carelessly inscribed or imperfectly preserved laws. Imagine such a state of things even in the days of Israel's kings. Supposing, in the days when the law was written in consonants only, Rehoboam, who was an especially harsh king (1 Kings 12:10), had chosen to read, as a penalty for an offense, G L S instead of G L, claiming that the law was probably mutilated *at the particular point* where he had chosen to add that S to its consonants. This would have made all the difference between GaoL (jail) and GaLLowS; we take an English word for illustration. Now it is just such perversions as these against which God has undertaken, on the assurance of Jesus Christ, to protect us. That is not unreasonable, is it?

121. We have before us such a case as this, in this supposed law of retribution upon all womanhood, because Eve sinned. The "sentence," *I will multiply . . . thy conception,"* has wrought terrible havoc with the health and happiness of wives; because, so read it has been understood to rob woman of the right to determine when she should become a mother, and to place that right outside her will, and in abeyance to the will of her husband, —at least, the law has been read thus, because of its connection with what follows in this passage. This word is spelled, in Hebrew HRN,—but that is *not* the correct Hebrew way to spell "conception." The latter occurs, and correctly spelled, in Ruth 4:13 and Hosea 9:11, and nowhere else. The real word, "conception," as it occurs

in the above passages, is spelled HRJWN. This word in Genesis comes two letters short of spelling the word. All Hebrew scholars know this. For instance, Spurrell says: "It is an abnormal formation which occurs nowhere else in the Old Testament." Our highest lexical authorities (Brown, Briggs and Driver) call it a "contraction, or erroneous." Indeed! and is one half the human family to be placed at the mercy of the other half, on such a flimsy claim as this! So could Rehoboam have sent a man to the gallows, instead of sending him to gaol, by such a method of manipulating the law. We stand for our rights, as women, on the assurance of our Lord, that *no word* in Divine law has lost any of its consonants, or angles of a consonant; and on our Lord's promise we can demand a very different rendering of the word. While it is possible that the W of this word might be omitted in this particular formation, the J is a *consonant* of the root, and cannot be lost or omitted, *particularly* at the end of a phrase where the voice pauses or rests for awhile upon it; such is the Hebrew rule in an instance like this. The Septuagint gives the correct reading here, which is, *"thy sighing,"*—the whole sentence meaning, then, *"A snare hath increased thy sorrow and thy sighing."* Many ancient authorities agree with the Septuagint.

LESSON 16.

GOD'S WARNING TO EVE.

122. The N. T. teaches us that *"He that committeth sin is of the devil . . . Whosoever is born of God doth not commit sin . . . In this the children of God are manifest and the children of the devil"* (1 John 3:8-10). Eve repented; but there is no inference that Adam repented at this time, for he was expelled from the garden. What must have happened, after this? Before Cain could have been born (Gen. 4;1) either Adam must have repented and become again the child of God, or Eve must have turned from God and followed Adam out of Eden. The fact that Cain was a murderer certainly argues that Eve followed Adam.

123. Eve was, then, the first woman to forsake her (heavenly) kindred for her husband. She reversed God's marriage law,—*"Therefore shall a man forsake his father and his mother, and cleave to his wife."* Had Eve

remained steadfast with God, Adam might, through the double influence of God and Eve, have returned to God. Marriage might have been consummated by Adam, the husband, forsaking the devil, his father, and cleaving to his wife, thus returning, like the prodigal he was, to the heavenly Father's home.

124. God spoke warningly to Eve at this time, telling her that she was inclining to turn away from Himself to her husband, and telling her that if she did so her husband would rule over her. The correct rendering of the next phrase of Gen. 3:16 is this: *"Thou art turning away to thy husband, and he will rule over thee,"*—not as it has been rendered, "Thy *desire* shall be to thy husband." This assertion, as to the correct meaning of the phrase we shall now prove. As we have said before, a misinterpretation of a passage of Scripture can be proved by the misfit. The usual construction put upon the language of this verse fits accurately nowhere; the correct interpretation fits all around.

125. The original word used here is *teshuqa,* and as it only occurs three times in the Hebrew language, its sense must be fixed (1) by studying its relation to other words in the sentences where it occurs: (2) by studying its derivation and structure: (3) and by studying the way it is rendered in the ancient versions of Scripture.

126. To study its relations to other words, we will leave it untranslated, but, write it in its proper sentences, inserting the noun equivalents for the pronouns used.

Gen. 3:16,   "-and-to-Adam,   Eve's *teshuqa.*"
Gen. 4:7,   "-and-to-Cain,   Abel's *teshuqa*"
                                        (or perhaps sin's *teshuqa,*
Sol. Song 7:10, "-and-to-the-Church Christ's *teshuqa*"
                                        (as usually interpreted).

Now compare. No verbs are expressed. The conjunction is one for all and also the preposition. This is true of the Hebrew original also. In fact there is no variety in the three sentences, excepting in the proper nouns implied in the pronouns used. The sense of the three passages must be similar.

127. All the stress of teaching woman's supposed obligations to man is in the *"shall be,"* which is *supplied* by the translators. The force of the mandatory teaching, then, rests upon a *hiatus* in the sentence. If it be contended that the context proves that this is an imperative, then the previous sentences must be imperative, or the

55

following. *Must* woman bear children in *sorrow*, whether she wishes to rejoice or no? *Must* the serpent bruise the heel of the woman's seed, whether he will or no? As to the following clause: *Must* man rule woman, whether he will or no? We think women have more liberty in Christian countries than heathen because man loses the disposition to rule his wife when a Christian.

If this be a commandment of God, and man must rule woman, the more carnally-minded a man is the better he keeps that sort of "law!" But the Apostle Paul says: *"The carnal mind . . . is not subject to the law of God, neither indeed can be"* (Rom. 8:7). Thus we see that the context does *not* prove that this *"shall be"* of the sentence translated, "thy desire *shall be* to thy husband" is imperative. We can assert positively that this sentence is a simple future or present, warning woman of the consequences of her action. So it is rendered in all the ancient versions; never as an imperative. As a prophecy it has been abundantly fulfilled in the manner in which man rules over woman, especially in heathen lands. But Jesus Christ said, as much of women as of men: *"NO ONE can serve two masters."*

128. Compare again: The word *teshuqa* does not necessarily refer to the appetite between male and female, for it would then be out of place in the second sentence. And it does not necessarily imply the subordination of Eve to Adam, as the marginal reading of the A. V. puts it; for then, in the third sentence, Christ is subordinated to the Church, or according to the other interpretations of the Song of Solomon, the man is, at any rate, subordinated to the woman.

Nicholas Fuller, an eminent Oriental scholar, wrote an interesting chapter on this subject in a Latin work entitled *Theological Miscellany*, published in 1612. In reply to those who hold that the sense of the passage is, "the appetite of the wife is about to be in the power of the husband and subdued by him," he says: "Just as if nothing would be longed for by the wife excepting what would be pleasing to the husband. Absurd notion! Others again wish the appetite to be understood as that by which a woman seeks marital dominion. And yet it is not very probable that this yoke is sustained by spontaneous longing for it . . . This is not effected by longing, then, but it is suffered because not declined. Besides, Scripture saith not, 'The appetite of the wife shall

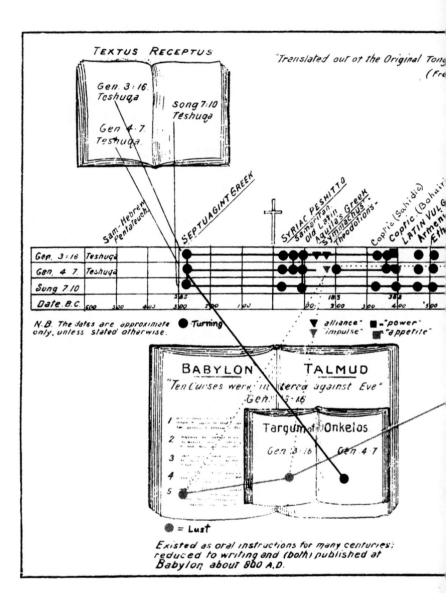

Arabic.

Wycliffe's English.

Pagninus Version. (Latin)

Coverdale's English 1535.

Matthew's (Rogers')

Cranmer's

Tyndale's

Geneva Bible

Douay.

Authorised, 1611.

Revised Version

DATE UNCERTAIN

800   900   1000   1100   1200   1300   1380   1528   1535 . TO . 1611   1884

1400   1500   1600   1700   1800   1900 A.D.

□ = "direction."

◇ = "moderation."

MODERN ENGLISH VERSIONS.

O = "let it be subdued."

RED ● = GRAY

BLUE ● = BLACK

DESIGNED

BY KATHARINE C. BUSHNELL

be inclined to the dominion of the husband,' but 'to the husband' himself. Wherefore, if *teshuqa* is allowed to be translated 'appetite' certainly this appetite is common and by nature reciprocal, and bending each in like manner to the other. Therefore, it displays a more equitable condition of life than dominion. Nay, moreover, if this form of speech declares the appetite for a ruler, Christ would adopt the Church as His ruler, for in the same manner the Church speaks, when, of Christ as a Spouse, in Canticles 7:10 it says, '*I am my beloved's, towards me is His appetite,*' as indeed they would there translate."

Lewis' note in Lange's Commentary declares: "The sense of this word [*teshuqa*] is not *libido,* or sensual desire."

129. As to the structure, and derivation of *teshuqa,* apparently it is derived from the verb *shuq,* meaning in its simplest form "to run." The prefix, *te,* gives the word an abstract sense, and it corresponds to our termination,—"ness," in such words as "goodness," "kindness," etc. The ending *a,* is added to give the word the feminine form usual to Hebrew abstract nouns. If this word is taken from the intensive form of the verb, it would bear the sense "to run repeatedly," that is "to run back and forth." But to keep running back and forth would necessitate frequent turning, and hence the word might easily have the derived sense of "turning;" and an abstract noun be derived therefrom, not meaning a literal "turning," but a quality of the character, a "turning," The sense "desire" has come to us from the Talmud, in the "Ten Curses of Eve." All the most ancient versions, as we will show in our next, give the idea of "turning," and that alone, for this Hebrew word "*teshuqa.*"

LESSON 17.
THE ANCIENT RENDERINGS OF *TESHUQA.*

130. The SEPTUAGINT GREEK version of the Old Testament is the most important of all the versions. It is also the most ancient. Tradition says it was the work of seventy-two Jewish scholars, and its name means "seventy." Made at Alexandria, about 285 B. C., certainly more was known about Hebrew then than at any time since. The version was much in favour among the Jews until the Christians used its translation of the prophecies to prove that Jesus was the Messiah, when it fell under Jewish displeasure. Nearly every quotation from the

Old Testament to be found in the New, is an exact reproduction of the Septuagint reading. This accounts for N. T. quotations not seeming always accurate. Dean Stanley says: "If there ever was a translation which, by means of its importance, rose to a level with the original, it was this. It is not the original Hebrew, but the Septuagint, which is the Bible of the evangelists and the apostles of the first century, and of the Christian Church for the first age of its existence . . . Whatever may be the value of the Hebrew text itself, or its value in the present Jewish Church, or the present Church of Western Europe, the Septuagint was the text sanctioned probably by our Lord Himself, certainly by the apostles." The Pentateuch of the Septuagint is especially esteemed for its accuracy. This version renders *teshuqa* into the Greek word *apostrophe* in both passages in Genesis: and *epistrophe* in Canticles. The former word, *apostrophe,* is familiar to us all: it means "turning away," and the latter, "turning to." The teaching is, that Eve is turning away from God to her husband, and, as a consequence of that deflection, Adam will rule over her.

131. Next in order of excellence is the SYRIAC PESHITTO of the second, or perhaps first, century after Christ. This version gives the same sense, rendering, *"thou wilt turn,"* (Gen. 3:16); *"will turn"* (Gen. 4:7), and *"turning"* for the third passage. We have only the Pentateuch in the SAMARITAN version. It translates both the passages in Genesis, *"turning."* The OLD LATIN version gives *"turning"* in all three places. We have a COPTIC (Sahidic), of not great value, which gives the same rendering for the first and third passage; and the more valued BOHAIRIC COPTIC which so renders the passage in the first two. These two copies are not complete Bibles, but fragments. The AETHIOPIC version of about 500 A. D. renders all three passages by words signifying "turning." In fact, as regards the third passage, all the ancient *versions* without any exceptions whatever, give no other sense but *"turning"* for *teshuqa*.

132. Now as to some variations in the rendering of the passages in Genesis: The Talmud, as we have shown, sets forth the teaching that God pronounced "Ten Curses" upon Eve; but the Talmud is not a translation

[Later Note:] We may count here also the ARMENIAN versions, I think, of the fifth century which affords the sense "circuit" for all three passages,—see Chart with Lesson 19.

of the Scriptures, but a compilation of the traditions of the Jews. The fifth, sixth and the ninth of these "curses" supply the sense *"lust"* for the Hebrew word *teshuqa,* together with the teaching that woman must center her "desire" upon her husband alone; his "desire" could wander away to other women. From this immoral teaching the English rendering has its sole original authority, so far as we have been able to trace, after very much research. After the Septuagint came into disfavour with the Jews, AQUILA, a proselyte to Judaism, in close touch with Jewish scholars of the second century after Christ, made a Greek translation of the Hebrew, to offset the errors, as was claimed, of the Septuagint. His translation does not exist, so far as known. But Origen compiled a work called the Hexapla, in which he gave the variations between the Septuagint and Aquila's renderings. According to the Hexapla, Aquila has rendered this word *"coalition,"* or *"alliance"*—a not unnatural sense, since Eve is represented as turning from God to form an alliance with her husband. Origen gives information also in his Hexapla of two other Greek versions made shortly after Aquila's, both of them, likewise, under the influence of Judaism. Of these, SYMMACHUS follows Aquila in Gen. 3:16, according to some authorities, but other manuscripts use another Greek word here, namely, *horme,* "impulse," and there is strong testimony that this latter word was employed by Symmachus in Gen. 4:7. But as to the passage in Canticles, we have no light beyond the inference that since Origen called attention to no variations at this point, these Greek translations agreed with the Septuagint. We have not yet mentioned the third Greek translation: All we know of THEODOTION'S renderings is, that he used *"turning"* in Gen. 4:7.

133. Jerome's LATIN VULGATE was made about 382 A. D. He went to Palestine and studied Hebrew under Jewish rabbis. He renders the first pasage, *"Thou shalt be under the power of a husband, and he will rule over thee."* The first phrase is mere guess-work; it is no translation of the original words. The second passage reads, *"his appetite,"*—whatever that may mean in a relation between brothers. The third passage reads, *"his turning."* The ARABIC is of most uncertain date; probably not earlier than the tenth century. It renders

the word *teshuqa* in the three places, respectively, *"direction," "moderation"* and *"turning."*

134. A TARGUM is not a translation, but a paraphrase,—the Synagogue explanation of the sense of Scripture. The TARGUM of ONKELOS, or Chaldee Paraphrase, was published at Babylon, and therefore would conform quite closely to the traditions embodied in the Babylonian Talmud which teaches the "ten curses of Eve." This Targum—the most reliable one—relates only to the Pentateuch. It renders, *"lust"* in the first passage, and *"turning"* in the second. A very unreliable Targum, accredited wrongly to "Joseph the Blind," of about the eleventh century, renders *"lust"* in the third passage.

135. Wiener says: "The coincidences of truth are infinite. In other words, the true hypothesis explains *all* difficulties." Let us apply this scientific test to our claim that *teshuqa* means "turning:"

Aquila and Symmachus assume that Eve "turns" to make an alliance with her husband, hence they translate "alliance." Or, according to other readings, Symmachus assumes that the "turning" is rather, as yet, an impulse, than an act,—he translates "impulse." (This Greek word for "impulse" does not necessarily imply a sensual impulse. It is used in Acts 14:5, and translated "assault," and in James 3:4,—not rendered in the A. V., but the R. V. reads: *"whither the impulse of the steersman willeth."*) The Arabic reasons, "If Eve is about to turn away from God, it must be in some direction;" so it renders, "direction." Jerome plainly shows he does not know what *teshuqa* means, but since the latter part of the phrase refers to the man's part,—*"he will rule over thee,"*—he concludes that the beginning of the passage must refer to woman's position, and renders, *"Thou shalt be under the power of a husband."*

136. Likewise, the sense "turning" reconciles the three passages one with another, whereas the sense "desire" puts them in utter conflict. Eve is "turning" from God, and He warns her that if she does this, she will fall under the dominion of Adam. Abel is "turning" toward Cain, in all the confidence of a younger and unsuspecting brother. God warns Cain prophetically that this confiding approach of his brother will be a temptation to slay

him in his defenselessness. The third passage is a joyful boast of the bridegroom's favor and attention, *"He
is turning to me."*
137. Prof. H. G. Mitchell of Boston University, in his
book, *The World Before Abraham,"* has well represented
the general sense of the phrase translated, *"thy desire
shall be to thy husband."* He says,, "This interpretation,
however, is not altogether satisfactory. The word here
used is found only in two other places in the O. T., Gen.
4:7 and Cant. 7:10. In the former of these two passages, if it means anything, if must mean mere inclination, or something equally removed from sensuality: and
in the latter, where a man is the subject, it has the force
of affection, devotion. There is therefore ground for
the opinion that the author in this passage intended to
make Jehovah say that the very tenderness of the
woman for the husband would [eventually] enable him
to make and keep her his inferior."

LESSON 18.

HISTORY OF THE TRANSLATION OF *TESHUQA.*

138. Were the teaching true that all women must suffer
pain and servitude for the sin of Eve, then it were
pertinent to ask, Why must they suffer thus,—because
they are Eve's offspring? Are not men equally the offspring of Eve? The only answer is, "Because they are
female offspring." But who made them female offspring,
—women or God? GOD. Then are we taught that God
is punishing women, *not* for their own fault, *not because
they are sinners,* not even because Eve sinned; God is
punishing women for what He Himself made them,—
because they are women, not men. Away with such an
attack upon God's reputation for justice! And further,
the idea that "sorrow," in this verse means labour pains,
or periodical suffering in women, is far-fetched; the
same word is used of Adam in the very next verse. This
word is not used for such suffering anywhere in all the
Scriptures.
139. Since this passage in Genesis, *"Thy desire shall be
to thy husband,"* has been the cause of much immorality
among men, in the cruelty and oppression they have inflicted upon their wives; since this false translation has
been the cause of much degradation, unhappiness and suffering to women; and since this translation has been

61

made the very keystone of an arch of doctrine subordinating woman to man, without which keystone the arch
itself falls to pieces; and since the Apostle Paul's utterances on the "woman question" are always interpreted as
though this perversion of the sense of Gen. 3:16 was
his accepted foundation upon which he builds his super-
structure, it behooves us to review again the history of
the ancient translation of the word *teshuqa,* and this we
will do with the aid of the appended table:

RENDERING OF *TESHUQA* IN ANCIENT VERSIONS.

Name of the Ancient Version.	Approxi-mate date	Translation of *teshuqa.*		
		Gen. 3:16.	Gen. 4:7.	Cant. 7:10.
1. SEPTUAGINT GREEK	285 B. C.	*turning*	*turning*	*turning*
2. SYRIAC PESHITTO	100 A. D.	*wilt turn*	*wilt turn*	*turning*
3. Samaritan, of the Pentateuch *only*	to	*turning*	*turning*	*lacking*
4. The Old Latin	200 A. D.	*turning*	*turning*	*turning*
5. Sahidic	300 A. D.	*turning*	*unknown*	*turning*
6. Bohairic	350 " "	*turning*	*turning*	*unknown*
7. Aethiopic	500 " "	*turning*	*turning*	*turning*
8. Arabic	uncertain	*direction*	*moderation*	*turning*
VERSIONS MADE UNDER RABBINICAL INFLUENCE:				
9. Aquila's Greek	140 A. D.	*alliance*	*unknown*	*unknown*
10. Symmachus' Creek	160 " "	*alliance*	*impulse†*	*unknown*
11. Theodotion's Greek	185 " "	*unknown*	*turning*	*unknown*
12. LATIN VULGATE	382 " "	*power*	*appetite*	*turning*
PURELY RABBINICAL TEACHING:				
BABYLON TARGUM Pentateuch *only*		*lust*	*turning*	*lacking*
Babylon Talmud	800 A. D.*	*lust*		

From this Table we readily see that of the twelve
ancient versions, 10 furnish us with the rendering
"turning", in at least one passage.

Of the 28 known renderings of *teshuqa,* in the
above Table, the word is rendered *"turning"* 21 times.

In the 7 remaining renderings, only 2 seem to
agree; all the others disagree.

140. With such testimony as this before us (and we
have quoted every ancient version we have been able to

---

* We give this date for the publication of the Talmud on the
high authority of Prof. D. S. Margoliouth, M. A., of Oxford, in
his valuable work, **Lines of Defense of the Biblical Revelation.** The date has often been fixed as early as 300 A. D.
† or alliance.

62

find, and none of importance, as likely to shed the least light on the meaning of this word are omitted from the list),—we can see no justification for rendering this word "desire." Even the Babylonian Targum renders it *"turning"* in the second passage (Gen. 4:7), and thus lends its authority to this sense. Nothing but that rabbinic perversion and addition to the Scriptures, teaching that God pronounced ten curses on Eve (something that Scripture nowhere teaches) seems to be at the bottom of this extraordinary reading. A hint of such a meaning for *teshuqa* as *"lust"* seems to have crept into the Bible through Jerome's Latin Vulgate. But even he did not give the sense "appetite" for the word as relates to Eve, but as to Abel; and further, even Jerome adds his authority, in his translation of the third passage, to the sense *"turning"*, and for 3:16, in his writings,—see Additional Note.

141. But let us now trace the adoption of "desire" into the English versions. In 1380 appeared the first English version by Wycliffe. It was not made from the Hebrew original, but from the Latin Vulgate, and it follows its readings in all three places. The Douay Bible, of 1609, of the Roman Catholic Church, is also a reproduction of the Latin Vulgate. Putting these two on one side as mere translations of the Vulgate, we turn to the others.

142. After Wycliffe's version, and before any other English Bible appeared, an Italian Dominican monk, named Pagnino, translated the Hebrew Bible. The *Biographie Universelle,* quotes the following criticism of his work, in the language of Richard Simon: *"Pagnino has too much neglected the ancient versions of Scripture to attach himself to the teachings of the rabbis."* What would we naturally expect, therefore? That he would render this word "lust,"—and that is precisely what he does in the first and the third place; in the second, he translates, "appetite."

143. Pagnino's version was published at Lyons in 1528. Seven years later, in 1535, Coverdale's English Bible appeared, published at Zurich, probably. Tyndale's version, in sections, had appeared in the time between Pagnino's and Coverdale's, published at Cologne and at Worms. It is to be noted that these were days of persecution, when no English Bible could have been published in England, and this may in part account for

these versions being influenced by Pagnino. At any rate, from the time Pagnino's version appeared, every English version, excepting the two Vulgate translations we put on one side, has followed Pagnino's rendering for the first passage, up to the present day. As to the second passage, Cranmer's Bible (1539) first introduced "lust" into this place, which was later followed by the Geneva Bible, and the Authorised and Revised versions. But Tyndale, Coverdale, Matthew (John Rogers) and Cranmer all retained "turning" in the third passage. But the three latest Protestant Bibles, Geneva, Authorised and Revised, have obliterated all trace of any other sense but "desire." The reading of the older English Bibles which follow Pagnino is, *"Thy lust* (or lusts) *shall pertayne to thy husband."*

144. Now will you please turn to the Title Page of your Bible. If you have an Authorised Version, you will read the assurance given to the reader, that the Book has been "Translated out of the original tongues; and with the former translations diligently compared and revised." If you have a Revised Version of 1884, it will claim to be "the version set forth A. D. 1611 compared with the most ancient authorities and revised." These assurances do not hold good, in this case where the status and welfare of one-half the human race is directly and vitally concerned; and the highest good of the other half just as vitally concerned, if even more remotely and less visibly. Pagnino's word has been retained against the overwhelming authority of the ancient versions.

ADDITIONAL NOTE.

It is to be noted that the Church Fathers seem to be ignorant of any other sense but "turning" for this word. We have noted that the following employ "turning," in one, two, or all three passages: Philo (a Jew,—not a Ch. Father died 50 A. D.), Clement of Rome (d. 100), Irenaeus (d. 202), Tertullian (born 160), Origen (b. 186), Epiphanius (b. 310 in Palestine), Jerome (b. 335,—in both Genesis verses, in spite of his own different renderings), Ambrose (b. 340), Augustine (b. 354) and Theodoret (b. 386).

In spite of the plain sense of the Greek words **apostrophe** and **epistrophe,** and the Latin rendering of **teshuqa, conversio** (all conveying, in their root, the sense of "turning"), the well known translation of the Church Fathers, published by T. and T. Clark of Edinburgh, renders the word "desire," in these **passages.** But these words cannot be lawfully rendered thus.

LESSON 19.

REVIEW WITH A CHART.

145. The lesson of the mistranslation of Gen. 3:16 is so very important that we represent the false rendering of *teshuqa* again, by means of a Chart which will readily fix its history upon the mind.

The scale running across the middle of the Chart is cut up into centuries by perpendicular lines. All to the left of the cross is B. C. in time; to the right A. D. One space of the scale, the bottom, numbers centuries, and gives the exact date of versions, so far as known; all the other dates are merely approximate, and some very uncertain. The top space of the scale represents the translation of *teshuqa* in Gen. 3:16, as we indicate at the left-hand end of the scale; the space next below gives the translation of the word in Gen. 4:7, and the third space, the translation in Solomon's Song 7:10— the only three passages employing the word. The translation of the word is carried along, throughout the history of the centuries, beginning with the first version of the Bible, the Septuagint, at 285 B. C. and ending with the Revised English Version A. D. 1884. The book up in the left-hand corner represents the original Hebrew text of our Bible, sending down light from above for us in this word *teshuqa*; the books below the scale represent the Talmud with the Targum sending up a perverted, immoral teaching from the "Ten Curses of Eve" (see pars. 105-106).

The blue balls represent the sense of *teshuqa* as "turning" in one form or another; the red balls the sense "lust." Where neither sense is employed in a version, we use another shape, and give the translation just under it, at the bottom of the scale.

At the point where this immoral teaching begins to find an entrance into the Bible (but not in the first but second passage, Gen. 4:7), in the second century, are three versions of the Greek made by Jews and Judaizers with the express object of emphasizing the teachings of the Jews, where they differed from the Christian teachings. We represent these by little wedges, driven into the place they occupy, on purpose to force an entrance for rabbinical teaching. Jerome who translated the Latin Vulgate Version, was instructed for his work by rabbis, and shows the same influence. Now count the blue balls, and see how they were universally used

65

until those wedges were driven in to break up the continuity. Note how a thin red line obtains entrance at this point, and gradually expands until the blue is entirely obliterated, in the Authorised and Revised Versions of the English.

Notice particularly that this teaching,—"thy *desire* shall be to thy husband," first got *full expression* through an Italian Dominican Monk, Pagnino (written Pagninus in Latin). Shortly after his version, several English versions appeared; and following his reading they use the word "lust," softened to "desire" in the later English versions. What do we know of his translations? Richard Simon, quoted in the *Biographie Universelle,* declares: "Pagnino has too much neglected the ancient versions of Scripture to attach himself to the teachings of the rabbis,"—just what we should have expected to learn. Following him, to the neglect of ancient versions, the English translators have not, in regard to Gen. 3:16, set forth the proper sense of *teshuqa.*

Observe that among the names of the versions above the scale, three are printed in capital letters,—the Septuagint, the Syriac and the Vulgate. Among scholars, the evidence of the exact meaning of a Hebrew word is generally considered conclusive, if these three versions agree, because, in the making, it is not known that they had any influence upon each other. These three versions agree on "turning" for the third passage, and the Septuagint and Syriac agree on all three passages. So much evidence as this, is practically conclusive as to the true sense of *teshuqa.*

LESSON 20.

UNSUBJUGATED WIVES.

146. We have much incidental evidence that Jewish women, before the captivity of Babylon especially, enjoyed much liberty, of which they were gradually deprived after that time. This subordination was in accordance, not with Scriptural, but with rabbinical and pagan teaching. So soon as it became necessary for the common people to have their own Scriptures translated and interpreted for them, man began to interpret those writings according to such teaching, to the detriment of

woman.* Let us cite instances of the freedom and dignity of Old Testament women.

147. Rebekah had no child. As often happened in Bible characters, being destined to become the mother of an important personage, (i. e.,—Jacob), no child came until it was conceived of *spiritual* desire, expressed in prayer (Gen. 25:21),—not merely of natural desire. A few months later, she went to enquire of the Lord concerning a perlexing state of affairs, and was told that she would have twins, and the elder was to serve the younger (Gen. 25:22-23). The elder was Esau and the younger Jacob. Rebekah's story teaches us: (1), God may reveal His mind, even in matters of greatest moment for both parents, to the mother alone. And hence (2), God does not intend that the husband shall invariably lead, in carrying out His will.

148. But this is quite contrary to the theological fiction as to the import of the "headship" of the husband. For instance: We open a Bible commentary, much in use at the present time, and highly praised in our Christian periodicals for use in the family (that of Jamieson, Faussett and Brown), and read: "As a moon in relation to the sun, so woman shines not so much with light direct from God, as light derived from man." . . . "In grace much of her knowledge is mediately through man, on whom she naturally depends." . . . "The woman was made by God mediately through man, who was, as it were, a veil or medium placed between her and God." . . . "Through him it (the veil) connects her with Christ, the Head of man." As though Christ were not the Head of believing women! This contradicts 1 Tim. 2:5, where "men" is of common gender.

149. If the Bible commentary tells the truth, why did God send Deborah to show Barak his duty, and not Barak to show Deborah (Judg. 4:6)? Why did the angel of the Lord instruct Manoah's wife about their coming child, rather than send Manoah to his wife with the instructions (Judg. 13:2-7)? Why did Hilkiah the priest, and Shaphan the scribe, with several other high dignitaries of the Royal Court, go, at the instance of the king himself, to inquire of Huldah about the Law, instead of going to Huldah's husband, her "sun?". Or,

* All but educated Jews lost, largely, their knowledge of Hebrew during the seventy years of captivity in Babylon. After their return, the Oral Law came into being (Nehe. 8:8) which is the basis of Targums and the Talmud. See par. 6.

67

instead of Huldah being required to go to these "suns," the priest, the Scribe and the high dignitaries of the Royal Court, to obtain her light about God's Law (2 Kings 22)? Why were women sent to the apostles to tell them of a risen Lord, instead of their husbands being sent,—from whom, according to the Commentary, these women must have received their light and knowledge? Or, why were not the apostles sent to the women to tell them that Christ was risen, if indeed women must receive their Divine light "mediately" through men? In these cases, and more that might be cited, the "sun" went to the "moon" for light, and got it.

150. In Genesis 21:11 we are told that it was "very grievous" to Abraham to do what Sarah demanded. Did the Lord remind her that she must rather obey him? No; He told Abraham that he must obey Sarah. The authority was vested, not in a "sex," but in the one who took the right moral view on the question of polygamy. And so it always will be; God is with the *right;* not the sex. Then recall the case of Abigail (1 Sam. ch. 25.) She knew her husband was a foolish and worthless man, and frankly said so. She did not even consult him when she took *"two hundred loaves and two bottles of wine, five sheep ready dressed, five measures of parched corn, a hundred clusters of grapes, and two hundred cakes of figs,"* and gave them to David, knowing full well that her husband had just refused to give David anything. Under ordinary conditions, had she had a worthy husband, she would not have done this. Nabal did not measure up to the occasion, and his masculinity counted for nothing, as to authority over a wife wiser than himself. The whole Bible story goes to show that Abigail did the right and prudent thing in going against what she well knew was her husband's will, to do what she could not have done with his knowledge. She showed moral courage. She averted a dire calamity. David praised her for it, and Scripture shows its approval,—for, *"It came to pass that about ten days after, the Lord smote Nabal that he died."*

151. As we have said, It is rabbinism—Judaism commingled with paganism, born in the "days of mingling" (par. 86),—which placed the badge of inferiority and servility upon woman. Let us give an illustration:

Originally woman had her place in the regular Tabernacle services, either as priestess or Levite. This is now conceded by Bible scholars, as proved by the technical term used in Exodus 38:8 and 1 Samuel 2:22, translated *"serving women."* Now this term was altered to "fasting women" by the translators of the Septuagint Greek, and the phrase in 1 Samuel containing the words entirely dropped. To use the words of Prof. Margoliouth of Oxford, "The idea of women in attendance at the Tabernacle is so odious that it has to be got rid of." The other ancient versions followed suit in purposely mistranslating the word as "prayed," "thronged," "assembled" there. Our A. V. renders "assembled," but the R. V. rightly renders it "served."

152.   After a close line of reasoning, unsuitable for this place, but which we produce in later lessons, Prof. Margoliouth proves this charge which he makes.* He concludes, "It is evident that by the time when the Septuagint translation was made, the idea of women ministering at the door of the Tabernacle had become so odious that it was wilfully mistranslated."

"Wilfully mistranslated" is very strong language to use, since that mistranslation has remained in the versions of the Bible until our Revisers corrected it. We prefer that such a statement should stand in the language of an eminent male scholar, rather than in our own words; therefore we quote him.

153.   Occasionally a Bible expositor comments on the *seemingly* narrower sphere allotted to women under the Gospel than was accorded them under the law. Kalisch says: "The New Testament is . . . even more rigorous than the Old; for whilst it commands the woman *'to learn in silence with all subjection, but not to teach, nor to usurp authority over the man, but to be in silence,'* she was in the Old Testament admitted to the highest office of teaching, that of prophets, as Miriam, Deborah and Huldah."

154.   But we may well suspect such an interpretation of the Bible as makes the Gospel appear less kindly, less liberal, more contemptuous toward women than the Old Testament law, and which represents women as less able, by grace, to conquer the vices of the sex and rise above

---

* Nearly every subject mentioned in this lesson is dealt with more extensively in future lessons. Here we design to make but the single point,—the freedom of women in the O. T., where, if anywhere, we should expect "the curse of the law" (Gen. 3:16) to operate.

them, than the law enabled them to do. There must be something wrong in such a representation. We should constantly bear in mind, in studying these Lessons, the point we have made: It was during the "days of mingling," especially, that the teaching got hold of the mind of the Jew, that his wife, merely because of her sex, was his inferior. It was during these days that the first translation of the Bible—the Septuagint Greek version—was made. This version, in some places, incorporated in its renderings the idea of woman's inferiority; and all other versions since have followed suit, more or less. "Men only need," says Dr. Beard, "to bring to the Bible sufficiently strong preposessions, sufficiently fixed opinions, to have them reflected back in all the glamour of infallible authority" (*Beard's Hibbert Lectures*, p. 192).

LESSON 21.
A SPLIT IN THE FIRST FAMILY.

155. Please note that after Cain, the first-born of Adam, had murdered Abel, and become a fugitive, he seems to have been lost to his parents. Gen. 5:1 begins: *"This is the book of the generations of Adam,"* and proceeds as though Seth were his first-born. The rationalistic critics assume that a fresh historian takes up the narrative here, who was ignorant of the fact that Adam had had sons previously to Seth. The theory leads away from interesting historical light. At this point we find the first great division of the human family.

156. The descendants of Cain are given in Gen. 4:18-22; the descendants of Seth, in Gen. 5:6-32. Please read these two lists. Notice that some of the names are the same, or very similar—as might be expected in related families—but they do not apply to the same individuals. Lamech, father of Noah, lived at a much later period than Lamech, the father of Tubal-Cain, the murderer and polygamist. Tubal-Cain whetted "cutting instruments," (R. V.) which his father probably used in killing a man, or threatening to kill one, and in intimidating the two women whom he had taken from their kin. He "took" his wives, in the days when men were supposed to go to their wives to marry them, and to remain in their homes. This implies violence, as it does also where the same form of expression is used in Gen. 6:2. We have pointed out some of the social wrongs growing out of this violation of God's marriage law.

157. Christ said: *"What God hath joined, let not man put asunder."* Now we inquire, "What did God join, when He gave that marriage law which Christ repeats? First and foremost, he joined a man to his wife's kindred, by the words, *"For this cause shall a man leave father and mother and cleave to his wife."* In the second place, God joined the husband to his wife, as indicated by the words,—*"and they shall become one flesh."* The R. V. is correct here, in translating, "shall become," instead of "shall be." Both the Hebrew of the O. T., and the Greek of the N. T. say "become," not "be."

158. The next case of violence towards women, after Lamech's, is that recorded in Gen. 6:1-11,—rather, many cases. *"The sons of God saw the daughters of men that they were fair; and they took them wives of all that they chose,"*—runs the story. The late and learned Sir J. W. Dawson has written an interesting article on this subject for *The Expositor* (Fifth Series, Vol. 4, 1896). We will quote him, as the subject has peculiar interest to women. He mentions three principal theories that have been set forth to explain the obscure phrases, "sons of God," and "daughters of men:" *First,* Angelic beings entering into matrimonial relations with women of the human race. This is the ridiculous and pagan theory adopted into Jewish apocryphal writings during the "days of mingling," and set forth by Tertullian, which has a fascination for men of a certain cast of mind. Dean Stanley and others make use of it to explain why women were to veil in worship, as we shall show when we come to the discussion of that topic. To this theory Dawson rightly replies: "It is at variance with all the other statements of Scripture respecting angelic beings, and with our Lord's declaration that they [angels] neither marry nor are given in marriage.* [It is to be

---

* We shall again encounter this superstition that angels sinned with human females. Therefore we think it well to add these words from the learned Prof. Peter Lange of Bonn University: "In its relation to the philosophy of religion the angel hypothesis would have the effect of confounding all the ground conceptions of revelation, and obliterating its distinctions. It authenticates a fact which perfectly destroys all distinction between revelation and mythology, between a Divine miracle and magic, between the Biblical conception of nature, as conformity to law, and the wild apocryphal stories. . . With what sort of superstition this angel-interpretation had already connected itself in early times, we may learn from the twenty-second chapter of Tertullian's **Apologetic.**"

noted, here, that the single word which men translate "given in marriage," conveys no thought of the *giving* or of the *selling* of daughters, in the original words of the Bible]. *Second,* "Sons of God" were men of eminence and position who formed matrimonial alliances with women of inferior rank. To this theory Dawson says: "The second hypothesis appears to be trivial and insufficient to produce the effect assigned to the occurrence," which was the production of a powerful but wicked race of giants. "Giants" (Nephilim) and "mighty men of renown" (warriors, etc.) he argues, are not born of inferior mothers, chosen on this supposition, in preference to superior women of this tribe called "sons of God." *Third,* They were Sethite men allying themselves with Cainite women. Dawson pronounces this theory "rational and natural," and yet rejects it for a *fourth,* which, we agree with him, is far preferable to all others.

159. Says Dawson: "I have ventured to suggest that the 'sons of God' (*Elohim*), in our primitive record are really Cainites, and the 'daughters of men' Sethite women." At first thought, the hypothesis seems untenable. Why should descendants of the murderer, Cain, be called "sons of God" when the daughters of the good Seth are merely denominated, "daughters of men?" "Sons of God" seems better to describe the descendants of Seth. But listen to his explanation: "After the fall, a Saviour had been promised, who was to be the Seed or progeny of the woman, and Eve most naturally supposes that the child to whom she has given birth is this "Coming One' [see par. 79]. From the time of this utterance we may assume that the name Jehovah becomes that of the coming Redeemer, and is associated with that of Elohim (God), who has promised the Redeemer. Thus the name Elohim represents God as Creator: the name Jahve [Jehovah] God as the promised Redeemer . . The point that we now note is that this distinction existed from the time of Eve, though only in the days of her grandson Enos did men formally invoke [or proclaim] Jehovah as God (Gen. 4:26). This is the testimony of the record, and we are bound to receive it in this sense, whether we believe it or no."

160. It would seem then, that just as today in China the Catholics are known as *"Tien Drü* people," and the Protestants as *"Shang Te* people," according to the name they employ in addressing God in worship, so in those

ancient times the Cainites who refused to acknowledge Jehovah, and addressed Elohim alone in worship, got the name of "sons," that is, worshippers of God. It will elucidate this point yet more, in passing, to explain that members of a guild, or order, are often called "sons" of that order, as "sons of the prophets"; and the worshipper of an idol as the son of that idol (though less often). "Ben-haded" signifies a worshipper of Hadad (1 Kings 15:20; see also Malachi 2:11). The Cainites were then, so to speak, the Unitarians of that remote age. If they pretended even to believe in the Coming One they did not "call on" him. Dawson thinks they did not believe in Him,—or rather, renounced Him.

161. Dawson continues: "It is Jehovah who remonstrates with Cain, and after the murder of Abel denounces his conduct, apparently without effect; and henceforth Cain may be said to have gone out from the face of Jehovah, which implies much more in the way of religious separation than mere departure from a local shrine, and at the same time he leaves his parental home and goes forth to found a new tribe of men distinguished from Adam."

162. "In a religious point of view the Cainites are not represented as cultivating the worship of the Redeemer—Jehovah. They probably still retained the nature-worship [which Cain adopted from the first] of Elohim . . . Of the Sethites, on the other hand, we have mainly the record of their invoking Jehovah while walking with Elohim, of their retaining a hope of redemption from the fall, though it seems certain that towards the end of the antediluvian period they also degenerated, in a religious point of view, probably in consequence of the intermixture with Cainites, mentioned before. This intermixture, however, is stated to have originated in the aggressions of the Nephilim among the Cainites, who captured wives from the feebler Sethites. Feebler because not furnished with instruments of brass and iron. This, I think, is implied in the expression, 'took to them wives of all they chose,' that is, at their own will and pleasure, and without regard to the primitive law of marriage, which provides that a man should leave father and mother and cleave to his wife."

LESSON 22.

FIRST SINS AND THEIR FRUITS.

163. The more frequently a vice is indulged the greater its tyranny. Hence, the older a sin the stronger its sway over the moral character, the more blinding its effect upon the intellect, and the less likely is it to be recognized as a sin. Now we must consider the first sin of the human race, its longest indulged vice. This sin will be the chief characteristic of Antichrist, when he comes. He *"opposeth and exalteth himself against all that is called God, or that is worshipped; so that he sitteth in the temple of God, setting himself forth as God."* (2 Thess. 2:4, R. V.)

164. The first indulged temptation,—that is, Adam's willfully indulged sin (Eve repented), was to be *"as God"* (Gen. 3:5, R. V.; "gods" is incorrect, for Adam, as yet, had heard of but one God to envy). What must have been the inevitable result of Adam's continuing to indulge the desire to be "as God?" These two already had equal dominion over all the earth; so Adam, in his desire to be "as God," had no one else to be "as God" to, but to Eve. He would wish, therefore, to extend his dominion by subjugating Eve to his rule. This is precisely what God warned Eve against, if she for a moment, in the weakness of affectionate attachment, turned away to Adam. But we infer Eve did this, with the predicted result.

165. The sin of the male in loving the preeminence began so early in the world's history, and has prevailed so persistently, as to gain respectability, in accordance with the teaching expressed by the poet Pope:

> "Vice is a monster of such frightful mien,
> As to be hated, needs but to be seen.
> But seen too oft, familiar with its face,
> We first endure, then pity, then embrace."

Over and over, Jesus Christ rebuked this sin in His disciples, but the rebuke seemed to fall on uncomprehending ears. Matt. 18:1-5; Mark 9:33-37; Luke 14:8-11; Luke 20:46, should all be read before we proceed further. This was the last sin among His Twelve that Jesus rebuked when on earth, Luke 22:24-27. In these passages there is not a hint that the duty is to be limited to one sex. So far as the teaching of Jesus Christ is concerned, it seems to matter little whether it be the sin of woman exalting herself over man, or man over woman; it is not the *sex* which is rebuked, but the *sin itself*. Jesus does not speak merely with reference to man's attitude towards man, but man's attitude towards all. In Christ *"there is neither bond nor free."* *"Ye know that they . . . exercise lordship . . . But among you it shall not be so."* Matt. 20:25, 26; Mark 10:42 etc., are rules for the future Church, not merely for the Twelve.

166. Strange to say (yet not so strange when we consider Pope's lines), we are all able to see the hatefulness of a woman's attempt to exercise government over her husband, but beyond that point our moral sense has become dulled. Because the government of a man over his wife is customary, it seems natural and quite proper to us. Modesty, meekness, humility, become woman; these virtues became Jesus Christ; but as to men in general, there are doubts with many as to these being virtues at all in them.

We may take courage. Up to very recent times a slave class was looked upon as a necessity and slavery as legitimate. Some men were born, it was supposed, to be slaves; others to be their masters; and the world could not go on without the two classes. That misconception was exploded, and the world goes on quite comfortably. So long as slavery existed, men thought they found warrant for it in the Word of God. But the number who thought so came to be a decreasing number. Just so, the number of those who imagine they find, in the Word of God, warrant for the dominion of the male over the female, is an ever-decreasing number.

167. The third chapter of Genesis, rightly translated and interpreted, reveals to us the fact that lordship of the husband over the wife, which began when man sinned, was Satanic in origin. Knowing this, and the strong force of a long-indulged habit, it need not surprise us if we discover that men have gone to their Bibles (as they did on the slavery question), to find warrant for what they were already doing, not to find a clue as to what they should do.

168. Again we turn to William Law, who says: "As a less evil, and to prevent a greater, God divided the first perfect human nature into two parts, into a male and

female creature. . . . It was at first the total humanity in one creature, who should in that state of perfection, have brought forth his own likeness out of himself, in such purity of love and divine power as he himself was brought forth from God. . . . This purity of love and delight in the image of God, would have carried on the birth of humanity, in the same manner, and by the same divine power, as the first man was brought forth; for it was only a continuation of the same generating love that gave birth to the first man."

169. "The first step therefore towards the redemption or recovery of man, *beginning to fall,* was the taking of his Eve out of him. . . . God took part of his nature out of him, so that the eye of his desire, which was turned to the life of this world, might be directed to that part of his nature that was taken from him. And this is the reason of my saying before, that this was chosen as a less evil, and to avoid a greater; for it was a less degree of falling from his first perfection to love the female part of his own divided nature, than to turn his love towards that which was so much lower than his nature. And thus, at that time, Eve was an help that was truly and properly meet for him."

170. We have no reason for inferring here that this interest and desire of Adam for the animals about him, of which the writer speaks, was sensual, in our use of that term; but Adam was beginning to lose delight in communion with God, to take a correspondingly greater interest in the natural creation about him; he was becoming more material in his interests. God would instruct him that they were not suitable as his companions and equals, by supplying him with a help meet for him. *"But for man there was not found an help meet for him,"* was the verdict, after Adam had surveyed all the animals, and named them. But to what purpose this division of man into male and female, that through the woman half, in cooperation with the divine will, deliverance from sin might come, unless God's primal intention in it was THE INDEPENDENCE OF THE FEMALE *from all dominion but God's?* And what could more completely frustrate this beneficent plan than to teach her that God demands that she submerge her identity in man?

76

171. We have preferred to quote the teachings of a highly esteemed and widely known theologian; gifted as a writer to a very unusual degree; reputed as a veritable saint; removed by his very sex from all imputation of sex bias in his opinion,—a view that he considered to be necessitated by the general tenor of Scriptural teaching as to the fall and redemption of man. We believe that his view will appeal to the consciousness of every thoughtful woman as at least far superior to the more generally-accepted rabbinical view, especially after a careful re-reading of the first three chapters of Genesis. We do not set forth William Law as an infallible guide; but we do contend that his very holiness of life may have enabled him to examine impartially and expound clearly the simple teaching of the Bible at this point, where the blindness of sex-bias and of self-interest would lead others astray. Certain we are that the ordinary rabbinical view, that woman rests under the curse of God, a slave to the base passions of men, is both cruel and immoral, as well as being contrary to the plain teachings of Scripture. Almost any view of the matter would be more creditable to a Christian, which at all agreed with the Scriptures, than the one at present generally taught.

LESSON 23.
SWEEPING CONCLUSIONS FROM SMALL PREMISES.

172. Here are three quotations from the late Dean of Canterbury, the Very Rev. Payne-Smith, which we would do well to ponder: (1). "A bad translation of this book" (he means the Bible; and we hold that it has been badly translated on "the woman question"), exercises a depressing influence upon a nation's civilization: a good translation is one of the great levers in a nation's rise." (2). "Give men what proof you will, but seldom do they find more than what it suits them to find. If what is said agrees with their preconceived notions, well; if not, they reject it." (3). "Men never do understand anything unless already in their minds they have some kindred ideas, something that leads up to the new thought which they are required to master."

173. In all these remarks Payne-Smith has special reference to the work of translating and interpreting the Word of God. Now add to these the words of Dr.

Beard which we have already quoted (par. 154),* and with a realization of the contempt in which, in past ages, women have been held by men, there is no reason to marvel that, with the best motives of honour and honesty, men have often, even to the present time, been unable to see the truth of God regarding women, as revealed in the Word. My copy of Smith's *Bible Dictionary,* under the topic, *Law of Moses,* subhead, *Husband and Wife,* makes this sweeping assertion as regards women: "The power of a husband [was] so great that a wife could never be *sui juris* [a law unto herself], or enter independently into any [!] engagement even before God." The whole proof of this astounding assertion, as given by the writer of these words, is Numbers 30:6-15. This is not a solitary instance by any means in theology of "tracing the ever-widening spiral *ergo* from the narrow aperture of a single text."

174. Please open your Bibles to this passage. The first instance cited is that of a daughter, in the father's house, vowing a vow. The two kinds of vows here mentioned seem to include vows of abstinence and vows of giving. The nature of some of these vows is described in Gen. 28:20, a vow to give; and I Sam. 14:24, Psa. 132:3, 4, 5, vows to abstain. Here we have the provision: *"If a woman voweth a vow . . being in her father's house in her youth; and her father heareth her vow . . and holdeth his peace at her: then all her vows . . shall stand. But if her father disallow her* in the day that he heareth; *none of her vows . . shall stand: and the Lord shall forgive her, because her father disallowed her."*

175. Now please observe: first, the express reading of this statute permits a daughter to make a vow on her own initiative: second, the father could only disallow that vow by action *taken immediately upon the information reaching him;* third, there is no provision *requiring her* to carry the information that she has made the vow to her father. Moses' statute relating to this matter would not be broken, then, should a girl make a vow entirely independently of her father, without his knowledge or consent.

176. It is quite likely, as Gray asserts (*The International Commentary*) that in the use of the words "in her

---

*"Men only need to bring to the Bible sufficiently strong prepossesion, sufficently fixed opinions, to have them reflected back in all the glamour of infallible authority."

youth," "childhood is scarcely contemplated, the child, whether male or female, probably being assumed to be incapable under any circumstances of making a vow. The class contemplated . . . would consist of young marriageable but unmarried women." Now let us suppose a case. Without arguing that it would be *right* for a girl to conceal her vow, we can imagine that a young woman might, if her mother were ill, say, "Oh, Lord, heal her, and I will take to the Tabernacle for sacrifice this choice little lamb." The mother gets well, and the grateful daughter, having an uneasy feeling that her father will not consent, goes quietly and makes her offering, not letting him know that she has made such a vow.

177. The father hears of the deed accidentally, and rushes after the daughter. But already the priest, who is covetous, has offered the lamb, and taken his share, without caring to know whether the father consents or not. The angry father then makes his way to the head of his tribe, and lays the case for the recovery of a lamb before him. Now judge of this Mosaic statute from precisely the same standpoint that we would judge a law of this country today, and what would the lawyer say to the father?

178. "I am very sorry for you, sir. You have lost a fine lamb. Your daughter has done wrong, and the priest has taken advantage of the situation. But I am bound to say, the law will not help you out, and I cannot advise you to bring the case into court. I think that statute sadly needs amending. You see, it makes no provision *requiring* consultation with the father before a vow is made by a daughter; and again, it does not *oblige her* to let her father know, when she makes a vow. He has to find out in the best manner he can; and if he does not find out in time, he has to take the consequences, and there is no redress, and will be none until we get this law amended."

179. But that Mosaic statute never was amended; so when Dr. William Smith, in his Bible Dictionary, asserts that a woman "could never be *sui juris,* nor enter independently into any engagement even before God," and quotes this law to prove it, he has quoted a Mosaic Law which proves nothing of the sort. For as we shall presently show, the case of the wife is very similar.

The provision made here is somewhat like a certain provision relating to the solemnization of marriage in the United States, where the publication of the banns in advance is not required. At the marriage ceremony, in the presence of the witnesses and assembled guests, the minister utters the following: "If anyone knows cause, or just impediment, why these two should not be joined together, let him declare it here and now, or forever after hold his peace." Someone *might* know a real cause, a very just impediment, but if that certain person did not know when the wedding took place, or neglected to be on the spot to object, what could he do afterwards? Just so, the father of the girl who "vowed a vow" under this Mosaic statute,—excepting that the Mosaic law did not even provide that the officiating priest call for objectors to the sacrifice. To claim all that Dr. Smith does under this statute for the subordination of the daughter to the father, or the wife to her husband, would be as great an exaggeration as to claim that a young man in the United States "could never be *sui juris* or enter independently into any engagement even to marry a young woman."

180. This statute was never enacted with the object of strengthening a father's rule over his daughter, but for quite a different reason, i. e., to protect the inexperienced, and to protect property from covetous priests, who might influence the inexperienced to make rash vows. The conclusion of the matter, in case the father disallows the vow is as follows: *"The Lord will forgive her." Why* is she forgiven; because it was a rash vow? The Bible does not so state. Because she has repented of not consulting her father beforehand? The Bible does not so state. Because she has repented that she did not inform her father of the vow she made? The Bible says nothing about such offences here, as it certainly would have done, had the law been designed to strengthen the father's power over the daughter. *"The Lord shall forgive her because her father disallowed her,"* the text says.

"If there be first a willing mind, it is accepted according to that a person hath, and not according to that he hath not"* (2 Cor. 8:12). This is the teaching of this Mosaic statute.

(*To be Continued.*)

LESSON 24.

SWEEPING CONCLUSIONS FROM SMALL PREMISES.

(Concluded).

181. Leviticus 27:1-25 tells us a great deal about the nature of vows. These might consist of the offering to the service at the Tabernacle of (1) persons: (2) cattle; (3) houses; (4) and fields. There was also the more unusual vow of abstinence, probably referred to in Numbers 30:13, in the words, *"binding oath to afflict the soul."* This word for *"bond,"* verses 3, 4, 5, etc., in Numbers thirty, is found nowhere else in Hebrew, though the corresponding verb *"to bind,"* is not uncommon. It goes with the womanly nature to practice these forms of abstinence and self-affliction in all religions; and in this chapter, at this point, we may find a merciful provision to put a restraint upon excesses in such vows, needed in the case of women, but not so much in the case of men.

182. Vows, though *entirely voluntary in the making,* could not be left unperformed, Deut. 23:22, 23), no matter how rash (Lev. 5:4), without incurring guilt. *The Speaker's Commentary* tells us: "A large proportion of vows would always relate to the presentation of . . . offerings," Such offerings, together with other offerings, went to the support of the Tabernacle service, and to the maintenance of the priesthood,—so that covetous priests would have an interest in their kind and richness. We have an extreme case of this covetousness recorded in the sons of Eli, I Sam. 2:17.

183. Says the same writer quoted above: "It is probable that this fresh legislation [relating to women's vows] was occasioned by some case of practical difficulty that had recently arisen, and it is addressed by Moses to the heads of the tribes; who would in their judicial capacity have to determine questions on these subjects: and would also represent the class specially interested in obtaining relief . . . from vows made by persons in their families who had no independent means." We could have said all this ourselves, but then we might be accused of going beyond the legitimate inferences to be drawn, to conform them to our conclusions.

184. There is real significance in the fact that widows and divorced women were held, like men, to full responsibility for their vows. Hence we know that it was no mere teaching of the subordination of woman to man which led to this piece of legislation. The word translated "widow" means in the Hebrew *femme sole,* that is, "the solitary woman," and would doubtless have applied also to any mature unmarried woman of those times who owned property. These were supposed to have absolute control over their own property, to vow it away (Num. 30:9).

185. In those days as in these, the young daughter and the wife would not have much property under their own control, and hence the father and husband would stand in such relation to them as to be able, to a large extent, to control their vows. But as we said in our former Lesson, this statute in no wise obliges the woman to consult her father or husband before determining to make a vow, or determining the form or value of her offering. Nor does the statute compel or direct her to convey the intelligence to her male relative as to the vow she has made. In fact, the precise form of words used would seem to imply as much. According to Grey, verse 4 should read, "—and her father comes to hear her vow," and the *Speaker's Commentary* says, further, "It would almost necessarily be brought to his knowledge when the time for the performance of it arrived,—if not sooner." The real object, then, of these statutes, is *to provide a proper time* when the one *who controlled* the family property might show reason why he objected to relinquishing that control to the extent that daughter or wife might make a suitable offering; and doubtless his refusal to relinquish that control could be justified only by his showing that the offering was in some sense not suitable, to the satisfaction of the "heads of the tribles," to whom the enforcement of the statute had been committed by Moses.

186. The objection must be made *"on the day that he heareth,"* in the case of either father or husband (verses 5, 12). This expression is defined further in verses 14, "from day to day," an expression which means "within a few days." In the case of the husband, who was dealing with a woman of sufficient maturity to be his wife, it is significant that if he "broke her vow," (for that is the

precise meaning of the word "made void"), after he had been silent for awhile, *"then he shall bear her iniquity,"* verse 15.

187. But someone will say: "Why did not Moses give the mother and the wife an equal control over the son's and the husband's vows? Then the case would be equal, and equality of the sexes maintained." Moses did not *create* this matter of control by the husbands and fathers; and he could *not* have created an equality of this sort, between women and men, had he wished it. Here is where the mistake is made, in quoting Moses as the *author* of these things. Law is made to control lawlessness; its object is negative; law cannot by enactments, *create a non-existent good.* It inheres in the nature of things that women who marry and devote themselves to domestic pursuits must be more or less dependent upon the business activity of their husbands, just as men are dependent upon the domestic activity of their respective wives. And so must the young daughter be dependent on the father's business activity.

188. These vows extended to the right even to vow away children to the Tabernacle service. The case of Hannah who vowed away her son Samuel, compared with the case of Jephtha, who dedicated his daughter to perpetual service as a virgin at the Tabernacle,* is most instructive. Jephthah, all men would say, vowed without consulting the mother of his daughter, Judg. 11:30; and likewise Hannah's husband does not seem to have been consulted, when she vowed, any more than Jephthah's wife, 1 Sam. 1:9, 10, 11. If the mother of Jephthah's daughter seems to have had no part in this dedication of his daughter, so the father of little Samuel seems to have had no part in Samuel's dedication. This account of the dedication of a son to a life-long pursuit, without the father being described as taking any part in the same, is strikingly *unlike* the theological description of those times, which declares that the wife "could not be *sui juris,* or enter independently into any engagement even before God;" and we believe that if the Bible had wished to teach any such thing concerning those ancient days, the story of *Hannah*

---

*We accept Dr. Adam Clarke's refutation of the popular idea that Jephthah's daughter was sacrificed as a burnt offering; she was merely dedicated to the Tabernacle service with a burnt offering, and this is all Jephthah's vow implied.

would have been written after this fashion: *"Having fully gained her husband's consent,* Hannah's 'vowed a vow and said,' . . . 'If thou wilt give unto thine handmaid a man child, then, *with my husband's permission, we will together* give him unto the Lord;'" and verse 22 would have read, "I will not go up until the child be weaned, and then," *since you are willing,* "we will bring him, that he may . . . abide there forever." And she and the father, Elkanah, would later have stood before Eli, while the father said: *"My wife prayed for this child . . . therefore, at her earnest desire I have consented to dedicate the child to the Lord."* But nothing of this sort is recorded, and therefore we have asserted that Dr. Smith teaches Bible students to draw sweeping conclusions from small premises, in the conclusions he draws from Numbers 30. Read over again our Lesson on "Unsubjugated Wives" (pars. 146-154), and realize afresh how misleading such teachings are, as to the Bible.

LESSON 25.

SHALL WOMEN KEEP SILENCE?

189. The Apostle Paul speaks twice, in his first Epistle to the Corinthians, concerning the public ministry of women,—in 1 Cor. 11:3-16, and 14:29-40. We shall treat of the second utterance, as the simpler, first. Please read these two passages in turn, and note that they occur *in the same letter,* and if the writer was not interrupted, he wrote the second in the next breath after the first, that is, one could not have been written more than fifteen minutes or a half hour after the other. This point is important. Next note that *if St. Paul veiled women* he did not silence women, for, according to this interpretation he ordered them to veil only when prophesying or praying, not at other times; so that, if they were silenced they were left unveiled, so far as Scripture teaches. Yet the general idea and teaching is that Paul *both* veiled and silenced women.

190. Now turn to the second passage: Fix your attention, for a moment, on verses 31-36. Does it not seem strange that unless Paul *means* "all," he should have repeated "all" three times over? It is probable that the women far outnumbered the men in these early churches,

held in the homes of the people,* for they have usually
outnumbered the men throughout Church history even
since meetings have been held in public churches. Now
if only a small fraction of the attendants (the mature
men released from business so that they could be at
home for meetings), were allowed to prophesy (Paul says
nothing about mere *Sunday* meetings), then why did the
Apostle say, *"Ye may all prophesy, one by one, that all
may learn, and all may be comforted?"*

191. Again, at verse 34 he says, *"It is not permitted
. . . as also saith the law."* *Who* did not permit it?
Where was it not permitted? The O. T. says *absolutely
nothing* from Genesis to Malachi to forbid women to
speak. No "law" can be found anywhere in the Bible
forbidding women to speak in public, unless it be this one
only utterance here by St. Paul. And besides, we know
perfectly that the O. T. permitted women to speak in
public (Num. 27:1-7), and Jesus Christ did also, without
rebuke, Luke 8:47, 11:27, 13:13.

192. What is actually *known* about the situation which
occasioned the writing of this Epistle to the Corinthians?
We gather from the Epistle itself that the Corinthian
Christians had written Paul a letter (7:1) and he is
answering it. There were divisions among them (1:11).
He had enemies at Corinth, who disputed his right to be
called an Apostle (9:1), and criticised him and his companions for leading about a woman with them (9:5) and
he declares that "we" have as much right to do it as *"the
other apostles, and the brethren of the Lord, and
Cephas."* Who was this woman? Doubtless Priscilla,
who with Aquila her husband had left Corinth, in company with the Apostle, shortly before (Acts 18:18),—
the woman whom Paul mentions before her husband.
He actually dares to put this woman's "head" on behind!
How that would scandalize the proprieties of modern
theology! She was, all are bound to agree, a very able
person, and well known to *"all the churches of the Gentiles"* (Rom. 16:4), and how could that be if she was
altogether silenced and veiled? Paul was probably writing this very Epistle in her home at Ephesus (1 Cor.
16:19). Here we have the proper setting for these
words addressed to the Corinthians.

---

* The meetings of the Corinthian Church were probably held
in the house of Gaius (1 Cor. 1:14; Rom. 16:23).

193. Aquila was a Jew of Pontus in Asia Minor, converted to Christ, and his wife probably also a native of Asia Minor (Acts 18:2). Here women were held in great honor, as Professor Sir W. M. Ramsay of Aberdeen University clearly shows in his valuable books, *The Church in the Roman Empire,* and *The Cities and Bishoprics of Phrygia.* This woman would expect to take her position as on a perfect equality with her husband, and the attempt to do so on her part would at once arouse the ire of the Palestinian Jews who pursued Paul wherever he went, the so-called "Judaizers," bent on winning the Church back to Judaism. We believe this is what stirred up the "woman question" at Corinth, and led to Paul's two famous utterances in that Epistle.

194. Says Prof. Ramsay: *"The honours and influence which belonged to women in the cities of Asia Minor form one of the most remarkable features in the history of the country. In all periods the evidence runs on the same lines. On the border between fable and history we find the Amazons. The best authenticated cases of Mutterrect* belong to Asia Minor. Under the Roman Empire we find women magistrates, presidents at games, and loaded with honours. The custom of the country influenced even the Jews, who at least in one case appointed a woman at Smyrna to the position of* archisynagogus" ("ruler of the synagogue"). Again he says: *"Among the Asian Jews, women took an unusually prominent place."* But later, when Priscilla was at Corinth, she was in a totally different atmosphere, as regards the position of woman. Here, all she did would be subject to severe criticism by the "Judaizers," and by the Jews, who must have hated her for having instructed Apollos so well that he was converting many of their number to Christianity (Acts 18:26, 28, and 19:1); and St. Paul could not have given a woman such prominence under any circumstances without angering the Jews,—for the latter (of a later date at least, and probably by this time), forbade that women should even *learn* the Scriptures, much less teach them.

195. For candid scholars admit that, according to the best manuscript authority Acts 18:26 should read as in the R. V. (not as in the A. V.)—that is *"Priscilla and Aquila expounded"* unto Apollos the Way of God; and

---

* Matriarchy, see pars. 53 ff.

Dean Alford says, "There are certain indications that he himself [Aquila] was rather the ready and zealous patron than the teacher; and this latter work, or a great share of it, seems to have belonged to his wife, Prisca or Priscilla. She is ever named with him, even in Acts 18:26, where the instruction of Apollos is described." When first met with, and comparative strangers to St. Paul and Luke, the husband is mentioned first, according to usual custom (Acts 18:2,) but quickly the order changes: after eighteen months' acquaintance (Acts 18:11) Priscilla is mentioned first (Acts 18:18, 26; Rom. 16:3; 2 Tim. 4:19) with a single exception (1 Cor. 16:19).

196. We are not accustomed to look to German sources for broad-minded statements as regards women, therefore we the more readily turn in that direction for a statement as to Priscilla's position in the Apostolic Church. Prof. Harnack of Berlin says "In any case she must have been associated with and more distinguished than her husband. That is verified from Acts 18:26 and Romans 16:3, convincingly. For according to the former passage not only Aquila, but she also instructed Apollos. One is allowed to infer from it that she was the chief instructor; otherwise she would scarcely have been mentioned. And in the Roman Epistle Paul calls her and Aquila—not the latter only— his *fellow-laborers in Christ Jesus.* This expression, not so very frequently employed by Paul, signifies much. By its use Priscilla and Aquila are legitimized official Evangelists and Teachers. Paul adds, moreover the following: *'Who for my life laid down their own necks; unto whom not only I give thanks, but also all the churches of the Gentiles.'* To what heroic service the first half of this clause refers we unfortunately know not. From the second part it follows that the Christian activity of the couple was a genuinely ecumenical work. Why *'all the churches of the Gentiles'* were obliged to thank Priscilla and Aquila Paul does not say." Then Dr. Harnack adds in a footnote, quoting the views of Origen and Chrysostom as in accord with his own, "That the thanks of the Gentile churches relate only to the fact that Priscilla and Aquila saved the life of the Apostle is to me not probable."

(To be Continued.)

87

LESSON 26.

SHALL WOMEN KEEP SILENCE?

(Continued.)

197. Different attempts have been made to reconcile Paul's directions about women *"praying and prophesying"* in Chapter 11 of 1st Corinthians, and the seeming command, *"Let the* [not your] *women keep silence in the churches,"* of Chapter 14, such as the following: (1) "Paul is meeting a purely local difficulty of some sort, in these latter words, of no importance outside of Corinth, or to us in our day." *Objection*: We must not quickly assume that any point in Scripture has only a local application (though sometimes such is the case), lest we weaken the authority of the Bible. (2) "Paul changed his mind, and decided in the end to forbid women speaking at all." This is the usual claim made by present-day expositors. *Objection* 1. He changed it quickly, then, with scarcely time for fresh consideration or fresh light, or deep thought on so momentous a subject, which has surely affected for all time, in a most profound manner, the progress of the Christian church. *Objection* 2. A merely human writer might even be so fickle as this, though one could at least expect, under such circumstances, some intimation of a change. But, if these words are inspired, the Holy Spirit who prompted the writing of these words could never be so fickle; the Spirit knew from the first sentence of the Epistle all that was to follow, and did not need to correct His mind. (3) "He forbids the women 'babbling' and 'chattering' in church, but does not forbid them prophesying." *Objection*: Those who hold this view generally refer to the disorderly way women in Eastern churches, recently out of heathenism, conduct themselves. But there is no proof that Corinthian women misbehaved after this manner. But the most serious obstacle to the last view is this: The Greek word here "to talk" (*laleo*), may be employed in the sense of "to babble", but the Apostle never uses it in this sense elsewhere, and he uses the word 23 times in this very chapter for solemn utterance under Divine inspiration. (4) "He only forbids them to speak to ask questions; they must do that at home." *Objection* 1. It is not known that even men asked questions in church, as the Jewish men did in the synagogue. *Objection* 2. As to asking questions of their husbands at

home, some of these Corinthian women would be widows, some perhaps divorced on account of their Christian faith, some with Jewish husbands, some with heathen husbands, some not married at all. And so would it be in the Church throughout all subsequent ages of its history. Paul is represented as sending all these to their "husbands." If Paul did so foolish a thing, he drove some back to heathenism for spiritual help; others back to Judaism for spiritual help; many others he deprived of all opportunity to get their questions answered, since they had no husbands. In fact, a majority of the Christian women would have been left in ignorance of important spiritual truths, by such a ruling. We do not believe Paul went about giving the Bread of Life to all men, and a stone for bread to many women, after this partial manner.

198. Besides, he makes use of the phrase, *"it is not permitted,"* clearly implying that others besides Paul have, before him, forbidden this thing, yet, *not one trace of any such prohibition can be found anywhere in the Bible, until these very words of Paul.* This raises the important question, where and by whom was it not permitted? Gen. 3:16 is the only reference to "the law" given in the marginal references, and it will not do for two reasons. (1) If husbands command their wives to speak in public, then they *must* speak, if Gen. 3:16 means, *"Thy desire shall be to thy husband,* and *he* shall *rule over thee."* (2) But few of the Corinthian Church members, if indeed any of them, would know this sense for Gen. 3:16, since they used the Septuagint Version. St. Paul quotes this version almost exclusively in this Epistle; he only once quotes clearly the Hebrew text, in his seventeen references to the O. T. Therefore the Corinthians would read the verse, "Thou art turning away to thy husband, and he will rule over thee,"—a sense that has no application to the Corinthian passage.

199. Before reaching the superficial conclusion that St. Paul's one utterance about "silence" closes the mouth of every Christian woman or that Paul meant it so, read the account of Miriam (Ex. 15:20); of Deborah (Judges chs. 4 and 5); of the immense assembly of important personages addressed by the daughters of Zelophehad (Numbers 27:1-7, where it is expressly said the Lord approved of their message); the reference to Huldah the prophetess (2 Kings 22); the references to women

who prophesied in song (1 Chron. 25); and to women who *"prophesy out of their own heart,"* where the rebuke is as to *what* is prophesied, not as to the prophesying itself (Ezek. 13:17.) This incidental mention of a considerable body of women prophets, implies the existence of many women prophets who were not false. Then read in the N. T. of Anna, (Luke 2:36-38); of the women Christ *caused* to speak in public (Luke 8:47, Luke 13:13); the utterance of Peter as to women prophesying (Acts 2:16-18); and the reference to Philip's daughters (Acts 21:9).

200. Next ask yourself this question: If this one only utterance of St. Paul's is to be set up as a Scriptural "law" to silence women, then what is to be done with the hundred and one other "laws" in the O. T. opening the mouths of women,—such as "Let the redeemed of the Lord say so," "Praise ye the Lord" (repeated about a hundred times in the Psalms alone), "Make a joyful noise unto the Lord," "Declare His doings among the people," "Let everything that hath breath praise the Lord," "Tell of all His wondrous works?" For it is simply impossible for men to set up an effectual claim, that all these admonitions and exhortations in the O. T. were meant for themselves only. It was not so understood or taught for thousands of years. This over zeal of certain religious teachers for such an interpretation of a *single* sentence of Scripture as sets at defiance a hundred or two of other Scriptural utterances (rather than an attempt to harmonize the one with the many), should warn us against accepting their interpretation too hastily. Why, for instance, have not such sticklers for a literal and universal application of a single phrase here been equally sticklers for a literal and universal application of Paul's authority where he says it is good for unmaried females to remain so (1 Cor. 7: 8, 34, 35)? But no! they are usually the very persons who advocate marriage and domestic pursuits as the one and *only* calling for women. Why do they not claim that the phrase, "Let *all the earth* keep silence before Him," (Hab. 2:20), should close, not only the mouths of women, but of the entire church?

201. St. Paul, here in the words, "it is not permitted" refers to some rule *outside,* not inside Scripture. The question is, where shall we find this rule of silence? The great German lexicographer, Schleusner, in his Greek-

Latin Lexicon, declares the expression *"as also saith the law,"* refers to the Oral Law of the Jews. Here are his words: *"The oral laws of the Jews or Jewish traditions . . . In the old Testament no precept concerning this matter exists,"* and he cites Vitringa as showing that it was *"forbidden by Jewish traditions for women to speak. in the synagogue."* But think again! It is not likely that the Apostle Paul would quote the traditions of the Jews. and refer to them as "the law," and as constituting a final authority on a matter of controversy in the church. He spent a large share of energy battling against these very "traditions" of the Jews, as did his Master, Jesus Christ. Paul warns against *"giving heed to Jewish fables, and commandments of men, that turn from the truth"* (Tit. 1:14). No, the Apostle Paul is here quoting *what the Judaizers in the Corinthian Church are teaching,*—who themselves say women must "keep silence" because Jewish law thus taught.

202. That the Talmud, unlike the Old Testament, did remand women to silence admits of no doubt. "Out of respect to the congregation, a woman should not herself read in the law." "It is a shame for a woman to let her voice be heard among men." "The voice of a woman is filthy nakedness." These are some, out of many, of its sayings. As to asking questions: A wealthy Jewess ventured to ask once, of the great R. Eleazer, "Why, when the sin of the golden calf was but one only, should it be punished with a three-fold death?" We imagine the question was beyond his stock of knowledge, for he replied: "A woman ought not to be wise above her distaff." One Hyrcanus protested, aside, to R. Eleazer, because the lady who was thus reproved might withhold her tithes, in retaliation, and they amounted to considerable. R. Eleazer replied: *"Let the words of the law be burned rather than committed to women."* This was accepted as a sort of judicial utterance, for future generations, among the Jews.

(*To be Continued.*)

LESSON 27.

SHALL WOMEN KEEP SILENCE?
(Continued.)

203. To repeat: We are driven to believe *the Apostle was not uttering his own views* in verses 34 and 35 of

1. Cor. ch. 14, which read: *"Let the women keep silence in the churches: for it is not permitted unto them to speak: but let them be in subjection, as also saith the law. And if they would learn anything, let them ask their husbands at home: for it is a shame for women to speak in the c h u r c h"* (R. V.) We believe this is the language of Judaizers at Corinth, which has been reported to Paul, and which Paul quotes to answer back in the words: *"What! came the word of God out from you? or came it unto you only?"*—with what follows to the end of the chapter.

204. Now for the evidences that Paul quotes the Judaizers here, and then answers that false teaching as to women keeping silence: First re-read what we said in par. 192-6 on The Situation in Corinth,—the prejudice that had been aroused there against Paul's having Priscilla "laboring in the Gospel" with him. These Corinthians had written Paul a letter, all agree to that; Paul was answering a lot of points that had been submitted to him for decision, in this Epistle. Listen, please, to what Prof. Weizsäcker writes, in his book, *The Apostolic Age of the Christian Church,* of this First Epistle to the Corinthians, and Paul's method: "And now [at chapter 7] begins a new letter, or at any rate a new section of the letter . . . What follows, therefore, bears a wholly different character; the language is now comparatively calm, official, instructive and hortatory, and treats of a whole series of affairs belonging to the life of the Church. And as an answer to the Church's enquiry, the discussion furnishes a subject new in form as well as in matter. *The reference to the question is repeated whenever a new point is taken up . . . Under each heading* a discussion is given as has been desired, and therefore the matters are discussed one after the other and each by itself."

205. Now let us see what this means. At 6:12 occur the words, *"All things are lawful unto me."* Paul is here expressing not his own views. This is his quotation from the Corinthians' letter to him; he has quoted it as a subhead, to answer it. This he does in the next sentence, *"But all things are not expedient."* Then he repeats the "heading" again, in order to give another answer, namely: *"But I will not be brought under the power of any."* The Corinthians were justifying license by these words, because Paul had taught, *"Ye are not*

under law, but under grace." At 10:23 he again reverts to their claim, *"all things are lawful,"* and repeats his first answer, then adds a third reply, *"All things edify not."* Again, at 8:8, he takes words (probably his own originally, but being misapplied), *"Meat commendeth us not to God,"* from the Corinthians' letter as his text, and comments on them thus: *"But take heed lest this liberty of yours become a stumbling block to the weak."* We could give other instances where commentators trace Paul's quotations from the letter from Corinth, using each as a "heading" to his discussion of the points involved, but it is unnecessary. We merely wish to show that this idea that Paul makes quotations from the letter he has received and is answering, is no novel idea, invented by us to suit a prejudiced view. Prof. Sir Wm. Ramsay says, on this subject: *"We should be ready to suspect Paul is making a quotation from the letter addressed to him by the Corinthians whenever he alludes to their knowledge, or when any statement stands in marked contrast either with the immediate context or with Paul's known views."*

Our case answers to all of these tests. Following our guide, we will apply the three points of Prof. Ramsay's rule. I. "Whenever he alludes to their knowledge:" Paul alludes to their knowledge in verse 37; and in 38 he declares if anyone still remains ignorant of his meaning he is past being enlightened. II. "When any statement stands in marked contrast with the immediate context:" Verses 34, 35 are in marked contrast to verse 31 and to verse 39, for it is impossible to hold that Paul's use of the word "brethren" applies only to the male sex. III. "When any statement stands in marked contrast with . . Paul's known views:" A command on the part of the Apostle for women to "keep silence" would put him in direct conflict with what must be inferred from what he has just written in chapter eleven, about women veiling.

206. Paul's reply to all this caviling of Judaizers and their efforts to strengthen their case by quoting the Oral Law of the Jews, is: *"What? came the word of God out from you? or came it unto you only?"* Then, in verses 37-40, he expresses his own mind, which is the mind of the Holy Spirit, on the subject. Psalm 68:11 (R. V.) declares: *"The Lord giveth the word; the women that publish the tidings are a great host."* The

"word," therefore, when women prophesy, comes out from God, and comes unto women. Expositors attempt to show that here the expression "the word of God," in Paul's language, refers to church customs. But such an expression has never been used in this sense. This is far-fetched. The expression "the word of God" and "the word of the Lord" have a definite and specific sense in the N. T., as referring either to the Gospel, or to prophetic utterances given from above. See Luke 3:1, 2, *"In the fifteenth year of the reign of Tiberius Caesar . . the word of God came unto John the son of Zecharias in the wilderness."* Thus, Luke 5:1; John 10:35. Compare 1 Kings 12:22, 1 Chron. 17:3, Jer. 2:1, Ezek. 34:1, Jonah 1:1. See Paul's use of the expression, Rom. 9:6, 1 Thes. 1:8, 2:13, 2 Cor. 2:17, 4:2.* Paul's contention is, that since the spirit of prophecy, which is "the word of God," did not, as its very terms imply, come forth from anyone but God, to attempt to control prophecy by restrictions as to who may utter it, means a dictating to God as to what instruments He may employ. As a matter of fact, Scripture teaches us that "the word of God" has come to kings (1 Sam. 10:10), to a child (1 Sam. 3:11-18), to an ass (Num. 22:28-30), and also to women (Judges 4:6, 2 Kings 22:15, 16, Luke 1:41, 42, etc.).

207. On the day of Pentecost, the Spirit was poured out upon "all flesh," that is, not upon every human being, but as is precisely told us, upon old and young and upon male and female alike. And in these words, *"What? came the word of God out from you? or came it unto you only?"* Paul seems specially to refer to that day of Pentecost, when about 120 persons, many of them women (Acts 1:14, 15), were assembled, and the Holy Spirit, that is, the spirit of prophecy, came upon "each of them" (Acts 2:3), and they all *"began to speak . . . as the Spirit gave them utterance;"* and Peter said, *"This is that which hath been spoken by the prophet Joel . . . your daughters shall prophesy . . . and upon my handmaidens . . . will I pour out of my Spirit."* So that there is no possibility of denying that at the time of the inauguration of the present Gospel dispensation, the

---

* Prof. Harnack declares that the expression in our passage (1 Cor. 14:36), **"the word of God,"** means, "the new preaching which went forth from Jerusalem, and then from other places." See for example the use of this expression four times over in Acts 13; and **"the word of the Lord"** twice in that same chapter.

"word of God" "came out" from God, not from man, and it *"came unto"* women, and not unto men only. This is Paul's indignant protest against these Judaizers, who, by quoting the Oral Law of the Jews would silence women, and interfere with Divine order.

208. The Apostle then declares: *"If any man think himself to be a prophet, or spiritual, let him acknowledge that the things that I write unto you are the commandment of the Lord."* He here contrasts "the commandment of the Lord" with the "precepts of men," which the Oral Law of the Jews taught. In other words, a true prophet, or a spiritual person, would perceive, Paul claims, that his ruling in this matter accorded with Scripture, while the ruling of the Jewish rabbis did not. What was Paul's ruling? It was given just before, in directions relating to veiling in worship, which clearly show that he permitted women both to preach and to pray in public. He gave the same permission in his universal rule but a moment before, at verse 31: *"Ye ALL can prophesy . . . that ALL may learn, and ALL may be comforted."*

(*To be Continued*).

LESSON 28.

SHALL WOMEN KEEP SILENCE?
(Concluded).

209. Paul claims that he gives his own ruling, as to the conduct of women in church, on *"the commandment of the Lord"* (I Cor. 14:37)." By this statement he may refer to some special revelation to himself, such as led him, on a previous occasion, to say: *"There can be neither Jew nor Greek, there can be neither bond nor free, there can be no male and female: for ye are all one in Christ Jesus"* (Gal. 3:28, R. V.). But since he states that if they are spiritual they will perceive this matter, he probably refers either to the whole tenor of Scriptural teaching, with its hundreds of exhortations, given without regard to sex, that the redeemed should proclaim the goodness of the Lord to others, or to the Great Commission, *"Go ye into all the world and preach my Gospel to every creature,"* spoken to women, as well as to men, Luke 24:22, 33-48, Acts 1:8, 14, etc., or to the definite commandment set forth in Isaiah 40:9, which, if correctly translated for us into English, would read:

95

"*O woman that bringest good tidings to Zion, get thee up into the high mountain; O woman, that bringest good tidings to Jerusalem, lift up thy voice with strength; lift it up, be not afraid; say unto the cities of Judah, Behold your God.*" We will treat of this verse at greater length later on. This preaching by women was prophesied of in Psalm 68:11, and in Joel 2:28, 29. The fulfilment of the prophecy began on the day of Pentecost, as we are clearly instructed by Peter's words, Acts 2:16-18. And Paul declares that the spiritual will know this.

210. The words, "*If any man be ignorant, let him be ignorant,*" are, according to Winer, "A renunciation of further effective instruction."

He concludes his instructions with verses 39 and 40: "*Wherefore, my brethren, covet to prophesy, and forbid not to speak with tongues.*" This would seem a peculiar ending for an argument *forbidding* women to prophesy, but a very appropriate one with which to end a reproof to those who thus forbade women. We must remember that the word "brethren" was much more like "sisters" in Greek than in English. The difference would be equivalent only to that between "sisteroi" and "sisterai," and besides, masculine and feminine nouns and adjectives very generally had the same form in New Testament Greek. It is only by an effort of thought that women take the word "brethren" to themselves; but not so the Greek word "adelphoi" which New Testament women would quite naturally apply to themselves, and instinctively. Imagine Paul saying: "Let the women keep silence . . . wherefore covet to prophesy." "Let the women keep silence . . . wherefore forbid not to speak." Why, they represent Paul as concluding a commandment to keep silence with an exhortation to speak out; they represent him as forbidding to speak in one breath, and in the next commanding others: "Forbid not to speak." Is this consistent? But let us imagine he has just reproved men for silencing women: then it naturally follows that he should say to all, both men and women, "covet to prophesy." Imagine him rebuking those who would *forbid* women speaking: and then we would expect him to say, "Forbid *not* to speak." This view makes of Paul's language a consistent whole.

211. The expression "*covet to prophesy*" deserves special attention here. It is the positive admonition of that

which is negatively put by the Apostle in 1 Thess. 5:19, 20: *"Quench not the Spirit; despise not prophesyings."* It relates not properly to the individual, but to the whole church. "Covet the *to-prophesy*," is the literal reading, and it means "covet the prophesying,"—that is, the gift itself,—not simply for oneself but for others also; covet the existence of the gift in the church, by whomsoever exercised. Paul has used this word "covet" before, at 1 Cor. 12:31: *"Covet earnestly the best gifts: and yet I show unto you a more excellent way."* No one will dispute that women should heed these words as far as to seek that way of "charity." Then why should they not also heed the beginning of the verse, and "covet the best gifts," among which is prophecy,—for Paul teaches that this is the best (14:5)? Again, at 14:1, we are told to *"Follow after charity and desire* (it is this same word "covet") *spiritual gifts, but rather that ye may prophesy."* Here again, are women to believe that they are to *obey* the first half of this commandment and as diligently *disobey* the second half? The BIBLE does not tell them to treat its commandments thus: and if expositors do, how do they come to know more about the matter than what the Bible teaches? But the Bible warns: *"Every word of God is tried . . . add thou not unto His words, lest . . . thou be found a liar"* (Prov. 30:5, 6, R. V.).

212. In fact, by using that word "covet" more than once, Paul touches the sore spot in this objection to women prophesying, on the part of Judaizers, namely, *Jealousy.* This Greek word "to covet" (zelein) means likewise "to envy," "to be jealous," and "to be zealous." By using here the same word that their Greek Bible (for the Corinthian Church would use the Septuagint Greek Version) uses in Num. 11:29, the Apostle would turn their minds to the lesson taught there. God took the spirit that had before rested upon Moses alone and gave it to his seventy elders. Joshua was "jealous" for Moses' honour, but could say nothing, because God had done it, and it came about in the *regular* way, upon those who were in the Tabernacle.

213. But two of the elders were out in the camp, at the time, yet they began to prophesy also. This gave Joshua a pretext for the display of his jealous spirit, for there was something *irregular* in it, he thought. He ran to Moses saying, *"My Lord Moses, forbid them."* But

Moses read in him the real spirit that prompted the desire to forbid the prophesying, and replied: *"Art thou jealous* (the same word Paul uses) *for me? And who shall make ALL the people of the Lord prophets, when the Lord hath put His Spirit upon them?"* Thus (according to the Septuagint) he prophesied, as Joel did, of that general outpouring of the Spirit upon "all flesh" that is God's plan for the Gospel dispensation. But that which God Himself does can never be forbidden as irregular or out of order. In God's own time, says Moses, ALL shall have the privilege of seeking to be prophets, and he only is out of order who attempts to thwart the will of God, through envy or jealousy. Hence, St. Paul says, *"all may prophesy,"* 14:31.

214. The Judaizers at Corinth were really in a rage of envy at the Church, being jealous of its increasing influence under Pentecostal power ,and they were eager to bring Christianity back within the confines of Judaism again. Many of these Judaizers were in the church as "false apostles" (2 Cor. 11:13) to destroy it. Others were honestly, but mistakenly, working to the same end, but with better motives. But none of them could hope to influence the Christians to return to obedience to the traditions of the Jews, by attacking things that were manifestly *regular.* Like Joshua, the only opportunity lay in something *irregular,* and this they readily found, in the public prophesying of women.

215. The Oral Law had said: *"It is a shame,"* and the Judaizers took up the cry that *"The women must keep silence . . . they must ask their husbands at home . . . it is a shame for a woman to speak in the assembly; the Oral Law of the Jews says so,"* etc. All this was written to Paul from Corinth. He copies it out for his text. He shows up its sophistries, exhorts his converts to be jealous of this gift of prophesying in their church, and not to forbid anyone to speak in tongues. He shows us the motive of the objection to women as "jealousy," and closes with the words, *"Let all things be done decently and in order."*

LESSON 29.

THE SOPHISTRY OF THE VEIL.

216. We can prove that the usual interpretation of St. Paul's words about veiling is wrong, because it is a mis-

fit all around. Please read over carefully 1 Cor. 11:1-16, and keep your Bibles open to the passage, while we study it. The usual sense (not ours) put upon these words by expositors, beginning with verse 3, we give in the language of Dr. Weymouth's Modern English translation: (3) "I would have you know that of every man, Christ is the Head, that of a woman her husband is the Head, and that God is Christ's Head. (4) A man who wears a veil praying or prophesying dishonours his Head; (5) but a woman who prays or prophesies with her head uncovered dishonours her Head, for it is exactly the same as if she had her hair cut short. (6) If a woman will not wear a veil, let her also cut off her hair, but since it is a dishonour to a woman to have her hair cut off or her head shaved, let her wear a veil. (7) For a man ought not to have a veil on his head, since he is the image and glory of God: while woman is the glory of man. (8) Man does not take his origin from woman, but woman takes hers from man. (9) For man was not created for woman's sake, but woman for man's. (10) That is why a woman ought to have on her head a symbol of subjection, because of the angels. (11) Yet, in the Lord, woman is not independent of man nor man independent of woman. (12) For just as woman originates from man, so also man comes into existence through woman, but everything springs originally from God. (13) Judge of this for your own selves: is it seemly for a woman to pray to God when she is unveiled? (14) Does not nature itself teach you that if a man has long hair it is a dishonour to him, (15) but if a woman has long hair it is her glory, because her hair was given to her for a covering? (16) But if anyone is inclined to be contentious on the point, we have no such custom, nor have the churches of God."

217. MISFIT 1. Now please note, first of all, that at verse 10, first clause, Dr. Weymouth substitutes something totally different from what the text says. The text reads, *"ought to have power,"* while Dr. Weymouth, following the usual interpretation, says, "ought to have . . . a symbol of subjection." The original word for "power," here, is *exousia,* meaning authority, right; the same word for "power," and preposition for on, *epi,* (often translated "over"), with the same construction, will be found in many places,—for instance, Rev. 11:6, *"They have power over waters to turn them to blood."*

and likewise in Matthew, Mark, and Luke, in the sentence, *"The Son of Man hath power on earth to forgive sins."* Furthermore, the original text here has never been called into question; the reading is as simple as it could possibly be, *"The woman ought to have power over* [rendered "on" in the English Versions] *her head."* No scholar questions this.

218. At this place, the Authorised Version introduces the longest Marginal Note to be found in the whole Bible. Where Paul says, *"ought to have power,"* the Note reads, "That is, *a covering in sign that she is under the power of her husband."* This is certainly a most extraordinary substitute for the words of Scripture. Had it read merely, that she was to be *"under power,"* even that would have been a contradiction of the explicit statement of St. Paul; but they add to this contradicting thought: The woman is not only expected to *yield* to authority, instead of *wielding* authority, but also to "wear a sign" that she renounces the authority Paul gives her. And not only is she to renounce that authority, but to renounce it *in favour of a particular person,* —her *husband.* The *BIBLE*—St. Paul—says nothing of this sort, but the Marginal Note, and the Bible Commentators teach it. For our part, we think it suspicious because that *husbands,* not wives, have discovered this extraordinary meaning for St. Paul's words. If indeed a woman should wear "a sign of subjection" (and scholars can produce *no Scriptural proof* that a veil *is* a sign of subjection), then why should it not rather be a sign of subjection to God, whom she serves in prophesying, or whom she addresses in prayer? Why is the *husband* thrust in by husbands, at this point? Dr. J. W. Thirtle makes the sensible remark here, "The context puts in no plea for anyone outside the woman: it is THE WOMAN'S OWN AUTHORITY that is in question, and the Apostle defends it with his decisive OUGHT." [The capitals are Dr. Thirtle's.]

219. This phrase in verse 10 is manifestly a conclusion —the *ergo*—of all the foregoing arguments of the passage. Now we ask, If *you* were arguing a point, would you, or would you not, know the point you were arguing? Certainly you would know it. And would you know how to state your point? Certainly, even if you could not argue it, for you have your right mind. St. Paul was a highly intelligent person, and to pretend that

he knew how to *argue* a point, but could not *express* the point in plain words, is puerile. Whether Paul knew how to argue clearly or not, he knew how to state what he was arguing about, or St. Paul's intelligence was far below the average man's. And when we believe that St. Paul was inspired by the Holy Spirit in what he wrote, then we must yield at once that verse 10 *means what it says,* and we dare not reject its teaching for the *"vain traditions of men."*

220. Of the usual interpretation here, Sir Willliam Ramsay, our present-day most widely accepted authority on St. Paul, says very truly, "Most of the ancient and modern commentators say the 'authority' which the woman wears on her head is the authority to which she is subject—a preposterous idea which a Greek scholar would laugh at anywhere except in the N. T., where (as they seem to think), Greek words may mean anything that the commentators choose." Here, then, in the usual interpretation, is a *Tremendous Misfit.*

221. MISFIT 2. As to the second clause of verse 10, *"because of the angels,"* a very common explanation, given by Dean Stanley for instance, one of the Translation Committee that produced our Revised Version, is that the angels and women fell into sin together, and therefore, he says, "Woman ought not to part with the sign that she is subject, not to them, but to her husband. The authority of the husband is, as it were, enthroned visibly upon her head, in token that she belongs to him alone, and that she owes no allegiance to any one else besides, not even to the angels who stand before God's throne." This teaching (1) contradicts Heb. 2:2. *"The word spoken by angels was steadfast, and every transgression and disobedience received a just recompence of reward."* (2) It assumes that angels are *males,* whereas they are sexless,—Mark 12:25. (3) We have already, in par. 158 and note, disposed of the superstition that angels sinned with women. (4) Christian women belong to Christ, who purchased them with His own blood,—not to their husbands. (1 Cor. 6:19, 20).

222. MISFIT 3. Verse 4. Commentators set forth two or three views here: Men dishonour their own heads by wearing "a token of subjection." If so, then Christ dishonoured His head when *"He took on Him the form of a servant."* Why are not men called upon to imitate

101

Christ's humility? Another view is, that *because* Christ is man's Head man must not veil in His presence. This is more nearly correct. But if man must unveil before Christ, because Christ is man's Head, in the same sense Christ is woman's Head, and therefore she will dishonour Him unless she unveils in His presence. And if it is because of "headship," then, since man is woman's head, she should, for the same reasons, unveil before man. Here then is a double reason why women should unveil.

223. But next, in verses 5 and 6, we come to a clear statement which has given occasion for the assumption that Paul is arguing for the veiling of women, not against their veiling. Can we get an explanation for the words, *"Every woman that prayeth or prophesieth with her head uncovered, dishonoreth her head."* which can be reconciled with St. Paul's logic for unveiling? We promise a satisfactory explanation in due course. Please note that the penalty, *"Let her be shown or shaven."* is softened to *"let her cut off her hair,"* by Dr. Weymouth, though it is not at all what the words mean. It is too much, even for these hardy expositors, to claim that Paul actually commanded the church to punish unveiled women after this fashion.

(To be Continued.)

LESSON 30.

THE SOPHISTRY OF THE VEIL.

(Continued).

224. MISFIT 4. Verse 7 reads, *"A man ought not to cover his head, forasmuch as he is the image and glory of God."* And so is woman, in precisely the same sense, —*"In the image of God made He him, male and female made He them"* (see pars. 23-25),—and hence she ought not to cover her head. Any argument drawn from the "image" idea must apply surely quite as equally to woman, who was created at the same time as man, and by the same act. It is the spirit of phallic worship which contends that this image inheres in physical *sex*, not the spiritual characteristics. And if a man ought not to veil before God because he is "the glory of God," then woman should not veil before man because she is "the glory of man." Here then is set forth again a double

reason for women *unveiling*.. Yet the commentator declares this an argument for the veiling of woman.

225. MISFIT 5. Verses 11 and 12, if they mean anything, are an argument that men and women are to be dealt with exactly alike, are on precisely the same level *"in the Lord"* (that is, after they become Christians); these words cannot be fitted to an argument placing woman under the power of man, or legislating specially for her apart from man, in the Church of God.

226. MISFIT 6. Verse 13, *"Judge in yourselves."* Rather, *"among yourselves."* This phrase should end verse 12; see 10:15. According to the usual representation of conditions at Corinth, St. Paul would never have said this, in connection with verse 13, unless he *meant* that *the men* should judge for the women; and there is not a scrap of evidence that he meant any such thing, especially since he had already said that the woman ought to have authority over her own head. We will describe these *conjectured* conditions at Corinth in the words of Dr. Ernest Von Dobschütz, Prof. N. T. Theology in the Strasburg University, written in 1904: "Corinth was full of prostitutes. The temple of Aphrodite on the fort alone possessed over a thousand *'hierodules,'* (temple slaves), a dedicatory gift to the goddess from men and women, as Strabo tells us. We cannot discover the character of the female element in the Christian church. It is very certain that many honourable women of better standing were Christians . . . But the Christian community could not have lacked persons who before their conversion followed dishonourable pursuits any more than it lacked slaves . . . Should the honourable matron, used to a strict morality, sit, not only next her slave, but also next a former prostitute? Should the former lay aside her veil, which she was accustomed to wear outside the house, or should the latter assume it? Were the freedom and equality with men, which were conceded in public life to the *hetaira,* to hold good, or the chaste seclusion and subjection prescribed by usage for the honourable wife? The Gospel recognized the full equality of man and woman in religion, more clearly perhaps than was the case in pagan cults, or even in Judaism itself. Did not the claim of women to equality of position within the Church follow? As usual, the freer and more progressive tendency gained more acceptance."

227. Then the writer draws a picture of the women all arrayed against Paul, proving themselves his worst enemies in the Corinthian church, and adds: "He (Paul) becomes impassioned whenever he has to speak of their 'emancipation,' which nothing could bring to reason . . . Paul insists on veiling. He declares their position of subordination "demands an external sign, 'because of the angels' lest they [the angels] should lust after the woman, who belongs to her husband alone."

228. Let us women exercise a little common sense here. These temple women, dedicated to the goddess of sensuality, Aphrodite, were slaves. They went bareheaded, having shaved heads. Some were *supposed* to have been converted, and to have entered the church; and the question arises, shall the "honourable women of better standing" be allowed to copy slave-prostitutes in dress and manners? They are determined to do so, and defy Paul's authority, while the latter "becomes impassioned whenever he has to speak of their 'emancipation'." Could anything be more ridiculous? Free women, because emancipated, wishing *to ape slaves!* Imagine women of our Southern States, after Lincoln's Emancipation Proclamation, or their own enfranchisement, being provoked thereby to copy the dress of the negresses!

229. This is all *pure conjecture.* There is not a scrap of historical evidence that the women at Corinth *wished* to unveil, and there exists considerable evidence to the contrary. But were it true, and St. Paul had such difficulties to contend against, then he would never have said, *"Judge in yourselves,"* but "The *men alone* must judge for the women."

We believe that the remainder of the verse is a simple statement: *"It is comely that a woman pray unto God uncovered."* Moses, when veiled before the people, always unveiled when he went back into the Tabernacle to commune with God,—Ex. 34:34; Thence Paul rules that the women, even if not free to unveil before men, will be doing a very proper thing to unveil before God (2 Cor. 3:18). We must bear in mind, here, that a change from question to statement does not involve the change, in Greek, of the order of words, (such as from "is it" to "it is"); and punctuation is a matter of more recent days than Paul's time (see par. 17).

230. MISFIT 7. Verse 14 purports to be a question asking, *"Doth not nature itself teach you that if a man*

have long hair it is a shame?" Now every candid person must answer this question with a "No." It is not nature, but the barber who keep's man's hair short. In China, millions of men wear long hair, and nature has never taught them that it is a shame. Furthermore, the last time the Corinthians saw the apostle Paul before he wrote this Epistle, he himself had long hair (Acts 18: 18); and to the Jew, accustomed to religious vows (Num. 6:1-21), long hair, religiously speaking, was more of a "glory" than a "shame." Additionally to this, the native Corinthians would have thought this a strange question to submit to them, for they would boast* that they were descendants of the "long-haired Achaeans," celebrated as such on almost every page of that most famous and most ancient Greek poem, Homer's Iliad. Therefore we do not believe that St. Paul asked a question, here. His simple statement of fact, "Nor doth nature teach you," has been changed into a question by the uninspired men who put in the punctuation marks centuries later than St. Paul wrote these words. As a question, this is a Tremendous Misfit. It contradicts a fact of nature; it makes St. Paul inconsistent in his practice with his teaching; it is an entirely unsuitable question to submit to Achaeans.

231. MISFIT 8. Verse 16, *"We have no such custom."* What custom? Most commentator's assume that this means, "We have no such *defiance* of custom, as women unveiling." But this is not what Paul says, but the exact contrary. We cannot insert "defiance of custom" in the place of "custom" without introducing a contradiction. Paul is talking of some custom, which he repudiates. What is it? Veiling, of course; this is the only custom mentioned (unless it be that of wearing long hair, a custom for women; or wearing short hair, which was the usual custom for men,—and no one thinks it means these latter). Paul has been talking, almost wholly, of the custom of veiling, and he now says, *"We have no such custom."* He renounces the custom. This verse cannot be easily reconciled with the teaching that St. Paul is here strengthening a prevalent custom.

232. Now we have discovered that every portion of St. Paul's argument (if we change the punctuation of verses 13 and 14), and certainly his plain statement that

---

* Whether the boast were true or not, we need not discuss here.

women *"ought to have authority"* over their own heads, fits better to an argument for *unveiling* than for veiling. But there remain the statements in verses 5 and 6, where Paul says that the woman who unveils dishonours her head. Can they be explained to accord with the idea that St. Paul is not teaching the veiling of women? We promise a satisfactory explanation to that effect in due course. But before we leave our present topic, we must consider how at variance with common sense and true religion as well as sound logic is the whole tenor and spirit of this traditional misinterpretation of St. Paul. So true is this, that after standing for its teaching, as to the main points (those that appeal to the vanity of the male sex, and the love of dominion over the female sex), then men apologize that such (worthy) points are not supported by worthier arguments on the part of St. Paul, —as though the Holy Spirit could not have caused the Apostle to set forth God's *good* reasons for veiling women, had God wished women to be veiled! (See further on for the apologies pars. 346-353).

(To be Continued).

LESSON 31.

THE SOPHISTRY OF THE VEIL.

233. To impress the need of a more intelligent interpretation of this passage, we must give some further idea of what has been taught by commentators. If after this general survey the student still clings to the traditional misinterpretation, it will not be for the lack of knowledge that something better is sadly needed.

234. *"The image and glory of God."* The comments here must needs remind one of the words of the Psalmist, *"Verily every man at his best estate is altogether vanity."* Dr. Agar Beet says, "Man is an outshining of the splendour of God. By looking at him we see in dim outline what God is." Dr. Kling, "Paul indicates the godlike rule and lordly majesty which the position of man as the head of his wife involves." He explains the meaning of *"the woman is the glory of the man"* thus: "In her management as his housewife, the exalted position of man is manifest." Men would have made precisely the same sense out of the words, doubtless, if Paul had said instead, "The man is the glory of the woman." Dr. Cruden says, "Since God would have the male sex

106

to be a kind of representation of His glory, majesty and power, a man ought not, by hiding his face, . . . to conceal the glory of God shining in him." Dean Stanley says, "Man, therefore, ought to have nothing on his head which represents so divine a majesty—nothing on a countenance which reflects so divine a glory." Dr. Adam Clarke says: "Man is, among the creatures, the representative of the glory and perfections of God . . . So woman is, in the house and family, the representative of the power and authority of the man."

235. Dean Alford says, "Man is God's glory: He has put in him His majesty, and he represents God on earth; woman is man's glory: taken from the man, shining not with light direct from God, but with light derived from man." Jamieson, Faussett and Brown, in their commentary, say: "As the moon in relation to the sun, so woman shines not so much with light direct from God, as light derived from man. . . . Through him it [the veil] connects her with Christ." But quaint old Dr. John Lightfoot, who at many points gives the best interpretation of the passage extant, is the funniest of them all on two phrases in it. He says, here, "A woman praying not veiled, as if she were not ashamed of her face, disgraceth man her head, while she would seem so beautiful beyond him, when she is only the glory of man; but man is the glory of God." To be sure! When the "moon" succeeds in outshining the "sun," of which it is merely a reflection, it is time for the "sun" to cry, "Disgraceful!" To sum up, these men affect to be more wise than Moses, who *wist not that the skin of his face shone."*

236. As to the veil, some declare that it is to be worn as an "authorization" to pray and prophesy; others, that it is a "power," because worn by married women, who are raised in dignity because married. (How about a Christian wife of a libertine or drunkard?) But the attempt to substitute the idea of "subjection"—no power —for the word "power" is shameful. Prof. Lias, for instance, editor of the *Cambridge Bible for Schools,* for this Epistle, makes this remark: "The abstract is put for the concrete, the authority itself for the token of being under authority." If it be allowable to treat this verse so, then we may read elsewhere, "The Son of Man hath a *token of being under* authority," instead of reading that He *"hath power"* to forgive sin. *"Behold I give you power . . . over all the enemy,"* might then be read,

"Behold I give you *a token of being under the power of the enemy*,"—and other passages may be corrupted after the same manner. Edwardes, quoted by Weymouth and others with approval, substitutes "subjection" for "authority," declaring, in explanation that "Authority and subjection are opposite sides of the same fact." Certainly they are, and so are love and hate, black and white, honesty and dishonesty, the truth and the lie, and those who substitute "subjection" where the Word of God reads "authority" change the truth of God into a lie.

237. As to the phrase, *"because of the angels*," Bishop Ellicott's commentary says, "They are good angels, and should not be tempted" by the sight of a woman's face. Stanley adds to the thought by saying that women must defy the authority of even the angels before God's throne. But if women had done so badly, no Christ would have been born; there would have been no Gospel for men to preach. To such views, Dr. Agar Beet rightly replies, "If the angels of God are in danger of being led into sin by the sight of a woman's face, the angels of God are much weaker, in the matter of sensual desire, than are average Englishmen of the present day." In all this, we are to *suppose* that angels are all of the male sex; that they cannot see through a woman's veil; and that women have no other opportunities for "tempting angels" excepting when praying or prophesying in church. Others teach that the angels come to church to see if the women are veiled or not,—not the best motive for church-going. Still others, that "angels" mean "spies." But Dr. John Lightfoot taught that these "angels" were "messengers of espousals"—go-betweens seeking mates for young men; and St. Paul rules that girls have a right to unveil their faces, *to catch husbands!*

238. As to Paul's transition from the veil to hair, in general the expositors *assume* that the woman's hair indicates where the veil should go, and translate the Greek preposition *anti* (always implying substitution, or barter) as "for," when it should be rendered "instead of,"— *"hair is given her INSTEAD OF a covering."* Alford gives us the logic of this teaching:

"When we deal with the properties of the *artificial state,* of *clothing the body,* we must be *regulated by nature's suggestion*: that which she has indicated to be left uncovered, we must so leave; that which she has covered, when we clothe the body, we must likewise cover. This is the argument." The italics are Alford's. His reasoning is surprising indeed, when reduced to the syllogism,—as contradictory as most of the reasoning on this passage:

"That which Nature has left uncovered, we must so leave."
Nature has left the face of woman "uncovered."
Ergo: "We must leave" the face of woman "uncovered."
Again:
"That which nature has covered, when we clothe the body we must cover likewise,"
"Nature has covered" the face of man—with a beard.
Ergo: "When we clothe the body" man "must cover" the face "likewise."

239. Having convinced himself that Paul teaches in this passage the supremacy and splendour of the male sex, next the commentator grows ashamed of the weakness of the reasoning which leads to these conclusions, and apologizes, not for himself, but for St. Paul. The lameness of Paul's logic is due to "his early training in the great rabbinical schools." "He is not free," says Sir Wm. Ramsey (for example), "from the beliefs and even the superstitions of his age. . . . In the non-essentials he sometimes, or often, remains impeded and encumbered by the tone and ideas of his age. . . . The instructions which he sometimes gives regarding the conduct of women are peculiarly liable to be affected by current popular ideas . . . Where both angels and women are found in any passage, * Paul is peculiarly liable to be fettered by current ideas and superstituitons."†

The truth is, had some of these expositors been one-tenth as broad as St. Paul on the "woman question," and honest besides, we should never have been taught these pitiful, puerile and ego-centric perversions of Paul's meaning. If there had been any reasons for ordering women to veil in church, would not the Holy Ghost have seen to it that those reasons were properly voiced by the Apostle, whether Paul approved of the ruling personally or not? The Holy Ghost—the Spirit of truth—does not descend to sophistry, to induce women to do the will of God; and when we find sophistry in association with the Word of God, we may rest assured that it is always because of man's unlawful manipulation of the Word; it cannot belong to the original text.

---

* As though Paul had about a thousand passages relating to "angels and women" instead of one!
† More of these apologies for Paul's logic are given later,— pars. 346-351.

LESSON 32.

PAUL'S REAL TEACHING AS TO VEILING.

240. The real purpose of this passage, 1 Cor. 11:1-16, was to stop the practice of men veiling in worship, as Dr. John Lightfoot so ably contends. The Jewish man veiled as a sign of reverence before God, and of condemnation for sin. This sort of head covering was called a *tallith,* and is worn, to this day, "by all male worshipers at the morning prayer on week days, sabbaths and holy days: by the *hazzan* at every prayer before the ark: by the reader of the scroll of the law when on the *almemar;*"—so states the *Jewish Cyclopaedia.* The *hazzan* is the chief functionary of the synagogue, and the *almemar* is the reading-desk. The Romans also veiled in worship, and the Corinthian church was made up in large part of Roman converts. The testimony disagrees as to whether Greeks veiled in worship, or did not. The question therefore arose, were women to be *forbidden* veiling, as the Christian men, or not? Paul, in the passage, (1) forbids men to veil (since *"There is now no condemnation to them which are in Christ Jesus")* ; (2) permits women to veil; (3) but guards against this permission being construed as a command to veil, by showing that *ideally* the woman should unveil, before God, man, and angels; (4) shows that there is special propriety in women unveiling when addressing God in prayer; (5) declares that (contrary to the teaching of the Jews) there is nothing for a woman to be ashamed of in showing her hair, for it is a "glory" to her; (6) and disavows veiling as a church custom.

241. St. Paul's words are to be interpreted as follows:

3. But I wish you to understand that of every [Christian] man Christ is the Head; but of a wife the husband is a head [also] ; and God is Christ's Head.

4. Any [Christian] man praying or prophesying, having his head covered [as is required among the Jews, in sign of guilt and condemnation] dishonours his Head [Christ, who has atoned for all his sins].

5. But any wife praying or prophesying bareheaded dishonours her [other] head [her husband], for it would be one and the same thing as [having] her head shaved.

6. For [Jewish law provides that] if a woman is not covered, let her be shorn. Now if it would bring disgrace to a woman to be shorn or shaven, let her be covered.

First of all we wish to say, where the practice has ceased of veiling in sign of guilt and condemnation before God and His law, this whole teaching, in its literal sense, has no application; the veil has no significance, and can be worn or rejected in worship. But the spiritual teaching remains, that among those who believe that Christ has made for them a full and SUFFICIENT atonement, *any badge* that signifies guilt or penance for sin is out of place, for women as much as for men. This is the lesson for all Christians to learn. Women need to especially learn a lesson here; what have they to do with wearing a badge of servility to the male, because of Eve's sin? Has not Christ atoned for Eve's sin also? Does that remain as the *one* point where Christ's atonement failed?

(Verse 3) We add the word "Christian", to verse 3, because, as Chrysostom says: "He cannot be the Head of those who are not in the Body . . . so when he says 'of every man' one must understand it of believers." We add "also" because woman could not be a believer at all, and in the Body, unless Christ were likewise her Head. The word used here and throughout this passage, for man, is *aner,* meaning "the adult male, or husband." Dean Stanley rightly explains, *"Anthropos* ["man" without regard to gender] would have been the natural word to use with reference to Christ . . . but for the sake of contrast with 'woman' he has changed it to *aner."* But there is a further reason: according to the Oral Law of the Jews the *aner* alone was obliged to wear the *tallith.*

(Verse 4) "*Every man* (aner) . . . *having his head covered dishonoureth,*" not "his own head, by wearing the token of subjection," as expositors say, but dishonoureth Christ. The symbolic language of "headship" having just been introduced, in all fairness it requires its application to what follows. Besides, Paul taught actual "subjection" of man to man, and to religious leaders, Eph. 5:21, 1 Cor. 16:16, and hence could *not* teach that the mere symbol of "subjection" was not to be allowed the male. The meaning is, "every man . . .

111

having his head covered dishonours Christ his head,"
by wearing the *tallith*.

242. (Verse 5) If I should describe how I had burned
down a house, I should have small chance of escaping
punishment by a mere denial, later, that I had done so.
A sufficient proof that I had done the deed is "But you
have even told *how* you did it." So here; a description
by the person as to *how* a thing may be done nullifies
the force of a seeming denial by that same person of
that deed. Says Dr. A. J. Gordon: *"It is quite incred-
ible that the Apostle should have given himself the trouble to prune a custom which he desired to uproot, or
that he should spend his breath in condemning a forbidden method of doing a forbidden thing."* These words
prove conclusively to an unprejudiced mind that Paul
did not silence women praying and prophesying in the
churches, as is claimed in the ordinary interpretation
of 1 Cor. 14:34.

"Dishonoureth her head," i. e., her husband rather
than her own head, in analogy to the argument of verse
4. This is because she would lay herself open to the
charge (before Jewish law at least), of being an adulteress, and such a charge is always considered dishonour-
ing to a husband. In what sense it would amount to
having the head shaved, the next verse explains.

243. (Verse 6) *"For if the woman be not covered,
let her be shorn."* Paul refers to the Oral Law of the
Jews. Says Lightfoot: He *"does not here speak in his
own sense but cites something usual among the Jews."*
It admits of proof that such was the Oral Law. A
woman *"sinner"* is described in the Talmud as "she who
transgresseth the law of Moses and the Jewish law."
The gloss explains: " 'The Jewish law, that is, what
the daughters of Israel follow though it be not written"
(i. e. the Oral Law). The question was asked: "How
does she transgress the Jewish law? Answer: *"If she
appear abroad with her head uncoverd, if she spin in
the streets,"* etc., etc., through a long list. For the
offences here enumerated, one of which is uncovering
the head, it is prescribed that the wife should be divorced
"with the loss of her marriage portion." (*Kethuboth,
fol. 7, col. 1*). Furthermore, in that section of the Talmud called *"Sotah,"* which treats of unchaste women,
under the sub-head, *Of the duty of Repudiation of a
Wife* for adultery, we learn that this DUTY rested upon

a Jew whose wife was seen abroad with her hair *"not done up"*, i. e. not covered. Thus we learn that a Jew, even if favorably disposed towards his wife's profession of Christianity, and towards the practice of unveiling in worship, might be compelled by his relatives or the synagogue authorities, much to his regret, to divorce his wife, if she unveiled. The rest of the story, as to what would be done with the woman who unveiled, and thus furnished sufficient proof of "adultery" to compel her husband to repudiate her, we learn from Dr. Edersheim's *Sketches of Jewish Social Life, p. 155:* "It was the custom in case of a woman accused of adultery to have her *hair shorn or shaven,"* at the same time using this formula: "Because thou hast departed from the manner of the daughters of Israel, *who go with their head covered* . . therefore that hath befallen thee which thou hast chosen." An unveiled Jewish wife might, then, be tried for adultery; and when so tried, be "shorn or shaven." Paul here cites this obstruction to *commanding* women to unveil, but he *permits* it (verse 10).

"Now if it is a shame,"—The word translated "but" (*de*) readily admits of the translation "now" in this sense, see Jno. 6:10, 19:23, 1 Cor. 15:50 etc. That is, if it be a case in which disgrace and divorce would follow, she is permitted to cover the head,—*"Let her be covered."*

244. A little historical evidence at this point ought to go a long way. If the Apostle, as is so often assumed, was accustomed to forbid women unveiling, how did it come to pass that women "sat unveiled in the assemblies in a separate place, by the presbyters," and were "ordained by the laying on of hands," until the eleventh canon of the Church Council of Laodicea forbade it, in 363 A. D.? I give the account in the words of Dean Alford in his comments on 1 Tim. 5:9; the same admission is made by Conybeare and Howson in their *Life of St. Paul,* and stands undisputed in church history.

(To be Continued).

LESSON 33.

PAUL'S REAL TEACHING AS TO VEILING.
(Concluded).

245. The Apostle considers it his duty, however, to go further, and tear away any remaining prejudice among

Christian men, against women unveiling. Verses 7-9 are intended for this purpose, showing what "headship" in Christ means to the believer, and that woman's relation to man is not unlike man's relation to God (and woman's to God also, for that matter), so that the same argument that would lead to his unveiling before God applies to her unveiling before man.

Verses 7-9 mean,—

7. For a [Christian] man ought not to veil the head because he is the image and glory of God. But woman is [also] the glory of man.

8. For man is not originally from woman [as from a despised and inferior source], but woman is from man.

9. Nor was the man created for the woman [to help her], but the woman for the man [to help him,— see par. 34].

Poor, fallen, sinful man does not bear God's image and likeness simply because he is a *male!* God is not male or female, so that one *sex* bears His image more than the other. It is the glorified Jesus Christ who bears that image and manifests that glory (Heb. 1:3). It is only *in Him* that humanity takes that standing before God. He is our Representative, our Head. It is because Christ, the Head of the redeemed man, is in heaven, there *"to appear in the presence of God for us"* (Heb. 9:24), that man is permitted to cast aside all tokens of guilt and condemnation on earth. As for us, *"All have sinned, and come short of the glory of God."* *"But woman is the glory of man,"* for she reflects credit on him. This is what the Apostle meant when he said of the Thessalonians, *"Ye are our glory"* (1 Thess. 2:19, 20); "glory" means "an outshining,"—the very opposite state of a veiled person. Read its Scriptural import in Prov. 17:6; 20:29; Psa. 3:3; Isai. 13:19; 20:5; 60:19; Ezck, 20:; Luke 2:32; etc.

246. But why is Paul so interested in this matter as to veiling or unveiling in worship? In what way did it dishonour Christ? 2 Cor. 3:16-18, gives interesting light as to Paul's teaching and Jewish practice. The Jew was expected to wear the *tallith,* in worship, as a sign of guilt and condemnation before the law; but Paul tells us that *"When it* (the Jewish nation) *shall turn to the Lord, the veil shall be taken away."* It was not the veil itself, but *what the veil signified* to Jewish converts, that

made it objectionable. The atonement of Jesus Christ had removed guilt and condemnation, from the heart of those who trusted the sufficiency of the atonement. And growth in grace depended upon trust in the removal of these, and hence the unveiled face. *"We all with unveiled face, beholding as in a mirror, the glory of the Lord are changed into the same image, from glory to glory."* This truth applies to women as well as to men.

Verses 10-16

247. For this [additional] cause ought the woman to have authority over head [to unveil it] because of her angels [who always behold God's face].

11. Nevertheless, in the Lord, [i. e. among believers,] the woman is not [to be legislated for] apart from the man, nor the man from the woman.

12. For just as woman came out of man, so is man [born into the world] through woman and all Christians born of God. Judge of this matter among yourselves.

13. It is proper for a woman [at least] to pray unto God unveiled.

14. Nor is there anything in the nature of hair itself that teaches you that if a man wear it long it is a dishonour to him, while if a woman have long hair it is a glory to her, for her hair has been given her instead of a veil.

16. But if anyone thinks to be contentious [in defence of such a custom as either men or women *veiling for worship*], let him know that *"we have no such custom, neither the Churches of God."*

248. We come now to the 10th verse, of which Dean Stanley says: "In the difficulty of its several parts, it stands alone in the New Testament, unless we except, perhaps, Rev. 13:18, or Gal. 3:20." But the only difficulty encountered is to *make* Paul say the *precise opposite* to what Paul clearly says here. That has indeed proved a difficult task. The real sense can be found through humility of spirit, where egotism fails. When the disciples asked the Lord which of them would be greatest in the kingdom of heaven, Jesus set a child in their midst, and informed them that until they humbled themselves as such they could not even enter that kingdom. From the child He transferred the lesson to *"one*

of these little ones that believe on Me," i. e. to the believer humblest in rank among them, saying, *"Take heed that ye despise not one of these little ones; for I say unto you, that in heaven their angels do always behold the face of My Father who is in heaven,"* Matt. 18:10. The words in verse 10 bear the translation, *"because of her angels,"* the definite article in Greek often having the force of a possessive pronoun, and thus the verse should have been rendered. Paul taught that "angels" were inferior in rank to redeemed man, 1 Cor. 6:3. They are ministering spirits to us ,Heb. 1:14. Yet the most despised women's angels stand before God, with no intervening veil, and behold His face. Shall not woman be permitted to do as much as her "ministering spirits" are allowed to do? Man unveils because Christ, his Head, is unveiled before God. Woman "ought to have the right" to unveil because not only is Christ, her spiritual Head, unveiled before God, but man, her matrimonial head, also; and, if this were not enough, then her ministering spirits *"do always behold the face"* of God. This is the Apostle's argument. Shall man attempt to require that woman veil out of respect for his authority (?)¹ over her? Not when God does not require man to veil out of respect for God's authority over man.

249. To meet the prejudices of man against woman, the Apostle has been obliged to discuss the sexes apart from each other, as though set in contrast, and he must now renounce this conception as unchristian. Verses 11 and 12 declare there is no such disunion *"in the Lord,"* but, as he says in Gal. 3:28, *"There can be neither Jew nor Greek, there can be neither bond nor free, there can be no male and female: for ye are all one in Christ Jesus"* (*R. V.*).

(13) Then the apostle declares: *"It is proper that a woman pray unto God uncovered."* This is Paul's simple statement of fact, and not a question. Greek does not alter the order of the words of a sentence to distinguish a question from a simple statement, as we do in English. We only need to alter the punctuation (of uninspired and recent invention), to change from one to the other, since there is no interrogative word in the sentence.

(14) *"Nor* doth even the nature itself* [of hair] *teach you," etc.* Our idiomatic English would say, to express the same idea, "There is nothing in the nature of hair itself to teach you,"—a simple statement that appeals to everybody's common sense, while, as a question, this is an absurdity. The entire Chinese nation of men disproves the statement of theologians that Nature gives women long hair and men short hair. No artist would dare paint a portrait of Jesus Christ with short hair. Is His hair "a shame" to Him?

250. But why does Paul discuss hair here? Because he has just said it was a fitting thing for a woman to uncover the head in prayer, and Jewish women would find it most difficult to overcome a false sense of shame in doing so, or in seeing other women do so, since uncovering the hair in public amounted to proof of adultery in Jewish estimation (par. 243).

(16) Then comes Paul's concluding statement, that if anyone is going to contend for either sex veiling for worship, or women for modesty, *"We have no such custom"—veiling,*—though we may have to make allowance for it, out of regard for the welfare of women, to save them from "disgrace." John Stuart Mill has wisely remarked: "To pretend that Christianity was intended to stereotype existing forms of government and society, and protect them against change, is to reduce it to the level of Islamism or of Brahmism."

LESSON 34.

HOW DID "POWER" BECOME A "VEIL?"

251. We can trace the teaching that "power" means a "veil" no farther back in history than to Valentinus. He flourished first at Alexandria, and founded the Valentinian sect of gnostics. He went to Rome in 140 and died at Cyprus in 160. At Rome he was excommunicated from the church. Clement of Alexandria (b. 150) and Origen (b. 186), both of Alexandria, passed on the teaching. The date of birth of Valentinus is unknown, but presumably it was within 35 years of the death of

---

* A British Biblical scholar has pronounced my rendering of the Greek word *oude* by "nor even" in this affirmative sense, "a somewhat peculiar presentation of the case", but "not impossible." Let Greek scholar turn to 1 Cor. 5:1; 1 Cor. 14:21; 2 Cor. 3:10 (A. V.); Gal. 2:3; 6:13; Heb. 8:4; 9:18, and judge if the peculiarity is not Paul's, rather than mine.

St. Paul. Clement tells us that Valentinus was a disciple of one Theudas (of whom we know no more), who was acquainted with St. Paul. This is dubious.

252. Irenaeus (b. 126) wrote a book which is still extant against heresies, and in it he describes the gnostic teachings of the Valentinians. They taught that there was a primal goddess, *Bythus,* (depth, profundity), who bore thirty *aeons,* (ages ever-beings). These were arranged in groups of eight, ten and twelve, and were in pairs,—male and female. Together they constituted the *Pleroma* (fullness). All this nonsense they pretended to find hidden in the meaning of the first three Gospels, and in Paul's Epistles. They claimed that Paul referred to their *Pleroma* where he says *"throughout all ages."* Thirty *aeons* were shown by the Lord beginning to preach at thirty years of age; twelve *aeons,* by the Lord being twelve years of age when He disputed with the doctors in the temple, and by the twelve apostles. The other two groups, ten and eight, were shown by the eighteen months that Jesus spent on earth after His resurrection! Thus they parodied and corrupted Scripture, as is well known.

253. The initiation ceremony of the gnostics was taught to be a re-union of mortals with celestial consorts of the opposite sex. Naturally, the veil would be desirable to somewhat screen the rites,—for the gnostics fell into gross sensuality. Both men and women veiled. Irenaeus tells us that this is what Valentinus and his associates taught as their warrant for these rites: A certain goddess escaped the *Pleroma,* and apart from her male consort conceived and brought forth a formless being called *Acamoth* (Hebrew for "wisdom;" sometimes she is called *Sophia,* Greek for "wisdom"). *Acamoth* goes through a series of experiences, always sinking lower and lower into degradation. Then her celestial consort, called *Soter* ("Savior;" also blasphemously called Jesus, Paraclete and Christ), goes to her rescue with a band of seventy angels. Irenaeus thus continues the account: [We will insert *"Soter"* always, as the name of her consort.]

254. "As he approaches, *Acamoth,* filled with reverence, at first veiled herself through modesty, but by and by, when she had looked upon him with all his endowments, and had acquired strength from his appearance, she ran

to meet him. . . . That *Soter* appeared to her when she lay outside the *Pleroma* as a kind of abortion, they affirm Paul to have declared in his Epistle to the Corinthians, *"And last of all He appeared to me also, as one born out of due time."* Again, the coming of *Soter* with his attendants to *Acamoth*, is declared by him in like manner in the same Epistle, when he says, *"a woman ought to have a veil on her head, because of the angels."* Now that *Acamoth*, when *Soter* came to her, drew a veil over herself through modesty, Moses rendered manifest when he put a veil upon his face."

In another place Irenaeus tells us that sometimes the teaching was, "Beholding the angels along with *Soter*, she did . . . conceive their images." Theodotus the gnostic says, "Seeing the *masculine* angels with *Soter*, she put on a veil." The whole mass of fables is saturated with sensuality, which we do not care to repeat, *Acamoth* was typified in the twelve-year old daughter of Jairus, whom Christ raised from the dead, etc.

Another Valentinian, is mentioned by Clement of Alexandria as teaching "The woman ought to *wear* a power."

At this place in history, then,—among Gnostics — we find the very first interpretation of "power" as "a veil."

255. To suit their teachings along other lines that we have not space to go into, the Valentinians corrupted "not one thing" (*oude hen*) into "nothing" (*ouden*) in John 1:3, and put a period after "nothing", beginning John 1:4, "That which was made in him was life," They then altered the first "was" into "is"; and the word "Son" to "God," in John 1:18. They changed John 12:27 "What shall I say?" into "What I shall say, *I know not."* This shows how daring they were. Yet they had such influence in the primitive Church that the very men who denounced their corruptions of Scripture, such as Irenaeus, Clement, Hippolytus, etc., often inadvertently fell into the use of some of them, in quoting these verses.*

256. After this, it seems superfluous to inquire whether the Valentinians would hesitate to corrupt this verse of St. Paul's, if there was a sufficient motive for it. And there was a motive,—viz., to find Scriptural war-

---

* These facts we gather from the highly valuable work of Dean Burgon, "The Revision Revised," and of Burgon & Miller, "Causes of Corruption in the Traditional Text of the N. T."

rant for the use of the needed veil to obscure the sexual initial rites of their sect. We cannot clearly determine from Irenaeus' language whether or not he intended to denounce as a corruption the word "veil." The gnostics may have influenced him in the same way that, as we have said, he fell into the use of their corruptions elsewhere, even when he denounced them. "Power" could not be made over into "veil" in Greek. The first word is *exousia* and the second *kalumma*. But the transition from the one to the other could easily be accomplished in the Coptic language.

257. We remind you (see par. 254), that Clement, Origen and Valentinus were of the same place—Alexandria, Egypt—which was the birthplace likewise of the gnosticism of which Valentinus was, in his days, the chief exponent. The native tongue of these three men was Coptic, and "power" bore a close resemblance to "veil" in that language. In an imperfect or dim manuscript of a Coptic translation of Paul's Epistle, one word could readily be mistaken for, or altered into the other Here are the two words: ογερϣιϣι , ογερϣογν. The first, *ouershishi*, means "power, authority," the second, *ouershoun*, means "veil."

258. And again we remind you that it was Clement of Alexandria and Origen of the same place who confirmed by quotations the idea that "power" meant a veil,—first taught by Valentinus when as yet he was considered worthy of membership in the primitive Church.

259. While Valentinus and his followers did not have the precise Coptic version of the Scriptures now in existence, it is almost certain they had earlier Coptic versions of portions of the N. T., for it is easily demonstrable that their false teachings and corruptions have left their traces on the present Coptic version. No other ancient version has attempted to substitute "veil" for "power" but the Coptic, in which it could be easily accomplished. The Coptic N. T. recently issued by the Clarendon Press lies before me as I write. A footnote at this verse states that fifteen Coptic manuscripts read "power," and "four or five" veil. Here we must leave the matter. Some may think this insufficient proof that the idea of a veil crept into the interpretation through a readily accomplished Coptic corruption. But until we obtain light to the contrary, we hold this belief.

(To be continued.)

LESSON 35.

HOW DID "POWER" BECOME A "VEIL?"

(Concluded)

260. Now it is easy to assume that these ancient variations, due to gnostic corruptions as a matter of fact, lend authority to the view that "power" in this one and only place in the whole world means a veil. A similar assumption—the authority of *mere* antiquity—has caused the Revisers to give the gnostic perversions of John 1:3, 4, in the margin of the R. V. (and Dean Burgon vigorously protests against such superficial work in textual criticism), but since any such assumpton throws this entire passage in Corinthians into the category of rabbinical casuistry and makes it necessary to apologize for Paul, we refuse the teaching. That "power" means a veil, here, but *has never meant that before or since in all human history,* and a veil means subordination to the male sex, is pleasing to ego-centric males, but absurd to the mind of the ordinary man. The commonly accepted interpretation of this Corinthian passage bears on its face the evidence that at the beginning men started out to prove a foregone conclusion by it.

261. Next after Clement and Origen of Alexandria, Tertullian of Carthage promulgated the teaching, and his influence on Christian theology was so powerful that we need not trace the teaching farther on towards our own time. In fact, his exposition of St. Paul's meaning is, in a general way, the one set forth to the present day by the commentaries.

262. Through doctrinal drill, we of the West have become accustomed to regard the veil, *as recommended by Paul,* as a sign of subjection to one's husband, but in daily life no one so regards it, and it is easy to show that the Scriptures do not so teach. The only instance in the O. T. that could be so construed is that of Rebekah (Gen. 24:65) when she meets Isaac; but that is interpreted in accordance with the misinterpretation of Paul (see par. 561).

263. Tamar did not veil in any such sense (Gen. 38:14). Hannah prayed unveiled at the Tabernacle (1 Sam. 1:13); the virtue of Sarah and of Rebekah would not have been threatened by Pharaoh and Abimelech had they habitually veiled; and St. Paul and St. Peter would

not have rebuked women who dressed their hair too elaborately, had they come to church veiled (1 Tim. 2:9, 1 Pet. 3:3). As Smith's *Dictionary of the Bible* says, "With regard to the use of the veil, it is important to observe that it was by no means so general in ancient as in modern times. Much of the scrupulousness in respect to the use of the veil dates from the promulgation of the Koran, [in the 7th century A. D.], which forbade women appearing unveiled except in the presence of their nearest relatives."

264. Tertullian was a courageous defender of the Christian faith, a man of learning and of powerful intellect. He was not altogether bad, though he said some very wrong things about women. Had he been altogether bad, he could not have influenced the ecclesiastical mind of later generations to the remarkable degree that he did. But he was not converted from paganism until thirty years of age, and before that time he had led a profligate life on the streets of Carthage, his native city. He was a jurist by profession, and never got past the lawyer's habit of trying to carry his point in an argument by sophistry, if it could not be done by honest logic. Much that he said, particularly about women, we doubt if he himself really believed, but he wished to carry his point.

265. As to Tertullian's method of treating Scripture, Maurice, in his *Ecclesiastical History* says, "Every page almost of Tertullian would furnish terrible instances of the irreverent torturing of Scripture to his own purposes —of a resolute determination that it shall never contradict or weaken any purpose of his—all the while that he professes to take it as his judge and guide." Other writers testify to the same effect.

266. Tertullian visited Corinth, and was delighted to find, as he represents it, that in the Christian church not only matrons but young girls were veiled. Probably he exaggerated the case, but if so, it seems far more likely that this was necessitated by the great wickedness of Corinth (and especially, in view of Paul's *concessions* as regarded veiling) rather than, as Tertullian represents, because of their exaggerated obedience to Paul's wishes, in extending the veiling even to young girls. If, as Dobschütz and the majority of expositors represent (see pars. 226-228), St. Paul could scarcely bring the Corin-

thian women to obedience and to the veil in his own day, what reason have we for believing that they would be universally yielded to his wishes in this matter, a full century and more after Paul was in his grave?

267. Tertullian returned to Carthage determined to see every Christian matron and maiden of N. Africa veiled. His ideas of purity were entirely mechanical.—so much of the sight of woman, so much uncleanness, both for the man and the woman,—particularly for the woman or girl who had shown her face. He gave an address about the Veiling of Virgins which must have at once brushed off the last traces of "the bloom of innocence" from the cheek of virgins who heard or read it.

268. Tertullian, living in Roman Carthage, must have been familiar with the Valentinian gnostic teachings about veiling, backed by the perversion of Paul's words. He was also familiar with the Apocryphal teaching that angels sinned with women. He seized upon the two, and launched that very exposition of Paul's passage which is set forth by most expositors (with individual modifications) to the present day. He alone, perhaps, had weight and influence within the church sufficient to secure its perpetuation (see pars., 158, 158n.).

269 Here are a few quotations from his various writings:
"I pray you, be you mother, or sister, or virgin, or daughter . . . veil your head! If a mother for your son's sake; if a sister, for your brother's sake; if a daughter, for your father's sake. All ages are imperilled in your person . . . Wear a rampart for your sex, which must neither allow your eyes egress, or ingress to other people . . . If any are so deaf as not to be able to hear through a covering, I pity them." . . . "Arabia's female heathen shall be your judges, who cover not only the head, but the face also, so entirely that they are content to leave one eye free, to enjoy rather half the light than to prostitute the entire face.". . . . ' 'Because of the angels'—What angels? If he means the fallen angels of the Creator, there is great propriety in his meaning. It is right that the face which was a snare to them should wear some mark of humble guise and obscured beauty . . . But even though they were females already contaminated, whom these angels had desired, so much more 'because of the angels' would it have been the duty of

virgins to be veiled, as it would have been more possible for virgins to have been the cause of angels sinning: . . . So perilous a face, then, ought to be shaded, which has cast stumbling-blocks so far as heaven."

270. This misinterpretation of St. Paul would not be recognised as even remotely Christian, if placed in pagan environments. Imagine yourself in a far country, unacquainted as yet with its religious customs. You go with your guide to a place of heathen worship, from which women are not (as is usual) excluded. You see the women all veiled, at least they draw their veils over the face and mumble behind them when they speak or pray. You ask, "Why do not these women lift their veils when speaking; then we could hear what they say?" Your guide replies, "Our great prophet says they must veil when praying or speaking in public." You ask, "But does he bid them veil at other times?" "No; only at worship, when if they will not veil, he orders them to be punished by having their heads shaved." "Why is this?" you ask, to receive the astonishing reply, "In some way, I cannot explain just how, they seem to tempt the good angels in heaven to fall into sin with them, and therefore must veil when in public worship,—some claim it is to show that women must not obey angels lest the angels command them to sin; others that angels must not see their faces lest they be seduced to sin." You take out your notebook, probably, and prepare the skeleton of a letter to your church paper at home: "These heathen . . . their inane and insane jealousy of their wives . . . leading them to view good angels with suspicion of the basest sort . . . stupid superstition as to the sin of angels and the danger of it . . . unclean imaginations . . . following their wives with jealous fears particularly in the matter of religious worship, when one would think a woman safe, if ever . . . strange to say they fear holy angels, as to the virtue of their wives, more than demons or men," etc.

The church follows no such instruction and practice as this, and is it not time to repudiate such teaching?

LESSON 36.

HEADSHIP IN THE OLD TESTAMENT.

271. In our last lesson, St. Paul says, "Of a wife the husband is a head," to translate the words exactly.

What does he mean? Precisely what we should mean if we said, "The husband is ahead of his wife." He does not say in what respect he is ahead; he does not say that he always will be ahead; and St. Paul no more creates or ordains that headship of the husband, than he ordains or creates the headship of God over Christ, by saying, *"The head of Christ is God"* (1 Cor. 11:3). And though he says this latter of Christ, it cannot therefore be lawfully inferred that Christ remains less than God since His ascension, or was inferior to God before His birth.

272. Now we must proceed slowly to study O. T. "headship." Look at the O. T. reference in the margin (the only O. T. reference cited), where these words occur regarding the headship of the husband,—Gen. 3:16. The only other place where the husband is said to be the head of the wife, Eph. 5:23, refers in the margin also to Gen. 3:16 only. No other word can be found throughout the O. T. which seems to support the interpretation that men are to govern their wives. But we have already shown (par. 198) that at Corinth the church used the Septuagint Greek version and would read Gen. 3:16, *"Thou art turning away to thy husband, and he* will *rule over thee,"*—the same is true of those addressed in the Epistle to the Ephesians, for Paul's quotations are also from the Septuagint in this letter.

273. Now had we always read, as we should have read, *"He will rule over thee,"* instead of *"He shall rule over thee"* (pars. 124, 127; all the ancient versions testify that the verb is a simple future), ignorant, careless, or dishonest interpreters would not have thought to show that this "rule" was God-ordained. We remember seeing in a religious periodical, when a discussion of enlarging woman's activities in the Church was on, an editorial in opposition, which ended by quoting Gen. 3:16,—" *'He shall rule over thee,'* Remember, women,— shall, *shall, SHALL!"**

274. Prof. J. H. Moulton, in his *Grammar of N. T. Greek,* says: "The use of *shall* where prophecy is deal-

* "I think that the author is very right in frequently calling attention to the fact that the future tense in Hebrew is erroneously rendered in English by 'shall' instead of 'will.' The future tense, or aorist, never implies in the Semitic languages a sense of obligation. This remark highly befits the sentence 'He shall rule over thee' to which in par. 273 the writer is taking particular exception."—Dr. A. Mingana.

ing with future time is often particularly unfortunate. I have heard of an intelligent child who struggled for years under perplexity because of the words, *'Thou shalt deny me thrice.'* It could not therefore be Peter's fault, if Jesus had commanded him! The child's determinism is probably shared more widely than we think; and a modernized version of many passages like Mark 14:30— e. g., 'you will be renouncing Me three times'—would relieve not a few half-conscious difficulties." How different women would have felt if, from the beginning, they had read, *"he will rule over thee!"*

275. We question, then, the correctness of interpreting the words, "But of a wife the husband is a head," as meaning, "Of the wife the husband is the ruler." Gen. 3:16 proves nothing of the sort; it only prophesies what has been only too true,—that ever since Adam fell, his male progeny has sought to subjugate woman: and it is further demonstrable that to the extent that grace works in the heart of the male he loses the love of the pre-eminence and the desire to rule his wife. In general, Christian husbands do not seek to govern their wives, any more than Christian wives seek to govern their husbands. Then why should fossilized theologians be allowed to drag their antiquated notions across the pages of every Biblical commentary which is published for the use of Christians?

276. We inquire the meaning of the Hebrew word "head" (*rosh*). It often means "first in order." 1 Chron. 12:9 renders the word *"rosh"* as "first"; and in this sense, at least, man is the head of woman as having been elaborated as a sex first. "Head" is rendered "first" 6 times in the O. T. It is rendered "beginning" 16 times; "chief" 97 times; "company" and "band" 16 times; "captain" 10 times; and "ruler" twice only—in Isaiah 29:10 and Deut. 1:13. As to the first case, no particular reason appears for rendering the word, "rulers," so the Revisers change to "heads." This case, then, we put on one side. The other occurrence of the word is perhaps properly translated "rulers," although the Revisers change to "heads" here also. We will come to a consideration of this latter instance by way of a historical review:

277. When God separated Abraham and Sarah, his half-sister and wife, from their idolatrous relatives

(Josh. 24:2, 3), and sent them forth with the express object of founding a theocracy through them and their descendants, He virtually ordained Sarah, after matriar- chal custom, the ruling head of the tribe.* God changed the name of Abram to Abraham because he was to be a father of multitudes (Gen. 17:5). He said the same of Sarah also, (*"She shall be a mother of nations"*); but He said, additionally, *"Rulers of people shall be of her;"* and because of this fact her name should be, no longer Sarai, but the locally understood title of a female prince,—Sarah (Gen. 17:15, 16). Moreover, in the case of a family dispute, God expressly revealed to Abraham that he was to obey Sarah, in the strong language, *"In all that Sarah saith unto thee, hearken unto her voice"* (Gen. 21:12, R. V.). Abraham was given no name indicating that he was a prince, therefore Sarah's title was not a reflection from Abraham's glory. Of Abraham God said: *"I know that he will command his children and his house after him,"* but this is the rule of a father, not of a husband over his wife.

278. Furthermore, Prof. Robertson Smith claims that Sarah's name, according to matriarchal custom was handed down to her children as their family name in the word "Israel." The stem of the word is the same as the *sar* of Sarah's name. Jacob's victory when he wrestled with the angel, fulfilled in part the prediction that rulers should come out of Sarah. The Septuagint Greek and the Latin Vulgate read the angel's words as, *"Thou hast had power with God, and thou shalt prevail with men"* (see Gen. 32:28 marg. of R. V.), and the original Hebrew words would bear this rendering. Jacob's name was changed to one which means, "prince of God," and what was Sarah but a "prince" of God's own appointment? (Pars. 58-60).

279. But later the Israelites became slaves in Egypt, and all, both men and women, subordinates. But woman sinks lower than man under enslavement, the reasons being two, at least: (1) The handicap of children, making her ever easily her *husband's* subordinate, if he should take advantage of it for the purpose, acts even

---

* There is strong textual authority, which some scholars claim amounts to positive proof, for reading, at Gen. 20:13, instead of "God caused me [Abraham] to wander," the more striking sentence, **"God caused her [Sarah] to wander,"**—see par. 56, and comments on this verse in **"The Samaritan Pentateuch and Modern Criticism,"** by the Rev. J. Iverach Munro, M. A.

more terribly as a means of levelling down her status in slavery. (2) Her moral character suffers violence by the sensuality of masters. We see, then, how God started His theocracy with Sarah in high honour, as the head of the tribe, but when the Israelites emerged from four hundred years of slavery, the women would hold a different relation to their men,—they would be, for the most part, inferior to them. And each added captivity would hamper the progress of the women more than of the men; and Israel passed through many captivities.

280. When Moses led the Israelites out of Egypt, with the aid of Aaron and Miriam (Micah 6:4), he appointed men who were head and shoulders above their fellowmen, in wisdom and ability to share his rule over them. This his father-in-law had advised him to do (Ex. 18:21-26). The word used of "men" in this connection might have included women, but it is not at all likely that any beside Miriam would have been equal to the responsibility; and we believe that she already held a higher position than these appointed by Moses.

281. Now we come to the verse we wish to explain: Moses, reciting this incident, says: *"I took the chief* [Heb. "heads"] *of your tribes, wise men, and known, and made them heads* [same word, again] *over you, captains* [that word *sar*] *over thousands,"* Deut. 1:15. They were ahead already, *in ability,* and therefore Moses made them "heads," captains *in government.* So referring to this same incident, Moses says, Deut. 1:13, *"I will make them heads,"* and the word is rendered in the A. V., *rulers.* This is that single instance in the O. T. where the word "head" necessarily implies ruler, and is therefore so translated. And why were men, at this time made "rulers," over women? For the simple reason that, owing to the ruin of woman's character by slavery, men were ahead of women.

LESSON 37.

HEADSHIP IN THE NEW TESTAMENT.

282. The "head" in the symbolic language of the Revelation (where alone it is used in pure symbolism in the N. T., aside from the headship of Christ and of the husband), does *not* signify rule. The red dragon has *diadems* on his seven heads to signify rule (Rev. 12:3);

the Beast has *diadems* on his horns (not on his heads) to signify rule (Rev. 13:1); the *diadem,* not the head, is a symbol of rule in these instances. The heads in each case signify divisions; the diadems, rule. The teaching is that all divisions of rule unite in the dragon, and in the Beast, in turn; they obtain universal sovereignty. In Rev. 17:9, 10, we read: *"The seven heads are seven mountains, on which the woman sitteth: and they are seven kings"* (R. V.). This refers to the Beast and the Scarlet Woman on the Beast. Here the symbolism is support. Seven mountains support the foundation of this great city, and seven kings support her rule (Rev. 17:18). The Woman rules these "heads;" they do not rule her.

283. "Head" (*kephale*), in the N. T. is used in the same way as "head" (*rosh*) in the O. T. for "chief," in speaking of Christ as the *"head of the corner"* in six different passages; but these are quotations of, or references to, Psalm 118:22, *"The stone which the builders refused is become the head stone of the corner."* The head or corner stone gave support to the entire building, and was usually of immense size for this purpose; it also bound the sides of a building together. So Christ is the support of His church, and binds its members together into one (Eph. 4:15, 16; Col. 2:19).

284. We have shown (pars. 248-250) that St. Paul is not teaching the subordination of wife to husband, in 1 Cor. 11:3-16, unless it be implied in the one phrase, "of a wife the husband is a head;" and we waived the discussion of this symbolism until the present time. As we have already said, the only other place where it is stated that the husband is head of the wife, is Eph. 5:23, and there we are told in what sense he is head,—*"as Christ also is Head of the church"* (R. V.). Christ is the cornerstone of the church,—its support, Builder. For Christ is no mere stone; He lives, and Christians are represented by St. Paul as growing *"up into Him in all things, which is the Head, even Christ"* (Eph. 4:15). And Colossians 2:19 describes Christ as *"the Head, from which all the Body by joints and bands having nourishment ministered, and knit together, increaseth with the increase of God."* Neither of these passages refers to Christ's government. They represent Him as the support, nourisher and builder of the Body, its Saviour.

285. But Eph. 1:22 does speak of Christ's Headship as a reign. God *"hath put in subjection all things under His feet"* (*R. V.*); and the preceding verse informs us that this means that all *"principalities and powers"* are put under Him. But where is His church? The opening verses of the next chapter tell us. We have been quickened, and raised up with Christ. The Church is not, therefore, under His feet, in this headship of *governments;* it is designed that the Church share His rule, —Rev. 1:6; 3-21; 20:4, etc. We are taught that God gave Him *"to be Head over all things to the Church."* He is God's gift *"to the Church"* that we might share His headship over all things; as Dean Alford says here: "He possesses nothing for Himself . . . but all things for His Church, which is in innermost reality *Himself,"* —speaking, of course, of the mystical Body.

286. Christ began to found that Church when He said, *"Tarry ye in the city of Jerusalem until ye be endued with power from on high,"* then, *"Go ye into all the world,"* . . . *preach* . . . *teach* . . . *baptize."* (See Luke, Mark and Matthew). Men and women listened to the command; women tarried and got the power as well as men (Acts 2:3, 4); but men said: "No! Paul teaches that woman is merely a symbol of the Church; man a symbol of Christ. Therefore woman must not preach; must not teach; nor have power, or she will destroy the symbol." Symbol of a strange church this! Woman with no message for the world; no converts to baptize; veiled like Judaism; stripped of power.

287. I have a friend, who belongs to a sect which teaches these things. A devout niece who belonged to the same sect confided in this lady that the Spirit often moved upon her with such power, in meetings, that she did not know how to refrain from speaking out; it was like a "fire in her bones." Her aunt could but advise her, *"We ought to obey God rather than men."* Following her aunt's advice, the next time the Spirit constrained her she did speak out, Sitting far at the back, her husband by her side, the "brethren" sitting with downcast eyes, thought that her husband had spoken so thrillingly. They allowed themselves to be moved mightily by the message; and had an unusually "melting time," that morning. Then, after meeting, they learned that a *woman* had done this! In consequence, this "symbol of a church," who happened to be not quite like a church *"twice dead and plucked up by the roots"*, was driven out of the sect.

288. No church can long survive the silencing of its women. The church which silences women will be found to silence the Holy Spirit. A sect, or sex, or race which attempts a monopoly of the Spirit's voice and power, will find that the Holy Spirit will flee far from it. Woman is destined to have a very large share in the preaching of God's messages, and in bringing souls to Christ, for did not God promise, long ages ago, as regards woman, that her seed should bruise the Serpent's head?

289. No teaching of the New Testament has ever been more cunningly perverted than this concerning the "headship" of the husband. Does Christ jealously keep the Church from rising into His power: or does He say, *"Behold, I give you power?"* Does He say, "This is *My* throne, keep away!" to the Church; or does He say, *"To him that overcometh will I grant to sit with Me on My throne?"* Christ's delight and His constant exhortation is for us to share His throne-life with Him. If we fall short, it certainly is not because He has ever shut the door to our attainment of it. He is not jealous of His own exaltation; He only secured it (for He had it before He came to earth), in such a manner that He might bring it within our grasp also.

290. But are we not to *obey* Christ? Yes, most certainly; obey Him *because He is God,* because he is *King of kings;* and these a husband *is not,* and he should not usurp Christ's prerogatives. Christ said: *"Be not ye called Rabbi: for ONE is your Master, even Christ; and all ye are brethren."* . . . *"Neither be ye called masters; for ONE is your Master, even Christ."* Woman's *spiritual* Head is *also* her King; and so is man's spiritual Head. But woman's *matrimonial* head is not her king,— he is only a fellow-disciple and fellow-servant of the King; and the King has laid down His rules as to the conduct of fellow-disciples towards one another: *"Ye know that the princes* [rulers] *of the Gentiles exercise dominion over them, and they that are great exercise authority upon them. But it shall* not *be so among you: but whosoever will be great among you, let him be your minister: and whosoever will be chief among you, let him be your servant"* (see Matt. 20:25; Luke 22:25).

291. When the Word says, *"the husband is the head of the wife,"* by the pen of St. Paul, it merely states a fact; those were the conditions under which women lived *at that time.* The husband was, in those days, the head of the wife simply because he held the superior place. In days when a man could divorce his wife *"for every cause"* (Matt. 19:3; and even Christ's own disciples demurred when Christ declared this was not right), there could be no doubt that women were compelled to be ignorant, inferior and very cheap. The rabbis taught that it was lawful for a man to divorce his wife if she even burned his food. Hence the Apostle says. "Be a head, as Christ is a Head of the Church,—to help your wife upward to your own level,"—for it is only as man imitates Christ in his conduct that he can remain in the Body of which Christ is Head. Therefore the woman should "imitate" (1 Cor. 11:1, R. V.) St. Paul, and the others in worship. And the man has certain duties to perform toward his wife which are analogous to what Christ purposes to do for His Church, for its elevation, until it shall *"reign in life with Christ Jesus."* This is the headship of the husband that Paul speaks of. He would never encourage the husband to imitate Adam and Antichrist in trying to be *"as God,"* to woman, and to interfere with Christ's authority over His own servant,—woman.

LESSON 38.

WHAT DOES "SUBJECTION" MEAN?

292. This and our next chapter should be studied with both an Authorised and Revised Version at hand. Two words are constantly confused in reference to woman's duties, "subjection" and "obedience." But these words do not in the original Greek cover the same scope of meaning, although sometimes subjection may go all the lengths of blind obedience. The verb "to be in subjection" is from *hupo,* meaning "next after" or "under," and *tasso,* "I arrange," and means "to arrange after" or to "arrange under,"—as soldiers are arranged, file after file, or under a captain. The noun "subjection" is not found (in Classical Greek), outside the N. T. and we are left to infer that it was coined to describe a relation peculiar to believers. Had the word merely meant "obedience," such an invention would have been needless.

The verb itself is comparatively rare outside the Bible. The A. V. often translates it as "obey" and "submit," but the R. V. carefully translates these words as "subjection" and "be in subjection" wherever they occur, distinguishing them in sense from "obedience." See the difference between the A. V. and R. V. at 1 Cor. 14:34, Tit. 2:5, etc.

293. The true sense of the word describes the Christian grace of yielding one's preferences to another, where principle is not involved, rather than asserting one's rights. Schleusner's Greek-Latin Lexicon to the Septuagint declares that this verb does not always "convey the thought of servile subjection." Jesus, as a boy, was *"subject to His parents,"* yet we know that He did not even consult them when He was *"about His Father's business,"* Luke 2:49, 51.

294. Two men cannot be long in partnership in business unless willing to be "in subjection" to each other. They must each yield preferences; they must *"in honour prefer one another;"* they must harmonize their views, one to the other, or else they will soon be obliged to separate. They cannot better the situation if a question arises and one assumes the right to command the other. To obey orders like this is not "subjection" but servility, and man refuses to be servile, for that would be degrading to character. This indicates the difference in sense between the two words, as applied to the relation of believers. In 1 Cor. 15:28 we are told of a time when Christ will become *"subject"* to His Father. But we certainly know that Christ will never be less than equal with the Father in the Godhead. There was a time when, as Son of man, for our sakes, *"He took on Him the form of a servant,"* but since then, *"God hath highly exalted Him,"* and He will never again become reduced in rank, nor will He ever pass under the Father's coercion. This word speaks of loving harmony, not of impassable ranks, superior and inferior.

295. That "to be in subjection" does not mean "to obey" necessarily, is shown because the Apostles, who so plainly taught "subjection" to the *"higher powers,"* Rom. 13:1, 5; Tit. 3:1; 1 Pet. 2:13, were constantly getting into difficulty with these same powers through disobeying them. The Apostles were not guilty of the inconsistency of teaching one thing and practicing an-

other. When they could harmonize their conduct with human laws and not injure their work, they did so. But this very Peter who commanded, *"Be subject to every ordinance of man,"* when brought to account for a very manifest disobedience to the commands of the rulers of Israel, answered merely: *"We ought to obey God rather than men"* (See Acts 5:29). If "subjection" meant always all that "obedience" means, no monstrous tyrant could ever be dethroned by righteous revolution on the part of Christian citizens. Disobedience to human rule may become one's highest duty to God and our fellow-beings. "Subjection" would teach a humble, a concilatory spirit, not a servile one.

296. In Eph. 5:21, the Apostle says, in exhortation to all believers, without regard to sex, *"Subjecting yourselves one to another in the fear of Christ"* (R. V.). Peter says to all believers, without regard to sex, *"Yea, all of you be subject one to another, and be clothed with humility,"* 1 Pet. 5:5. These passages clearly enjoin "subjection" upon men, yet all feel instinctively that they cannot mean that men must pass under the arbitrary control of each other when they become Christians.

297. In Phil. 4:3 the Apostle Paul says: *"I entreat thee . . . help those women who laboured with me in the Gospel."* We know, from Rom. 16:1, 2, that Phebe had laboured with the Apostle, in certain ways of helping. In Rom. 16:3 Priscilla is called by Paul *"my helper,"* ("fellow-helper," R. V.) ; at verse 12, Tryphena and Tryphosa are mentioned as women *"who laboured in the Lord,"* also Persis, who *"laboured much in the Lord."* These are all women; yet the Apostle, at 1 Cor. 16:16 says: *"I beseech you, brethren . . . that you submit yourselves"* ("be in subjection," R. V.) . . . *"to everyone that helpeth with us and laboureth."* He had just come from Corinth, where he had been labouring with Priscilla and Aquila, and there, as well as at Ephesus, whence he sent this letter to Corinth, his chief helper was Priscilla. Here then is a very clear command which at least included men, to "be in subjection," to women, who were certainly included in the body of *"every one that helpeth with us and laboureth."* It seems clear that "subjection" in this case cannot mean exactly the same as "obedience."

298. Yet after all this, when we come to the three instances where the Apostle exhorts wives to be in sub-

jection to their husbands, one is considered almost heretical who questions whether this exhortation to "wives" means absolute obedience. The word "subjection," as we have shown, has not been interpreted as obedience where the relation is that of man to man, nor where the "subjection" may mean of man to woman, as in 1 Cor. 16:16. Furthermore, each time where the relation of wives to their husbands, of children to their parents, and of servants to their masters is prescribed, a careful distinction in the use of words is made. The word "obey" is generally used for servants and always for children, but the word "subjection" always for wives.* If the sense is the same, why such care in the choice of a different word? As to the duty of wives, see Eph. 5:22; Col. 3:18; Tit. 2:5 †(R. V.). As to children, Eph. 6:1; Col. 3:20. As to servants, Eph. 6:5; Col. 3:22,—in the R. V. in each case.

299. The Old Testament sense in which "to be in subjection" is sometimes used, is highly suggestive and instructive. Psalm 62:1 reads in the English, *"Truly my soul waiteth upon God; from Him cometh my salvation."* At verse 5 of the same Psalm, we read: *"My soul, wait thou only upon God".* In Psalm 37:7 we find the words: *"Rest in the Lord and wait patiently for Him."* The words *"wait"* in the first passages, and the word *"rest"* in the last are all three represented in the Greek version by the single word *hupotasso,* "be in subjection," while the literal sense of the Hebrew original word is "be silent unto." Compare this with 1 Peter 3:1, 2, where wives are exhorted to win unbelieving husbands by "subjection." Surely Peter is not here exhorting wives to blindly obey unbelievers, for if heathen, they would at once remand them back to the worship of the gods; if Jews, back to Judaism. Rather, they are to win them away from these by their *"manner of life," "without the word,"*—actions speaking louder than words. *"Coupled with fear,"*—such fear of God as would cause these women, so gentle, quiet and patient in daily life, to be as adamant in their truth to God; and the husbands so overawed by their quiet maintenance of principle, whereas they are so ready to yield to their husbands when principle is not involved, that the husbands dare not try

* 1 Pet. 3:6, a seeming exception, will be explained in our next Lesson.
† In Titus 2:5 "obedient" is a mistranslation for "in subjection."—see R. V.

135

to compel their wives to violate conscience, and thus are themselves gradually led into the Christian faith.

Where "subjection" is spoken of as a woman's duty, without further immediate specification, it has been too readily assumed that this means subjection *to a husband*. But many women even from Apostolic days, and certainly an increasing large proportion of women in latter days, have no husbands. In both 1 Cor. 14:34, "let them be in subjection"; and in 1 Tim. 2:11, "learn in all subjection," this O. T. idea of waiting on God, or the thought of a spirit of humility *towards God*, may be all that is intended.

LESSON 39.

MUST WOMEN OBEY?

300. The word "obedience," *hupakoe*, is quite different from the word "subjection." Its corresponding verb, from which it comes, is *hupakouo*, and means literally, "to listen to," with the derived sense of "to obey." It has always been translated "obey" in the New Testament excepting at one place, Acts 12:13, where Rhoda comes "to listen to" Peter's knocking. This word has been used nowhere in respect to the wife's duty to her husband, with one safe exception, in an illustration. In 1 Pet. 3:6 the Apostle points women to the example of Sarah, who *"obeyed Abraham, calling him Lord,"* or "Sir," as the same is often translated (Matt. 13:27; John 12:21, etc.). So did Jacob call Esau "lord," though it was God's revealed will that Jacob should hold the place of superiority; and Aaron called Moses, his younger brother, "lord;" and Moses called the striving Egyptians "lords" (Gen. 33:8, 14; Exod. 33:22; Acts 7:26) There was a rabbinical saying which Peter may have known and quoted, here: "The wife of Abraham reverenced him and called him lord." It is to be noted that Peter's admonition is "subjection;" his illustration is subjection carried to the point of obedience. When giving a pattern for incitement we are very apt to take an extreme case, "Be unworldly; as Francis of Assisi, a wealthy young man, who renounced all his inheritance, and lived on alms." By these words the *spirit* of Francis is the point urged; not the literal copying of his acts. So with Peter's words here. And that spirit becomes all Christians alike. *"In honour preferring one another."*

301. As far as Abraham and Sarah are concerned, we are left in no doubt as to this relation of obedience and respect being mutual and reciprocal; God commanded Abraham to call Sarah by the very respectful name of "Princess," Gen. 17:15; and the strongest passage in the Bible seeming to enjoin obedience, as between husband and wife, is at Gen. 21:12, *"And God said unto Abraham . . . in all that Sarah saith unto thee, obey her voice."* The Hebrew verb used here, translated into the English, *"hearken unto,"* is the same word translated *"obey"* at Gen. 22:18. It means "to listen to," as does the Greek word "to obey," but it has been translated "obey" in 89 places in the Old Testament, and carries the sense "obey" as proved by the context, in scores of other places, just as it does in this passage, concerning which there is no doubt that Abraham was to obey in what Sarah told him to do,—*"Cast out the bondwoman and her child."*

302. The question naturally is asked: "But in the unique relation existing within the marriage bond, is not the wife bound to unquestioning obedience?" We do not so read the Bible. Turn to Lev. 20:18, where exists a commandment to prevent unhygienic conduct within the marriage relation. There is no question here but that God held both man and woman equally responsible for trampling upon this hygienic law; and this could not have been the case had the wife been bound to unquestioning obedience to her husband in this matter. In both the Greek and the Catholic Church, we understand that in the marriage service the conditions laid upon the bride and bridegroom are identical. In the United States the word "obey" is seldom used in the marriage ceremony. If, under the Mosaic law, the obligations and responsibilities of the matrimonial relation were identical for man and woman, as the passage cited from Leviticus seems to prove, it is exceedingly difficult to believe that the Gospel message is meant to place women on a lower plane of moral responsibility than the Mosaic law did. See more on this subject, pars. 110, 111.

303. To sum up: It seems clear that Jesus Christ MEANT WHAT HE SAID in the words, *"No one CAN serve two masters."* It amounts to an impossibility, and God never demands the impossible. Mutual respect, honour, humility, meekness, forbearance, and the yielding of one's preferences, are incumbent upon all be-

lievers, to be exercised under all circumstances short of making allegiance with man such as one owes to God only. Sarah made a greater declaration than her limited intelligence in that age could have fully grasped, but God ordered Abraham to act in accordance with its inexorable law: *"The SON of the bondwoman shall not inherit with the son of the free woman."* Let us pass over the circumstances that led to that decision in the Household of Faith,—and an utterance on Sarah's part that has been misunderstood and misjudged, but we have not space to enter into it now,—and learn the lesson of the words themselves. God establishes no covenant relations with one in bondage. Moses' words to Pharaoh knew no variation: *"Thus saith the Lord, Let my people go, that they may SERVE ME."* They could not BOTH serve the Egyptians as bondsmen, and God. *"No one CAN serve two masters."* God would not take them into full covenant relations with Himself until they were FREE. It is so to-day. Thousands of Christians, held in bondage by human companions, are crying out for a clearer realization of covenant relations with God, and God's demand is ever the same: *"Let my people go, that they may serve me."* God may *remember* His covenant with our fathers, but nevertheless we are NEVER in full covenant relations with Him until FREE. And this applies to women as well as to men. The freedom or bondage of the mother, moreover, both Sarah and St. Paul declare, shall determine the status of the son. No son of a bond-woman, because of her spirit in him, can, as such, enter into full covenant relations with God. Fathers of sons, who hold their wives in sensual bondage, doom those sons to a *personal* sensual bondage. It is God's own law, then, that one sex *cannot get free* and the other sex remain in bondage. It is impossible to understand the enormous extent to which all Christendom has been morally crippled in its progress by the attempt to keep the female sex in bondage, especially to the husband's sensuality.

304. Let us remind ourselves again that when the women of apostolic times, who laboured with Paul in the Gospel, either listened to, read, or taught others from the text, Gen. 3:16, they must have understood and taught it as meaning, *"Thou art turning away to thy husband, and he will rule over thee,"*—for this is the reading of the Septuagint version, which they univer-

sally used, and this is the way early Church Fathers invariably quote the verse. These women would not have read, *"Thy desire shall be to thy husband, and he shall rule over thee."* Now without this verse, translated as we have it, and used as an index to Paul's meaning when he talks on the "woman question," we may well inquire how these women would have interpreted his words. What sense would Paul's language about women have conveyed to women who had not been taught "the curse of Eve?" To women who never knew that Genesis taught (?) that God subordinated woman to man at the time of the Fall? To women who had never heard that the Bible taught the wife to obey the husband, because Eve brought sin into the world? Or to a woman who had never heard that, according to the Bible, her "desire" must be under her husband's control? Such was the condition of mind of the Gentile women, at least, who heard Paul's letters read. They knew that their heathen religions taught that woman was her husband's subordinate. But they did not have this teaching from Gen. 3:16, and if not from there, then they found it nowhere in the Old Testament. How differently they must, therefore, have construed Paul's language!

305. In place of such teachings as this about woman's "desire," they would have, rather, the recently uttered sayings of our Lord, standing out to their minds with startling clearness, because so unlike their Gentile teachings: *"The kings of the Gentiles exercise lordship over them: and they that exercise authority over them are called benefactors. But ye shall not be so."* They were not to look upon this exercise of authority as a benevolent thing, but quite the contrary. *"No one can serve two masters,"* then how could a woman "serve" her husband and her God? And how could her husband be a "benefactor" to her, while exercising authority over her? *"Be not yet called Rabbi: for one is your Master, even Christ . . Neither be ye called Masters: for one is your Master, even Christ. But he that is greatest among you shall be your servant. And whosoever shall exalt himself shall be abased."* What a totally different sense have such words as these! And these are the teachings which would be much in the mind and thought of those early Christians, because so recently uttered by their Divine Master.

LESSON 40.

PAUL'S WORDS TO TIMOTHY ABOUT WOMEN.

306. Paul's advice about women, in a personal letter to Timothy, Bishop of Ephesus, written about A. D. 67 (see 1 Tim. 2:8-15), assumes importance to women mainly because its import has been greatly exaggerated. Paul merely states his own practice and gives his reasons, as a matter of advice. He does not command or exhort Timothy, or anyone else, to do the same. Here there is no *"as also saith the law,"* as in 1 Cor. 14:34, to be made use of as opposing the ministry of women; nor does he express an *"ought"* on the subject, as in 1 Cor. 11:10. Yet this, the third and last of the familiar utterances by Paul on the "woman question," has probably been more used than the others as a pretext for subordinating woman, ecclesiastically. But to exaggerate advice of this nature in a personal letter, into a law for the governance of all women throughout all time, means to destroy the naturalness of this personal epistle.

307. Because Paul says to Timothy, in this same letter, *"Use a little wine for the stomach's sake,"* no one is so foolish as to believe that all Christians for all time are expected to drink wine. Paul writes to Timothy (2 Tim. 4:13), *"The cloak that I left at Troas with Carpus, . . . bring with thee,"* yet expositors do not teach that we must all follow Paul's directions to Timothy, and fetch a cloak from Troas. To be sure, Paul was inspired, and often uttered, in these personal letters, exhortations, commands and perhaps requests, which we could not disobey without sin. But Paul was not so *limited* and *hampered* by his inspiration that he could no longer give *individuals advice,* and make *private* requests. He was not so hampered by his inspiration that he could not, like the rest of us, give advice of *temporary use only,*—advice unsuitable for all individuals to practice under all circumstances. Expositors who cannot see a difference between God's inexorable laws, or eternal principles of justice and righteousness, as described in personal epistles, and practice or advice suitable for the emergency only, are too literal in their mental make-up to be useful teachers for their age and generation. We have already quoted, but will repeat again, John Stuart Mill's thoughtful words of warning: *"To pretend that Christianity was intended to stereotype existing forms of*

government and society and protect them against change, is to reduce it to the level of Islamism or Brahmism."

308. For all that, when Paul merely says: *"I suffer not a woman to teach or to control a man"* (as it should be read), certain expositors declare that all women must for all time be discounted as teachers of the Word and must not, on any account, have any place of importance in managing church affairs. With what ardour they contend that Paul's *mere example* must be obeyed here! Do they thus ardently obey Paul's example themselves, in all matters? Let us see: Speaking of his own unencumbered state, Paul says, even in a general epistle (1 Cor. 7:7), *"I would that all men were even as I myself."* Yet men who would be scandalized by women daring to teach or preach, or to exercise authority, themselves, in opposition to Paul's plainly expressed wishes, marry. They disobey his plainly expressed example. The question is, *ought* they to obey Paul in this matter, or are they free to disobey, without sin? Listen to Paul's own answer to this question; at verse 28 of this very chapter Paul says, *"But and if thou marry, thou hast not sinned."* Therefore we know, on the Apostle's own words, that he *could* give advice which might be disobeyed with impunity. In 1 Cor. 16:12, Paul declares that he "greatly desired" Apollos to go to Corinth; but Apollos did not obey his wishes, yet Paul continues to call him "brother Apollos," just the same, and hopes that he will go later,—a wish that Paul would not have expressed, had he felt that Apollos was sinning in this disobedience of his wishes. Paul understood, if others conveniently forget sometimes, that "One is our Master," and that one is not Paul, but Jesus Christ.

309. All that is claimed by the Bible, for the Epistle to Timothy is that it was *meant for Timothy.* This all will admit, as to the "wine" and the "cloak" question; and we claim it for the "woman question," too,—for reasons that we shall presently state. Nevertheless, we are not hindered from seeing that Paul uttered many truths in this same Epistle to Timothy, that bear internal evidence that they are inspired with messages of value for all, and for all time,—words that breathe the same Spirit of prophecy and doctrine that characterizes the Bible in every part, and make it a Book to be both revered and obeyed. But it has been strong masculine

prejudice, in the past, which has led to this stress upon Paul's words about woman's part and place in the Church. When prejudice runs strongly in another direction, men are quite ready to disobey Paul's words, and to teach women to do the same. For instance, Paul says (1 Cor. 7:8): *"I say to the unmarried and widows, it is good for them if they abide even as I."* Do ministers of the Gospel, and theologians go about saying to unmarried women and widows, "You should heed Paul's words, and remain unmarried as he did?" Not at all, if there is one point on which prejudiced males would give advice to women who wished to preach, that point would be to "get married,—the home is woman's sphere." Their advice, then, on the "woman question" can run counter to Paul's teaching when their prejudices do also.

310. Now, for the evidences that Paul's advice to Timothy was not meant to control all women for all time, we must take time and space to get the historical setting. When Paul was arrested, (Acts 21), and taken for safety to Caesarea for trial (Acts 23), he there appealed unto Caesar (Acts 25:11), and was sent to Rome, where he arrived in A. D. 61, in the seventh year of Nero's reign. He was placed in charge of "the Captain of the Guard," who, profane history tells us, was Burrus, who treated him with some kindness, allowing him to dwell in his own hired house, and he preached to all that came to him,—though kept chained to his guard. In time, Paul came to have a church gathered about him, almost within the very household of the most infamous potentate that ever disgraced a throne (Acts 28:16-31).

311. When Paul reached Rome there was less hostility against Christians there than anywhere else throughout the Empire. Nero was young, and his tutors, Seneca the Philosopher, and Burrus, already mentioned, attended to matters of state, while Nero, for the most part, devoted himself to art. But soon a courtier named Otho corrupted the youthful Nero, and the latter fell madly in love with Poppaea, Otho's wife, a woman of desperate character, though a Jewish proselyte. She induced Nero to murder his own wife, Octavia, and marry herself. Thenceforward, his fall was very rapid, and his court became unspeakably vile.

312. Conybeare and Howson, in their most valuable book, *The Life and Epistles of St. Paul,* (in comments

immediately following the Epistle to the Philippians),
say of St. Paul: "He tells us [see Phil. 1:13] that
throughout the Praetorian quarters he was well known
as a pioneer for the cause of Christ, and he sends special
salutations to the Philippian Church from the Christians
in the Imperial household [Phil. 4:22]. These notices
bring before us very vividly the moral contrasts by
which the Apostle was surrounded. The soldier to whom
he was chained might have been in Nero's body-guard
yesterday; his comrade who next relieved guard upon
the prisoner might have been one of the executioners
of Octavia, and might have carried her head to Poppaea
a few weeks before. Such were the ordinary employ-
ments of the fierce and blood-stained veterans who were
daily present, like wolves in the midst of sheep, at the
meetings of the Christian brotherhood. If there were
any of these soldiers not utterly hardened by a life of
cruelty, their hearts must surely have been touched by
the character of their prisoner, brought as they were
into so close a contact with him. They must have been
at least astonished to see a man, under such circumstances, so utterly careless of selfish interests. Strange
indeed to their ears . . must have been the sound of
Christian exhortation, of prayers, and of hymns;
stranger still, perhaps, the tender love which bound the
converts to their teacher and to one another, and which
showed itself in every look and tone." We will continue
this sketch of Paul's times and surroundings in our next
lesson.

LESSON 41.

HISTORICAL LIGHT ON PAUL'S WORDS TO TIMOTHY.

313. The authors quoted before, Conybeare and Howson, continue: "But if the agents of Nero's tyranny
seem out of place in such a scene, still more repugnant
to the assembled worshippers must have been the instruments of his pleasures, the ministers of his lust . . .
The ancient historians have polluted their pages with
details of infamy which no writer in the languages of
Christendom may dare to repeat . . . Suffice it to say
that the courtiers of Nero were the spectators, and the
members of his household the instruments, of vices so
monstrous and so unnatural, that they shocked even the

men of that generation, steeped as it was in every species of obscenity." They tell of the death of Burrus, and of the fact that Paul now passed into the charge of one of these vile instruments of Nero who succeeded Burrus, and then continue: "Another circumstance occurred about this time, which seemed to threaten still graver mischief to the cause of Paul. This was the marriage of Nero to his adulterous mistress, Poppaea . . . We know from Josephus that she exerted her influence over Nero in favour of the Jews, and that she patronized their emissaries at Rome; and assuredly no scruples of humanity would prevent her from seconding their demand for the punishment of their most detested antagonist." However, Paul seems to have been acquitted, after a considerable time, to have gone from church to church, in Ephesus, Crete, Macedonia, Miletus and Nicopolis, and probably he was in Spain when he heard of the awful martyrdom of the Roman Church under Nero in A. D. 64.

314. Nero himself burned Rome, wishing to widen its streets and to build more modern houses. Tacitus, a pagan historian of those days, says: "The infamy of that horrible transaction adhered to him. . . . In order, if possible, to remove the imputation, he determined to transfer the guilt to others. For this purpose he punished with exquisite tortures a race of men detested for their evil practices, commonly called Christians . . . A number of Christians were convicted, not indeed upon clear evidence of having set fire to the city, but rather on account of their sullen hatred of their kind. They were put to death with exquisite cruelty, and to their sufferings Nero added mockery and derision. Some were covered with skins of wild beasts, and left to be devoured by dogs; others were nailed to the cross; numbers were burned alive; and many, covered over with inflammable matter, were lighted up when the day declined, to serve as torches during the night. For the convenience of this tragic spectacle, the Emperor lent his own gardens. At length the cruelty of these proceedings filled every breast with compassion . . . It was evident they fell a sacrifice, not for the public good, but to glut the cruelty and rage of one man only."

315. Prof. Ramsay says in his *Church in the Roman Empire* (page 240, 241): "This went on till the Roman populace was sick of it, and began to pity the sufferers

. . . But it can have been no inconsiderable number and no short period which brought satiety to a populace accustomed to find their greatest amusement in public butcheries, frequently recurring on a colossal scale . . . On these grounds we conclude that if Tacitus has correctly represented his authorities, the persecution of Nero, begun for the sake of diverting popular attention, was continued as a permanent police measure, under the form of a general persecution of Christians as a sect dangerous to the public safety." Ramsay quotes Sulpicius Severus, a historian of those days, who informs us: "This was the beginning of severe measures against the Christians. Afterwards the religion was forbidden by formal laws, and the profession of Christianity was made illegal by published edicts." Ramsay continues: "When Nero had once established the principle in Rome. his action served as a precedent in every province. There is no need to suppose a general edict or formal law. The precedent would be quoted in every case where a Christian was accused. Charges such as had been brought against Paul in so many places were certainly brought against others; and the action of the Emperor at Rome would give the tone to the action of the provincial governers" (p. 243-245).

316. This Epistle was probably written in A. D. 67. James, the brother of John, had been slain by Herod long before. James, the brother of our Lord, had been done to death by a mob, at Jerusalem; and Peter was at Rome to be crucified, or the deed had already been done. And Paul, having such intimate knowledge of conditions at Rome, 'as well as the enlightenment of spiritual perception, could well discern "the signs of the times," and hence his precautionary advice, which related largely to the protection of women from possible arrest. We have shown that, owing to the Jewish proselyte, Poppaea, and her influence over Nero, the Jews were in favor in Rome at this time, while the Christians were in the greatest peril. Prof. Ramsay makes the following significant remark: "If the Jews appeared to the Empire to resemble the Christians so much, and yet were treated so differently, the reason for the difference in treatment *must have lain in those points in which Christians differed from the Jews,* in the estimate of the Imperial Government" (page 355; the italics are our own),—and

at no point was the contrast greater, at this time, than *in the Christian treatment of women.*

317. For there were four points at any rate, in which this difference was very manifest: (1) In the aggressiveness of Christianity, while Judaism was proud, exclusive and unexpansive; (2) in the instruction of women as expressly permitted by Paul in our present Lesson, whereas the Jewish Oral Law taught that women were only to be instructed in their own special duties, but not in the law in general; (3) in the many conversions of women; and (4) in their activity in the Apostolic Church. On this latter point Lecky, in his *History of European Morals,* says: "The general superiority of women to men in the strength of their religious emotions, and their natural attraction to a religion which made personal attachment to its Founder its central duty, and which imparted an unprecedented dignity and afforded an unprecedented scope to their characteristic virtues, account for the very conspicuous position that female influence assumed in the great work of the conversion of the Roman Empire. In no other movement of thought was it so powerful or so acknowledged. · In the ages of persecution female figures occupy many of the foremost places in the ranks of martyrdom, and pagan and Christian writers alike attest the alacrity with which women flocked to the Church."

318. But this aggressiveness of Christianity, and activity of Christian women, would not only offend Jews, but the complaint against it, on the part of Jews, would make a deep impression, in time, upon the pagan mind and the Imperial Government. Roman law provided a death penalty for those of lower rank who won converts to their faith, and banishment for those of higher rank. Were the enforcement of this law once demanded, then every new convert would mean fresh danger for the Church,—and the aggravation would be doubled if that convert were the wife of an unbelieving husband, or the daughter of an unbelieving father.

319. In another place Lecky adds: "Another cause of the peculiar animosity felt against the Christians was the constant interference with domestic life, arising from the great number of female conversions. The graphic title of 'earpicker of ladies,' which was given to a pontiff of somewhat later period, might have been applied

to many in the days of the persecution; but to the Roman, who regarded the supreme authority of the head of the family, in all religious matters, as the very foundation of domestic morality, no character could appear more infamous or more revolting."

320. The same writer describes the general attitude of the pagan mind on this subject in the words of Plutarch: "A wife should have no friends but those of her husband; and as the gods are the first of friends, she should know no gods but those her husband adores. Let her shut the door, then, against idle religious and foreign superstitions. No god can take pleasure in sacrifices offered by a wife without the knowledge of her husband." Now let us continue in the words of Prof. Ramsay which have special reference to Paul's Epistles to Timothy and Titus: "The advice given by St. Paul as to the relations of the Christians to the society in which they are placed, IS ALWAYS IN ACCORDANCE WITH THE SITUATION WHICH WE HAVE DESCRIBED AS OCCUPIED BY THEM UNDER NERO" [page 246; the capitals are ours].
(To be Continued).

LESSON 42.

HISTORICAL LIGHT ON PAUL'S WORDS TO TIMOTHY.

321. Prof. Ramsay says, further, "The danger about 65-70 is that calumnies and false charges be circulated, and the Christians tried for these imputed crimes. In such trials recantation is not sought for, and would be no palliation of the crimes charged against the Christians" (p. 247). History has not left us ignorant as to the nature of these calumnies. We have seen that Tacitus spoke of the Christians as "a race of men detested for their evil practices." We should prefer not to give more precise information as to these calumnies, but it is essential to an understanding of Paul's words, to know what sort of slanders had to be met,—and they were precisely of that nature that would cause Paul to recommend (1), a separation of the sexes; (2), and that the women should be quiet for their own protection. Lecky, in the book we have already quoted from, states: "At a time when the moral standard was very low, they [all Christians] were charged with deeds so atrocious as to scan-

dalize the most corrupt. They were represented as habitually, in their secret assemblies, celebrating the most licentious orgies, feeding on human flesh, . . . [and worse]. The persistence with which these accusations were made is shown by the great prominence they occupy, both in the writings of the apologists and in the narrations of the persecutions. That these charges were absolutely false will now be questioned by no one" (Vol. 1, p. 414).

322. We must not forget that *an accusation* against a woman's virtue throughout all time, has generally been treated more severely than a *proved deed* of the same sort in a man. Moral conditions were most terrible under Nero, who actively encouraged his officers and soldiers in every conceivable form of vileness. Paul had an intimate first-hand knowledge of all these dangers to women, and he knew more; he knew what had actually transpired at Rome, when the little church (that had gathered round him in the friendlier days, only two or three years before) had been wiped out of existence by Nero's ferocity. We have only a glimpse, in a single sentence contained in a letter which Clement of Rome, a few years later, wrote to the Church at Corinth. We will give the sense of his words in the language of Archdeacon Farrar, from his book, *The Early Days of Christianity:* "Christian women, modest maidens, holy matrons, must be the Danaids or the Proserpine, or worse, and play their parts as priestesses of Saturn and Ceres, and in blood-stained dramas of the dead . . . Infamous mythologies were enacted, in which women must play their parts in torments of shamefulness more intolerable than death."

323. Some of the women who came to this fate for their confession as followers of the harmless and holy Son of God, we probably have heard of by name, in the 16th chapter of Romans, for therein Paul sends greetings to many women of Rome. We are glad to know positively that Priscilla escaped,—from the mention of her name in 2 Tim. 4:19. How the tender, loving heart of Paul must have bled when he heard the terrible news of women who had "laboured with him in the Gospel," women "of note among the apostles," women who had "succoured" him, or "bestowed much labour upon him,"—those to whom he had applied these and many other appreciative words, brought to such a

terrible plight as above described! And then his mind would sweep the entire field of his missionary labours, and he would see the same peril threatening, or the same shame being suffered, by his Christian sisters and female disciples everywhere.

324. But it must have rested with peculiar sadness upon the city of Ephesus, next in importance to Rome, where he himself had suffered persecution so sore that he describes it as having "fought with beasts," 1 Cor. 15:32. When Paul went up to Jerusalem, before ever he was arrested, as he passed through Miletus, he summoned the elders from Ephesus to meet him there, and said to them: *"Ye yourselves know, from the first day that I came into Asia, after what manner I have been with you at all seasons, serving the Lord . . . with many tears, and temptations, which befell me by the lying in wait of the Jews"* (Acts 20:18, 19). Thus he testifies to the spirit of hatred towards Christians which prevailed at Ephesus, where Timothy lived, to whom Paul's epistle is written. In Acts 19:23-41, we have an account of trouble there, when a certain Alexander was put forward by the Jews. What he would have said, had the mob permitted, we do not know; but when Paul writes his second letter to Timothy, he warns Timothy to beware of the man,—so we know there was at least one deadly and active Jewish enemy of the Christians at Ephesus, —the man who, later did Paul *"much evil"* (2 Tim. 4:14, 15), even probably going to Rome for the purpose of appearing against Paul at his last trial before Nero, when, alas! Paul was finally condemned and executed. It should cause no surprise, then, that Paul, under such exceptional circumstances, should caution Timothy, Bishop of Ephesus, against bringing women into prominence, or permitting them to come forward, under such perilous circumstances.

325. And, then, there was a peculiar peril to women, of which Paul would know, though Christian women might be ignorant of it. We will describe it in the words of Prof. Ramsay (page 399, footnote, of his *Church in the Roman Empire*): "The ingenuity of Roman practice had in A. D. 31 perverted a humane scruple . . . into a reason for detestable brutality [criminal outrage] to the young daughter of Sejanus;
. . . and this act constituted a precedent, which might defend numerous cases of similar brutality to Christian

virgins in later time. There is no reason to disbelieve these cases, as Neumann does. They are attested by too weighty evidence, though of course the fantastic developments given to them in later hagiography are inane. If such things were done to the innocent daughter of a Roman noble, why not to a Christian criminal?" Yes, and under Nero, why not to married women, as well as to virgins, if the keeper of the prison so chose? We know, then, that the situation which women Christians occupied under Nero was that of extreme peril, not only to life, but, as Church history shows, to virtue also. And we know that the peril to men who would indoctrinate women in the Christian religion, was great also,— for it led to the accusation of provoking family discord (par. 319).

326. To be sure, one should not carelessly assume that anything in the Bible is of exceptional and temporary import only. Yet we are now dealing with a personal letter, and advice given to one individual, and given in a time of exceptional peril.—and these facts ought to count for a great deal. Again, while we should not thoughtlessly assume that the Bible is to be read in the light of profane history, and corrected by it; nevertheless, the Bible, when carefully tested by well-known ancient customs or conditions set forth in reliable profane history, will be found to ring true to contemporary facts. We might have suffered a stagger to our faith in Paul's tenderness and prudence, if not a stagger to our faith in the Bible, if, in a time of such supreme peril to Christian women, Paul could be represented as urging women to the front of the fight, and putting on them equal ecclesiastical responsibilities with men,—when he knew that the cost to them would be far heavier than to men. Rather, we find in Paul's letter to Timothy precisely that sort of natural advice that a tender over-pastor under such conditions would give to one in charge of a church in his jurisdiction: "I should not allow a woman to teach or control a man. They are attacking our reputation for common decency, and we must meet it by separating the women from the men, and having them keep very quiet." All history testifies that women did not shirk martyrdom for Christ's sake, but Paul says: "However willing they may be, I do not permit it. We men must take the lead: Adam was first formed, then Eve, and besides, Eve, being immature, got in-

volved, unwittingly, in transgression through her immaturity and inexperience. So are our women immature and inexperienced; they do not even understand fully the terrible dangers that confront them." Thus might the Apostle who, ten years before, wrote to the Corinthians about women "praying and prophesying," and to the Galatians about the same time, to the effect that there could be no distinctions as regards sex in the Christian body, now consistently write after this manner to Timothy,—for he must have regard for the situation under Nero, and the relations of Christians to the social order about them. It seems to us far more sensible, then, to ascribe Paul's precautionary advice to the then existent perilous times, especially for women, than to go back to Eve, or to creation to find a reason.

LESSON 43.

PAUL'S WORDS TO TIMOTHY EXPLAINED.

327. We should translate and punctuate 1 Tim. 2:8-15 as follows:

Verse 8. I desire that the men pray everywhere lifting up holy hands, without wrath and doubting, and the women likewise [or "in like manner"].

Verse 9. [I desire women] to array themselves in a befitted *catastola*, with reverence and restraint, not with braids, or gold, or pearls, or costly garments.

Verse 10. But as becomes women proclaiming godliness, with good deeds.

Verse 11. Let a woman learn, quietly, in all subjection [to God].

Verse 12. Now I permit a woman neither to teach nor exercise authority over a man, but let her be in quietness.

Verse 13. For Adam was first formed, then Eve.

Verse 14. And Adam was not deceived [when he sinned]; but the woman, having [first] been thoroughly deceived, became [involved] in the transgression [of Adam],

Verse 15. And she will be saved by the Child-bearing [i. e., the bearing of Jesus Christ], if they abide in faith, and love and sanctification with self-restraint.

We should remember that St. Paul himself must, in such perilous times, be cautious how he writes. He could hardly say, in unambiguous language all that he could wish to express, without imperiling Timothy and his church.

328. Now for the explanation: Bloomfield says: "Here almost all modern expositors take the sense to be, 'And in like manner I wish women to adorn themselves,' etc. But there is no correspondence such as is expressed by 'in like manner.' Now as it is likely that the Apostle would address something to the women as well as to the men, on the subject of prayer, I agree with the ancient and a few modern expositors (as Grotius), that we must repeat not only 'I desire,' from the preceding, but also 'pray.' Grotius indeed repeats the whole sentence." Conybeare and Howson say, "After 'women' we must supply 'pray' (as Chrysostom does), or something equivalent (to take part in worship, etc.), from the preceding context." Prof. Ramsay (*Expositor*, Sept. 1909) says: "The necessary and inevitable sense of the word ["likewise"] is that the whole body of women is to be understood as affected by what has been said about men." In other words, Paul wishes that the women too would "pray everywhere," etc. Wrongly punctuated, as it is in our Bible, it teaches that women are to dress likewise to men praying with uplifted hands. Strange costume that!

329. *"Lifting up holy hands,"* was the customary attitude in public prayer, seeming to express a helpless appeal to God. A century later, Tertullian writes, "For Emperors we supplicate the true, the living, the eternal God, in whose power they are . . . *with hands extended* because harmless; *with head uncovered* because not ashamed; without a prompter because from the heart we ask long life and every blessing for them . . . Then, while we stand praying before God, let the *ungulae* [instruments of torture] tear us, the crosses bear our weight, let the flames envelope us, the sword divide our throats, the beasts spring upon us; the very posture of a praying Christian is a preparation for every punishment."—*"without wrath and doubting,"* because in such times, only grace could restrain wrath against their cruel tormentors; only strong faith could preserve from doubt as to God's goodness.

330. Verse 9. *"To array themselves in a befitting* catastola, *with reverence and self-restraint,."* Under the conditions of peril to women, it was very appropriate

for the Apostle to impress the need of a very unobtrusive costume for the women who took part in public meetings. Indeed it were well if the Christian women of our own day would obey the Scriptural injunctions regarding plain and unobtrusive dressing; women sin greatly in this regard. The *catastola* is mentioned in Scripture only here and in the Greek O. T. version at Isai. 61:3. It was a loose garment that reached to the feet, and was worn with a girdle. The word may be used as an equivalent for "garment", yet it seems more likely that the Apostle should have used this rare term (rare in Scripture), rather in its specific application. A spirit of *"reverence and self-restraint"* would ever prevent a woman from becoming a mere tool of fashion. The word "reverence (*aidos*) translated "shamefacedness," is used in only one other place in the N. T.,— Heb. 12:28. It was not necessary for the translators to concoct an "unmeaning corruption," as Dean Alford calls "shamefacedness," in order to describe what the word means, *because it applied to women.* The Revisers changed it to *"shamefastness,"*—an obsolete word without meaning to the average mind; excepting that both words convey the sense that women should always be ashamed of themselves. There was no such "travail in birth" to bring out a sense for the word when the word applied to men also, even when before God, "a consuming·fire."

331. Verse 10. *"But as becometh women proclaiming godliness, with good deeds."* The reference may be to Dorcas Acts 9:36. We must study that phrase rendered "professing godliness." It conveys an idea to modern thought such as "professing conversion," "religion," or "sanctification." But the N. T. word for what we call Christian profession is "confession,"—see Matt. 10:32, 1 Tim. 6:13. It is the Greek word, *homologeo,* or *exhomologeo.* But here we have a totally different word, *epaggelomai.* Two "g"s coming together are pronounced "ng" in Greek. This is a word from which we get "angel, messenger." The first letters, ep, are for the Greek preposition *epi,* "to." The verb means, "I bring a message to." The verb is often used as meaning "I promise," but though in the reflexive form, it takes a direct object after it, *something* is promised to *somebody.* But the word can hardly be separated from the idea of a "message;" and it is also far-fetched to imag-

ine it means to "promise *to be* godly,"—rather, it means to "promise godliness" to *someone else.*

332.   The only other passage in the N. T. where the word is translated "profess" is in this same Epistle (6:21), *"which some professing have erred concerning the faith."* Read the connection. It means that the "babblers" themselves "promised" these things to others,—that is, proclaimed them. Prof. Ramsay, in the *Expositor* (July 1909), says of this very word in 6:21, that it "regularly implies that the person mentioned came before the public with promises, in order to gain supporters; it is applied to candidates for municipal favour and votes in the Greek cities, who publicly announced what they intended to do for the general benefit, if they gained popular support."

333.   If this be the meaning "regularly implied" by the word, then why not here, where it relates to women? These women preachers would seek "to gain supporters," —not, however, for themselves, but standard-bearers of the Cross; and they "promise godliness" in place of a sin-burdened heart, to those who will accept the offer of salvation. In such a time of peril, women might not be safe teaching and controlling the work of men, for this would involve a certain freedom of manner between the sexes.   But there would be much less danger of scandal in women praying and speaking in the generally small meetings in private homes of the Christians, in which case all could testify as to what was said.   Indeed it is difficult to imagine that when men assembled in the home of some woman, who was their hostess, that they required their hostess to veil herself and lapse into silence before they began the meeting.   The practical difficulty would be to get hostesses to open their homes to men on such insulting terms. We must not think of great churches and cathedrals as existing when Paul wrote these words.

(*To be Continued*).

LESSON 44.

PAUL'S WORDS TO TIMOTHY EXPLAINED.
(Continued.)

334.   Verse 11: This verse is generally interpreted as teaching that all women are to learn God's law "in all

submission" to man's law. If such be the case, why not at once learn man's law wholly? If one were set to learn King George's law "in all subjection" to the Kaiser, one might seriously question whether it would not be more sensible to move out of Britain into Germany and study there, not in England. Such teaching as this contravenes the Lord's own warning, *"No one* [for so it should be translated] *can serve two masters; for he will hate the one, and love the other; or else he will hold to the one and despise the other."* The husband has not been mentioned heretofore, nor in this verse. The assumption that woman is to learn God's law in subjection to her husband's law is quite gratuitous. Paul does not say this. Supposing the woman is not married, or is a widow, or has been divorced (as many were in those days), from a heathen husband on account of her religion, what then? Read again par. 299.

335. But for the fact that we have had a long drill in a misconception, our inference from these words would be, that the woman who is learning the Word of God must have a spirit of "subjection" to God; or, perhaps, a spirit of subjection to the teacher (man or woman); Paul enjoins subjection and even obedience to religious teachers (1 Cor. 16:16. Heb. 13:17). We believe Paul here directs that a woman who comes asking to be taught the Christian religion is to be allowed to learn, but in "quietness," because, as we have shown, the teaching of women led to persecution,—and it must be understood that she comes with the serious purpose of harmonizing her life to the religion she is taught,—and that is all Paul's words mean. The matter must be conducted "in quietness," because the Jews would be angered thereby. The Jews had a different spirit towards the learning of women at this time: "Let the law be burned rather than committed to a woman;" "He that teaches his daughter the law, is as though he taught her to sin." This is the teaching of the Talmud. Dr. Edersheim, in his book, *Sketches of Jewish Social Life,* says: "Women were interdicted engaging in rabbinical studies and a story is related to show how even the wisest of women, Beruria, was thereby brought to the extreme brink of danger." Recalling then the fact that such teaching was angering to the Jews, and the aggressiveness of Christianity in making female converts angering to the Romans, we have a clear explanation why Paul would advise it to

be done "in quietness,"—and only to those who would learn "in all subjection,"—not to those who might wish to learn merely on account of mental inquisitiveness.

336. The word "silence" should be translated "quietness," and so it is in the R. V. The same word occurs in 2 Thess. 3:12, where Paul says: *"We command and exhort . . . that with quietness they work, and eat their own bread."* No one supposes that in this latter passage Paul commands the men to be dumb when about their daily task, but only that they attend to their own business, and make no unnecessary fuss about it. And so here, women are to learn 'in quietness," not in absolute silence. The quietness may be as much enjoined upon the one who is teaching as the one who is learning. It is not to be told abroad, or boasted of, by either teacher or learner, that the woman is learning. But yet, the woman is to be allowed to learn. That was a step far in advance of the practice of the Jews. That women might do this teaching will appear plain to the unprejudiced who read Titus 2:3, 4. In fact it is most likely that women taught the women.

337. Verse 12: *"But I suffer not a woman to teach, nor to usurp authority,"* etc., gives the impression that Paul forbade women, under all circumstances, to teach anyone whatsoever. This constitutes a contradiction of plain evidence. Paul *did not* forbid it, absolutely. He merely states here his own practice in times of fierce persecution and a fierce attack upon the moral reputation of the Christians,—under those conditions he did not allow women t ɔ *teach men.* But he not only allowed but enjoined women to teach women, for at this very period, he wrote Titus. Therefore that comma after "teach," in the A. V. and R. V. both, is out of place, and the verse should be read as though written: *"I suffer not a woman to teach [a man] or to control a man, but to be in quietness,"* that is, to teach women alone, and do even that quietly. Paul did not, at other periods in his ministry, forbid women to teach men. This is an exceptional, prudential measure to meet a dire necessity of perilous times. All are bound to agree that the order of the names, Priscilla and Aquila, proves that Priscilla was the more active and able of these two helpers of Paul. Their names should stand in this order, the woman's first (see R. V.) in Acts 18:26, where it is stated that they taught Apollos. That is, Priscilla was

his principal teacher (see pars. 195-196). Timothy, to whom Paul writes this Epistle, had a Gentile father (Acts 16:1), but a mother and grandmother who had instructed him in the Bible, and Paul congratulates Timothy on his good fortune in this regard, 2 Tim. 1:5. And yet, commentators who admit these facts freely, go on teaching us, by bad punctuation, that Paul absolutely forbids women to teach anyone at all. Then how could Paul say: *"For what knowest thou, O wife, whether thou shalt save thy husband"* (1 Cor. 7:16)? The word "usurp" in the expression, *"nor to usurp authority over the man,"* does not occur in the original; and the word "the," which also does not exist in the original text, is misleading. The insertion of "usurp" without warrant, in this translation, is an index of the spirit which has prompted the interpretation of this entire passage,—an assumption, against proof to the contrary, that it is man's exclusive right to teach woman and his right to rule her.

338. Verse 13; *"For Adam was first formed, then Eve."* This verse is interpreted as meaning that Adam was first *created*, then Eve. But the word here employed, *plasso*, is not the word for "create," the latter word is *ktizo*,—nor does it mean the same. My Greek lexicon says the word means, "to mould, form, shape,— to put in a certain form." It is translated "fashioned" Psalm 119:73 and Job 10:8, in the Greek verson (see par. 30). The lesson that Paul would teach is this: as Adam was first developed and then Eve, in the natural world, so must it be in the social world. There are social perils for women that men never encounter. The crime of all crimes—far worse than murder—cannot, in the nature of things, be committed against man; therefore, when woman's virtue is threatened, as it was in the Neronian persecutions, there is no question but man must go first. He can carry the contest forward with more safety where woman would encounter the greatest peril; therefore he should be the pioneer, the "head',, in attacking and destroying social conditions dangerous to woman's virtue. And again, the world over, apart from the spirit of Christianity, woman has been hampered and hindered in development. To the end that women might be controlled, the custom was early established of the male marrying a female of less mature years than himself; so that a *habit of immaturity* of mind and character has been cultivated in woman. This

was more the social condition in Paul's day than now. Paul speaks here of that immaturity and inexperience which the rival sex has brought about, and the obligations it imposes upon Christian men to take the lead in time of peril. But Paul's spirit is very different from the spirit of theology at this point. He promises *another condition* for the future of women, in the words—*"then Eve."* Eve, under the influence of Christianity, is to have her full social development. But theology has taught,—"Eve never!" and reproved her aspiration towards full development, as though it were a sin against God and nature.

339. Verse 14: *"And Adam was not deceived; but the woman being deceived was in the transgression."* Bishop Ellicott declares the sense of this verse to be; "He sinned, quite aware of the magnitude of the sin he was committing. Eve, on the other hand, was completely, thoroughly deceived." The word means more than "deceived," as translated,; it means "thoroughly deceived," in Eve's case, see par. 91.

(To be Continued).

LESSON 45.

PAUL'S WORDS TO TIMOTHY EXPLAINED.

(Concluded).

340. We have shown that in this very passage, which is generally interpreted as Paul's strongest denunciation of the public ministry of women, he expresses a wish that women should *"pray everywhere,"* and recommends a suitable attire for women "proclaiming godliness." "But," says an objector, "what about women learning 'in quietness?'" That evidently relates to a *learner,* not to a woman teacher, or preacher. "But women perhaps capable of teaching men are likewise told to be 'in quietness,' verse 12." Supposing, during the Armenian atrocities, or the Chinese Boxer uprising, because of some special peril to *men,* to which women were not exposed, a bishop had sent the following advice: "Let male preachers of the Gospel refrain from teaching women and controlling them, and be in quietness." Could that be justly construed as an interdiction of all male preaching *for all time,* if once it were known that at that time *special* peril to *men alone* existed? No; the use of such

an expression as "preachers of the Gospel" would lead one to infer that, when peace was restored, these men could pursue the vocation named with greater boldness. So here, once knowing that special peril for women alone existed, the use of the expression *"women proclaiming godliness"* would surely indicate this as their normal occupation under normal conditions.

341.   In verse 13, the Apostle declares that Adam, having been first formed, and hence being older than Eve, was "not deceived." Paul is not here comparing the *quality* of Eve's sin to Adam's sin; if that were the case the illustration would be out of place for application to Christian workers. All Paul's thought is centred on proper equipment for service in the Church at a time of great peril to the Church,—and he makes the point that in time of tempest an inexperienced and immature person should not be put at the rudder of the ship. Paul does not argue that a *wilful sinner,* like Adam, is of more value than a *deceived person.* Paul did not go about ordaining, in the Church, knaves to govern fools. He is dealing with Christians, all of whom have been forgiven their sins of the past, and therefore they are reduced to a common level in Christ's atonement (as he asserts, Gal. 3:28), though when it comes to Christian *service,* some are fitted for it and some are not; some are suited to take the lead, and some, because of immaturity of mind, and because exposed to peculiar dangers, should be more quiet.

342.   Paul refers here to woman's social condition of inexperience and immaturity, as leaving her vulnerable to deception, when she does not wilfully intend to go wrong. But this is his next thought: *"She shall be saved by* [or through] *the Childbearing."* Again, Paul is not here speaking of woman's salvation from sin, or from perdition. His mind is on offices in the Church to be filled only by persons already saved from sin. He has now turned away from the individual Eve, and says, *"the woman,"* that is, all womankind,—using a collective form, after which, in the following verse, he employs a plural pronoun "they." (This is Winer's interpretation here, and no better grammatical authority on N. T. Greek could be quoted). The thought then is, that woman, finding herself involved in a condition of social disorder brought about by transgression, will not escape as readily as man—her full development requiring more

time than his. Since man, even in that day, was less a victim of circumstances than woman, so in the Church must he shoulder the heavier responsibilities. This word 'saved" is often used in the N. T. of other than precisely spiritual or moral forms of rescue, see the marginal readings of Mark 5:23, Luke 8:36, in the R. V. Paul implies that woman's social rescue began in the birth of Jesus Christ; and we all know how Christianity, unhampered by the narrowness of man, is calculated to elevate woman, until in Christ she stands on his level (Gal. 3:27, 28),—rather, both, in Christ, as on His level.

343. Opinions differ as to the meaning of verse 15.

As to childbearing, we know that Christian women who know and trust Jesus Christ and the true God, may die in childbirth, just like unbelievers. Nor is another thought correct that some theologians set forth,—that women are saved from their sins and go to heaven if they bear children. Absurd! Has God placed before women a test for reaching heaven that any female animal can answer to? If this were true, then the childless widow, the old maid, and the barren wife, are all on the broad road to perdition, while ("tell it not in Gath!")¹ the reckless mother who omitted the preliminary marriage ceremony, is in the narrow way that leads to everlasting life. No! women are NOT saved from death in childbirth, nor are they spiritually saved merely by the animal process of giving birth to children. Women are saved from their sins, and are saved for heaven precisely on the same terms as men, and on no other and on *no additional* terms; for God is no respecter of persons. What Paul says here, as literally translated from the Greek, and as it appears in the R. V., is, *"She* [woman] *shall be saved by* the *childbearing,"*—that is, by the birth of a Redeemer into the world. This we believe is what is referred to in this verse,—see Prof. James Orr's remark, end of par. 515.

344. But Paul adds very important conditions beyond the mere birth of a Redeemer into the world, with which Christian women must comply before their *social* redemption will be wrought out, *"If they continue in faith and love and sanctification with sobriety"* (R. V.). Alas! women did not "continue." It seems clear that within fifty years after Paul's utterance, they had largely yielded their faith,—that they were to be saved on precisely the

160

same conditions as men sinners:. They accepted the mischievous teaching that in addition to meeting the conditions laid down for men sinners, they must do penance for the sin of Eve (as though Christ's atonement had not been sufficient for Eve's trangression). Faith went; love and loyalty to Jesus Christ and His atonement waned; and finally they accepted a precisely opposite condition to the one laid down by Paul so impressively,—*"with sobriety."* They have now, through the weary generations since, too often bent themselves to the task of winning approval from God, by yielding all their nobler instincts towards pure living within the marriage relation to the sensual "desire" of their husbands, in mistaken obedience to the misinterpretation of Gen. 3:16. The meaning of the Greek word translated *"sobriety,"* we set forth as "self-restraint" (see par. 327.) The word is *sophrosune,* and 4 Maccabees 1:31 tells us, *"sophrosune is the mastery of the lusts."* Several sayings in the Greek classics tell us the same. Paul declares, and we are sure it is the truth of God, this self-control is an essential in woman's social redemption. Woman can never be matured as a useful instrument in God's hands, or an efficient servant of His Church, until she comes to understand that "she is not her own; she is bought with a price," and it is neither her duty nor her privilege to *give herself* away to any human being,— in marriage or in any other way. Her bodily appetites are subject to God's control, and cannot be indulged in violation of conscience; any other teaching is but teaching woman how to be a pleasing slave. There is no social redemption for woman until the chain that binds her to the lusts of her own, and of man's flesh is broken, and she maintains the inviolability of free-will, as her *sustained attitude* towards every human being, including her husband. There is no method of moral improvement remaining, after the loss of a free will. To attempt to accept any means or method of salvation from sin different from or beyond the simple act of accepting Christ's atonement for sin,—be that act "circumcision," which Paul so strongly denounced, or woman's service in the lusts of the flesh, is to accept a condition in which *"Christ shall profit you nothing," "Christ has become of no effect unto you,"* Gal. 5:2, 3.

345. It is generally the case that after man has discovered a truth for himself, he is in danger through self-

interest of denying that the same truth applies to woman. Instance, the present-day political axiom that "taxation without representation is tyranny." Luther, who established for the Protestant Church the truism: "It is a great error to seek ourselves to satisfy God's justice for our sins, for God ever pardons them freely by an inestimable grace," never paused to think that as to women this is true also. To the present day, the women of the Protestant Church are taught by Bible commentators to keep to penance (seek to satisfy God's justice) for Eve's sin by silence in the Church and obedience to man.

LESSON 46.

NEEDLESS APOLOGIES FOR PAUL'S LOGIC.

346. Now what alternative have we to this view that Paul is giving advice suited to a great emergency,—and that he *is not* arguing for the perpetual silencing and subordination of woman? We have, according to expositors, the statement that the very Apostle who spent so much time combating the "Jewish fables" of the Judaizers, was himself very deeply dyed by the same school,—for it is impossible to escape from the representation that Paul indulged freely in frivolous Jewish sophistries here, unless we conclude that *someone else* has interlined Paul's teaching with interested sophistries. For instance, Calvin says of the argument, "Adam was formed first:" "Yet the reason which Paul assigns, that woman was second in the order of creation, appears not to be a very strong argument for her subjection, for John the Baptist was before Christ in order of time, and yet was greatly inferior in rank,"—and Calvin might have added: "Every man has a mother who was made before himself, and yet she is held to be his inferior." Or, if Paul referred to the primary act of creation, "Cows were made before men—even before theologians, —men must be subordinated to cows." For our part, we should sooner believe that the expositor has made use of unworthy sophistries than that Paul has done so.

347. According to the view that Paul is enforcing rabbinical teachings, as Kalisch says, "The New Testament is . . . even more rigorous than the Old; for whilst it commands the woman 'to learn in silence with all subjection but not to teach, nor to usurp authority over the

man, but to be in silence,' she was in the Old Testament, admitted to the highest office of teaching, that of prophets, as Miriam, Deborah and Huldah." But we would rather believe that the expositor is mistaken, than that the very term "Gospel,"—"Good News,"—proclaims oppression to women, such as was not enforced under Old Testament Law.

348. Sometimes the expositor, content with Paul's *ruling* but uneasy over Paul's *reasonings,* as he represents them, attempts to apologize. Says Prof. Reynolds of verse 13, "This may sound to our ears a far-fetched argument, when used to discountenance female usurpation of intellectual supremacy. It was, however, a method current at the time to look for and find in the Scriptures the concrete expression of almost all philosophical judgment." That sounds very wise. But we are accustomed to believe that the Holy Spirit prompted Paul's writing; and we do not believe the Spirit needed to study rabbinical rubbish to suggest a reason for silencing and subordinating women. Dire indeed must have been the want of a reason, before Paul could have contented himself to produce those attributed to him!

349. The Apostle who wrote the sustained logic of the Epistle to the Romans, and who either wrote the lucid arguments of the Epistle to the Hebrews, or was instructor of the one who wrote them, did not need to resort to what he himself spoke of with utter contempt, —"Jewish fables"—and warned Timothy to shun, to find a pretext for silencing women. If he did silence them, he had an *honest* reason for doing so, and could have found proper language in which to express that reason. A grave responsibility rests upon those who subject Paul to ridicule, and the Bible to suspicion as to its worth, by trying to support sophistries by lame apologies for Paul. We do not admit for one moment that either the Apostle or the Bible in general needs any apology. Let the expositor consent to give up the attempt to prove egotistical and foregone conclusions, and Paul's language becomes perfectly lucid and consistently Christian. We have shown that Paul did not argue for the subordination of woman to man; he did not argue that Eve was more guilty than Adam. He only recommended temporary "quietness" on the part of women in the Church because there was special peril to the Church and to

woman in contrary conditions. The Neronian persecutions were on, and the virtue of Christian women threatened.

350. Yet, still persisting in the inference that Paul silences and subordinates all women, for all time, Prof. Ramsay, in *The Expositor,* in the year 1909, pronounces Paul's language in this place, "A quaint example of the way in which the Jews were wont to derive arguments from Scripture, and to twist and torture its words, in order to support the opinions which they were stating. Even where Paul is expressing a truth which he sees clearly with direct and unerring intuition, he sometimes draws from the Old Testament arguments which to us seem tortuous special pleading and quite valueless as reasoning.' The Jewish mind reasoned in a totally different way from us; and by its line of reasoning often offends us. But we must not identify the truth of the opinion with the validity of the reasoning, or conclude that, because the argument is so unconvincing, the opinion is therefore untrue. Accordingly, we may set aside as not appealing to our minds, and barely intelligible to us, the argument drawn from the conduct of Adam and Eve. So far as it is intelligible, it fails to strengthen Paul's case in the judgment of modern readers. But his case is quite independent of the argument."

351. We are very glad that "in the judgment of modern readers" the case for the subordination and silencing of women, has not been strengthened by the arguments *attributed* to Paul, for we now take hope that the expositors will presently perceive that such flimsy arguments are not Paul's at all, but the work of manipulators of Paul's language. Paul has not twisted Scripture; rather, men have twisted Paul's arguments out of conformity with Scripture. But there is hope, if expositors once begin to acknowledge the twist in the language. Prof. Ramsay assumes that Paul's argument is bad, but his conclusion from the bad argument is true. But a bad tree cannot bring forth good fruit. When once the fact is recognized that man's dominion over woman is a piece of property vested in a faulty title-deed, men cannot struggle against a guilty conscience; and woman has God on her side of the contest. Hence we conclude that between the two courses, either to admit that Paul was arguing for something else, or to contend that Paul was arguing dishonestly, by twisting Scripture (for the

silencing and subordination of woman), it is far more honouring to Paul and reverent towards God and His Word, to repudiate the latter view of the case and to accept the former.

352. We have shown that a consistent, worthy sense can be found in Paul's words to Timothy about women, quite apart from the idea that he is upholding rabbinical sophistries. But Prof. Ramsay, not to quote others of like views, accuses Paul of "tortuous special pleading" in order to support the teaching (which belongs to rabbinism) that woman is subordinate to man. No one can deny that tortuous special pleading has been employed in enforcing such teaching by means of this Timothy passage. That fact is self-evident: but we deny that Paul is the guilty party, who has handled the word of God deceitfully. We lay the charge at the door of the "Judaizers" of the early church; and masculine interpreters, for (perhaps unconscious) self-interested reasons, have adopted that ready-made tortuous special pleading of the "Judaizers," whose mischievous influence in the church, Paul himself contended against daily throughout his entire ministry. He warned and prophesied against them as follows: *"I know this, that after my departing shall grievous wolves enter in among you, not sparing the flock"* (Acts 20:29). He denounced them and their teachings a score of times in his various epistles; and after Paul's day, Peter wrote warning the Christians against those who wrested the words of Paul's epistles "unto their own destruction," 2 Pet. 3:15, 16.

353. Paul declared of himself, in 2 Cor. 4:2, 3: *"Seeing we have this ministry . . . we . . . have renounced the hidden things of dishonesty, not walking in craftiness, nor handling the word of God deceitfully."* In order to accept the view that Paul fell into "tortuous special pleading" such as characterized the "Judaizers" of those days, we must believe, then, much more than merely that Paul "twists and tortures" (to use Prof. Ramsay's words) the language of Scripture. We must believe that the Holy Spirit who inspired Paul's writings, has given way to a lying spirit, and that when Paul makes this declaration concerning himself, he was not truthful; and we hold no such opinion of Paul.

LESSON 47.

CONCLUDING REMARKS ON THE HEADSHIP OF THE HUSBAND.

354. If the headship of the husband, then, does not imply government by the husband, why is the wife exhorted to "be in subjection" to her husband, rather than the husband to the wife? Because the real meaning of the word "subjection" refers, not to servility, but to conciliation. Where wrong exists, or is supposed to exist, the Christian method is always to exhort the wronged one to efforts to keep the peace, if possible, until the wrong-doer learns the better way. Read 1 Pet. 2:18-23 for light on this point: note the transition to 3:1, especially the word "likewise." The "subjection" urged is toward a wayward, not Christian, husband. So the Apostle Paul, in Ephesians, fifth chapter, exhorts the wife, who is the one likely to suffer wrong, to one set of duties, summed up in the word "subjection;" and the husband to another set of duties, because he is the one inclined to oppress. The husband is to show that love which gives itself for the good of another.

355. But the expositor wrongly interprets Paul's *intention,* in the use of the word "subjection." Let us illustrate: In China, for centuries past, mothers have felt compelled to bind the feet of their girls in order to prepare them for the matrimonial market. This custom is now yielding before the humane influences of the Christian religion, and mothers, with the support of the men of their families, refuse to bind the feet of their daughters, and often unbind their own. But the problem of having free feet is one thing to the daughter, whose feet have *never* been bound, and quite another to the mother, whose feet *have been bound* for years. The reason is, that the very bandages which have so weakened and crippled the feet, have, in the course of time, become an *essential support* to the weakened members; so that, when the woman medical missionary unbinds the feet of the Chinese mother, she must remove the old bandages, *and then put on fresh bandages,*—this time, binding each individual toe to its individual splint,—*only* until it can go free of all support.

356. Now this latter is a process of binding, but it is done with an *opposite view* to the original foot-binding.

It looks to the restoration of lost freedom, while the old process aggressively deprived of freedom. It is, moreover, in the very nature of things, a process wholly unsuitable to the girl whose feet have never been bound. Would it be fair, now, or truthful, because of this *temporary device,* looking to eventual complete freedom, which the doctor adopts, to represent the woman doctor as favourable to foot-binding? Yet, precisely after this manner has St. Paul been misrepresented by those willing to justify male rule. They ignore Paul's declared object; they are silent as to Paul's clear utterances elsewhere, as to *"the glorious liberty of the children of God;"* they disdain the guards Paul puts about his words, and pervert his meaning.

357. Such words as, *"There is neither Jew nor Greek, bond nor free, male nor female,"* convey small authority to their minds; but because Paul has twice reminded the wife that her husband is her "head" ("support," see par. 282), therefore would these expositors permanently rebind upon women the very burdens of oppression which Paul would remove from their bowed backs. This false representation of the Apostle's intention has led many people into irreverent ridicule of the Bible and Paul; and the perverters of Paul's meaning are responsible for this. Paul does not speak as an "old bachelor," but as the mouth-piece of God. Nor is he labouring under the blight of rabbinical training. Paul speaks under the influence of the Holy Spirit, and can be easily understood, with the Spirit's help, by those who care to understand him rightly. Any other representation of his words is irreverent.

358. The Apostle, then, realizing the difficulties under a pagan government, and under civil laws unjust to women, first declares that within the Church bandages of oppression must be removed, but that the bond of matrimony must be carefully conserved (*"Let marriage be held in honor of all"*); wives must be patient; and husbands be used as individual splints to each broken and crushed woman. The revolutionary ethics of a Christlike love would shortly accomplish all the rest. Like his Master, Paul came *"to proclaim liberty to the captive,"* by his Gospel message,—not to proclaim captivity to the captive. Paul's goal for women, as much as for men, is *"the glorious liberty of the children of God,"* and he declares it in many ways, again and again; and when

once that goal has been attained by women, the *method* is obsolete and meaningless. In Christian lands, in *real* Christian homes, special injunctions upon the wife to "be in subjection" to her husband, are out of place,— the method has accomplished its work; oppression is gone; the liberty is wrought out.

359. Let us turn now to Ephesians, fifth chapter in the R. V. Verse 22 reads, *"Wives [be in subjection] unto your own husbands, as unto the Lord."* Note first that the words we bracket are not in the original. The duty is the same one that was already laid upon all Christians by verse 21, and this does not design to extend the duties of the wife to indefinite proportions, but to limit them. The form is equivalent to Col. 3:18, concerning the same set of duties, *"as is fit in the Lord"*. Subjection, to Paul's mind, could go beyond what is "fit." For when false brethren came to him and gave him bad counsel, he declares, *"to whom we gave place by subjection, no, not for an hour."* Yes, this Apostle who taught all believers to "be in subjection" one to another, as did Peter also (I Pet. 5:5), declares even of Peter, *"I withstood him to his face, because he was to be blamed,"* (Gal. 2:3-5, 11). An *unqualified* subjection of one to another has never been enjoined upon man or woman Christian, by the Bible.

360. Very different is Milton's teaching from the Apostle Paul's, to women:
> *"To whom thus Eve, with perfect beauty adorn'd:*
> *'My author and disposer, what thou bidd'st*
> *Unargued I obey: so God ordains;*
> *God is thy law, thou mine; to know no more*
> *Is woman's happiest knowledge, and her praise.'"*

Such teaching as this puts man in the very place of God. It is the spirit of Antichrist who *"sitteth in the temple of God, setting himself forth as God"* (2 Thess. 2:4 R. V.). It also teaches woman that most hateful of all sins, to God, idolatry.

361. If the Apostle does not especially enjoin "subjection" on husbands, as such, it is because he has occasion to set forth more important duties on his part. Verse 23 of this passage in Ephesians tells him that, like his Lord, he is to be to his wife, *"the saviour of the body."* How free and chaste Paul intends her to be! Verse 25 teaches an utter self-renunciation, like Christ's, for her

168

sake. Verse 26, that by his own cleansed and sanctified fleshly nature, he is to *"sanctify and cleanse"* his wife's body, so as to be prepared in the end to present her spotless (verse 27) to Christ,—free from all moral injury by his conduct. Verse 28 teaches him to love his wife as he loves his own body, i. e., to nourish and cherish her. The opposite conduct—the oppression of lust—is to hate her. Verse 31: He (not she) is to forsake all others, and to cleave to her alone. See pars. 45-64.

362. Woman's only century, in the Christian Church, was during apostolic days, and a little while thereafter. Prof. Ramsay, in his valuable book, *The Church in the Roman Empire,* states: "The Universal and Catholic type of Christianity became confirmed in its dislike of the prominence and the public ministration of woman. The dislike became abhorrence, and there is every probability that the dislike is as old as the first century, and was intensified to abhorrence before the middle of the second century." With the growth of this abhorrence, we may rest assured that every conceivable effort would be made to find a warrant for silencing and subordinating women; and the "Judaizer" was at hand to point the method of torturing and twisting Scripture, especially Paul's words, into teaching the same. Here we have, in a few words, the history of that "tortuous special pleading" which enables conclusions to seem to be drawn from arguments presented by Paul; arguments which, if rightly read, and interpreted by unbiased minds, would lead to very different opinions of the Apostle Paul and his teachings on the "woman question."

LESSON 48.

"DIVERS WEIGHTS AND MEASURES."

363. Expositors of the Bible will never be able to understand, or to set forth a clear, consistent, correct interpretation of the Word of God as regards women until they abandon, once for all, the attempt to found the social, ecclesiastical and spiritual (as far as this life is concerned) status of Christian woman on the Fall, and found it, as they do man's social, ecclesiastical and spiritual status, on the atonement of Jesus Christ. They cannot, for women, put the "new wine" of the Gospel into the old wine-skins of "condemnation" before God's

law. The skins burst, the wine is spilled; and such "theology" is responsible for much "free-thought" among justice-loving persons, who confuse the teaching of the expositors with the teaching of the Bible,, and denounce the latter instead of the former.

364. The Lord says, through the mouth of Moses, *"Thou shalt not have in thy bag divers weights, a great and a small,"* Duet. 25:13; and Proverbs 20:10 teaches us: *"Divers weights and divers measures, both of them are alike abomination to the Lord."* It seems to us that divers weights and measures have been employed, occasionally, when translating the utterances of the Bible. For instance, the word for "minister, deacon," *diakonos,* is used, properly, of a helper of any sort who is not a slave. It occurs 30 times in the N. T., and is almost always rendered "minister." It is translated "servant" only 7 times and "deacon" 3 times, and "minister" 20 times. We will notice only those instances in which it *may,* or certainly does, refer to an ecclesiastical office,— Rom. 15:8; 1 Cor. 3:5; 2 Cor. 3:6; 6:4; 11:23; Eph. 3:7; 6:21; Col. 1:7, 23, 25; 4:7; 1 Thess. 3:2; 1 Tim. 4:6 (rendered "minister"). And Phil. 1:1; 1 Tim. 3:8, 12 ("deacon"). But in Rom. 16:1, where the Apostle Paul says: *"I commend unto you Phebe our sister, who is* diakonos *of the church which is at Cenchrea,"* referring, beyond all possibility of a doubt, to her status in the church, the A. V. translates "servant" (the R. V. margin translates "deaconess"). Bishop Lightfoot speaks of the mistranslation, "servant" in this place. He also gives strong reasons for believing that 1 Tim. 3:11 refers also to women deacons, and adds: "If the testimony borne in these two passages to a ministry of women in the Apostolic times had not been thus blotted out of our English Bibles, attention would probably have been directed to the subject at an earlier date, and our English church would not have remained so long maimed of one of her hands." We suppose the Bishop's thoughts went no further than to the thought of a needed order of "deaconesses," when he penned these words. But they apply with greater force all the way along to woman's full equality with man in the ministry of the Gospel,— for until that point is reached, the Church will ever be maimed of one of her hands in her struggle with the world, the flesh and the devil.

365. It was not until the middle of the third century that an order of women called "deaconesses" (*diakonissae*) became common in the churches of the East; they were scarcely ever known in the early centuries in the Western branch of the Church. Speaking of the rendering of this title attached to Phebe's name,—"deaconess," Bishop Ellicott says: "The proposed rendering 'deaconess' is open to the objection that it introduces into the N. T. the technical name (*diakonissa*), which is of later origin."

366. Conybeare and Howson, in their *Life of St. Paul*, (p. 240), call attention to the use, in connection with Phebe's name, of two words associated together in technical legal matters, in Paul's recommendation of her, which indicate that she was abroad on some important business with the courts,—possibly in behalf of the church. Yet with all this, our translators found no difficulty in levelling her down to the "servant" class. But Paul calls her, *not* a "deaconess" but a "deacon," a "minister." In the Apostolical Constitutions (a third century document of the Church), "deaconesses" are referred to; but here we have the "deacon" or "minister" of the Church. Paul uses precisely the same form of the word that he does in such passages as 1 Tim. 3:8, 12. This goes a long way toward proving that when he gave directions as to ordaining "deacons" he made no distinction as to sex, in his own mind. To be sure, he had to caution Timothy about ordaining any men who were polygamous (women were not likely to have two husbands), which gives such passages more of a masculine twist than they otherwise would have had.

367. What Paul says of Phebe as a *prostatis* (translated "succourer," literally meaning "one standing before"), proves that she was of no *inferior order* in the Church. Had the words been given the *strong cast* into which they are run, when (supposedly) spoken of men only, in 1 Tim. 3:12, we should be reading here about Phebe, in our English Bibles: *"I commend unto you Phebe our sister, minister* [or deacon] *of the church which is at Cenchrea; . . . for she hath been a* ruler *of many, and of myself also."* This is the noun form corresponding to the verb translated "rule" in the Timothy passages (1 Tim. 3:4, 5, 12; and 5; 17), where Paul is supposed to be commanding that these men "rule well" their own households. We have only to say that if these men are to "rule" their households, then Paul tells us that Phebe ruled himself and many others; but if it be impossible to concede that Paul was ruled by a woman, then it is equally impossible, by every law of truthful and just translation, to prove that these passages in Timothy instruct men to "rule well" their households. The translators cannot have it both ways. The Greek noun used of Phebe, *prostatis*, means a "champion, leader, chief, protector, patron." Phebe held the same relation to the church at Cenchrea, that Paul says church officials should hold to their own children and household,—that is, they should take good care of them; these passages have no direct reference to rule, or government. In Tit. 3:8, 14, the word is translated "maintain." When a man is told to "stand before," his family "well," men translate the word "rule." When the Bible tells us that Phebe is a "stander-before" they translate "succourer."

368. Now let us again draw a contrast, between this word "to stand before" translated "rule," when spoken of men, and a certain word translated "guide," because spoken of women. Men often talk of the father and husband as the "final authority" in the home. What says St. Paul on the point? The Greek word for "despot" (*despotes*) furnishes us with our English word. Its meaning is precisely the same in Greek as it is in English. It means an absolute and arbitrary ruler, from whom there can be no appeal. It was the title slaves were required to use in addressing the master who owned them as property. Please read all the passages in which this Greek word *despotes* occurs. It is rendered "Master" in the following places: 1 Tim. 6:1, 2; 2 Tim. 2:21; Tit. 2:9; 1 Pet. 2:18; "Lord" in Luke 2:29; Acts 4:24; 2 Pet. 2:1; Jude 4; and Rev. 6:10.

369. *Oikos* is a very ordinary word in Greek, meaning "house." These two words, *oikos* and *despotes,* unite to form the word *oikodespotes,* which, as you can see, means "master of the house," and it is so rendered, Matt. 10:25; Luke 13:25 and 14:21. Now the Apostle Paul makes use of a verb corresponding to this noun *oikodespotes,*—namely, "to master the house,"—*oikodespotein.* He says, 1 Tim. 5:14, *"I will that the younger women marry, bear childern,* oikodespotein, *give none occasion to the adversary to speak reproachfully."* After the analysis of this word, we can all see

how it should have been translated. The A. V., however, translates, *"guide the house"* the R. V., with a little more justice translates, *"rule the household."* Now whom, *if anyone,* does St. Paul make the "final authority in the home?" The woman. But we believe that Paul would teach that God alone is final authority in a Christain home.

370. The lesson is this: Expositors having once convinced themselves that Nature (they would not own to doing it themselves), has outlined a certain "sphere" for woman, whereas man is at liberty, under God, to outline his own "sphere;" and having convinced themselves that the Apostle Paul places teaching, preaching and governing outside women's "sphere,"—whatever supports this view as to woman's "sphere" is slightly (and sometimes more) exaggerated in our English translation; and what would stand out as proof against this masculine preconception is toned down in translation. This making use of *"divers weights and measures"* is an abomination in the sight of God (see pars. 616-644).

LESSON 49.

OUR FAITH MUST REPOSE IN THE ORIGINAL TEXT.

371. We have called attention to some of these misinterpretations, as well as mistranslations of the Bible, as to women. But a certain type of mind is sure to reason: "What am I to believe, then? And *whom* am I to believe?"—as though it were ever intended that our faith should rest in human beings,—uninspired, as these translators are, as well! Let us hope, however, that the majority of those who will read these Lessons will rather say, "We must never rest until we have seen to it that a sufficiently large number of young women are kept in training in the sacred languages, so that women can always command a hearing, as to the precise meaning of such passages in the Bible as relate to the interests of women specially. Thus only will women's temporal and spiritual interests receive their due consideration." Better, *far better,* that we should doubt every translator of the Bible than to doubt the inspiration of St. Paul's utterances about women; and the justice of God towards women; or, above all, to doubt that "Christ hath re-

deemed us" (women) "from the curse of the law" (Gal. 3:13).

372. Recalling Dean Payne-Smith's words about Bible interpreters, "Men never do understand anything unless already in their minds they have some kindred ideas," it is not worth our while to complain that men have not always seen truths that had no special application to their needs, either in interpreting or in translating the Bible; we merely wish to point out wherein there is need of changes. Supposing *women only* had translated the Bible, from age to age, is there a likelihood that men would have rested content with the outcome? Therefore, our brothers have no good reason to complain if, while conceding that men have done the best they could alone, we assert that they did not do *the best that could have been done.* The work would have been of a much higher order had they first helped women to learn the sacred languages, (instead of putting obstacles in their way), and then, have given them a place by their side on translation committees.

373. The same writer says, again: "A bad translation of this book [the Bible] exercises a depressing influence upon a nation's advance in civilization: a good translation is one of the great levers in the nation's rise." We believe that the very reason why we see so large a proportion of the women of Christendom, in our day, given over to fashion and folly, is precisely because they have never been given a proper and dignified work in the advancement of God's kingdom,—since the first century of the Christian Church. And the true value of woman's powers will never be known so long as her self-respect is destroyed by teaching her that she rests under God's curse, and is bound to remain in perpetual subordination to her husband, even when he happens to be a fool or a scamp; and this is what the Church unconsciously teaches in its sweeping assertions as to woman's "subordination" to her husband,—never pausing to define (even if this were true), *what sort of a husband* is entitled to act as her superior and ruler.

374. The end of Gen. 3:16 reads: *"He will rule over thee,"*—a prophecy that has been abundantly fulfilled. There is no third person imperative form of the verb in Hebrew, and the ancient versions testify that this expression is a simple future (see pars. 273-274). But

what has transpired? It is rendered *"He shall,* as though imperative. We repeat Prof. Moulton's words: "The use of *shall* when prophecy is dealing with future time is often particularly unfortunate. I have heard of an intelligent child who struggled under perplexity for several years because of the words, *'Thou shalt deny Me thrice.'* it could not therefore be Peter's fault, if Jesus commanded him! The child's determinism is probably more widely shared than we think" . . . "for instance, in such a passage as Mark 13:24-27 we have *shall* seven times where in modern English we should undeniably use will." Can we even imagine the wonderful lightening of the burden, if women opened their Bible merely to read *precisely* what the Hebrew says of man: *"He will rule over thee?"* Or, if instead of reading, *"No MAN can serve two masters,"* we could read what Christ meant,—*"No ONE can serve two masters."* But in cases of the latter sort, where the common gender is expressed by the masculine form, the masculine interpreter and translator is accustomed to take as exclusively his own so much as he seets fit; and to translate as of common application that which prejudice dictates that he may safely accede to women also,—though he may hotly deny the imputation. He is wholly unconscious of any such offence against the truth, merely because no woman is allowed to sit by his side, when translating, to recall him from the error of his ways. Archdeacon Farrar says: "A translator has the need of invincible honesty if he would avoid the misleading influences of his own *a priori* convictions." Speaking of "the fierce temptations which the faith of the interpreter must resist," he illustrates it by Luther's throwing his inkstand at the devil, when doing such work. He continues, "Few are the translators, fewer the exegetes . . . to abstain from finding in the Bible thoughts which it does not contain, and rejecting or unjustly modifying the thoughts which are indeed there."

375. This being the truth as regards translations, what are we to do? "Learn to read and judge of the original for ourselves," is our first answer. But all women *cannot* do this, even if they would. Then we would reply in the words of an eminent Scotch divine, "If we find even in the Bible anything which confuses our sense of right and wrong, that seems to us less exalted and pure than the character of God should be: if after the

most patient thought and prayerful pondering it still retains that aspect, *then we must not bow down to it as God's revelation to us,* since it does not meet the need of the earlier and more sacred revelation He has given us in our spirit and conscience which testify of Him." We must remember that no translation can rise much above the character of the translator,—who must be chosen, not simply because of his reputation for unprejudiced honesty, but for learning too. He cannot properly render what has not as yet entered in the least into his own consciousness as the truth; and the Holy Spirit invariably refuses to seal to us as *truth* that which is *error.* Rather, He will warn us against accepting the error, even though it appears on the page of our Bible translation.

376. But surely, enough has been revealed to us, in the poorest translation, for the securing of our spiritual salvation, and communion with God,—so we need not be disturbed, if, after doing our very *best,* we feel, at a given passage, uncertain. The likelihood is that every translation falls to a lower level than it would, but for the personal faults and personal prejudices of the translators. But as Bishop Butler has said, "The age-long misinterpretations of the Bible are no more disproof of its authority, than the age-long misinterpretations of Nature are any disproof of its Divine creation."

377. We must recall that every translator of the Bible, throughout Church history has been a male;* and sex bias came into existence very early in human history. In fact the sin in the garden at once affected the love between the sexes, and Adam sought to show excellence beyond Eve. Says the German divine, Dr. Lange, in his Commentary on Genesis: "The guilt proper is rolled upon woman [by Adam], and indirectly upon God Himself . . . The loss of love that comes out in this interposing of his wife is, moreover, particularly denoted in this, that he grudges to call her Eve or my wife . . . 'That woman by my side, *she* who was given to [be with] me of God as a trusty counsellor, *she* gave me the fruit.' " . . . "An acknowledgement of sin by Adam, but

* This statement is not absolute; women (a few) have translated a part of the Bible, or the whole. But their work is ignored, and allowed to perish. But we refer here to those translators who have been on Translation Committees, or whose work has been allowed a place of influence in the Church.

not true and sincere." Secondly, Adam generated, by his unholy ambition, a desire to be *"as God"* which will never cease to exist in human nature until that Wicked One *"sets himself forth as God,"* in the very Temple of God, and is destroyed by Christ's second coming. And since sex bias is of old, and also the masculine desire to rule, every version of the Bible, beginning with the first one—the Septuagint Greek version—reflects from its pages the sinful nature, in this regard, of those who have made the translation. It is beyond our province, however, to enter upon all the versions,—only upon the English.

LESSON 50.

LESSONS IN HUMILITY.

378. Servility and weakness are two contemptible vices. They have been too often recommended to women clothed in the names of "humility" and "meekness," to which virtues they are as opposed as north is to south. Presently we shall have a lesson on that badge of royalty, meekness; today we will risk a charge of being unoriginal by giving a lesson in "humility" in the language of Rev. Andrew Murray and Rev. Wm. Law.

379. Surely it is hardly necessary for us to explain here that there are, and always have been male Christian teachers who, like the above-mentioned Christian ministers, by example as well as precept, have shown the beauty and importance of these virtues in men as well as women. Let us say, *once for all,* that in noting the general unfairness and unscripturalness of masculine expositors, it is not incumbent upon us to pause at each step in order to call attention to exceptions. Suffice it to say, such expositors *are* exceptions, as far as the "woman question" is concerned. We are glad to make use of the language of the above-mentioned male religious teachers, as showing that our representation of the hatefulness of the sin of the love of preeminence in no wise goes beyond what good men have taught.

380. Says Mr. Murray: "No tree can grow except on the root from which it sprang. Through all its existence it can only live with the life that was in the seed that gave it being. The full apprehension of this truth in its application to the first and the Second Adam

177

cannot but help us greatly to understand both the need
and the nature of the redemption there is in Jesus."

381. "When the Old Serpent . . spoke his words of
temptation into the ears of Eve, these words carried with
them the very poison of hell. And when she listened,
and yielded her desire and her will to the prospect of
being as God, the poison entered into her soul and blood
and life. . . All the wretchedness of which this world
has been the scene, all its wars and bloodshed among the
nations, all its selfishness and suffering, all its ambitions
and jealousies, all its broken hearts and embittered lives,
all its daily unhappiness, have their origin in what this
cursed, hellish pride, either our own, or that of others,
has brought us." . . . *

382. "Even as we need to look to the first Adam and
his fall to know the power of sin within us, we need to
know well the Second Adam and His power to give
within us a life of humility as real and abiding and over-
mastering as has been that of pride . . . In this view
it is of inconceivable importance that we should have
right thoughts of what Christ is, and of what may be
counted His chief characteristic, the root and essence
of all His character as our Redeemer. There can be
but one answer: it is His humility. What is the incarnation but His heavenly humility, His emptying Himself
and becoming man? What is His life on earth but
humility? 'He humbled Himself and became obedient
unto death.' And what His ascension and His glory,
but humility exalted to the throne and crowned with
glory? 'He humbled Himself, therefore God highly
exalted Him.' In heaven, where He was with the
Father, in His birth, in His life, in His death, in His
sitting on the throne, it is all, it is nothing but humility.
Christ is the humility of God embodied in human nature; the Eternal Love humbling itself, clothing itself in
the garb of meekness and gentleness, to win and serve
and save us. As the love and condescension of God
makes Him the benefactor and helper and servant of all,
so Jesus of necessity was the Incarnate Humility. And
so He is still in the midst of the throne, the meek and
lowly Lamb of God."

---

* **Humility,** Rev. Andrew Muray, chapter 2.
    We need hardly say, in this connection, that it was not,
however, through Eve that the desire to be "as God" became
current in the human family,—see Lesson 12.

"If this be the root of the tree, its nature must be seen in every branch and leaf and fruit. If humility be the first, the all-including grace of the life of Jesus,—if humility be the secret of His atonement,—then the health and strength of our spiritual life will depend entirely upon our putting this grace first too, and making humility the chief thing we admire in Him, the chief thing we ask of Him, the one thing for which we sacrifice all else . . . Until a humility which will rest in nothing less than the end and death of self; which gives up all the honor of men as Jesus did, to seek the honor that comes from God alone; which absolutely makes and counts itself nothing, that God may be all, that the Lord alone may be exalted,—until such a humility be what we seek in Christ above our chief joy, and welcome at any price, there is very little hope of a religion that will conquer the world."

383. "I cannot too earnestly plead with my reader, if possibly his attention has never yet been specially directed to the want there is of humility within him or around him, to pause and ask whether he sees much of the spirit of the meek and lowly Lamb of God in those who are called by His name . . . and his eyes will be opened to see how a dark, shall I not say a devilish pride, creeps in almost everywhere, the assemblies of the saints not excepted. Let him begin to ask what would be the effect, if in himself and around him, if towards fellow-saints and the world, believers were really and permanently guided by the humility of Jesus."

384. Mr. Law says: "Pride and humility are the two master powers, the two kingdoms in strife for the eternal possession of man. There never was, nor ever will be, but one humility, and that is the one humility of Christ. Pride and self have the all of man, till man has his all from Christ. He therefore only fights the good fight whose strife is that the self-idolatrous nature which he hath from Adam may be brought to death by the supernatural humility of Christ brought to life in him,—" *Address to the Clergy, p. 52.*

385. What an utter contrast to such teaching as this, of the grace of humility, is that sort of artificial instruction forbidding man to wear "the sign of subjection" because he is *"the glory of God;"* and which would put a veil on woman "in sign that she is under the power of

179

her husband" (inserted by those who wish it were in the Bible, into the marginal reading of 1 Cor. 11:10)! In the first teaching there is that which seals it to our inmost consciousness as *truth;* in the second teaching honest men and women cannot find rest for the sole of the foot. We all know something is wrong with it; and the falsity of the latter teaching must ever be suspected so long as it is set forth. Had uninducted women read and pondered Paul's language for the first time, we are perfectly safe in saying it would never have occurred to them that Paul meant anything so extraordinary.

386. Men, by such teaching, vaunt themselves as the superiors of wife and mother. Women have not the right to content themselves as nourishers of such masculine weaknesses. *"Thou shalt in any wise rebuke thy neighbor, and not suffer sin upon him,"* Lev. 19:17, is the teaching even of the Old Testament. The words of Jesus Christ are even a more stern commandment: *"Take heed to yourselves: if thy brother trespass against thee, rebuke him; and if he repent, forgive him,"*— Luke 17:3. There is something most weak and unworthy in woman's acquiescence in man's pride and egotism, for the sake of not incurring man's displeasure. But at the same time let us see to it that when men vaunt themselves in our presence we do not add a wrong spirit to the wrong conduct on their part, and angrily speak otherwise than in kindness. Above all, let us not "sin their sin" and be guilty of the same offense, by vaunting ourselves. We will be accused of this, at any rate, even if we should do no more than our duty and administer rebuke.

(To be Continued).

LESSON 51.

LESSONS IN HUMILITY (Concluded).

387. We will let another define "humility". Andrew Murray defines it as "nothing but that simple consent of the creature to let God be all, in virtue of which it surrenders itself to His working alone." Speaking of Christ, our example, he says: "His humility was simply the surrender of himself to God, to allow [God] to do to Him what He pleased, whatever men might say of him, or do to him."

388. Please notice thoughtfully a certain qualification in each of these definitions. In the first the creature *"surrenders itself to GOD ALONE;"* this is humility: in the second Christ does this, *"whatever men around Him might say of Him, or do to Him."* Now I ask, Is woman taught that it is "humility" for her to conduct herself after any such manner? Let us see. As to the first point, take, for instance, Dean Stanley's teaching (par. 221): "The authority of the husband is enthroned visibly upon her [the wife's] head in token that she belongs to the husband alone, and that she owes no allegiance to anyone besides, not even to the angels before the throne of God." Now Mr. Murray's definition as to humility speaks of GOD ALONE; Dean Stanley's definition of a wife's duty, as an allegiance to MAN ALONE. The first defines "humility;" the second defines "servility." Since true humility *excludes* surrender to man (according to Mr. Murray), it is perfectly evident that exclusive allegiance to man would prevent a woman from exercising true humility.

389. But this allegiance, or surrender, to man is not merely servility. Let us seek to discover what it really is. Supposing, in days of old, Queen Elizabeth had gone in procession through the streets of London, and a man had stepped forward and waved the Arms of Mary Stuart on a banner before her face,—what would have happened? This much at least: the cry of "treason" would have resounded through the air; we need not picture the further consequences.

390. A dispute for the throne has existed, between God and man, ever since in the Garden that ambition was fired in humanity to be "as God"; to be sure, it is a very foolish and impossible ambition on the part of man, which God, but for His long-suffering, might have ended long ago. Its culmination will be in the Lord's return to *"slay with the breath of His mouth"* this *"man of sin"* who sets himself forth *"as God,"*—2 Thess. 2:3-8. But this dispute is on, and what part in it shall women take, for at such a time the situation is both sensitive and critical? What will God wish His women to do? Dean Stanley answers in effect. "Let women show their humility, their willingness to take a lowly place; let them put on a veil to show they owe no allegiance but to MAN ALONE,—not even to God's own messengers, the angels before God's throne."

391. What madness for women to do this! And call it "humility!" What can be more arrogant, more bold and impudent, than to appear before one's awful Monarch tricked out in such a manner as to demonstrate to His Majesty and all His Court, that one is in allegiance with His rival? But Dean Stanley did not mean to teach all this, in so many details. Then what did he mean? Who knows, but Satan? Satan knew very well how to clothe an insult to God in the garments of "humility" and "womanliness." We observe that when an expositor and preacher of the Gospel wanders out of his path of duty "to preach Christ" as woman's one example of conduct, and preaches "womanliness" instead, he sets up an idol of his own creation for women to worship; he turns himself to folly. We imagine such expositors would have been pleased had God sent into the world, an additional *female* Christ, to set women a *female* example; but since God did not see fit to do so, women are under obligation to endeavor, as best they are able, to follow the "manly" example of Jesus Christ, and leave the consequences with God. This is woman's truly humble place. Any other is sham humility.

392. What was Christ's attitude toward man, seeing HE ALONE is woman's pattern? John 2:23-25 tells us plainly: *"Many believed in His name, when they saw the miracles which He did. But Jesus did not commit Himself unto them, because He knew all men, and needed not that any should testify of man: for He knew what was in man."* Let women do the same; they have here a very safe example to follow. What we know of "trust" in man must not go so far as to include the vitiation of our surrender to GOD ALONE. "What! a woman not trust her husband! Why, every husband *loves* a trusting wife; let her lean all her weight upon him. This is ideal marriage; any less trust than this will bring discord into the family." Possibly it will; in some cases, the husband may quarrel with his wife unless she trusts him to this idolatrous extent. A trust that *must* be exercised towards a husband, who threatens discord otherwise, is of the world's own kind. The Lord Himself said, *"I came not to send peace, but a sword."* We believe that family concord can be better preserved *apart from* a trust on the part of the wife which amounts to idolatry of her husband; but if not, let discord prevail: at least, leave the result of absolute sur-

render to God alone in the hands of Him who requires it of every human being.

393. There is a "trust" of which one can properly approve,—a reciprocal tie and duty between husband and wife. But this matter of the surrender of one's entire person and conscience to the keeping of another human being is *idolatry*.—a *deadly sin* against God. Love does not require it. Never man loved as Christ; never man trusted himself to man less than Christ did. The more He surrendered Himself to God, the more humble He was; and the less He committed Himself to man. Mark how He kept His conduct free from all human influences.

394. Even as a child of twelve, He lingers behind in the Temple, at His own discretion. His mother searches in vain for Him for several days. When found and reproached by her, He utters not a word of regret; rather, a gentle reproof that she did not at once know that He was "about His Father's business" (Luke 2:49). To be GOD'S ALONE meant literally to Him to be not man's in the least. Later in life, His mother and brothers come to Him when teaching, apparently to take Him away from the crowd. He does not even leave His place to speak with them, but utters a declaration of entire independence, as to *natural* kinship, in favor of spiritual ties (Matt. 12:46-50).

395. While letting God do what He pleased with Him, He made no concessions to man, "whatever men around might say of Him." How differently women have been taught! At every step expected to ask themselves, "How will this look, for a *woman?*" As though woman should do everything with reference to her *sex*, rather than with reference to her God!

LESSON 52.

WHAT IS MEEKNESS?

396. Meekness has nothing whatever to do with the vices, cowardice and weakness. No one can be meek who is not of royal blood; hence the quality is little understood, and, for the most part, confounding it with weakness, it is taught to women and children and slaves, and despised in men. As truly as our humility has its source in our attitude towards GOD ALONE, so has

the virtue of meekness. The first means loyalty to God ALONE as alone to be obeyed; the second means loyalty to GOD ALONE, as our Judge and King.

397. To be humble and obey God alone will surely bring tribulation to any human being, sooner or later. It is only a question of time, and we will discover that some human law contravenes God's laws. We are often told that the days of persecution are past and ended. But why have they ended? Because man has concluded to accept man's laws as God's whole will for him. He argues that the laws of his country must be accorded unquestioning obedience; that the laws of a husband must be met by unquestioning obedience by the wife; but it is as true to-day as it ever was that "traditions," i. e., man-made laws, ever "make void the commandments of God" at all inconvenient points, and it ever will be so.

398. Let a man or woman determine to wholly follow the Lord, and trouble brews for that person, and such will either get into tribulation, or effect a compromise to escape it. Now let us imagine such an one, who, like his Lord, gives uncompromising testimony, by word and deed, against all sham customs and wicked human legislation. Trouble follows, and now comes the opportunity for meekness. As the man determined to obey God ALONE, now must he allow God ALONE to defend him and avenge his wrongs, growing out of his obedience and loyalty. If the man do this, he is meek; if he turn to human means of defense or vengeance, he is not meek. Only those who know the King as Father, and have royal blood in their veins, are sufficiently "highborn" (because born of God) to endure the test. For this reason *meekness is that one virtue which has little reward until the Millennial Age,* excepting inward rest (Matt. 11:29).

399. What means that silence of Jesus before human potentates? *"Jesus held His peace,"* is the record of His conduct before the Sanhedrin, Matt. 26:63. Yet He did answer at one point—when He testified that He was the Christ, the Son of God (v. 64). A little later, Pilate asks Him, *"Art thou the King of the Jews?"* and He answers with a strong affirmative, but no other questions (Mark 15:2-5). Later, Jesus stands before Herod: *"He questioned Him in many words; but He*

answered him nothing," Luke 23:9. On one point He gives clear testimony, namely, He is the lawful King of the Jews, and the Son of the King of Kings; but He gives no testimony against His persecutors, nor in His own defense. His case has already been submitted to the Supremest Court for adjudication, and it is not within their power (John 19:11).

400. To Him there was but one kingdom, His Father's. His royal blood, and sojourn in a land of which He was not a citizen, forbade His submitting His case to their courts. Not that He was antagonistic to human laws, executed by human rulers, for the children of this world. But such laws were not intended for the children of the heavenly King,—certainly not for the only-begotten Son of that King. His royal blood was not to be overlooked.

Now does this conduct on His part show weakness or strength of character? There can be but one answer. This loyalty to a Royal Father on the part of Jesus Christ, both in His *obedience* to God alone, and appeal to God alone, is His crown of humility and meekness. Isaiah described it in the words, *"As a sheep before her shearers is dumb, so He openeth not His mouth"* (53:7). This meekness is displayed in the conduct of Moses, in that incident which sets him forth as *"meek above all the men upon the face of the earth."* Here we have, as Dr. Lange has said, "An intimation that he endured in silence and committed his justification to God." And God at once took up Moses' defence (Numbers Ch. 12).

401. As Christ's conduct in the court of human potentates, so was His manner towards common men: *"Who, when He was reviled, reviled not again; when He suffered, He threatened not; but committed Himself to Him [God] that judgeth righteously,"* 1 Pet. 2:23. He recognized but one King; He knew but one Judge; He knew but one Enforcer of law, just as He knew but one law (the Word of God) to be enforced; and God was His own interpreter and enforcer of His law.

402. It requires the utmost balance of Christian character to maintain such an attitude as this towards God and towards man; on the one hand, towards the Christian's King; on the other, towards the rule founded upon military power for this world. The Apostles tell us,

185

"Submit yourselves . . to the king . . unto governors," (1 Pet. 2:13, 14;) *"Let every soul be subject unto the higher powers,"* and *"Put them in mind to be subject to principalities and powers"* (Rom. 13:1; Tit. 3:1). Christ enforced the same lesson, Matt. 5:41, by saying that when compelled to go one mile we must be ready to go two; if sued at court and forced to give his coat to an oppressor, the oppressed must not retaliate, but give his overcoat also. To do this for love's sake, for harmony's sake and for Christ's sake, and yet to recognize always the limitations that God's law places upon man-made laws, and obey first the higher law,—this is a narrow path to tread. And yet we know He trod it. We must follow in his footsteps.

403. He was questioned once in order to determine His attitude towards human governments, and He disclosed it at once. He merely drew a dividing line, as it were, between what is honest and what dishonest: *"Render unto Caesar the things that are Caesar's; and unto God the things that are God's"* (Matt. 22:15-22). For the privilege of using Caesar's money, without which they could not purchase the necessaries of life, pay *an equivalent* to Caesar, and *no more*.* But let that sense of obligation cease when Caesar is paid; and let the recognition of that debt involve no disloyalty to the ONE KING—GOD, in whose image ·we stand, in Christ Jesus. No dynamite of human invention can ever embosom within itself such revolutionary powers as "meekness" such as this. An intangible spiritual force, it is utterly baffling to crude cannon and rifle of human government, while it always puts the enemy in the wrong, even in his own estimation. Unregenerate man is always an angered and malicious coward in the presence of such a virtue. No wonder the Bible assures us that *"the meek shall inherit the earth,"* in the age to come.

404. No fear but God will "avenge His own elect" who trust Him to right their wrongs. Christ so trusted, while His enemies cried, *"His blood be upon us, and*

---

* The earliest Christians refused absolutely to fight for Rome. A Lutheran pastor has lately expressed what amount of compensation the Kaiser requires of his subjects, in these words: "The crime of the nation against the individual, is not that it demands his sacrifices against his will, but that it claims a life of eternal significance for ends that have no eternal value."

upon our children." And so it was, one of their own Jewish historians being the witness. Josephus tells us that within less than forty years after Christ's death, the streets of Jerusalem, in siege, were impassable by reason of the dead, while the palaces of Jerusalem were packed from floor to ceiling with corpses. At the same time, as many Jews hung on crosses outside the city, as wood could be found on which to impale them. What wonder that, seeing the approaching avenging of His innocent death, Jesus prayed for His tormentors, and wept over the doomed city, crying, *"O that thou hadst known, even thou, at least in this thy day, the things that belong unto thy peace!"* (Luke 19:42, R. V.).

LESSON 53.

MEEKNESS AND HUMILITY FOR WOMEN

405. We do not say, therefore, that women are not to be humble and meek; they must be, to please God. We have shown, however, that meekness is not weakness, nor humility servility. Both meekness and humility supersede man's government with God's. And woman must do this to enter into the kingdom of God. It is *under God's rule alone* that these virtues grow; outside of God's exclusive government they are not found. Their very source of existence is in entire dependence upon GOD ALONE, and that necessitates entire independence of other control.

406. We owe duties to each other, and women owe certain duties to their husbands; we are perfectly clear on that point. We are not to avenge ourselves, as God's children, when oppressed or defrauded; Christ did not. The wife must be Christlike when wronged by her husband. God has commanded this non-resistance, and women must practice it, even if some men do but preach it to women for self-interested reasons.

407. But all this is to be done *"as unto the Lord, and not unto men,"* done because God commands it, in spite of the fact that man may command it for selfish reasons. But this class of duties is to be offset by other duties which, if fulfilled with equal faithfulness, will save the character from degradation,—from a degradation into weakness and servility, which would surely follow were this second class of duties neglected. Herein lies an illustration of the Apostle James' warning: *"Whosoever shall*

keep the whole law, and yet offend in one point, he is guilty of all,' James 2:10.

408. Let us illustrate: It is recorded that men did not learn how to fly, with all their efforts, until first they discovered the important fact that the wind never drives steadily forward in its prevailing direction, but advances and recedes,—so that there is always present a to and fro motion of the air. It is by turning first this wing and then that, to allow for these contrary currents to play upon its wings, that the bird, and birdman, rise in the air. Just so, we rise in virtue by keeping *our balance* amid the duties of life; and we may sink, for want of proper balance, if any duty is overlooked or neglected. An unbalanced virtue becomes quickly a source of degradation. Let us keep all points but one of the law, and we will soon begin to fail.

409. Humility and meekness, then, will not elevate the character unless they are *real;* and unless balanced by other equally important virtues. And it has been by the exclusion of these other duties as "unwomanly" that woman has been allowed, not to rise, but to sink, through her mere non-resistance of evil. Let this one current of non-resistance prevail alone, to the exclusion of their off-setting duties, and the woman sinks, as would a bird trying to fly with one wing. This accounts for much of the degradation of womanhood which we see around us.

410. But what are these balancing duties? We must turn to our Pattern, Jesus Christ, to find out. Again we must remind ourselves that women have but *one pattern* to follow, and at this point her feet have often been led astray from the path of woman's duties. God did not send a *female* Christ into this world to guide woman in a *female* manner, by setting her a pattern of *"womanliness;"* He only sent a man *"made of a woman,"* alone, and therefore sufficiently womanly and sufficiently manly for each sex to find in Jesus Christ a perfect *Pattern,* for both sexes, in all the duties of life. Let woman fail to completely follow this Pattern, and she is as much a failure, as a Christian, as is the man who fails to completely follow His example in all things.

411. In all the Bible no sin is held up to human contempt more than Esau's. Now we can readily imagine that Esau, after he had *sold out his birthright,* might attempt to bolster up his self-respect by putting a gloss

188

of virtue over his sin. "See how I loved Jacob! See how self-effacing I have been! Behold my meekness! In my humility I gave my brother the chief place." But God would say to all this, *"Jacob have I loved, but Esau have I hated."* God turns away with loathing from the sin of the self-indulgent shirk. Such "virtuous" veneer is not thick enough to hide woeful self-indulgence as its mainspring. Women need to study well the lesson. Woman was created as a help "meet," sufficient for man; and because it was "not good" for him to be alone. And later, by all he had lost *she* was left sole heir of a great inheritance,—to furnish the seed for a better race. She has fulfilled her call in part, by the virginal birth of Jesus Christ. Its complete fulfilment implies a large spiritual progeny growing out of the spiritual activity of woman. She must not sell her birthright (for it is the same one, except greater, that Esau sold), by a vicious self-effacement.

412.   That is sham virtue in woman which lends a cloak or gives stimulus to vice in man. *"By their fruits ye shall know them."* That which begets virtue in others *is* virtue; that which begets vice *is vice.* A wifely self-immolation which encourages masculine sensuality is vice. A feminine "humility" which gives place for the growth of masculine egotism is vice. Women need to ponder these things, and their responsibility (as the mothers and trainers of the men of the world), for the *lack* of gentleness, meekness, humility and chastity among men. Women must train their sons in *all* these virtues.

413.   There stands a mysterious prophecy, relating to woman, which no scholar who accepts the rabbinical view as to the inferior rank of woman in the divine economy is capable of understanding or interpreting. The guesses at its meaning would fill a considerable niche in a museum of literary curiosities. We refer to Jer. 31:22, which is translated: *"How long wilt thou go about, O thou backsliding daughter? for the Lord hath created a new thing in the earth, A woman shall compass a man."* But, as there is no word for the article ' a" in the Hebrew tongue, we are at liberty to read the last phrase, "woman shall compass man," or, more literally, "female shall compass male." The verb "wilt . . go about" (חסק), in the first clause of this verse, is found only in one other place in the Hebrew, Solomon's Song, 5:6, where it is translated "withdraw;" but following the marginal reading of the

R. V., it means, more properly, in the form used, "to turn [oneself] away." The second verb of the verse, translated "backsliding," means also "to turn," and is translated "turn" in the previous verse. Now it is the third verb, translated "compass," which has puzzled men most of all; it has led to a lot of different translation and interpretations; the verb (סבב) seems to mean also to "turn about." It is generally translated "compass." Now what does the whole verse mean? (1) The precise form of the latter verb is translated "led about," in Deut. 32:10, *"He found him in a waste howling wilderness; He led him about, He instructed him."* (2) Once again "new" is an adjective, used in the sense of "something new." We suggest this rendering: *How long wilt thou keep turning away, O thou turning away daughter? for the Lord hath created [something] new in the earth, Female will lead male about.* In other words, it seems God's design that the "new woman" in Christ Jesus, shall no more "turn away," as did Eve, to her husband, but remaining loyal to God alone, and true to her destiny as the mother of that Seed,—both the literal, Jesus, and the mystical Christ, the Church,—shall lead man about,—out of the wilderness of the inefficiency of egotism into the glorious liberty of the children of God. For, who shall specially conquer Satan, if not the sex to whom God gave the honor from the beginning of being in eternal enmity against Satan, in the promise, *"I will put enmity between thee and the woman?"* But woman must be truly meek to fulfil this her promised destiny.*

414. But none of God's promises are the mere reading of fate. That which God promises will never be fulfilled excepting to those who *seize the promise.* God overrides no human will. But as woman has passed through a long night of travail to bring forth the sons of men on earth, so shall God render to her double for all she has undeservedly suffered through the cruelty and slight and disrespect of man, by giving her a very large share in the work of saving the world through the preaching of the Gospel, if woman will not despise her birthright.

*Prof. Mingana remarks here, "I do not believe that your translation is certain, although I feel convinced that the English version is here hopelessly wrong."

LESSON 54.

THE NEWLY-DISCOVERED CHAPTER IN WOMAN'S HISTORY.

415. We will now resume the study of the early dignity of woman. Please read again Lessons 7 and 8. Prof. W. Robertson Smith, late professor of Arabic at Cambridge, wrote a book, called *Kinship and Marriage in Early Arabia,* which has special interest for Bible students, because it deals with a people closely related to the Hebrews in both language and customs. Speaking of *ba'al* marriage (the sort which involves subordination on the part of the wife), he says: "The husband in this kind of marriage is called, not in Arabia only, but also among the Hebrews and Armenians as well, the woman's 'lord' or 'owner' (*ba'al,* Hos. 2:16), and wherever this name is found we may be sure that marriage was of the second type, with male kinship,* and the wife bound to her husband and following him to his home. It will be convenient to have a short name for the type of marriage in which these features are combined, and, as the name Baal is familiar to every one from the Old Testament, I propose to call it *ba'al* marriage, or marriage of dominion, and to call the wife a *be'ulah,* or subject wife (Isaiah 62.4).

416. For the contrasted type . . . we ought to seek a name expressing the fact that the wife is not under her husband's authority but meets him on equal terms." He proposes *sadica* for this purpose. It comes from *sadac,* the gift given *to a wife* by her husband, upon marriage, as contrasted with the gift to the *father,* in the purchase of a wife by her *ba'al.* Sadica marriage he describes thus: "*The woman receives the husband in her own tent, among her own people . . the children are brought up under the protection of the mother's kin, and are of her blood.*" On the other hand, "*The wife who follows her husband, and who bears children who are of his blood has lost the right freely to dispose of her person; her husband has authority over her, and he alone has the right of divorce.*"—this is *ba'al* marriage.

417. What W. Robertson Smith calls sadica marriage, the earliest form of marriage, is generally called *beena*

---

* As Lesson 7 shows, the primal form, or type, of marriage was characterized by female kinship.

marriage,—the word which is applied in Ceylon at the present time to the marriage in which the husband resides with his wife's family. Robertson Smith's word is descriptive of such marriages among the Arabs only. He sometimes uses one term, sometimes the other (for reasons we need not enter into), and hence the need for our defining both. The proper term for this primitive form of marriage (in which the man forsakes his parents for his wife, not the woman for her husband) is "the *Christian* marriage," since it was not only enjoined by God's primal social law, but reiterated in the authoritative language of Christ Himself, at the same time and in the same sentence in which He forbade divorce for any cause but adultery (Matt. 19:4, 5); and is further declared by St. Paul to typify Christ's self-renunciation in behalf of His Bride, the Church, Eph. 5:31, 32.

418. But our interest for the moment centers around the fact that God *did not* Himself subordinate Eve to Adam, and all women to their husbands, as has been claimed by the Church throughout many centuries. Man gradually brought about that subordination to himself, and it has been accomplished so late in human history as to leave traces of its history, and also remnants of the other form of marriage. From understanding, at last, that Eve was a believer; and that there is more to the promise, or threat, made to Satan, *"I will put enmity between thee and the woman"* than that men should hate snakes (!), we are left without any clew to any sense or reason why God *should* subordinate Eve to Adam. And we are glad to know that many sociologists are at work on the many evidences that *"in the beginning"* woman was *not* subordinate.

419. The first to publish investigations along the line of woman's early dignity was Herr Bachofen, a Swiss jurist,—in 1861. His work is very voluminous and confusing to those not well acquainted with the German language. We get his views from those who quote him. His work, called *Das Mutterrecht,* "the matriarchate," made a profound impression. The first English writer on the subject, Mr. J. F. McLennan, tells us: "Bachofen announced to the world, for the first time, the discovery that a system of kinship through females had everywhere preceded the rise of kinship through males . . . The honor of that discovery, the importance of which, as affording a new starting-point for all history, cannot

be overestimated, must, without stint or qualification, be assigned to him."

420. Bachofen's ideas as to how this dignity of women came about are very curious. Starting on the theory that general promiscuity at first prevailed, he declares, "Women grew disgusted with promiscuity, being nobler and more sensitive than men, appealed to force [an Amazonian movement], put down this vice and established monogamy in its place, and, by right of conquest, held the first place in the management of human affairs. Their children bore the family name of their mothers, and all the relationships to which rights of succession attached were traced through women only. Further, they assigned to themselves, or had conceded to them, the political as well as the domestic supremacy." This is a considerable exaggeration of the actual facts, and his theory of a sex war has not been accepted, as accounting for female dignity. The Bible gives strong evidence in another direction.

421. The term *matriarchate* is an exaggeration, excepting as applied to small communities, occasionally: There has been no general government of men by women, such as men have now established over women; but there has existed a widespread equality of the sexes in early times. Yet the word matriarchate is so constantly used that we adopt it, but with this explanation. We must not get tangled in the theory of strident evolutionists that the human family began in promiscuity, instead of monogamy,—as the Bible plainly teaches the latter. Even such evolutionists as Darwin and Herbert Spencer disclaim the theory of general promiscuity. The latter says: "I do not think the evidence shows that promiscuity ever existed in an unqualified form."

422. Evolutionists desire to show, next, that female kinship (in which children are recognized as belonging to their mothers, not their fathers) and dignity developed from polyandry, which would, of course, cause confusion as to fatherhood. But the Bible teaches us definitely that the human race began in absolute monogamy, with the family as a unit—not the tribe—and that woman's place was secured for her by God Himself, who ordained that marriage should disjoint man from his kin. The evolutionist view is degarding to womanhood, since it represents the gradual subjugation

of the female sex as a high road to human progress. Thus Bachofen taught: "It was the assertion of fatherhood which delivered the mind from natural appearances [that the child was kin to its mother], and when this was successfully achieved, human existence was raised above the laws of natural life. The principle of motherhood is common to all spheres of animal life, but man goes beyond this tie in giving pre-eminence to the power of procreation, and thus becomes conscious of his higher vocation. . . Victorious fatherhood thus becomes as distinctly connected with heavenly light as prolific motherhood is with teeming earth."

423. But we note that it is *fathers,* not mothers, who so teach and that the "Light of this world" said once. even of religious instructors—not merely physical but spiritual fathers—*"Call no man your father upon the earth; for One is your Father, which is in heaven,"*— Matt. 23:9. While as concerning motherhood, He who brought down the heavenly light, and who was speaking in behalf of the truth, not in behalf of His sex, or any other sex, said: *"Whosoever shall do the will of my Father which is in heaven, the same is my mother."* (Matt. 12:50). So long as the prophecy stands, *"The Seed of the woman shall bruise the serpent's head,"* woman, as mother, physical or spiritual, will have a Divine right to special dignity, if only she will not, like Esau, despise her birthright.

LESSON 55.

ENDOGAMY AND EXOGAMY.

424. In order to understand and appreciate the testimony of the O. T. to the early dignity of woman, and how her subordination was brought about, we will need first to give some space to a description of how woman's early dignity was discovered,—in other words, what constitutes proof in this case.

425. Mr. J. F. McLennan soon followed Bachofen with a book on *Primitive Marriage,* now incorporated with his *Ancient History,* dealing wholly with this same subject. He writes most interestingly, informingly, and for the most part logically. Beginning with the symbol of capture in the marriage ceremony, he shows, convincingly, that such a symbol never could have come to

be considered an essential part of the marriage ceremony unless as the outcome of a previously existing *actual capture* of the bride. He describes, first, those peaceful marriage ceremonies which still retain the *symbol* of capture, as they may be witnessed to the present time (or existed in the near past) all over the world. Then he describes the *actual capture* of the bride, as it has prevailed or does prevail at the present time.

426. A single illustration or two, of each kind, will serve our purpose. Description of a wedding among the Circassians: "The wedding day is celebrated with noisy feasting and revelry, in the midst of which the bridegroom has to rush in, and with the help of a few daring young men, to carry off the young lady by force; and by this process she becomes his lawful wife." He quotes from Lord Kames, who in 1807 describes the following custom as prevailing in Wales: "On the morning of the wedding day, the bridegroom, accompanied with his friends, who are mounted on horseback, demands the bride. Her friends, who are likewise on horseback, give a positive refusal, upon which a mock scuffle ensues. The bride, mounted behind her nearest kinsman, is carried off, and is pursued by the bridegroom and his friends with loud shouts. . . When they have fatigued themselves and their horses, the bridegroom is suffered to overtake his bride."

427. This symbol of the capture of the bride, as an essential part of the marriage celebration, existed among the Romans and Spartans as well as among other ancient peoples. It exists among the Bedouins, Tartars, certain African tribes, the North and South American Indians, and among many other peoples. In some places a transitional stage between actual capture and a friendly agreement may be observed. The bride is actually taken, after which the bridegroom enters into friendly negotiations with her people to keep her. It is not unlikely that Shechem, in Genesis thirty-fourth chapter acted up to his best light as to the proper method of obtaining Dinah for his wife,—though shockingly, from our modern standpoint.

428. *Real capture* of the bride prevails among certain tribes of American Indians. Such customs existed up to recent times in other places, such as Deccan and

Afghanistan. But notably it prevails among the aboriginals of Australia, where a man will first stun a woman with a club and carry her off half-dead and unconscious, to make her his wife. A horrible description of another method of capture among the Australian blacks is given: "Sometimes two men join an expedition for the same purpose, and then for several days they watch the movements of their intended victims, using the utmost skill to conceal their presence. . . They wait for a dark, windy night; then, quite naked, and carrying their long 'jag spears,' they crawl through the brush until they reach the vicinity of the camp-fires, in front of which the girls they are in search of are sleeping. . . Then one of the intruders stretches out his spear, and inserts its barbed point amongst her thick flowing locks. Turning the spear slowly around, some of her hair speedily becomes entangled with it; then, with a sudden jerk she is aroused from her slumber, and . . feels the sharp point of another weapon pressed close against her throat. . . She knows that the slightest attempt at escape or alarm will cause her instant death, so . . silently rising, she follows her captors. They lead her away . . . tie her to a tree, and return to ensnare their other victim in like manner. Then they hurry off to their own camp, where they are received with universal applause."

429. McLennan reasons thus, by exclusion, upon these facts: "If members of a family or tribe *are forbidden* to intermarry with other families or tribes, and free to marry among themselves, there is no room for fraud or force in the constitution of marriage. The bride and bridegroom will live together in amity among their common relatives. . . A woman will become the wife of a suitor peaceably. If a suitor forces her, or carries her off against her will or that of her friends, he must separate from these to escape their vengeance:" the symbol of capture could not, hence, have arisen among tribes which marry *within their own tribe.* The form of marriage within a tribe McLennan calls *endogamy,*—a name widely adopted by later writers on the same theme.

430. Next, McLennan points out the existence of tribes which practice *exogamy,* by forbidding marriage between members of the same tribe. Such tribes oblige their young men to secure wives from other tribes,—

and in those primitive conditions tribes are always at enmity one with another, so that the method of securing a bride outside one's own tribe must be by capture, excepting in those cases where the man joins the wife's tribe. He calls attention to the frequent existence of exogamous tribes, and argues that even when the mere symbol of capture remains it is a proof of a previously-existing actual capture. Then he proceeds to account for the *origin* of that curious custom of exogamy, which obliges men to marry outside the tribe to which they belong. He declares: "Perhaps there is no question leading deeper into the foundations of civil society than that which regards the origin of exogamy." Up to this point McLennan's logic has been so clear and convincing as to carry all with him, excepting as to a theory of primal promiscuity. But as to the origin of exogamy few writers agree with him, or with each other.

431. The Khonds of Orissa consider marriage within the tribe incestuous, and punish it by death. Certain Russian tribes are exogamous. The same can be said of Circassians, who are forbidden to marry within fraternities which may consist of thousands of members. Native Siberians cannot take wives within their own tribes, nor Kaffirs, nor some tribes of India. Traces of similar exogamous laws exist among the American Indians, in Australia, and they existed among the early Celts. The remarkable thing about these laws of exogamy is that these peoples are always at war, one with another, and women for wives can be secured by no other means than capture.

432. We make no attempt to complete the list of the exogamous peoples which exist, or are known to have existed. As to tribes which employ the symbol of capture, we may mention, further, the American Indians, the blacks of Australia (who also practice actual capture), the Maoris of New Zealand, the inhabitants of many of the islands of the Pacific, Mongolians, Russians, Deccans, Afghans, and formerly the Irish, French, Welsh, and other peoples of Europe and Asia. McLennan says that this wide-spread symbol of capture "carries us back to a remote antiquity when marriage and prowess in war were closely associated." Yes, indeed, had this unbeliever in the Bible turned to the 4th chapter of Genesis, he would have found proof of his statement.

LESSON 56.

THE ORIGIN OF EXOGAMY.

433. McLennan says, "Perhaps there is no question leading deeper into the foundations of civil society than that which regards the origin of exogamy." Prof. Robertson Smith declares that "the origin of exogamy has not yet been explained." Lord Avebury (Sir John Lubbock) in his book, *Marriage Totemism and Religion,* tabulates the various views regarding the origin of exogamy and marriage by capture, real or symbolic. These we will condense:

434. (1) Plutarch's adopted by Tylor: Exogamy was a political expedient meant to strengthen the tribe by foreign alliances. But, since the symbol of capture implies a former real capture by force at its beginning, exogamy must rather have strengthened animosities, not alliances; but the practice may have been adapted to this purpose later. The case of Shechem and Dinah would illustrate this,—Genesis 34.

(2) McLennan's and Morgan's view: Exogamy arose in the scarcity of women, due to the prevalence of infanticide. Mr. Andrew Lang rightly answers, "The prevalence of infanticide at the supposed very early stage of society is not demonstrated . . . even if it existed it could not create a prejudice against marrying the few women within the group."

(3) Müller: The symbol of capture was due to coyness,—i. e. the bride "could not surrender her freedom unless compelled by violence." But what about the mock resistance offered by the male relatives, instead of the bride?

(4) Bachofen: A social reform, due to the moral sense of women. It is not likely that a sex war has ever prevailed, in which the women have subordinated all the men.

(5) Westermarck: Exogamy arose out of "an instinct" against marriage of near kin. But this marriage of near kin existed before exogamy. In primitive times, among many peoples, notably the Persians and Egyptians, even brothers and sisters married. Abraham married his half-sister. Rather, the instinct against the marriage of near kin has been a development out of the law against incest. Exogamy forbade much more

than marriage with mere kin. It interdicted marriage between members of the same group or tribe.

435. (6) Exogamy was arranged by chiefs to prevent the marriage of near relations. This view is supported by Herbert Spencer, Dr. Frazer and others. But the same objection as above can be brought against it. The law against exogamy is too sweeping for the mere evils of incest.

(7) M. Fustel de Coulanges: Force, or pretended force, in the capture of a bride, arose from the supposed necessity of the bride's resistance to transference from one's family gods to the gods of another family or tribe. This view is not considered tenable.

(8) Lang and Reinach: It arose from *totemism,*—something difficult to explain in a few words; but its main feature is that tribes name themselves after certain animals and thereon base a sort of family tree. But totemism does not always prevail where exogamy is found; and besides the totemism is often a later development than the exogamy.

(9) Lord Avebury: At first, communal marriage (promiscuity) alone prevailed; then, secondly when a warrior captured a woman he owned her exclusively; thirdly, two classes were thus created (a) the women of the tribe held in common by the men of the tribe, and (b) captive wives, who enjoyed the protection of one man, and thus rose to dignity; fourthly, women within the tribe would long for dignity, and men for exclusive property: fifthly, this would increase the practice of capturing wives. It has been strongly declared by other writers that the capture of a woman, at this stage of affairs, would not give the capturer exclusive right over her. What reason is there for believing that the men within a tribe would not fight as much over a captive woman as over a woman born in the tribe? Again, while a woman might long to belong to one man only, there is no ground for believing that a woman captured from an enemy's tribe, and owned exclusively by her captor, would be so well treated, being his absolute property and slave, that the women within their own tribe would long for her status.

436. At any rate, the practice of exogamy must, in some manner, be related to the fact of scarcity of women. And now please note one thing: It is the rule for these writers to conceive that first of all promiscuity

prevailed; and secondly, that polyandry followed,—that is, the state in which women have more than one husband. But, with characteristic blindness (as it seems to us), to the faults of the masculine sex, not one of them suggests that *polygyny*—the possession of more than one wife by a husband—has anything whatever to do with the scarcity of women within a tribe.

437. These writers seem to assume that by inclination these men are monogamous, or, at least, that after a man has made good his need of a wife he rests satisfied. But what is farther from the actual facts? The scarcity of women within a tribe may be brought about in two ways: the actual number of women may be wanting which would supply one woman to each man, or there might exist an unequal distribution, caused by the women of the tribe being monopolized by its more powerful members. What would happen then? The men who lacked wives would go forth to capture them from the enemy's tribe; and presently there would exist a law, promulgated by the chief men of tribes, that the women of the tribe belonged to them; the other men must capture women for themselves.

438. The unbalance, then, which leads to the law of exogamy, may be not in an *actual* scarcity of women, or due to a hypothetic infanticide, or anything of the sort, but to an *artificial* scarcity due to a monopoly. These writers are evolutionists who often repudiate the light to be found in the early chapters of Genesis. We will not be so foolish, for we have most important information given us in those chapters. The unbalance goes even further back than one produced by a monopoly, for that monopoly is due to an unbalance in sensual desire, which we can probably trace back to Adam. Lamech, by violence, seized upon two women of his tribe, and that because he had inherited from Adam, through Cain, sensual desires which he did not choose to control. When he took two wives, instead of one out of the tribe, that would have left one man wifeless, excepting that, in this case, Lamech killed a man of the tribe. But in the case of other men, emboldened by Lamech's example, the widowed men would not be killed.

439. Now we have the steps of social development plainly before us, on the authority of God's Word:

First, monogamy, with female kinship, the Creator's own ordinance. Marriage should disjoint man from his kin, and not woman from her kin. But Cain's progeny spread sensuality and violence over the earth, for Cain's sons invented "cutting instruments," that is, weapons of warfare (R. V.), and introduced polygamy into the tribe. This monopoly of women within Cain's tribe, by its more powerful members, would force those who lacked wives, if sensual, to capture women from other tribes, and thus the law of exogamy would be established. The sixth chapter of Genesis, then, describes the beginning of exogamy. The descendants of Cain, or *"sons of God"* (read carefully, Lesson 21), deprived of wives from within their own tribe, *"took them wives of all that they chose"* from the daughters of Seth, and soon *"the earth was filled with violence."*

LESSON 57.

THE REAL CAUSE OF EXOGAMY.

440. A point in the evidence from profane history that exogamy has had its origin in polygyny (the humbler members of a tribe being driven to seek wives outside the tribe because the stronger, or head men, had monopolized the women of the tribe for their harems), is the fact that very generally the royal classes have not been expected to obey such restrictions. In early times even brothers and sisters of royal blood married; and such is the custom among certain African tribes to this day. Dr. Frazer, in his book, *Totemism and Exogamy*, informs us that in both Assam and Africa, among exogamous tribes, the heads of the tribe marry members of their own tribe. It stands to reason, however, that should exceptionally pretty captive women be brought into a tribe, this would lead even its chiefs to join the next expedition to capture women from the tribe whence the attractive captives came. Thus we are told, Gen. 6:1, 2, that it was when the Cainites *"saw the daughters of men* (Sethite women) *that they were fair"* that they took them, and their progeny were *"mighty men," "men of renoun"* (see pars. 158-162*).
441. But of what practical moment is this matter?

---

* This statement and interpretation of Gen. 6:1-4, will not be understood apart from the exposition of Sir J. W. Dawson, given in pars. 158-162.

We answer, it is of great moment to women to grasp the immense difference between the teaching of evolutionists and the Holy Scriptures on the same facts. The teachings of the social evolutionists of the present day are very injurious to the progress of womanhood. The evolutionist rejects the teachings of the early chapters of Genesis, and would lead women to do the same, declaring the Biblical teaching to be degrading to women. But let us remember that what has injured women is the rabbinical and theological *perversion* of the real teachings of these early chapters. Women are in danger of throwing aside a priceless treasure because it has been presented to them under a repulsive cover; and evolutionists are exhorting them. "Throw it away! Throw it away! It is only rubbish."

442. But before we throw our document away, we will tear off the cover (its traditional interpretation and translation), and get to its original contents. And furthermore, we will compare with God's Word what evolution offers woman in place of it, for the early chapters of Genesis. The social evolutionists, for the most part, would begin the world's social history with a repulsive promiscuity; the Bible begins it with a picture of purest monogamy. The evolutionists next picture a state of polyandry for women; the Bible nowhere, from Genesis to Revelation, admits a picture of this degraded system of female life; polyandry has existed in this world, and may exist to-day, but never so extensively as to be a factor in great social problems. The evolutionist "evolves" female kinship out of polyandry, —a state in which the fatherhood of children cannot be determined; the Bible derives female kinship from an ordinance of God,—as binding upon Christians today (even though universally disobeyed), as the law against free and easy divorce.

443. God premised female kinship when He prophesied, "The seed of the woman shall bruise the serpent's head;" He founded the law of female kinship earlier, when He said, *"Therefore shall a man leave his father and his mother and cleave to his wife."* The evolutionist, by implication if not often by actual statement, pictures the growth of male kinship and the gradual subjugation of the mothers of the human race as progress; the Bible shows that the same is a defiant going against God's expressed will. The evolutionist is silent as to

the part that an initial polygyny has played in bringing about lamentable conditions, but has much to say that is misleading about polyandry; but the Bible shows the very early development of polygyny among men, and gives us a clear picture of its outcome—the capture of women,—the beginning of exogamy—as closely related to the sensuality and violence of men. Women, as a class, have never been pictured in Bible history as given over to the degrading habits of polyandry,—the nearest approach being an occasional woman of evil life. Such misrepresentations belong to rabbinical misrepresentations of the character of Eve and of women in general; or to pagan conceptions of womanhood; or to the theory of modern evolutionists, who have, once for all, committed themselves to the employment of picturing everything of the past as worse than the present, and cut the foot to fit their shoe,—in other words, shape the living truth to their dead theory.

444. McLennan states, in relation to the early dignity of womanhood: "All those signs of superiority on the woman's part were the direct consequence (1) of marriage being *not* monogamous or such as to permit of certainty of fatherhood; and (2) of wives not as yet living in their husband's houses, but apart from them, in the houses of their own mothers." Writers on this theme agree with McLennan as to the first point, while we, on Scriptural authority, strongly dissent. Female kinship was *not*, in early times, kept to the front merely because male kinship could not be determined, owing to the practice of polyandry. God Himself, by express ordinance founded female kinship. Nature also establishes female kinship, and it has only been by a "reform against nature" (that horror which is so odious to the eyes of all believers in masculine domination), that man has ever displaced female kinship and enthroned male kinship,—by gross cruelty and systematic tyranny, as we shall presently show. We agree in part with McLennan's second point. Certainly immense advantages accrued to the human race—primarily to women and children—by the early practice of disjointing the husband from his kin, and not the wife from her kin in marriage. Some of these are enumerated in par. 45.

445. All these writers seem to agree that exogamy, in its rise, is closely related to the capture of wives, and the capture of wives to a scarcity of women. But none

of them, excepting Herbert Spencer so far as we know, suggest that that scarcity might arise out of the practice of polygyny,—as we believe the Bible clearly shows. The problem with them, is, how to account for exogamy *after* having once agreed together that female kinship was born of polyandry. Let them once drop this hypothetic polyandry as accounting for female kinship, and accept the belief that nature and nature's God established female kinship, and a perfectly clear and simple case can be made out. We believe the otherwsie objectless, unsavoury stories of the blaspheming, polygamous Lamech and his self-vaunting poetry, and of the depredations of Cain's tribe on the daughters of Seth, have their place in the Bible because they instruct us in the initial steps of social degeneration. They are meant for clews to great social problems. Here (in the opening chapters of Genesis) we trace disease—the moral disease, sin, back to its initial symptoms. To be able to trace a disease through all its variations back to its inception, generally affords the secret of its conquest.

446. To review and sum up: Accepting the Biblical account as authoritative, (1) The human race began with the family (not the tribe, or clan, as evolutionists teach) as its unit; (2) it began in pure monogamy, Matt. 19:4; (3) with female kinship, Matt. 19:5; (4) but Cain bequeathed to the race sensual and domineering characteristics; (5) as a result of this bad inheritance, strengthened by bad example (Gen. 4:24) Cain's descendants invent "cutting instruments" (R. V.), and use them as weapons of warfare, first within the tribe, —the stronger members of which monopolize more wives than one, if they choose; (6) thus the weaker men are driven to unite themselves to wives in the (at first) friendly Sethite tribe, but still keeping up friendly relations with their Cainite brethren; (7) seeing Sethite women "that they are fair," the stronger men begin the capture of Sethite women, Gen. 6:1, 2, and thus exogamy, as a custom, is established.

447. Again we emphasize, as a lesson to be drawn from these considerations, the need of women translators and Biblical expositors to collaborate with men. There are, equally in each sex, certain sex prejudices and certain sex limitations that unfit either sex to be the sole custodian of divine truth for the opposite sex. In this instance, as in other instances, the predominance

of male expositors of the Bible and the predominance
of male expositors of scientific and archaeological facts,
lead both bodies astray as to their deductions from
plainly demonstrable teachings of nature, ancient history, customs and the Word of God.

LESSON 58.
FURTHER PROOF OF WOMAN'S EARLY DIGNITY.

448. It is but a meager account which we have in the
Bible of the ages between Noah and Abraham. The distance in time is spanned by the tenth and eleventh
chapters of Genesis. But we have light on this period
in archaeological discoveries. The Tel el Amarna tablets,
the Code of Hammurabi (King Amraphel of Gen.
14:1), and the numerous discoveries about Nineveh, in
Babylonia, Egypt and other places, have combined in
enabling scholars to reconstruct the manners and customs, to a considerable extent, of these peoples of early
ages.

449. First in time, we had information that in Egypt,
of ·old, women occupied a very dignified position, in
public as well as in private affairs; but this was supposed to be a quite exceptional fact. But after Bachofen's book appeared, and others, particularly McLennan's well-reasoned work, in which he traced the signs
of that early dignity of women, and gave investigators
new clews to follow out into past facts, historians and
others have interested themselves increasingly in this
newly-discovered chapter in woman's ancient history.

450. We are not turning aside from legitimate Bible
study, as regards woman's place in the divine economy,
in bringing these facts to the front, for they help us
the better to understand numerous incidents in the Bible
as regards women. Nothing is of more importance to
the Christian woman to-day than to understand that
God did not Himself subordinate woman to man. He
merely prophesied that such subordination would follow as the fruit of sin in this world. The subordination
of woman to man is *not* the result of God's ordinance;
it is the fruit of wrong-doing; and, as such, the fruit
can be no more God's doing than the bad tree.

451. Ancient history proves that woman, in earth's earliest ages, was not subordinate. As to Egypt, we shall never forget the profound impression made on our own mind by a review of the long line of ancient monarchs in stone, to be seen in the Gizeh Museum, a few miles from Cairo, near the pyramid of Cheops. Beginning at the end where the most ancient were placed, we noticed that the queen sat by the side of the king, of equal size and importance. A few centuries down the line, the queen had become smaller than the king. The representations were all rudely true to life, and we could not but conclude that for some reason the man had taken to marrying a wife not as mature as himself; and beginning to bear children in her immaturity, the development of woman's stature had been arrested. Further on towards our own days, the queen —now more properly only the king's wife—sat on a lower level than his eminence; the queen had become the subject of the king also. Lastly, the queen was no longer carved out of a stone block; she was merely scratched in portraiture upon the pedestal of the stool upon which he sat, or upon the arm of his chair or throne.

452. Now here was a story which could not lie. No man had carved more than one or two of these stones; they had not been carved under the same dynasty; no architect had conceived the plan of the whole; no sociologist, no theologian had written this history of womanhood; no romancer had woven the tale. It was cold fact, in cold stone. And that revelation of the ages tells us that the Egyptian woman was, of old, a dignified personage; she gradually lost that dignity; her fall was not all at once; it was accomplished only gradually, through the working of ages of custom. How very different this is from that theological teaching that while the nations were as yet unborn, God placed their mother, Eve, under servitude, so that, by divine ordinance, every woman excepting Eve has been born in servitude!

453. Turning to Isaac Myer's work, *Oldest Books in the World*, we quote what he says about ancient times in Egypt: "The mother of the deceased is usually shown with his wife, and his father rarely appears. The custom as shown by the funeral steles, was to trace the descent of the dead on their mother's side, and not, as we do,

on the father's. This produced also the curious effect that the father of the mother was considered the natural protector." "The position of woman both in religion and in government was elevated in ancient Egypt." Mr. Myer reproduces teaching which was found on what he calls *"The Papyrus of Balak, No. IV."* He dates the writing about 3,000 B. C. The words are in the language of a god, addressing some mother's son: "I have given thee thy mother who has borne thee; she gave herself a heavy burden for thy sake . . When thou wast born after thy months [of gestation], she was truly subjected to thy yoke, for her breast has been in thy mouth during three years. As thou grew marvellously, the disguist of thy untidiness did not turn her heart against thee. . . [Now] that thou hast married, . . have an eye on thy child, raise it as thy mother did thee. Do not do what she would reprove in thee, for fear that, if she raises her two hands towards God [against thee], he will hear her prayer."

454. Dr. J. H. Breasted, in his *History of Egypt* says: "Under the Old Kingdom [which he would place about 3,000 B. C.], a man possessed but one legal wife, who was the mother of all his heirs. She was in every respect his equal. . . The natural line of inheritance was through the eldest daughter, though a will might destroy this." To these statements, and many more kindred ones which we might quote, we know of no reliable historian who would take exception.

455. We turn now from Egypt to ancient Babylonia, to learn the same things, as regards the early dignity of woman. Formerly it was supposed that Hebrew was the oldest language, and no people were older than the nation from whence Abraham came. But before the Babylonians were the Sumerians; and Prof. Sayce tells us in his book, *Babylonians and Assyrians*: "Two principles struggled for recognition in Babylonian family life. One was the patriarchal, the other the matriarchal. Perhaps they were due to a duality of race; perhaps they were merely the result of the circumstances under which the Babylonians lived. At times it would seem as if we must pronounce the Babylonian family to have been patriarchal in its character; at other times the wife and mother occupies an independent and even commanding position. It may be noted that whereas in the old Sumerian hymns the woman takes the precedence of the

man, the Semitic translation invariably reverses the order: the one has 'female and male,' the other, 'male and female.' " Again he says: "Women could hold civil offices and even act as governors of a city." Again we read the same lesson,—in Babylonia WOMAN WAS BORN FREE!

456. Let us not distract our mind at present with mental discussions as to the *desirableness,* or otherwise, of such social conditions. At present we put these facts of history forward wholly for the sake of making one point perfectly clear and convincing,—viz., *Woman was NOT subordinated, at the beginning of human history through the wrong-doing of Eve.* At the dawn of authentic profane history, which must have been much later than Eve's day of course, we find woman holding a position so dignified and honoured, both in family and public life, that men are constrained to name it a matriarchate. If this be so, then the theologian has not read his Bible correctly, in his supposition that he can trace the subordination of woman all the way back to Eden, and to a day when the blight of God's curse fell upon Eve. We have shown, and will show further, by the teaching of the Bible itself, that such a conception is not consonant with the general spirit of the Word, and that such a sad day as *God's* curse of womanhood never dawned on human history.

This matter may seem of so little consequence to male Bible expositors that they are more than willing even to this day to ignore the "woman question" in their teaching, and allow the case to stand as *God's blight on the sex,* when it is wholly the result of man's wrongdoing. Thus Adam was more than willing to ignore the Serpent in the Garden, and lay the responsibility of his own wrongdoing at the door of the Almighty,—as he did when he said, "The woman whom thou gavest to be with me." But such continuance in an evil way will not escape God's eye, inasmuch as the teaching that all women are left under condemnation because Eve sinned is more a slight and disrespect shown towards Jesus Christ, the Atoner for ALL SIN, than a slight and disrespect shown towards women.

LESSON 59.
FURTHER PROOF.—Continued.

457. To continue the record as to old Babylonia: In the *History of Sumer and Akkad*, by L. W. King, of the British Museum, we read: "Tablets dating from the close of Ur-Nina's dynasty [B. C. 3,000] show the important part which women played in the social and official life of the early Sumerians." He describes a plaque which has been found, among others, on which Lidda, daughter of the king Ur-Nina, stands in the first place of honour, facing the king, while the crown-prince is represented as attending his sister.

458. Now let us turn from this part of the world to Asia Minor. Here, on the testimony of the investigator, Prof. Sir Wm. M. Ramsey, are abundant evidences of an early "matriarchate,"—so-called. But again we say, we must not misunderstand the real import of this word. Men are apt to name anything which savours of an equality of the sexes, in these days, a "petticoat government." The matriarchate does not convey to our minds the idea of a rule of women over men; it merely implies the absence of an exclusive government by men,—the existence of that saner, righteous state, in which the governing privilege is invested in the *competent*, without regard to sex.

459. In Prof. Ramsay's *Church in the Roman Empire* we read: "The honours and influence which belonged to women in the cities of Asia Minor, form one of the most remarkable features in the history of the country. In all periods the evidence runs on the same lines. The best authenticated cases of *mutterrect* [the matriarchate] belong to Asia Minor. Under the Roman Empire [in Asia Minor] we find women magistrates, presidents at games, and loaded with honours. The custom of the country influenced even the Jews, who in at least one case appointed a woman at Smyrna to the position of *archisynagogos*" [chief of the synagogue]. We could quote much more, and from Prof. Ramsay's other books, —especially his *Phrygia*, but this is sufficient for illustration; it puts the whole case in a nutshell.

460. Next we turn again to Prof. W. Robertson Smith (see par. 415). Here we learn facts concerning the Semitic races, to which the O. T. Hebrews belong. In

his preface to *Kinship and Marriage in Early Arabia,* he says, "The object of the present volume is to collect and discuss the available evidence as to the genesis of the system of male kinship, with the corresponding laws of marriage and tribal organisation, which prevailed in Arabia at the time of Mohammed; the general result is that male kinship had been preceded by kinship through women only, and that all that can still be gathered as to the steps of the social evolution in which the change of kinship law is the central feature corresponds in the most striking manner with the general theory propounded . . in the late J. F. McLennan's book on *Primitive Marriage.*"

461.   Elsewhere he says: "Mother-kinship is the type of kinship, common motherhood the type of kindred unity, which dominate all Semitic speech." Now, how was that mother-kinship secured? All these writers whom we have quoted propound the evolution theory that it arose out of polyandry, in which state fatherhood cannot be certainly determined. But let us repeat: We are *not driven to a theory* to account for mother-kinship; the Bible tells us it was of God's own ordinance,— *"Therefore shall a man* ["husband" is the precise word used] *leave his father and his mother, and shall cleave unto his wife."* Prof. Smith says: "The common old Arabic phrase for the consummation of marriage is . . 'he built [a tent] over his wife.' This is synonymous with 'he went in unto her,' and is explained by the native authorities by saying that the husband erected and furnished a new tent for his wife . . Though the wife of a nomad has not usually a separate tent to live in, a special hut or tent is still erected for her on the first night of marriage. In Northern Arabia this is now the man's tent, and the woman is brought to him. But it was related to me . . . as a peculiarity of Yemen [a southern tribe] that there the 'going in' takes place in the bride's house, and that the bridegroom if home-born must stay some nights in the bride's house, or if a foreigner must settle with them. This Yemenite custom . . must once have been universal among all Semites, otherwise we should not find that alike in Arabic, Syriac and Hebrew the husband is said to 'go in' to the bride, when as a matter of fact she is brought in to him" (p. 198).

462. He continues: "As the ceremony of the tent is common to all the Semites, the kind of marriage to which it points must have begun very early, and with this it agrees that among the Hebrews, as Mr. McLennan has pointed out, there are many relics not only of female kinship but of an established usage of *beena* marriage. In Genesis 2:24 marriage is defined as implying that a man leaves his father and his mother and cleaves to his wife and they become one flesh. These expressions seem to imply that the husband is conceived as adopted into his wife's kin—at any rate he goes to live with her people. This is quite in accord with what we find in other parts of the patriarchal story. Mr. McLennan has cited the *beena* marriage of Jacob, in which Laban plainly has law on his side in saying that Jacob had no right to carry off his wives and their children" (p. 207).

463. We will leave Prof. Smith for a moment, and pause to review the very interesting arguments by means of which Jacob's wives justify their forsaking the parental roof,—Gen. 31:14, 15. First: They had no inheritance in their father's house. This was contrary to the custom under *beena marriage,* with which was associated not only female kinship, but also the rights of inheritance through females; but the covetous Laban was keeping all the property as his own, to the exclusion of his daughters' rights. Second: Under *beena* or *sadica* marriage, the bridegroom made his gift to the bride, for the privilege of marrying her; but under *ba'al* marriage the bridegroom purchases his wife. These women complain of their father Laban, *"He hath sold us, and quite devoured the price paid for us"* (R. V.) In other words, they claimed that the entire wages of Jacob's fourteen years of service to obtain his wives belonged *to them,*—not to Jacob, and certainly not to their father Laban. Their argument for leaving their mother's roof (as doubtless it would have been called in those days), was not at all what one hears in these days.—"He is my husband; I must follow him." Rather, they argue that since their own father will not give them an inheritance, they will be better off to forsake him for Jacob. They in no wise recognize it as a duty to follow a husband away from the parental roof (see par. 56). It is a quarrel about *ba'al* marriage being substituted for *sadica* marriage by a covetous father.

464. McLennan calls attention to the following interesting sidelights on woman's position among the ancient Hebrews: "When Abraham seeks a wife for Isaac, his servant thinks that the condition will probably be made that Isaac shall come and settled with her people," Gen. 24:5.* Upon this Prof. Robertson Smith remarks: "He might have added other things of the same kind; the Shechemites must be circumcised, i. e., Hebraised, before they can marry the daughters of Israel; Joseph's sons by his Egyptian wife become Israelites only by adoption; anl so in Judges 15 Samson's Philistine wife remains with her people and he visits her there. All these things illustrate what is presented in Gen. 2:24 as the primitive type of marriage; but perhaps a still more convincing proof that the passage (Gen. 2:24) is based on a doctrine of *beena* marriage and mother-kinship lies in the very name Eve.—*The mother of all living.'*" To this we add the further strong warning which God gave to Eve: "*Thou art turning to* [to follow] *thy husband, and he will rule over thee.*"

LESSON 60.

MORE ABOUT WOMAN IN THE EARLIEST AGES.

465. Whether the waters of the Flood covered the entire earth's surface, so that no inhabitant of the earth survived, will always probably be a matter of dispute, and we need not enter into it. Suffice it to say that the account in Genesis does not require this view, for the expression "the whole earth," or "land," often means only as we use the expression—the entire region under consideration. It is said "all countries" came to Joseph for corn; but that does not mean that they came from far-distant China or Japan; and that at the time Christ was born the king commanded "all the world" to be enrolled,—but it is certain that the Chinese were then in existence, and did not come.

466. It is enough, for our purpose, for us to follow those eight souls who alone escaped of all those who were visited by the greatest flood this world ever saw,—Noah, his three sons, and the wives of the four men.

---

* But in this particular instance Abraham, having been himself called out from among these idolatrous relatives, will not permit Isaac's return to them,—Gen. 24.6.

And we notice that no name is given of any of these women. Owing to the wars for the capture of women, by force of circumstances women and girls must be concealed (as was the case in India, after the Mohammedan invasion), and fall out of notice, and take necessarily a subordinate relation to their menfolk. Nothing is said against them; nothing is said in their favor. Women, as men's subordinates are nonentities; they cannot be reckoned as good or bad, because morality and immorality both alike have their origin *in free choice.* When a master robs a subordinate (as every master does, in fact) of free choice, the virtues or vices, as they may seem, in the subordinate, are the virtues or vices of the master. So a God of justice must ever reckon them. Woman in control of another is a moral cipher,—unless she *chooses* to renounce her will for another's; then she is base by choice.

467. Japhet, after the flood, lived most remotely from the home of the Hebrews, occupying the "isles," or "coast-lines," "of the Gentiles." This means the coast-lines of the Mediterranean towards Asia Minor and Europe. His name is mentioned last, not because he was youngest, but more remote. Ham was next in age, and maintained a closer affinity to the Hebrews, his sons peopling Northern Africa and Canaan. Shem was the youngest son, though named first in Scripture. In reading the 10th chapter of Genesis it is difficult to discern when actual "sons"—descendants of Noah are meant, and when geographical regions or nations, named from these sons, are referred to. This is an interesting point for us to remember.

468. We may draw an instructive comparison here between the use of the word "son" for a region and "daughter" elsewhere in much the same sense. "Cush" is another name for Ethiopia; "Mizraim," a name for Egypt, and "Canaan" merges into the land of Canaan. If we turn to Joshua 15:45, 47; 17:11; Judges 1:27, etc., we will find "daughter" used for "town." Elsewhere we will find "daughter" used for "city" and for the people of a country,—see, Isa. 1:8; 23:10. But these expressions do not refer to regions or cities in any other sense than *primarily* to their inhabitants. Throughout the Old Testament the custom is far more frequent of addressing the inhabitants of a place collectively as "daughters" than "sons." In other words, whatever is

addressed primarily to the inhabitants in the *feminine gender* cannot by any kind of truthful logic be said to be meant for *men exclusively, or principally.* The observance of this simple rule of interpretation, in reading the Scriptures, would lead to remarkable revisions in the commonly-accepted ideas of woman's "sphere." This Scriptural practice of addressing whole cities and nations of people is not a mere meaningless human "custom" observed by the Holy Spirit who inspired the Word; it is a divine maintenance of the usage which naturally follows upon the law which God originally established, of reckoning kinship through females (see par. 64).

469. Canaan is called the "son" of Ham. We explain this as meaning that descendants of Ham settled in that land to which, later, Abraham of the Semites came form Chaldea. Here, among the Phoenicians McLennan has traced the system of female kinship also. Now glancing back over the ground we have covered, it will be seen to be precisely those portions of the globe peopled by the descendants of Noah. In all these regions we can trace the matriarchate,—in Babylonia, Assyria, Arabia, Egypt, and Canaan. Also we have traced it among the inhabitants of Asia Minor to which Japhet migrated,—and it can be traced in many European countries.

470. As another line of evidence of an original female kinship, take the very common word for "brother" (*adelphos*) and "sister" (*adelphe*), used scores of times in the Greek Testament, and translated, in its collective and plural form, "brethren," It applies to the "Seed of the woman," in the sense of the mystical body of Christ; the seed of the One who was born of woman. The word means literally, "from one womb." In profane Greek literature it dates from kinship through women. There is no related term in Greek answering to *adelphos* and implying kinship through men. At Athens, in early times, a man could marry a daughter of his father, but not of his mother,—just as Abrahm did, Gen. 20:12; and for the reason that she was *not* his *adelphe,* *n*or he her *adelphos.*

471. McLennan cites many passages in Homer indicating that kinship was reckoned through females among the early Greeks, and that woman held a place of real dignity. The gradual decline of woman's place can be

traced, until, in Solon's time, the next of kin on the father's side to the fourth degree succeeded to an inheritance before any kin on the mother's side. Mr. Gladstone who was a great student of the Homeric poems, and other Greek literature, says: "In truth it would seem not only as if before Christianity appeared, *notwithstanding the advance of civilization,* the idea and place of women were below what they should have been, but actually as if, with respect to all that was most essential, *they sank with the lapse of time."*

472. The Spartan women retained their dignity longer than other races of the Greeks. And of the Lycians, Herodotus, the historian, who wrote about 459 B. C., says: "If anyone asks his neighbor who he is, he will declare himself born of such a mother, and will reckon up the ancestors of his mother." Referring to the gradual decline in the position of Grecian women, McLennan utters these words (and let women learn their lesson): "We see that *no causes* [the italics are ours] could well have produced it, so long as relationships through women preserved their old importance. On the other hand, we can discern a sufficient cause for that degradation in the gradually increasing preponderance of male kinship, and in the changes in the marriage system . . which made possible that preponderance." To this conclusion most modern writers on sociology would agree,—viz., that the status of womanhood will rise or fall, and her social elevation or degradation be determined, by no other matter so much as by whether or not the relationship between *mother and child* has its rightful recognition in law and custom.

473. Far from the regions which the three sons of Noah inhabited, female kinship can also be traced. Among the Aboriginals of Australia children take the family name of the mother. The same is true of American Indians, of certain hill tribes in India, and it was true of the Celts of ancient Britain. Among the Limboos, an Indian tribe near Darjeeling, the boys only become the property of their fathers by the latter paying a small purchase price to their mothers. It is quite possible that some of these practices associate themselves with polyandry. But we know that God's primal social law which dissociated the husband from his kin, not the wife from her kin, since it was concomitant with pure monogamy, was a far more potent weapon for the

defence of woman's dignity. And as to the descendants of Noah, we have every reason for assuming that among them female kinship would be the direct outcome of an effort to obey God's own law of marriage.

LESSON 61.

KINSHIP RECKONED THROUGH WOMEN.

474. Prof. W. Robertson Smith says: "Where there is kinship only through women, bars to marriage can, of course, arise only on this side; and not seldom it is found that after fatherhood has begun to be recognized, a relic of the old law of kinship subsists in the laws of prohibited degrees, which still depend on mother-kinship." He illustrates this survival by the case of Abraham, who married his half-sister on his father's side—Gen. 20:12, but doubtless would not have married a sister on his mother's side. He could have cited other instances: Nahor married his niece by a brother,—Gen. 11:26-29; and Amram, father of Moses, married his father's sister,—Ex. 6:20. Later in history, Tamar declares that her father, King David, would have consented to her marriage with her half-brother on her father's side,—2 Sam. 13:13. But at a still later period, the practice of taking to wife a sister by the same father, not the same mother, is rebuked by the prophet Ezekiel (22:11) as the equivalent of "humbling" the woman. He will not recognize it as legitimate, though earlier in human history even the great Abraham did the same. Prof. Smith classifies this later rebuke as a survival of female kinship customs, and it seems reasonable, for otherwise there was no occasion for the singling out of the offense against a father's rather than a mother's daughter; the latter offense against incest laws was not likely to have been committed at this late period. (See Additional Note).

475. When evolutionists apply their theories to the rise and progress of the idea of kinship, one is reminded of the maxim of an American humourist: "It is better to be ignoraant about a few things than to know such a terrible lot that ain't so." McLennan describes the dawn of human intelligence as to kinship after the following fashion: "The earliest groups can have had no idea of kinship. Once a man has perceived the fact of consangunity in the simplest case—namely, that he has

216

his mother's blood in his veins, he may quickly see that he is of the same blood with her other children. A little more reflection will enable him to see that he is of the same blood with the children of his mother's sister. And in process of time, following the ties of blood through his mother, and females of the same blood, he must arrive at a system of kinship through females." We will not follow him down through the ages of evolution of masculine intelligence until it comes within sight of kinship through males. The remarkable thing to our minds is, that so many other male writers have accepted his first statement as solemn truth!

476. Men alone could imagine a time when mother and off-spring were ignorant of mutual kinship. Kinship is something which was orginally hidden from the "wise and prudent" and revealed to sucklings and mothers. There never was a period in the history of the human race when babes did not know which woman to cry for when hungry: or when a mother had given birth to a child without recognizing her blood-relation to the same! Nor have mothers ever forgotten, in later years the children, grown to manhood and womanhood, who brought them into the agony of childbirth.

477. The description of such processes of mind as this, through which grown men confess they must have passed, in order to arrive at a fixed comprehension of kinship, is food for thought for women. Women needed to pass through no such "process" of growing intelligence on this subject. The first case of the knowledge of kinship can be learned from the Bible,—but not by evolutionists who despise the book. When Eve's first-born came into the world she exclaimed, "I [not we] have gotten a man!" We suppose there was, as yet, no word for "baby." She named him Cain—"gotten"—for SHE had gotten him. She knew, of course, her blood-relationship to the child; to *not know* this was impossible. But she probably did *not* know that Adam was related to the child also: and apart from her instructions on the point when at last he learned it, Adam must have forever remained ignorant of the fact that he was the father of his children, and that they were his kindred also.

478. Thus the Creator gave woman the start of man, by—who knows how many hundreds of years?—in the

race for laying in a claim to kinship with children. Here is a most important sociological fact: Woman, however low she may be in intelligence, unless actually insane or imbecile, *always knows which children are her own,* whereas the father of a child (1) must either sit at his wife's feet, humbly to attain to this intelligence, by her instruction; or (2), he must repose confidence in her fidelity to him; or (3) else he must make her his captive, or at least put her under constant watch to secure the desired information. But man does not wish to acknowledge this dependence upon woman for a knowledge of kinship to his own children. He would rather picture the dawn of intelligence in McLennan's fashion—ignore the fact of the superior intelligence of women at this point.

479. What a state of helpless unintelligence it is! Contrast the progress of masculine intelligence through the evolution of centuries, with the fact that the cow never bellows for the wrong calf, nor does even the snake swallow the wrong brood of baby snakes at the approach of danger. Man, after long years of existence, as a man, on the earth, finally arrives to an intelligence as to kinship,—that is, according to the theory of evolution-its; but, accepting that evolution theory, for the sake of the argument, woman, long before her appearance as a human being on the earth, while yet a cow, or a snake, had full intelligence as to her relationship to offspring of her own kind.

480. We do not say these things to create a smile, but to point some morals of supreme importance to woman's progress. Now let us add this further thought: However man has arrived at his intelligence as regards his kindred, that knowledge will, in no way, aid him in *keeping the thread of kinship* for succeeding generations. Here too woman alone holds the key of knowledge. He must continue to acquire his knowledge of his kinship to those about him, or of the past and of the future generations, in precisely the manner in which he first acquired it. There are but two ways in which man may acquire such knowledge: (1) By trusting the faithfulness and truthfulness of woman, or (2) By placing woman under incessant espionage or in prison.

481. Throughout the heathen world, wherever men have put in a "prior claim" to the rights of parentage,

the second method is practiced. There are millions of women and girls in the world today under incessant espionage, or else they are as truly the prisoners of their husbands as the criminals of this country are prisoners of the State. Through no fault of their own, but merely because men propose to claim superior parental rights, is this cruelty practiced upon women. There are twice or three times as many women in China as in India whose children men have claimed as exclusively their own. They have acquired the ability to take the off-spring from their mothers by insisting, through many ages, that women should be secluded, or should, instead, cripple themselves by foot-binding. And if women did not do this self-maiming, they branded them as women of evil life,—and then any man could take possession of them. Thank God these cruel customs show signs of early decay! But as *force* is renounced by man then *faith in woman* must take its palce, as a means of knowledge of kinship on the part of man.

482. Virtue in woman, as in man, is a prime quality; but that virtue could have been much better conserved, in the vast majority of cases, by customs which would leave the wife closely joined up to her own kin, under the espionage, if such were necessary, of her own relatives. Nothing better than this arrangement could have been devised for keeping women virtuous, and the Creator Himself devised it. But man has set it aside, and invented many cruel customs for accomplishing the same result,—the virtue of women. And this has been done not because he values morality in itself (he holds a lower standard of purity for himself), but to keep in continuance knowledge with which his Creator never endowed him apart from woman,—a record of male kinship.

ADDITIONAL NOTE.

Regarding the late Prof. Robertson Smith's teachings, as quoted in these Lessons, Dr. A. Mingana, also a professor of Ababic (at Manchaster University, England) writes me: "The late Prof. R. Smith has missed an important link in the chain of his argument. The Arabic word meaning **relation-ship is Nasab**, and is used exclusively of women. Among the Arabs, therefore, there was no relationship by man at all. The same may be said of relationship among the Arameans with whom the word **Hyana** is also used of women only and never of men. So you see that the relationship among the early Semites was certainly **exclusively** through women.........
"The only verb (or rather word) used to express relation-ship by man is among the Arabs 'Asab, but the word means simply 'to gather together for **battle, to muster for fighting**,' and the only word used among the Arameans is **Karebutha**,

which means **neighborhood,** or **Nashutha,** manhood,' and both refer to the idea of an 'alliance for battle,' without the smallest idea of relationship. This is an important point for your thesis."

[The Professor, in each case, gives the Arabic and Aramaic words in their original characters, but it has not been practicable to reproduce the script in this book, nor would it serve a very useful purpose to do so.]

LESSON 62.

THE TRANSITION TO MALE KINSHIP.

483. McLennan declares: "The fact of consanguinty must have remained long unperceived, as other facts quite as obvious have done." But we cannot possibly accept any such assertion as this, excepting as referring to the ignorance of the male sex. Again he says: "It will be a curious chapter in history which successfully narrates the progress of the revolution by which the passage from the earlier [female kinship] to the latter [male kinship] systems was effected." That chapter will be more than "curious;" for every page of it will be found stained with deeds of treachery, brutality, capture, imprisonment, outrage and murder, inflicted upon women.

484. "Where conjugal fidelity was secured by penalties," he continues, "we should expect to find the system of kinship through males would appear." The sentence may sound mild, but we have enumerated some of the "penalties" inflicted upon women by men who, in ages past, captured women from their own kindred, and thus established kinship through males (see par. 428). Again he says: "We shall see further on how numerous the known causes are in which the progress [?] to male kinship and the patriachal system was a progress having polyandry for one of its stages. *The other main highway of progress* [?] *must have lain through the system of confining wives* [as prisoners to their husbands]—a system probably established by exogamy and *the practice of capturing wives."* [The italics are ours.]

485. Sir George Grey describes what these caputres by men mean to the women of the Australian blacks: "Even supposing a woman to give no encouragement to her admirers, many plots are always laid to carry her off, and in the encounters which result from these, she is almost certain to receive some violent injury, for each of the combatants orders her to follow him, and in the event of her refusing, throws a spear at her. The early

220

life of a young woman at all celebrated for her beauty is generally one continued series of captivity to different masters, of ghastly wounds, of wanderings in strange families, of rapid flights," etc. We need not continue the scene. This is what the system of capturing wives means to young girls and women.

486. We do not agree with McLennan's reference to polyandry (plurality of husbands), as leading to female, kinship as we have repeatedly shown; polyandry as a general system cannot be proved to have existed. Polyandry never could have exerted any great influence in the development of social conditions,—if for no other reason than because it is suicidal to the race; it quickly leads to sterility. On the other hand, polygyny began very early in human history,—with Cain's immediate descendants, the Bible tells us, and it remains as a very general system among men to this day, and since it does not lead to sterility it greatly increases men's offspring, and it led to the capture of wives, because of an unequal distribution. These things being so, we claim that this horrible capture of women has been *the method* by means of which female kinship has been displaced by male kinship.

487. Perhaps we should say that McLennan makes a lame effort to demonstrate polyandry among the Hebrews, citing in proof the regulation that a man should marry the surviving widow of his brother (Deut. 25:5-10), in case the brother died without issue. We mention the extraordinary view because many other writers have endorsed it, and it has even crept into some commentaries. Herbert Spencer ably confutes the claim, saying in conclusion, "We cannot, then, admit that the practice of marrying a dead brother's widow implies pre-existence of polyandry, and cannot accept the inference that out of decaying polyandry higher forms of marriage grew up." With this statement we are in hearty accord.

488. "There could be no *system* of kinship through males if paternity was usually, or in a great proportion of cases uncertain." This is a self-evident statement, yet we fear women have never recognized the full force of it. It means in effect this: Male kinship can be perpetuated by only one of two methods, as we have said. The first way,—by espionage, imprisonment and penalties,—signifies great cruelty to women. The second

method, when it secures kinship through males alone (as recognized in law, or custom), signifies an exploiting of woman's virtues—fidelity and truthfulness—to deprive her of her God-given right.

489. However we look at the matter, then, what McLennan calls "the highway of progress" from female to male kinship, is wet with woman's tears and blood, and strewn with her shackles and prostituted virtues. What woman can, for a moment, believe that God ever meant that such a transition should have been brought about? Nay, rather, He warned woman against the *first step of concession* in that direction, when He said to Eve, *"Thou art turning to thy husband, and he will rule over thee."* There was no provision, in God's plan, for that sentimentality which talks of the loveliness of that devotion in a young bride which causes her to forsake her kindred to follow her bridegroom—almost a stranger as yet—to the ends of the earth. Such devotion is not out of place in the wife who has been long enough married to have proved that her husband is trustworthy. Such devotion in a young bride has landed hundreds of them —perhaps thousands—in houses of shame,—for the "husband" has turned out to be a mere slave trader, or the sort of creature who expects to live off his wife's earnings, driving her to vice to support him. The natural protectors of the young should not relinquish their task in the case of a trusting bride, until they are satisfied that the bridegroom is trustworthy. This was God's ordinance in marriage.

490. It is in the laws of succession, particularly, that we see to what an extent male kinship prevails. During the reign of King Edward VI (1547-1553), British civil and ecclesiastical courts combined in the assertion that the son of the Duchess of Suffolk was no kin to his mother. In other ways the same point is made clear. A British woman is not a "parent" of her own child, within the meaning of the law at the present time.

"The system of kinship through females only was succeeded by a system which acknowledged kinship through males also; and which in most cases passed into a system which acknowledged kinship through males only," says McLennan. Our present civilization is now deeply shadowed by this system, as embodied in civil law. Thanks to the softening influences of Christianity, men· are often better than the law, as an offset to the many worse than the law.

491. The system of kinship through males alone is known by the name *agnation*. McLennan describes agnation, in Roman jurisprudence, as follows:

"All the children of a married pair were agnates, as well as all the grandchildren through sons, but the grandchildren through daughters were not in the number of agnates. The children of the same father through different mothers were kindred, but the children of the same mother by different fathers were not relations to any legal effect. The sons of brothers were kinsmen, but the sons of sisters, or of brother and sister, were no relations; for a woman's children were held to be not of kin to their mother but of their father."

The pagan argument to establish this, was put by Aeschylus (500 B. C.) in the mouth of Orestes, who killed his mother to avenge his father's death at her hands: "The bearer of the offspring is not the *author* of it, but only the nurse. . . It is the male who is the author of its being; while she, as a stranger for a stranger, preserves the young plant for those for whom the god has not blighted it in the bud. And I will show you proof of this assertion; one *may* become a father without a mother. There stands by a witness of this in the daughter of Olympian Zeus, who was not even nursed in the darkness of the womb." (Mythology teaches that Athene, or Minerva, sprang full-armored from the head of Zeus, or Jupiter.)

But in due course God sent forth His uncreated Son, *"made of a woman"* (Gal. 4:4), without male agency,— an unanswerable argument as to the importance and Divine ordinance of female kinship.

LESSON 63.

"WHO SHALL DECLARE HIS GENERATION?"

492. We must abandon, then, the views set forth by such writers as Sir Henry Maine, of an older school, who declares: "The elementary group is the family connected by common subjection to the highest male ascendant." That male ascendancy he calls the *patria potestas*. Later investigations demonstrate that previously there had been female dignity. We re-state the proposition: "The elementary group is the family, held

223

together by equal parents, with the children in subjection to them." We have said before that we do not believe that God designed that either adult parent should rule the other; we do not concede that such rule of an adult is necessary; it destroys domestic peace, and the happiness of the subordinated one. McLennan makes this useful remark, to which women should give heed: "The system of kinship through mothers only, operates to throw diffculties in the way of the rise of the *patria potestas,* and of the system of agnation." We believe God designed that system of kinship through females only precisely for that purpose; to put a check upon that ambition to which He foreknew Adam would give rein,—to have power, to be "as God," in the matter of ruling over others.

493. *"Who shall declare His generation?"* asks the farseeing prophet Isaiah (53:8), in regard to the coming Messiah. Most scholars agree that the sentence should have been translatd, *"Who considered His generation,"* and the R. V. so renders it. The precise import of the question is a matter of uncertainty among expositors.. Some refer it to the untimely death of Christ, which rendered posterity in His case, impossible. But would He have had human and fleshly posterity had He lived? Unthinkable! This sense seems to be conveyed by the A. V. translators. But this word rendered "generation," singular number, never seems to admit such a sense as "posterity." It means rather a single generation, or period. Therefore, *"Who shall declare His generation, for He was cut off out of the land of the living,"* can hardly signify, "He could have no posterity because of an untimely death."

494. The R. V. seeks to meet the need of a clear sense by supplying two words to the original text. It reads, *"As for His generation* [contemporaries], *who among them considered that He was cut off out of the land of the living?"* Concerning this Dr. Skinner, in the Cambridge Bible says of the original word for "generation" (dor) that "it is never used with any such significance as 'length of life,' or 'life-history,' or 'posterity.' . . . We may render with the R. V. 'and as for His generation who (among them) considered,' etc. Yet the construction. as a direct object of the verb is so much the more natural that any suggestion would be. acceptable which might enable us to retain it." We offer such a

suggestion, in the light of the recently recognized fact (so long ignored), that God's primal social law provided for female kinship, rather than male kinship, and that God prophesied that the Seed of the *woman* should bruise the head of the Serpent.

495. The suggestion is this: There being no neuter gender in Hebrew, the word for "generation" is masculine in form; but following English usage we should translate the pronoun "it," not "he." *"Who considered His generation, for* it *was cut off out of the land of the living."* And so it was; by setting aside female kinship, and reckoning kinship by males only, no place was left to record the unique generation of Christ Jesus, of a woman only. Isaiah, seeing this fact by prophetic vision, marvels that no man "considered" that the cutting off of female kinship from the earth would involve the cutting off of the generation of that One of whom Isaiah himself had previously prophesied (7:14) that He was to be conceived and born of a virgin. (Read the Additional Note at the end of the Lesson).

496. Satan, at any rate, had considered that coming time. He did not forget the prophecy, *"I will put enmity between thee and the woman, and between thy seed and her Seed; it shall bruise thy head, and thou shalt bruise His heel."* He knew that the woman was to bear seed in some special and unusual manner, to which man was not to be so closely related. And this generation would mean the birth of his conquering Enemy into the midst of mankind. What wonder if he determined, far in advance of the event, to plan that when it came to pass it should be scarcely "considered" at all by man? What wonder if he wrought upon the pride and ambition of men to be reckoned as the sole source of the generations of men on the earth, and upon their ambition to perpetuate their own names, instead of that of their mothers, from generation to generation? The deed was accomplished, but female kinship was not displaced by male kinship excepting by most cruel, oppressive and immoral methods.

497. Man did not consider, nor did Satan intend he should, that in cutting off the generations of woman from their genealogical tables of the living, he would leave no room for the record, in unquestionable terms, of the greatest event that could ever transpire in human

history. Joseph's name—the name of one in no way related to Jesus Christ by ties of blood, must do duty as Jesus' sole "parent," in the eyes of the law.

498. Two genealogical tables are given for Jesus Christ,—one in Matthew, the other in Luke. The first ends in the name "Joseph," and the second begins with "Joseph." The tables are not alike, at some points, nor are either of them a satisfying demonstration that Jesus Christ was of the House of David, whatever they may prove of Joseph's lineage. That in Matthew, first chapter, is supposed by many to be Joseph's own; that in Luke, third chapter, Mary's own, excepting for the name of Joseph. But this genealogical table ends with "Adam," who was that one member of the human race who, being older than Eve, cannot by any logical possibility be in the line of the descendants of Eve, within which line Christ was promised, and came. If we cannot *prove* the validity of the *evidence,* how can that evidence prove the case? If the witness that "this was the Son of God" rested *solely* upon these attempts to prove it by these tables, we should be badly off. These tables have, viewed in this light, proved to be to this extent stumbling blocks.

499. But understanding, as we now do, that man "cut off" the generations of woman from "the land of the living" to place his own name in her place, we see, in this confused attempt to establish a "generation" for the man Christ Jesus, Seed of woman alone, a confirmation and fulfilment of Isaiah's prophecy, which confirms rather than weakens faith. And women have the consolation of knowing that their Redeemer shares with them the dshonour. Her Saviour, and His mother Mary, suffered the greater affront in this wrong to womanhood; and man but struck at the foundations of his own faith in the Redeemer, by providing no proper place in the records of human births for that Name at which eventually every knee shall bow, that Name which, eventually, every tongue will confess,—voluntarily in loyal love and reverence, or involuntarily, in fear and dread.

500. Canon Payne-Smith speaks truly of Gen. 3:15 as containing "that promise, of which the whole of the rest of the Scripture is but the record of the gradual stages of its fulfilment." The grand seal of that promise was the virgin birth of Jesus the Christ; but just as,

when it came to His birth, no place was found for Him in the habitations of man (only among the lower animals), so was no place left for the record of the birth of the Most Holy among the records of the decent and honourable of earth. Female kinship would have made a place to receive Him among men. Male kinship required the makeshift of a foster "father."

And there is truth here for us to ponder. Male kinship, as recorded on earth rests *always* for proof, on hearsay evidence; female kinship, on *prima facie* evidence. Uncertainty must always haunt the former; and that is the great reason why it should never have been made the basis of human records.

ADDITIONAL NOTE.

Dr. Mingana makes the following note for me on this interpretation of Isaiah 53:8: "The Hebrew word [for "generation"] **Dor** is translated in Syriac by **Dar,** and curiously enough, the Syrian commentators understand this word as meaning "birth, genealogy," but mostly "the miraculous birth of Christ." See the still unpublished commentary of the Syrian Church entitled **Gannath,** p. 122 of MS 41 of the John Rylands Library. This is a distinct point gained for you."

LESSON 64.

THE MOST CERTAIN EVENT IN HUMAN HISTORY.

501. While men weakened the value of the genealogical table of Jesus Christ, by introducing the name of a foster father in the place of His only actual parent (a deed made necessary by the circumstance that male kinship had displaced female kinship, in public records), yet the actual event—that Jesus Christ was born into this world—rests upon a very sure historical foundation.

502. Does anyone doubt this? Then we wish to ask: Who ever made a *lie* so strong and stable that it could become the axis for all the *facts* of human events to revolve about? *Could* a mythical character traverse the stage of human action, and leave behind *it* a whirling eddy of all the *real personages* of history,—so that thereafter it would come to pass that every *actual event* would be reckoned as occurring 'Before-the-LIE" or "After-the-LIE?" But unless Jesus actually lived, this is precisely what must have happened. Perhaps one might even manage to invent a mythical character, and then give him a place so remote in human history that contemporary events could not be summoned in sufficient numbers to prove the historical representation a myth:

227

But Jesus Christ does not belong to this category. He belongs to a period of the world's history which is rife with historical records. And those very records have been, as it were, rent in twain, and compelled to re-arrange themselves in order as having happened before or after that virgin birth of the Son of God.

503. Pagans and Jews wrote of Jesus Christ as an actual historical character, close to His time on earth. We have the record of Josephus, who was born four years after the Crucifixion; Tacitus, born 22 years after it; Pliny, born 29 years after it, and Suetonius, born 37 years after it. Abraham Lincoln was born 109 years ago (I am writing at the beginning of 1923), and was assassinated 58 years ago. Would it be possible within this length of time, for us to be mistaken in our conviction that Lincoln ever lived on earth? So was it impossible for these unbelievers to mistake a mythical personage for a historical character. And besides, the two Talmuds of the Jews, and the Acts of Pilate stand forth as testimony to the life of Jesus on earth. None of the names cited in the foregoing list are identified with Christians in the least. Besides these, we have the writings of eight of His contemporaries, all but three of whom (Mark, Luke and Paul), were in immediate association with Him in His earthly career; and only enough difference in their witness as to who and what He was can be discovered as is needed to prove that the same hand did not write all the sketches.

504. But do not the Buddhists date *their* publications and events likewise on a basis of the life of the Buddha, Sakya Muni? They do,—in imitation of the method of almost the entire world, which bases its chronology on Jesus Christ's birth. But we need not fear the outcome. Listen to the statement of Prof. Cowell, professor of Sanskrit at Cambridge, on this subject: "Buddhism cannot be called an historical religion, if we mean by that term a religion whose origin is to be traced in contemporary annals. . . There are two separate streams for his history and doctrines [meaning Sakya Muni's] . . It is well known that there are twenty different dates for Sakya Muni's death, varying between B. C. 2422 and B. C. 543." On the other hand, while disgraceful quarrels and wars have prevailed between the unworthy professed followers of Jesus Christ, and they are divided into innumerable sects today, not one of these touch the

historical time of Christ. The whole world unites upon the one date.

505. Not that the precise day of the month, or month of the year, or even period of 365 days must be considered settled beyond all peradventure. But the *time* of His life on earth has never been lost, in the midst of changing chronologies, bringing in some confusion of a trivial nature. Dr. Horne tells us: "It is an extraordinary but singular fact that no history since the commencement of the world has been written by an equal number of contemporary authors. . . . . . The history of Alexander, King of Macedon and conqueror of Asia, is not attested by a single contemporary author; and the same remark can be made on the history of Augustus, Tiberius and others."

506. But can we believe in the *virgin birth* of Christ? Some teachers of the Bible can find no place in their scientific minds for the idea of a virgin birth, but that is because they are so ignorant of science. It has been known for long years by scholars that virgin birth was possible, at least in the lower ranks of animal life. The phenomena of virgin birth have received more attention of late years, with the improvement of methods for its investigation. The scientific name for virgin birth is *partheno-genesis*. *Parthenos* is the Greek word for "virgin;" *genesis*, the Greek word for "origin, birth." The scientific term means precisely what the English expression "virgin birth" means, and it describes precisely the same thing,—the production of offspring by unmated females.

507. Frogs' and hens' eggs will frequently develop partially, apart from fertilization (as we are accustomed to use the word). The same can be said of starfish and silkmoths. Some creatures that multiply in the ordinary way, if they are closely related to classes that multiply by parthenogenesis, will occasionally multiply parthenogenetically; to this order belong many butterflies. But they usually produce only males after this fashion. The fertilized eggs of the queen-bee will produce queens, while the unfertilized eggs will only produce drones. The same thing happens when the queen gets old,—that is, she only produces drones. Similar laws govern the lives of wasps and ants.

508. Some insects will at one season produce young in the ordinary way, and at other times by parthenogenesis.

Warmth seems to determine which, in some cases. Plant-lice are parthenogenetic in the summer, but only multiply in the ordinary way in winter; but by keeping them in an even temperature, plant-lice have been known to propagate parthenogenetically for fifty generations. Among some lower forms of insect life no males have ever been found. Among these the only method of propagation is by parthenogenesis. We must refer readers to works relating to this subject, such as Geddes and Thomson on *The Evolution of Sex,* books on bee culture, and articles in the encyclopaedias. This is not a scientific paper. We only wish to show that virgin birth is not an absurdity. Indeed there is a class of tumours of quite frequent occurrence in females of the human family, which some of our highest authorities have claimed to be attempts in the direction of virgin conception (dermoid tumors of ovarian origin).

509. On the subject of virgin birth in the human female, we cannot do better than quote the words of that scientific authority, Prof. Geo. John Romanes, M.A., LL.D., F.R.S., in his book, *Darwin and After Darwin,* foot-note, p. 119. It is expressed in scientific terms, but we must give it just as originally written,—or at least such portion as space will allow: "The earlier stages of par-thenogenesis have been observed to occur sporadically in all sub-kingdoms of the metazoa [creatures composed of more than a single cell—to these belong nearly all forms of life], including the vertebrata [back-boned], and even the highest class, Mammalia [animals which bring forth living young, and suckle them.] These earlier stages consist in spontaneous segmentation of the ovum; *so that if a virgin has ever conceived and borne a son, and even if such a fact in the human species has been unique, still it would not betoken any breach of physiological continuity* [in other words, it would not be a breach of the known laws of physiology]. . . *Such a fact need betoken no more than a sight disturbance of the complex machinery of ovulation,* on account of which the ovum failed to eliminate from its substance an almost inconceivably minute portion of its nucleus." We place in italics the words of most interest and importance to us. Could not our God have easily produced the "slight disturbance" quite independently of human means in the case of Mary of Nazareth, by His own entrance into humanity?

LESSON 65.

THE VIRGIN BIRTH.

510. We have demonstrated that a virgin birth does not contravene physiological law, though it may be exceptional; and that it might occur, in the case of the birth of Jesus Christ. It is very essential to Christian faith, and also essential to woman's dignity, to believe this. We have shown, in the words of Orestes, how the argument for male kinship exclusively was based by him upon the precisely contrary assertion,—namely, that as Pallas Athene (Minerva) sprang from the head of Zeus (Jupiter), it was demonstrated that the mother was nurse only to her child.

511. Though the argument has not usually been based upon this particular myth, yet its doctrine does prevail among men; and has determined decisions in law courts. Up to the present, laws which govern wedded life often proceed upon the fallacy that the mother is merely the pre-natal nurse of the father's seed. The precise physiological truth is so immensely different as to absolutely demonstrate (what nearly every human being knows by instinct), a nearer kinship between mother and child than father and child. That "reform" which displaced female kinship for male kinship was the greatest "reform against nature" this world has ever seen, and nothing but misery and social degradation, for man as well as woman, can follow in the train of the maintenance of such a systematic defiance of nature's laws and just claims. The virgin birth of Jesus Christ is woman's charter of rights in the matter of *kinship to her own offspring,* ever branding as false any counter-claim on the part of a father to superior property in their joint offspring.

512. Now we will listen to Prof. James Orr, of Glasgow, Scotland, as to the importance of the belief in the virgin birth to Christian faith. We prefer, in this case, the language of a scholarly man to anything of our own, lest feminine prejudices might be alleged. He has written a very concise, short essay on the subject for an American periodical called *The Fundamentals,* Vol. 1. From this we quote, but we would recommend the reading of an extensive, valuable book which he has written on the same topic.

513. "It is well known that the last ten or twenty years have been marked by a determined assault upon the truth of the virgin birth of Christ. . . because it is supposed that the evidence for this miracle is more readily got rid of than the evidence for public facts, such as the resurrection. The result is that in very many quarters the virgin birth of Christ is treated as a fable. . . It is likened to the Greek and Roman stories, coarse and vile, of heroes who had gods for their fathers. . . Among those who reject the virgin birth of the Lord few will be found—I do not know any—who take in other respects an adequate view of the Person and work of the Saviour. . . Rejection of the virgin birth seldom, if ever, goes by itself. As the late Prof. A. B. Bruce said, 'with denial of the virgin birth is apt to go denial of the virgin life.'"

514. "Those who take the lines of denial . . do great injustice to the evidence and importance of the doctrine they reject. The evidence, if not of the same public kind as that for the resurrection, is far stronger than the objector allows, and the fact denied enters far more vitally into the essence of the Christian faith than he supposes. . . It is, in truth, a *very superficial* way of speaking or thinking of the virgin birth to say that nothing depends on this belief for our estimate of Christ. Who that reflects on the subject can fail to see that if Christ was virgin born—if He was truly 'conceived,' as the creed says, 'by the Holy Ghost, born of the virgin Mary'—there must of necessity enter a supernatural element into His Person; while, if Christ was sinless, much more, if He was the Word of God incarnate, there must have been a miracle—the most stupendous miracle in the universe—in His origin?"

515. "One's mind turns first to that *oldest of all evangelical promises,* that the seed of the woman would bruise the head of the serpent. *'I will put enmity,'* says Jehovah to the serpent-tempter, *'between thee and the woman, and between thy seed and her seed; He shall bruise thy head, and thou shalt bruise his heel.'* (Gen. 3:15 R. V.). It is a forceless weakening of this first word of Gospel in the Bible to explain it of a lasting feud between the race of men and the brood of serpents. . . The 'seed' who should destroy him is described emphatically as the *woman's* seed. . . It remains significant that this peculiar phrase should be chosen to designate

the future deliverer. I cannot believe the choice to be of accident. The promise of Abraham was that in *his* seed the families of the earth would be blessed; there the *male* is emphasized, but here it is the *woman*—the woman distinctively. There is, perhaps, as good scholars have thought, an allusion to this promise in 1 Tim. 2:15, where, with allusion to Adam and Eve, it is said *'But she shall be saved through her* (or the) *childbearing'* (R. V.)."

516. "By general consent the narratives in Matthew (chs. 1, 2) and in Luke (chs. 1,2) are independent—that is, they are not derived one from the other—yet they both affirm, in detailed story that Jesus, conceived of the Holy Spirit, was born of a pure virgin, Mary of Nazareth, espoused to Joseph, whose wife she afterwards became. . A persual of the narratives shows clearly—what might have been expected—that the information they convey was derived from no lower source than Joseph and Mary themselves. There is a marked feature of contrasts in the narratives—that Matthew's narrative is all told from Joseph's point of view, and Luke's is all told from Mary's. The signs of this are unmistakable. Matthew tells about Joseph's difficulties and action, and says little or nothing about Mary's thoughts and feelings. Luke tells much about Mary—even her inmost thoughts—but says next to nothing directly about Joseph. The narratives are not . . contradictory, but are independent and complementary. The one supplements and completes the other. Both together are needed to give the whole story. They bear in themselves the stamp of truth, honesty, and purity, and are worthy of all acceptation." . .

517. "It is sometimes argued that a virgin birth is no aid to the explanation of Christ's *sinlessness*. Mary being herself sinful in nature, it is held the taint of corruption would be conveyed by one parent as really as by two. It is overlooked that the whole fact is not expressed by saying that Jesus was born of a virgin mother. There is the other factor—conceived of the Holy Ghost.' . . The birth of Jesus was not, as in ordinary births, the creation of a new personality. It was a divine Person—already existing—entering on this new mode of existence." . .

518. "The belief in the virgin birth of Christ is of the highest value for the right apprehension of Christ's

unique and sinless personality. Here is One who . . . .
free from sin Himself and not involved in the Adamic
liabilities of the race, reverses the curses of sin and death
brought in by the first Adam, and establishes the reign
of righteousness and life. . . . . As one of Adam's
race, not an entrant from a higher sphere, He would
have shared in Adam's corruption and doom—would
Himself have required to be redeeemd."

These quotations, although brief, will serve our purpose,—though, of course they cannot do full justice to
Prof. Orr's valuable article.

LESSON 66.

THE FOUNDING OF A CHRISTIAN FAMILY.

519.   According to the chronology of the O. T. ordinarily in use (Usher's), Abraham was born in 1996
B. C., and Sarah was ten years younger (Gen. 17:17).
This household of faith lived, then, about as long before
Christ as we live after Christ.   The same chronology
places Eve's day, when the promise of the conquering
Seed was given, at 4004 B. C., thus reckoning the time
of Abraham and Sarah as about midway between this
memorable promise and the birth of woman's Seed.

520.   From the days of Eve to Abraham (at first called
Abram), God had apparently taken no account of the
seed of the male, as having part in the progenitress of
the coming Messiah.   In the meantime humanity, at
least in that part of the world, had abolished the reckoning of posterity as to female descent; and much that
characterized the early female dignity was vanishing.
By some method trace must be kept of the coming Messiah, otherwise than the general designation that he
would be the Seed of woman; and now the light begins
to dawn as regards what *nation* He will be joined to
when He appears.   At the same time, it was in the purpose of God to prepare that nation to receive Him.

521.   Abraham, and his wife Sarah, were called away
from their idolatrous relatives (Gen. 12:1-5; Josh.
24:2,3).   Having arrived in Canaan, God began their
religious training, and to elevate their hopes and fix
them upon their future posterity.   We will do well to
study closely this preparation of a previously pagan
family as the head of all households of the true faith

for all time to come. This family may well be designated the first Christian family, for it was in training to believe in a coming Christ (as Eve did),—just as we believe in a Christ who has come and will come again.

522. We have often watched the erection of the very tall buildings which are so numerous in the large cities of America, and which are now appearing in increasing numbers on both sides of the water. Their construction is quite unlike that of smaller buildings. First of all, a far greater amount of earth is dug away, to make room for a deeply-laid and strong foundation; then every beam and rafter is of iron, well riveted together, after the style of bridge-building. God wished to found and erect the first household of faith as a pattern for Christian homes for all time. He dug deep; laid firmly His great foundation stones; and riveted all the beams of His building well together. Let us study how He operated.

523. God was promising Abraham a progeny as great as the number of the stars of the heavens, and at the same time not allowing Sarah to bear even *one* child. He took one hundred years to get Abraham ready to become a father, and ninety years to fit Sarah for motherhood. *"The ungodly are like the chaff which the wind driveth away,"* God says; and *"That which is born of the flesh is flesh."* There is no building of a respectable family on mere chaff. The Bible teaches us that when God wishes a numerous progeny He takes the regulating of the begetting of offspring into His own control. Everything depends upon *quality;* a great family of Ishmaelites or Philistines are no blessing to the world; and such a family is short-lived, anyway; vice and crime and war soon bring it near destruction.

524. *"Sarah, Abram's wife, bare him no children,"* (Gen. 16:1). On the one side was the promise of *"seed as the dust of the earth"* (Gen. 13:16) in multitude; on the other, a barren wife. What did it mean? Just this: *quality* is everything with God, even when *quantity* is the desired end. There had been, probably, first of all in Abraham, merely the sensuous delight in Sarah's beauty (Gen. 12:11-14), behind which lurked the desire of the flesh which had led the pagan Abram to marry his half-sister; then that had become mingled with a looking into the future, inspired by God's leading and

235

promises, and Abraham desired an heir to whom he could bequeath the wealth he had acquired, and who would perpetuate his name (Gen. 13:2; 15:3). Then God lifted his longings to fairer worlds than Canaan,— to *"a city which hath foundations, whose builder and maker is God"* (Heb. 11:10), and then, after his flesh was *"dead"* (Rom. 4:19) to all sensual desire, a son was born,—of the holy desire to bless the world, in fulfilment of God's promise, as to his seed (Gen. 12:3; 22:18), which holy desire met God's own desire to bless the world through Abraham and Sarah.

525. The case is a striking one, and reminds us that when Isaac married, Rebekah was allowed to bear no children, again, until fleshly desire was displaced by holier aspiration. The heir of the promises of Abraham, Isaac, *"intreated the Lord for his wife, because she was barren; and the Lord was intreated of him"* (Gen. 25:21),—and so Esau and Jacob came. In their turn, the promise made to Abraham, to bless all the families of the earth, was reposed in Jacob; and the wife of Jacob's choice, Rachel, likewise, found herself unable to bear children until she prayed for them; something more than sensual desire, or human ambition, must enter into the birth of promising offspring. *"God remembered Rachel, and God hearkened to her."* (Gen. 30:22, and she bare that one against whose character no fault is recorded, Joseph, a notable person, who saved his entire family from starvation; whose sons, Ephraim and Manasseh, were heads of the two tribes about which clustered the other eight which constituted the ten tribes of Israel; so that *"Israel,"* as distinguished from "Judah," is often called "Ephraim" in the prophets of the later periods of O. T. history (Jer. 31:18 etc.).

526. And thus it was again when God desired a deliverer for Israel. Samson's mother *"was barren, and bare not,"* and as an angel finally appeared to her and gave instructions as to the coming child, we have reason for inferring that she and her husband had prayer about this matter,—especially as we know Manoah, the father, prayed for more definite guidance as to the rearing of the expected child (Judges 13:8). Then we come to that rarely beautiful character, the founder of the schools of prophets, Samuel. He came, not in answer to fleshly desire, but in answer to Hannah's fervent prayers (1 Sam. 1:20). God, in this case also, hinder-

ing her from bearing children until her desire had become a sanctified one. Such may have been the experience of many other mothers, though not specially recorded, who bore great children in past times.

527. Now we go into the New Testament, to learn the same lesson from the experience of Elisabeth. God was about to make ready the Forerunner for Christ's entrance into the world. He chose the family of Zacharias and Elisabeth, and at once closed the way against a child of the flesh, that Elisabeth might give birth to one born of holy, unsensual desire. He waited long,—until all fleshly desire had ceased; then the angel was sent to announce: *"Fear not, Zacharias: for thy prayer is heard and thy wife Elisabeth shall bear thee a son. He shall be great in the sight of the Lord—and he shall be filled with the Holy Ghost, even from his mother's womb,"* Luke 1:13-15. Thus are great men born into the world; that is, men who are great in the sight of God, though the world may despise them, as Herod despised John the Baptist, imprisoning him first, and then beheading him.

(To be continued.)

ADDITIONAL NOTE.

There is a most striking contrast between God's purpose in His dealings with these parents of holy offspring, and the purposes served by the modern devices for "birth-control." Two phases of desire struggle for expression, and God decrees that for holy offspring the **fleshly** desire shall decay, and **desire for offspring,** spiritually expressed in prayer and supplications, shall supervene. On the contrary, the modern human devices would curtail expression of longing for offspring, and give full rein to irresponsible fleshly desire. "Base-born" indeed would be offspring of such unions, when finally permitted to come to birth.

LESSON 67.

THE FOUNDING OF A CHRISTIAN FAMILY.—

Continued.

528. But to return to that first household of faith: With all Abraham's wishes and prayers, as to a prospective heir, he had no mind to take any risk of his life to preserve Sarah, his wife. Before ever He obeyed God, and left his own kindred with Sarah, he put her under bonds to represent herself as merely his sister, to save his own life from all risk (Gen. 12:13), although, as his wife, she had already taken the risk of her own

life for Abraham's sake and for the sake of children,—
the risk that every woman takes who marries.

529. Sarah, at this period, lacked self-respect; and
Abraham had insufficient respect for her. He had also,
as yet, little faith in God, who, since He had sent
them forth to a distant land, would have protected them
both. We wonder if Abraham would have represented
himself as her "natural protector?" We think so; for
he says: *"Say, I pray thee, thou art my sister: that it
may be well with me for thy sake"* (Gen. 12:13). In
other words, "Please, Sarah, protect me from all risk to
my life, in order that your 'natural protector' may survive to protect you." The "protector" was protected by
his wife, and he survived, at the risk of the loss of both
wife and heir. See Gen. chapters 12 and 20. We see
something of this sort of "protection" in our own day.
God was Sarah's only protector; women would do well
to learn that *"cursed is the man that trusteth in man"*
(Jer. 17:5), but *"they that trust in the Lord shall be
like Mount Zion, which cannot be removed, but abideth
forever."*

530. Sarah ought not to have agreed to such an arrangement with Abraham, and she would not have done it
later in life,—if we read her character aright, in its
unfolding. But not knowing any better, God protected
her, and incidentally to that protection, she was given
as high a name as could be bestowed upon a human
being—*"messiah"*, "anointed",—given to Sarah who lived
ages before the great Messiah. 1 Chron. 16:22 and Psalm
105:15 read, *"Touch not mine anointed, and do my
prophets no harm."* The Hebrew-form "mine-anointed"
is generally taken as plural ("mine anointed ones," as
it is translated in the R. V.), but nevertheless it has
special application to Sarah and Rebekah. To Sarah,
since it was regarding her that God gave commandment
to Abimelech, and said, *"I suffered thee not to touch
her,"* Gen. 20:6. And to Rebekah, included with Isaac,
in a later Abimelech's* command not to touch them,
given doubtless under God's pressure,—Gen. 26:11. Of
no other persons is the same word spoken by God, at
this early period in history.

* This term Abimelech, meaning "father-king" was the
title (like Pharaoh in Egypt), of the rulers of the Philistines.

531. Before God answered Abraham's real, but as yet selfish desires, and gave him a son, He had one more lesson to teach him, by a not trivial operation upon a man of ninety-nine (Gen. 17:11), though not decrepit, as a man of those years would be in our day. It was likewise to be performed upon every male of his household; and after that operation, not before, they were in covenant relations with God. This was the act of circumcision. In Abraham's case, at least. "It was the fit symbol of that removal of the old man, and that renewal of nature which qualified Abraham to be the parent of the holy seed (Murphy). It is significant that whereas other nations and peoples have practiced and taught the circumcision of women also, this was not required by God, nor ever practiced among the Jews, among whom it signified entrance into covenant relations with God. The reason is not far to seek: long previously to this time woman had been entered into God's covenant, as progenitress of the coming Christ, in His declaration: *'I will put enmity between thee [Satan] and the woman; and between thy seed and her Seed; it shall bruise thy head, and thou shalt bruise his heel'* (Gen. 3:15).

532. Rebekah, Rachel, Leah, even Rahab and Ruth, not to mention other women of blood foreign to the descendants of Abraham, enter, without ceremony, into the list of ancestors of Jesus Christ. But no *male* enters that list, save on two conditions: (1) He must be a descendant of Abraham, and (2), like Abraham himself, must have passed through that mysterious ceremony which signified *"putting off the body of the sins of the flesh"* (Col. 2:11).

533. For an additional explanation of this exemption of women, we go back to the first chapters of Genesis, and what we have emphasized at the beginning. The sins longest indulged have the most tyranny over us. Adam desired to be "as God." Ambition and lust first of human sins controlled the human race, ambition to rule finding an entrance through Adam, and lust, in addition, through descendants of Cain. Before Abraham could become the father of a chosen race, these sins needed to be extirpated from his character.

534. We have shown the special dealings as to sensuality with Abraham, to perfect his character. Now as to

his domineering qualities: He had only pagan ideas of marriage at first, and by this time only scraps of that early dignity of womanhood remained. Without scruple, though a worshipper, of a sort, of the true God, he let Sarah be taken into Pharaoh's harem (Gen. 12: 14-20). Doubtless he thought those promises of an abundant seed could be as well fulfilled through any other *woman;* the promise had been made to *him,* and he did not think it included Sarah, or he could hardly have been so easy about disposing of her. And more than this, Abraham seems to have thought her his chattel. Making no effort to rescue her from captivity in Pharaoh's harem, he received many presents" in exchange for her; for Pharaoh *"entreated Abram well for her sake; and he had sheep, and oxen, and he-asses, and menservants, and maidservants, and she-asses, and camels . . . . And Abram went up out of Egypt . . very rich."* And all this at the cost of Sarah's moral well-being and risk of virtue, until Pharaoh restored her to him (Gen. 12:16, 13:1).

535. It was here probably at Sarah's cost that Hagar was obtained; and Hagar was a source of sorrow to the family, and of grievous sin. A childless wife, in the Orient, is set aside after a few years; and the only means of escape from such a fate must be obtained by the childless wife herself; because she could not present her lord with an heir, she must present him with a woman servant who could bear him an heir,—to be reckoned as the lawful wife's child. Books on the "Duties of Women," among the Chinese are embellished with instances of such wifely devotion as this, which is reckoned to be exceedingly "womanly."* The same is the case in India. One of the most vivid accounts of the ceremony, from a native standpoint, will be found under the title, *Uma Himavutee,*

---

* This, for instance: "Nine women of ten are jealous [of other wives, or concubines] . . . There are also many wives who are advanced in age and have no son, who are yet unwilling that their husbands should take concubines, content rather that the sacrifices to the ancestors [of the husband] should finally cease. There can be no punishment too severe for such women. Let them read the wise precepts of the ancients, and note the conduct of admirable and accomplished ladies as recorded in this book, and how can they help blushing [at their degeneracy]?" "In ancient times a wise Empress and virtuous concubines, laying aside selfishness, and with all-pervading kindness sought for the harem of their lord pure and accomplished ladies."

[From **"Records of Virtuous Women of Ancient and Modern Times,"** a book highly esteemed among the Chinese, translated, in part, by Miss A. O. Safford.]

in a book by Mrs. Flora Annie Steel, called *In The Permanent Way.* Every woman who wishes to understand Sarah should read it.

536. Much has been said in depreciation of Sarah's character because she gave Hagar her maid to Abraham (Gen. 16:2). We now know that the land of Canaan was, at this time, a dependency of the land from whence they came, the entire region being governed by Hammurabi (Amraphel, of Gen. 14-1). In 1901 a stone slab was discovered at Sura, upon which is engraved his code of laws. He ruled in the days of Abraham over all Mesopotamia, from the mouth of the rivers Tigris and Euphrates to the Mediterranean Coast, and Sarah but yielded to the requirements of the laws of her country in that which she did.

(To be continued.)

LESSON 68.

THE FOUNDING OF A CHRISTIAN FAMILY.—

Continued.

537. The legal requirements of King Hammurabi which Sarah obeyed read: "If a man has married a wife, and she has not granted him children, that woman has gone [shall go] to her fate [is to be divorced], if her father-in-law has returned him the dowry that that man brought to the house of his father-in-law," etc. (par. 168). Par. 138 of the same Code describes the conditions under which a man may "put away his bride who has not borne him children.' Par. 144 says: "He shall not take a concubine" if his wife "has given a maid to her husband;" and par. 146 says, if "she has given a maid to her husband and she has borne him children [and] that maid has made [should make] herself equal with her mistress," the mistress may reduce her to servitude again, but may not sell her. This is surely wonderful confirmation that Sarah's treatment of this whole matter, up to the time of Isaac's weaning, was precisely in accord with the legal provisions and customs by which the country was governed. But when Isaac was weaned, she took another course, and God, by express revelation to Abraham, confirmed her new departure as in the line of His will.

538. It is worth while for us to pause long enough to call attention to these very unjust and humiliating laws,

as relates to women, engraven on that stone which records the Code of Hammurabi, especially as that very Code is being commended by rationalists of the present time as more enlightened and more humane than the Mosaic Code,—which latter is often represented as a mere attempt to imitate the excellencies of the older Code. But women will prefer the Code of Moses, when once they enlighten themselves as to the vastly superior marriage laws of the latter. (See *Additional Note* at the end of this lesson.)

539. Sarah did go through the form of asking Abraham to bear a son by Hagar, but the act should be judged by the fact that a man had a legal right to divorce a childless wife, and she was now past seventy-five years of age. That Sarah had had reason to fear divorcement seems certain, because when Hagar became arrogant in her treatment of Sarah, the latter accuses Abraham of being himself to blame for Hagar's conduct, in the words: "*My wrong be upon thee.*" The Septuagint gives the idea conveyed by the words as, "*I am wronged by thee.*" Sarah is opening her eyes in new self-respect; she tells Abraham he had no right to have ever brought Hagar— the price of her humiliation—into the family; and then to have so conducted himself as to have created in her the fear of being divorced, through no fault of her own, but merely because she had not fulfilled for him the promises of God, that he should have a son. This is what we understand by her expression, and she adds: "*The Lord judge between me and thee,*" declaring her confidence that her position was just in God's sight.

540. And Abraham yielded, which he would not have done so readily had he not felt she was right. Then Sarah did the only thing allowable under the law; she attempted to discipline Hagar, and return her to the position of a handmaiden. Sarah was not willing that her household should be polygamous; the law cut Abraham off from the right of a *concubine* in the family, since Sarah had given him her maid to bear a child for Sarah (see par. 537). But Hagar would be nothing less than a wife, so she left the house, doubtless thinking Abraham, for the sake of his only child, would divorce Sarah and take her back in Sarah's place. Sarah made no effort to keep the child, so far as we know, which the law allowed.

541. The situation was hard for both Sarah and Hagar. Through fear that law and custom would set her adrift,

because a childless wife, she had yielded to the requirements of Hammurabi's legislative enactments, and provided a maid by whom to secure a son for Abraham; and
Hagar had taken advantage of Sarah's humiliated position,—to assume the position in the family of another
wife. Now Sarah begins to *think*, and that, on the laws
by which women are governed; and she charges upon
Abraham with the words: *"I am wronged of THEE . .
God judge between me and thee."* Doubtless Abraham,
like many another man, wished his wife would stop
dwelling upon the injustice of the laws which govern
women; and quit accusing him of wrong, if he merely
observed them.

542. Sarah's attempts to obey custom and law had
borne heavily upon a poor woman slave, too; and at first
Sarah perhaps did not see this; she *"dealt hardly,"* that
is, sternly—not likely abusively—with Hagar, to reduce
her to her former position in the family; but Hagar fled
with her child, rather than become a subordinate again.
As God protected Sarah, when Abraham left her in peril
in the harems of Pharaoh and Abimelech, so now He
appears for the protection of Hagar's interests (Gen. 16:
7-13). He gives her promises as to her progeny, but,
encumbered as she is with her own and Abraham's child,
as well as far from her own native land, God tells her to
return and submit as a servant to Sarah. God certainly
knew Sarah would not ill-use her; and Hagar had a right
to shelter and support, since the child was Abraham's to
support. The lesson for women to learn, from Sarah's
conduct in seeking a son for Abraham by such a method,
is this: Women who have superior advantages cannot
yield to enactments that are unjust to themselves without bringing greater injustice upon other women in less
fortunate circumstances. Sarah yielded to a wrong to
herself as a childless wife; the result was a worse wrong
to Hagar.

543. And furthermore, a wrong position of affairs can
seldom be put right without suffering to the innocent, or
at least without causing more suffering to others than
really deserved. The further incidents show this. When
Isaac was weaned a feast was given, at which Sarah
saw Hagar's son "playing." Some suppose we must
understand this to mean "mocking," and so the A. V.
translates (Gen. 21:9). This is not necessary. Sarah
was neither angered nor *jealous* of a rival's child. Had

this been the case, it is impossible that God should have endorsed, as He did, her conduct that day. Sarah had advanced greatly in character by this time, for we are told that *"through faith Sarah received strength to conceive seed"* (Heb. 11:11), and this implies no mean state of grace, for a woman barren from youth, and now past ninety. Sarah had become so enlightened that she revolted at any appearance of polygamy in her household, where Isaac was to be brought up,—for he had been given them to train for a very definite and holy purpose. Such surroundings were neither wholesome for Isaac nor Ishmael.

ADDITIONAL NOTE, The Code of Hammurabi.

Beginning with Lesson 71, we discuss the Mosaic laws, which at best were not ideal. But they were far superior to Hammurabi's in dealing with women. As an illustration we name the following:

Paragraphs 117 and 119 of Hammurabi's Code provide for the selling of wives and daughters for debt.

Par. 132 reads: "If the finger have been pointed at the wife of a man because of another man, and she have not been taken in lying with another man, for her husband's sake she shall throw herself into the water." Contrast with this the much-slandered *Trial of Jealousy* (Num. ch. 5), which allowed the suspected wife the protection of the Tabernacle until by voluntary confession, or an express miracle of God the suspected unchastity was revealed (if it ever was revealed by miracle—see pars. 585, 586). Exod. 21:22-25 provides that when, under certain circumstances, a woman is injured by a man, the penalty is "an eye for an eye, a tooth for a tooth," etc., that is, a woman's eye was worth what a man's was; the sexes were to be held of equal value. But under similar conditions, Hammurabi provides that the injurer was to pay (whatever the injury short of death) 10 shekels of silver to the woman's father; and in case of the woman's death, then *a daughter of the murderer* was to be put to death (par. 209).

This shows how completely daughters were reckoned as the chattels of their father's; and there was an express provision for sisters to become the property of brothers, after the father's death, in Hammurabi's Code, and these brothers could sell them for concubines.

A wife who became afflicted with disease could not be divorced, according to Hammurabi, but the husband could bring another wife into the house. Presently we shall show that, although polygamy prevailed to some extent among the Israelites, the Mosaic law *did not provide for it,* though garbled translations of one or two passages in our English and other versions seem to point the other way.

When rationalists contend for the superiority of Hammurabi's Code over Moses' we may feel sure that they are ignorant of their Bibles, whatever they may know of Hammurabi.

LESSON 69.

THE FOUNDING OF A CHRISTIAN FAMILY— Concluded.

544. Hagar's son is past fourteen, and Sarah demands that she and her son go elsewhere to live. Abraham demurs, but God commands him to comply. Nor were Hagar and Ishmael sent away without due provision for their support (Gen. 25:6), though Hagar gave herself up, for the moment, to needless despair, in which the Lord met and comforted her (Gen. 21:14-21). It was hard for Hagar to bear, for being a mere slave, she was not to be held responsible for having borne a child; but now, at any rate, she was emancipated. The setting of wrong conditions to rights made undeserved but unavoidable suffering for Hagar.

545. God cannot always elect,—that is, select—persons who are ideal, for they cannot be found. He takes faulty ones, but those capable of development. Such was the condition in which he found Abraham and Sarah. It is simply ludicrous to read some of the attempts that have been made by blundering expositors to explain away all the wrong things Abraham did: *"Abram's venture was not from laxity as to the sanctity of marriage, or as to his duty to protect his wife: it was from a presumptuous confidence in the wonderful assistance of God,"*—thus speaks Lange's Commentary. Such men, in their strained efforts to make Abraham appear

ideal from the day God called him, leave no place for that most valuable and much-needed lesson, as to the wonderful transformation of character which the grace of God can bring about in the faultiest person who will submit to God's authority, as Abraham began to do when he left his home in Chaldea.

546. The character of Abraham changed greatly under the moulding influence of divine grace, but we will not occupy the space to describe this transformation, for the reason that, as women, we are more interested in the character of Sarah, who, we hold, has been greatly belittled by the same commentators who will not admit that Abraham ever had many faults. Her character underwent a transformation quite as wonderful as Abraham's. Think what she was, as the servile female who went, apparently without protest, into the harems of Pharaoh and Abimelech, not knowing that she could ever come out undefiled; accepting polygamy weakly, if not happily. Like almost any Oriental woman of to-day, her husband's wish seemed as law, even when it bade her do that which was immoral, and which she may have utterly detested to do. She makes no complaint, but obeys.

547. Now study her character a little later, when she wakes up to resent the way she had been treated by Abraham in the matter of Hagar. She accuses Abraham as in the wrong, and appeals to God to judge between them. There were reasons why she might have been very cowardly at this moment, for Hagar was in the ascendancy just then, and was making the most of her position. Sarah might have reasoned: "I must not offend Abraham now, while Hagar seems so much more in his favour because of the boy." Doubtless Hagar counted on such a compromise. But Sarah was courageous, and met the situation boldly, calling upon Abraham to defend her in refusing Hagar the right to be a concubine, or a second wife, in the family,—for Sarah had yielded to the provisions of Hammurabi's Code on purpose to prevent this (see par. 537).

548. Then follows the later scene. Ishmael is older now, and Sarah demands that the last vestige of the semblance of polygamy be cleaned out of the household. If she again called on Jehovah to judge between her and Abraham, we do not know, but we do know that

when she made the demand, God told Abraham to obey what Sarah said, and it was done. If Abraham improved in character and saw the hatefulness of mixed marriage relations in the sight of God, it was under the joint training of God and Sarah. And later, after the old man had lost Sarah, and mourned deeply, her loss, he married one Keturah (Gen. 25:1). But though the word "concubine" is used in the sixth verse of this chapter, since Abraham did not marry Keturah until after Sarah's death, the word is not used in its ordinary sense, for, too, Hagar never bore this relation to Abraham.

549. But to return to Sarah: How are we to account for this development of such force of character, as that she has become quite "imperious?" Men usually do not like "imperiousness" in women; they think it "unwomanly" and they criticise Sarah because of this trait. But was it not of God's own planting and development, in Sarah's case? God called her "Mine Anointed" and God uses no idle words. He anointed her to be the Prince of the tribe, for God gives no empty titles. God commanded Abraham to cease calling her Sarai: *"As for Sarai thy wife, thou shall not call her name Sarai, but Sarah* (prince) *shall her name be,"*—Gen. 17:15. The older form "Sarai" meant the same as "Sarah" in Chaldea, but it did not in Canaan, hence the change.* Sarah means "prince." We do not say "princess," for the reason that the "—ss" has been used as rather a wifely termination among us, signifying the rank of the husband. Abraham was not called "Prince" by God. His name was changed from Abram to Abraham, "father of a multitude." Sarah was constituted by God a ruler, in her own right; she, not Abraham, was the anointed ruler of the tribe. Not because she was a *woman,*—not at all for that reason; but because she had better views than Abraham on the subject of social purity, and probably on other subjects.*

550. God had laid His hand upon a previously pagan family, to make of them a Christian household. He began by checking sensual tendencies in Abraham, taught him the benefits of monogamy, and respect for

---

* "I wrote a long note in **The Expositor** (1916, pp. 308-310), to the effect that Sarah meant 'my princess' and Sarah 'the princess.' The first word restricts the function of Sarah to Abraham, but the second generalizes it to all mankind."—Prof. Mingana.

his wife; wrought upon his instincts of fatherhood, and taught him to aspire to have a progeny that would bless the world, because of its excellencies. Furthermore, in receiving a special revelation as to the right course of dealing with spurious matrimonial relations (Gen. 21: 12), Abraham must have learned the lesson that the headship or leadership in a household turned not upon sex, but upon which one, husband or wife, knew best what to do. As for Sarah, He taught her He was her Protector and Deliverer from peril; trained her in self-respect; restored her to her place as the recipient of His promises when she had yielded it to another to secure a child for her husband; named her the Prince of her tribe, and anointed her for the office. We have shown that the oldest and most inveterate faults of man are the love of ruling and sensuality. Abraham's training was to correct these. Sarah's training was in dignity, authority and self-respect; and both in *faith*.

551. We may not do more than merely refer briefly to what a source of misfortune to the Israelites, God's people, the descendants of Ishmael always were. The Bible recurs to this again and again. The lesson of it all was summed up by Paul in the words: *"He who was of the bondwoman was born after the flesh; but he of the free woman was by promise . . . . as then he that was born after the flesh persecuted him that was born after the Spirit, even so it is now"* (Gal. 4:23, 29).

552. Abraham, in his waiting for the son of Sarah, became a notable instance (cited in Hebrews 6:12), of *"them who through faith and patience inherit the promises."* But few expositors have paused to consider the part of Sarah in the fulfilment of these same promises. She laughed at the possibility, when she first heard the promise, and made a remark (Gen. 18:12) which was given a sensuous turn in our translation, which is open to criticism. The expression is one common in the Orient today among women, and refers wholly to the 'pleasure" of having a child, very much desired, as the angel's own words show, for it puts the expression into plain words. *"Wherefore did Sarah laugh, saying, Shall I of a surety bear a child, which am old?"* Sarah was very old; she had also been barren all her lifetime. By faith Abraham waited patiently to receive the promise. Through faith Sarah rose above her age and her infirmity as well, and became, before

the eyes of Abraham, the living embodiment of those promises fulfilled. *"Through faith also Sarah herself received strength to conceive seed, and was delivered of a child when she was past age, because she judged Him faithful Who had promised,"*—Heb. 11:11. Abraham had the faith to expect and receive a child; Sarah, the faith to expect and *conceive* a child.

LESSON 70.

ISAAC AND REBEKAH.

553. Throughout Genesis, and in fact throughout the Bible, but decreasing in frequency, traces can be found of customs which characterized the early matriarchate. Many of these we are compelled to pass by for want of space leaving our readers to study them for themselves. But let us illustrate:

554. In the 24th of Genesis we read that when Abraham was old, after the death of Sarah, he called a trusted servant, and told him to go and search for a wife for his son Isaac among his *near relatives,* as we understand it, but on the *father's side* (verse 7), showing that still the idea of kinship through the *father* was scarcely taken account of. To be sure, the Bible nowhere forbids marriage between cousins, and this might be explained as only the ignoring of so remote a relationship as constituting no bar to marriage. But since Abraham had married the daughter of his own father (but not of his mother) in ignorance of any wrong in the matter (though it was strictly forbidden 450 years later by the Lord, Lev. 18:9), and in view of other points to be noted in this chapter, it is not improbable that up to this time the intimate relation between father and child was not given much importance, though we have noted how God was training the instincts of fatherhood in the character of Abraham.

555. This training was needful,—for there is nothing to be gained, and much to be lost, in the long run, by women as well as by men, in a weak tie between father and child. The child needs the protection and the support of a father; for the mother, so long as she is bearing children, ought to be circumstanced so as to be relieved entirely at these two points. And besides, she should have her own relatives to defend her rights,

should there be need, against a domineering or defrauding husband. But there has been an immense loss to both child and mother through weakening the tie between mother and child, *in order to set up the father-tie as a rival claim*. At first, as a result of ignorance and want of observation, the only tie clearly recognised was between mother and child; this was undesirable. Later, the kinship of both parents to a child came to be recognized; this was desirable. But later still, because of that love of power which has always more or less characterized the male sex, father-kinship displaced mother-kinship claims, before the law, and this is deplorable. Under the softening influences of Christianity, and more especially the fact of the Virgin Birth, the tie between mother and child came into recognition; but we have inherited from Roman law a legacy of abuses along this line which still often deprives the Christian mother of most palpable rights, in order to bestow them upon the father.

556. To return to Abraham: The servant said: *"Peradventure the woman will not be willing"—*. He said nothing about whether her parents would be willing; young women were free. On the other hand Isaac was not even consulted as to whom he wished to marry, so far as we know; his father settled that matter for him, and sent to get a wife for him whom he (a man of forty, Gen. 25:20), had never seen. The servant continued—*"must I needs bring* [take] *thy son again unto the land whence thou camest?"* (verse 5). Shall this man of forty be expected to go and reside with his wife's kindred, if the young bride so desire?

557. But in this case there were very important reasons why this should not be. The young woman's family was idolatrous (Josh. 24:2,3, and compare Gen. 31:30-34; 35:2), and God had called Abraham and Sarah away from this idolatry, promising to give their children the land in which they now dwelt (Gen. 12:1-5). Abraham knew his son would both lose this fair land for himself and his descendants, and would probably stray from the true God back into idolatry, if Isaac went back to Haran. Fidelity to God must be maintained at the cost of all claims of kinship, if necessary, so the servant was forbidden to take Isaac back to Haran.

558. When the servant arrived at Haran, and found Rebekah (Isaac's cousin on his father's side), at the

well, he gave her costly presents there, over one hundred dollars' worth,—a very large sum for those days. He did not reserve these presents to give to the father of the girl as purchase money. It is in later Bible days that we read of the purchase of wives (Deut. 22:29). The servant asks for room in Rebekah's *"father's house"* (v. 23), but Rebekah runs into *"her mother's house"* (v. 28), where her brother Laban is (and probably her father). Perhaps this signifies a division of the house into two parts, one for each sex. Perhaps it signifies that Bethuel had another wife and family. Again, perhaps it signifies that the same place is called by either name. The servant who was sent specially to Abraham's *own kindred,* on arrival would naturally (even if exceptionally) ask for the house of Abraham's nephew, not for the house of his wife,—one who was related to his master only as a niece by marriage.

559. But in view of the expression, "Sarah's tent" (see the next paragraph, and the interpretation put upon it by one so conversant with the customs of that land as Prof. Robertson Smith, and other late writers), it is not unlikely that in that sentence, *"The damsel ran, and told her mother's house these things,"* neither polygamy is implied, nor a strict separation of the sexes, but that the common family home is rated as the mother's rather than the father's. But in our own day, so far have we strayed from this dignity of woman that even when the wife is the actual and original proprietor of the house, the place will be called "Mr. So-andso's," so long as she has a living husband.

560. Afterward, in the house, the servant added to Rebekah's gifts (verse 53), and then gave good-will portions to Laban, her brother, and *to the mother,* who doubtless was expected to share with the father. This is no *purchase* of the bride from the father; the picture is very much in contrast to such a degrading scene. Mark the quiet part the father takes in this scene, as to the disposal of his daughter's hand, as compared with the mother. Laban is prominent, and officious, but for other reason than any custom; he is avaricious, and keenly alive to the approach of anyone who has riches, —as his entire after-history shows. Rebekah is not, in the end, taken away from home excepting after her express consent is obtained (verse 58). Finally, on arrival in Palestine, Isaac takes her into *"his mother's*

tent." Prof. Robertson Smith says: "Originally the tent belonged to the wife and her children, . . for Isaac brings Rebekah into his mother Sarah's tent, and in like manner in Judges 4:17, the Kenite tent to which Sisera flees is Jael's, not Heber's." Prof. Smith does not hold (with earlier expositors) that such expressions imply either polygamy or a separation of the sexes, but that property rights were vested with the wife. This ownership of the family home by the mother belongs to the early matriarchate.*

561. When Rebekah reached Isaac, *"she lighted off her camel"* and *"took a vail and covered herself,"*—not in "sign of subordination," as expositors would have us think, for that subordination did not exist. Nor was it as rendered, a "veil," for had veils existed at that early day, we may be sure Sarah would never have been imperilled by her beautiful face. The original Hebrew word signifies a "doubled" garment,—a mantle, shawl, to cover up the dust of her travel-worn costume,—see pars. 262, 263, and the Dictionary-Index at the end of the book, under *Veil*.

LESSON 71.

THE MOSAIC LEGISLATION WAS NOT IDEAL.

562. Many stumble at the Mosaic legislation because of its imperfections. Others will not admit but that everything the law of Moses allowed is allowed to Christians today. Often when we make clear the will of God touching moral conduct at some point, we are apt to question: "But why was this not embodied in the law of Moses? If it be true of these enactments, as is declared, that God *'spake unto Moses,'* then how can they express less than the full will of God?"

563. Concerning the subjects we have recently discussed, someone may say, "The Mosaic law makes no provision for female kinship; it would surely have done so, had that kinship been God's will." It is worth our while, therefore, to consider this matter, and the province of legislative enactments for the control of human conduct. The Mosaic statutes were not perfect; otherwise there would have been no room for their amendment,—for Jesus Christ to say, as He did, in the Ser-

* Dr. Mingana says, in regard to pars. 558-560, "Here also you have scored a good point."

mon on the Mount, *"Ye know that it was said to* [not "by," see R. V.] *them of old . . . . But I* [Jesus Christ] *say unto you,"* etc., Matt. 5:21-27, etc.,—each time making the rule stricter.

564. St. Paul, before us, trod this perplexing path of learning the province of "the law." In youth, he set about the task of establishing his own righteousness (Rom. 10:3, Phil. 3:4-6) by means of the law; and discovered that he did not attain to the law of righteousness (Rom. 9:31). Afterwards, he learned that *"The law made nothing perfect, but the bringing in of a better hope did,"* Heb. 7:19. Late in life, Paul wrote to Timothy: *"The law is not made for a righteous man, but for the lawless and disobedient;"* and he enumerates the various classes of offenders for whom the law was made, 1 Tim. 1:9, 10.

565. The lesson is this: Law is not an *elevating force;* it is a mere *check.* Paul did not find that its observance *elevated* him; it only temporarily acted in a limited way as a preventive of further degradation. Like a man who has fallen over the edge of a precipice; the bush at which he has caught may keep him from going to the bottom to be dashed to pieces, until help comes, and he is rescued. That bush cannot put him on his feet again at the top.

566. Nothing is more prominent in Paul's teachings than his warnings against trusting in "the law" for our elevation. There is need today for this warning, for still man is led on by the delusion which so long controlled Paul's life. And people of our day are continually trusting in some new law to improve social and political morals. When Paul talks of "the law," he in general means legislative enactments by which the Jewish commonwealth was governed. Some of these enactments are to be found in the Old Testament; some belonged to the Temple ritual; some were mere rabbinical deductions, based on rabbinical interpretations of the Scriptures.

567. "The law" to him was much what our legislative enactments are to us. Three classes of people can be found to-day in mistaken attitude towards human legislation. (1), Those who imagine that almost any degree of moral elevation may be accomplished in a people by means of good laws, efficiently enforced. We pronounce

this an entire mistake, on the authority of the Bible, particularly Paul's teachings. (2), Those who believe that since "we cannot make men moral by Act of Parliament," therefore the state of our moral laws is a matter of small moment. These are as mistaken as the former class. (3), Those who believe that all human legislation should be abolished; these are anarchists; their doctrine is horrible.

568. It is a matter of moment, then, for us to understand clearly what is the real province of human legislation as it relates to moral conduct. This is becoming a burning question for women, for they are not to be long outside the legislative body. Many Christian women are seriously questioning already whether they should or should not have a part in the political questions of the day. Whether, in fact, a Christian *woman,* at least, ought not to refrain from political tasks, as something unsuitable, and not in keeping with the higher ideals of the Christian life. Since human legislative measures so often fall short of the Christian standard, just as the Mosaic law does, have women any right to advocate anything but the very highest ideals? Do they not lower themselves by having anything to do with human legislation? Again they are perplexed by the question: Why did not Moses legislate more justly for women?

569. Let us show the province of legislation by the aid of a homely illustration: A heavily loaded cart is being dragged, laboriously, by a man, up a hill. That cart will represent human progress. The man pulling, will represent moral and religious instruction, including such means of grace as God has put forth for our help,— such as conversion, etc. Only one step is gained at a time, and there are many pauses,—in other words, the progress of the human race has interruptions. Now human legislation, as aid to human progress, may be compared to a stone, which is being used by a boy (the body of legislators), as a brake, so that when the pull ceases the cart will not run backward down hill again. At each pause in front, the boy pushes his stone close up against the wheel behind, and so he greatly helps the man in front.

570. It requires some skill on the part of the boy, in order to give the utmost help to the man in front. So

the genius of the statesman consists, largely, in his gift of divining public moral opinion,—in other words, in knowing the precise *moment when,* and the precise *point at which,* to apply legislation. The stone will do no good if placed too far behind the cart; in fact, it will do some mischief, for when the cart pauses, its action will be reversed for the want of a stay, and the cart will run backwards, and perhaps gain such momentum as to over-ride the stone entirely, and plunge to destruction. This is the sort of mischief which results from lax laws. Good laws may not make men good; but bad laws certainly demoralize men. A legislative enactment is "good," not necessarily because it is ideal —it may be far from ideal—but when it precisely meets the need of a brake, and prevents a nation from backsliding. And that law keeps "good" only as it keeps pace with the progress of the nation.

571. We scarcely need make further applications. Those who imagine that moral elevation can be accomplished by means of ideal legislation, may be likened to a boy thinking that his stone brake alone is sufficient to push the cart to the top of the hill. Those who advocate "no law" are generally hoping to see the cart plunge to the bottom. And those who imagine that our legislative measures should always correspond to the ideal set forth in the N. T., might put the brake high up the hill, far ahead of the cart. Moses' legislation was precisely suited to a people just emerging from slavery. It is not altogether suited to our needs. Yet, that slave people must have had some excellent traits, since some of Moses' statutes are in advance of our own progress. At any rate, we can now see that the pull at the front of the cart does not meet all our needs; the brake at the back is also necessary; and those Christians— whether men or women—do well who take an active interest in the making of laws that are "good" because precisely fitted to the progress of the people.

LESSON 72.
THE MOSAIC STATUTES AND WOMEN.

572. We have said that the Mosaic statutes, though designed for a people just emerging from slavery (and women are more degraded than men, usually under such conditions), were at some points in advance of our own

legislation. For instance, Lev. 20:10: The penalty for adultery was precisely the same for both sexes, and was not looked upon as a mere "accident" in a man (to use the language of Sir John Bigham, until recently head of Britain's divorce court). And that penalty was so severe that it must have solved the "illegitimacy" problem,—being death. The usual manner of putting to death was by stoning.

573. Lev. 12th chapter: A mother was in isolation 40 days with a new-born son, but 80 days with a new-born daughter. Three things are to be noted particularly here: (1). The actual term of "uncleanness" was only, respectively 7 and 14 days. According to the earlier covenant arrangement with Abraham, every male must be circumcised on the 8th day (Gen. 17:12). This religious ceremony would cut short the "uncleanness" in the male child. (2), The offerings made at the end of the full term were precisely the same for either sex, showing that one was rated as high as the other. (3), According to the Levitical law it was not in order to make the burnt offering, which was *self-dedicatory,* before the sin offering, which was *expiatory* (Lev. 8:14-18); but here is a remarkable exception; after childbirth the *sin offering* comes last, and even for the richest, was the smallest offering ever prescribed,—a pigeon. Now what may we deduct from these facts?

574. *Firstly:* From the expression, *"their purification"* (Luke 2:22, R. V., the A. V. being incorrect), used of the Virgin and her Child Jesus, this term of recovery by a process of purification, which followed upon childbirth, belonged to *both* mother and child; but as the 14 days' period of "uncleanness" itself was cut in half by another purification ceremony (circumcision), in the case of the male child, so would be the period of recovery, the six-and-sixty days. *Secondly:* Commentators have sometimes claimed the greater sinfulness of the female sex, because of the prolonged period of isolation after the birth of a female child. This is disproved by the fact that the offerings at the end of the period were the same in both cases. *Thirdly:* The mere fact of child-birth required no expiatory offering, or else it would certainly have come first. In other words, the mother could not have had access to God, to dedicate herself and child to Him, had there been any known sinfulness in her state, until first she had repented and

made expiation by a suitable offering for it. But at once she has access, and that in an exceptional sense, after child-birth, to God. Following upon this, a small sin offering is made, merely as a formal restoration, as it were, to her place among the worshippers, from whom she had been separated (not having enjoyed the privileges of the sanctuary), during her period of confinement.

575. Now having explained this matter, in accordance with the teaching of some excellent expositors, let us add: Even if the worst could be proved, i. e., that Moses taught it was far more wicked, or more unclean, to bring a female than a male child into this world, the process was very salutary for the female. By this time, in the world's history, women were being cheapened more and more. This statute of Moses was calculated to strengthen the tie between mother and female child, by their long isolation together—that tie which the patriarchy was doing so much to destroy. And the constant devotion to the child by its own mother, not a nurse, must have had a beneficial effect in starting girls with good constitutions, for the battle of life.

576. Lev. 15:16-18: (Please consult your Bibles). This statute regulated the ordinary habits of married life. Lange remarks: "The law must have operated as an important check upon sensual passions." Combine with this some further regulations of marriage, and we can readily see how carefully the health of Jewish women was guarded. Read Lev. 15:19-24, relating to unintentional defilement, and then Lev. 20:18, relating to deliberate disobedience. The latter incurred probably the death penalty, though some dispute whether "cutting off" means death; other equally learned scholars declare such to be its proper sense. These combined Mosaic statutes make it certain that Gen. 3:16 could never have meant, as interpreted in our day, that God placed the wife in such relations to her husband that his sensual demands must be her law.

577. Ex. 21:22-25: This makes considerate provisions for the protection of a woman who is about to become a mother, from the unintentioned, but nevertheless careless roughness of men. The woman, perhaps, of unusual nervousness, might rush to help, in the case of an attack upon her husband. At once they must recog-

nize her state and terminate the fight. If the fright caused evil consequences, the case came under the law for redress; if the woman was injured, precisely the same injury must be inflicted upon the man. An eye, to a woman, Moses declares, is worth as much as an eye to a man; her tooth is as valuable as his tooth, etc., etc. Here is an express provision that the value of woman's life shall not be rated lower than the value of man's life; nor her health less than his health. What hurt a man inflicted on a woman's body, that same hurt man must feel in his own body. Would that English and American women were as well protected in some regards as the Israelitish women of Moses' day!

578. Lev. 27:1-8. It is well for us to consider this passage next. In these days it is customary for the higher critics to set out two passages like the foregoing and this one, as contradictory,—written by two short-sighted men, who unwittingly contradicted each other's testimony as to the law; and the whole edited by a yet more stupid person who could not see the disparity. We have no sympathy with explaining the Bible as a mass of contradictions.

579. These "vowed" persons, who were "redeemed" from the actual expenditure of their time in the Tabernacle service, would naturally be "redeemed" on the basis of the value of their services to the Tabernacle. The chief occupation there was the slaughtering and offering of animals, and, while in the Wilderness, moving the Tabernacle from place to place. Old men, women and children would not be in much demand for such work. A boy would grow up to be of more use than a girl, in Tabernacle service. Anyway, the service would be very limited, after excepting what no one was allowed to do save a Levite. Hence the estimation was according to service or financial ability (v. 8) and had nothing to do with the value of life itself, or value in the sight of God, Who is *no respecter of persons.*

580. These are the laws, in part, concerning which Jesus Christ said: *"Think not that I am come to destroy the law . . . I am not come to destroy, but to fulfil. . . Whosoever therefore shall break one of these least commandments, and shall teach men so, he shall be called least in the kingdom of heaven."* These commandments indicate the lowest level, not the highest,

for the foundation of character. It was Christ's part, in the fullness of time, to build on these foundations, by the Sermon on the Mount, loftier edifices than Moses could in his day; and also to strengthen the foundations for these greater structures.

(To be continued.)

LESSON 73.

THE MOSAIC STATUTES AND WOMEN.

(Concluded.)

581. We must not thoughtlessly throw the coloring of our modern customs about the incidents of the far past, but must weight their sense by their own surroundings. In the case of the injured wife, treated of in our last, it may be natural to assume that the husband is allowed to exact a penalty of the injurer of his wife, as regarding it an injury to his own property (Ex.. 21:22). But the context does not support this view. The husband testifies, as the principal witness, as to how his wife was injured, and to what extent. This part naturally follows, because, it being a strife between himself and another man which led to the hurt, he was sure to have seen it, and, most likely, was the only witness besides the accused. He brings a suit, naming the amount upon which the conviction should be secured, while the accused *"shall pay as the judges determine."* Nothing is said as to money being paid to the husband,—similar to the expressions in verses 32 and 34 of this chapter.

582. So again in the case of a seduced girl. At the present time, the father is considered the injured party, before the law, because of her temporary disablement, if she becomes a mother. The Mosaic legislation bears an external resemblance to this, but on close examination, proves to be far more radical. The unmarried man who committed an open breach of the 7th commandment, *whether issue followed or not,* was compelled to marry the young woman without the right of subsequent divorce,—unless the father of the girl thought the man unsuitable for her husband, in which case he was obliged to pay a heavy dowry. Deut. 22:29 shows that the money was given the father, but even so, this was no compensation to the father because of the

loss of his daughter's services (as with our law), but it was paid on behalf of the girl; and she may not have suffered in the least as to interruption of service, since motherhood did not enter into the case as a factor, Ex. 22:16, 17.

583. Furthermore, if a man enticed a young woman betrothed to another, the offense ranked as adultery (in our sense of the word), and both were stoned, if there was ground to think her guilty as well as the man (Deut. 22:23-24). Scarcely any room was left, under the Mosaic statutes, for the problem of illegitimacy to arise at all. We must note here the difference made in the case of these offenses, whether committed by young men or young women. No punishment for the offense followed in her case, unless it was an instance in which the evidence was strong that she was *wilfully* implicated in the offense, and was at the same time betrothed to another. In his case, marriage was compulsory, whether there was issue or not, or, if not marriage because the father rejected him, then a heavy fine. Moses was no sentimentalist, to listen to pleas on the man's part, that he was an "innocent victim" of seduction. He was more scientific than in our day, when the fact is so frequently overlooked that the male offender cannot be an offender excepting wilfully; whereas there is often room for doubt as to the wilfulness of the young woman, when, at the same time, she has no means of establishing her innocence.

584. Deut. 22:13-21 has given rise to much perplexity among women, and if the 'tokens" were really such as they are generally thought to be,—natural tokens,—then the statute must be cruel, since *no proof,* either of innocence or guilt, can be established on such evidence [I speak now confidently, from the standpoint of a member of the medical profession]. Whiston's note on this passage, in his translation of Josephus (*Antiquities,* Book IV: Ch. VIII), is illuminating, and we will quote it in part: "These tokens . . . seem to be very different from what our later interpreters suppose. They appear to have been such close linen garments as were never put off virgins, after a certain age, till they were married, but before witnesses. . . . 2 Sam. 13:18."

585. But there are certain statutes of Moses, which show that the "cart" had made slow progress up the

hill, judging by the spot at which the "brake" was placed. One of these is the Trial of Jealousy, in the 5th chapter of Numbers. We are better able to comprehend the reason for this jealous espionage of their wives by husbands, from our knowledge of the tyrannical means by which the matriarchy had been supplanted by a later patriarchy, which prevailed in Moses' time. Moses' age was much closer to that transition period between matriarchy and patriarchy than our own, for we have frequent signs, in the Bible, not only of the matriarchal period but of the transition stage. Here is a remnant of that transition stage. Moses was compelled to recognize this jealousy, for men considered it right, even when there was no evidence upon which it was based.

586. Perhaps it is not in place to say that there could be no result from drinking "holy water" mixed with dust of the Tabernacle floor. But this much we can confidently say: No woman could be punished by this method short of a *divine miracle* of judgment. The procedure was calculated, (1), To extort, by fright, a confession of guilt, if the woman were really guilty. (2, To frighten women from the offense of committing adultery. (3), To compel a husband to cease his cruel jealousy; for if the wife passed successfully through the ordeal, humiliation would be his part, and odium would fall upon him if he continued to be jealous; whereas, if no means had been provided for terminating his suspicions, his wife might have suffered for an indefinite period of time. Vastly superior to this was the decree of Jesus Christ, which declared that the man must first be able to declare his own innocence before proceeding to condemn a woman for the sin of unchastity (John 8:7). And Moses's Trial of Jealousy, as we have shown (Lesson 68, *Additional Note*), was vastly superior to Hammurabi's law.

587. Another statute has mournful interest to women. The first wars were waged for the capture of women. Sociologists so declare, and the fourth and sixth chapters of Genesis are calculated to confirm this view. In entering the Promised Land, the Children of Israel were positively forbidden to intermarry with certain tribes, Deut. 7:3. But there was an exception: in other cases the warrior could make a wife of a female captive (Deut. 21:10-14). But the historical setting will enable

us to understand that Moses might not have been able to put the ideal any higher than this, without the revolt of his warriors, because men warriors, from early times, had been accustomed to reckon women as booty (Judges 5:30). Moses softens the lot of the captive woman as much as he can. She shall have a month, before marriage, *"to bewail her father and her mother,"* well provided for, under the roof of her captor. And afterwards, if he divorces her, he shall emancipate her, as well; he may not reduce her to slavery. The picture is dark enough, at best.

588. The scribes and Pharisees, of Christ's time congratulated themselves if they lived up to the precepts of Moses. Is it any wonder Christ said: *"Except your righteousness exceed the righteousness of the scribes and Pharisees, ye shall in no case enter into the kingdom of heaven"* (Matt. 5:20)? Their school of ethics allowed one a diploma of graduation at the point at which Pharisees ought only to have allowed one to matriculate. Let us take this warning to ourselves. Old Testament morality will not meet the requirements of Jesus Christ for our day.

LESSON 74.

THE OLD TESTAMENT AND POLYGAMY.

589. We must never forget that polygamy (more explicitly speaking, polygyny), from the Biblical point of view, is something quite different from that legal fiction which alone falls under the condemnation and punishment of our legal enactments. A man is quite able to live as a polygamist in modern civilization (and British law will even compel his more decent wife to live in the indecent relation with him, unless he, besides being a polygamist, inflicts "gross cruelty" upon her), and not be condemned as such. This is done by making the *ceremony* proof of the crime, instead of the crime itself. If a man can be proved to have gone through more than one marriage ceremony, during the life-time of the woman with whom he went through it the first time, he can be punished, not otherwise, generally.

590. But the Bible nowhere prescribes a marriage ceremony, nor can we find more than a slight trace of such ceremony in the Old Testament. Dr. Christian D.

Ginsburg says: "Cohabitation without any religious ceremony whatever constituted and consummated marriage among the early Hebrews." This gives us the true test as to what constitutes polygamy in its true and Biblical sense.

591. Prof. A. H. Sayce says: "The Biblical records have been put into a category by themselves, to their infinite harm. Commentators have been more anxious to discover their own ideas in them, than to discover what the statements in them really mean." Thus it was in early times as regards polygamy. The Jew sought a salvo for his own conscience as regarded the practice of polygamy, and thought he found it in the O. T. Christian expositors have preferred, for the most part, to accept the Jewish teaching that God did not, of old, discountenance polygamy,—indeed, that He even ordained it. It would carry us too far afield to fully discuss this question, but some points may be brought out of profit to us.

592. Without saying anything against the marriage ceremony (it is of the utmost importance for the protection of women and children in our day), yet we must not allow this mere *ceremony* to blind our moral sense as to the loathsome sin of polygamy. A polygamous man should not be permitted to shelter himself (as the law permits), behind the defense that more than one ceremony cannot be proved against him.

593. Take away, then, that sham test as to the crime, and we are bound to admit that there live in our midst today polygamists who are highly honoured, and seldom rebuked even by Christian men,—particularly if they happen to be monarchs, aristocrats, or men of great wealth. Their relations with women of loose morals are matters of public scandal; they answer to *every Biblical test*, as to their polygamy. And were these men of today subjects of Biblical record, they would be frankly pictured as precisely what they are, and the number and names of their wives and concubines might be given,—since Scripture takes no account of the marriage ceremony as a test or proof of the offence. We have already called attention to the (to us) misleading sense in which the term "concubine" is sometimes used in Scripture,—par. 548. It may not imply polygamy.

594. The Bible is nothing if not true to the truth, to which it will sacrifice the mere reputation of a hero ruthlessly, whereas the modern biographer may write up his hero, carefully concealing his "private life." For instance, David is pronounced a man of "integrity" *as a king,* 1 Kings 9:4, as the context shows; and "perfect," *as a king,* because he never went into idolatry, or led his people into it, 1 Kings 11:4; but the contexts show these to be political estimates; the same biographers show that David was faulty and sometimes criminal. Now because of these things, frankly written in the Bible, but carefully suppressed in the biographies of our day, though alas! too often equally true, have we any right to say that the Old Testament countenanced polygamy, whereas we who live in New Testament days do not? No; in these we suppress the truth, in those days the Bible acknowledged it. David was a polygamist. Putting aside shams, on the Bible test, how many of the "Christian" kings of the world, have been anything better?

595. There are only about a dozen instances in the Old Testament record, covering 4,000 years or so, where a man's wives are listed, and of some of these, we have no means of knowing but they were the second or third wives of *widowers.* We must not conclude too hastily that God ever thought polygamy was any less to be abhorred than He abhors it today. Indirect evidence of a thing is often proof of highest order. Years ago, we attended a service on Sunday morning at the Mormon Tabernacle in Utah, in company with a band of Christian missionaries. The comparatively inexperienced "preacher" who occupied the pulpit said: "A man should set a good example before his *wives.*" The slip made a sensation of uneasiness in the presence of "Gentiles." There are no such slips as this in God's speech, in His Book. *"Thou shalt not covet thy neighbor's wife,"*—not "wives," Ex. 20:17;—*"towards the wife of his bosom,"*—not "wives," Deut. 28:54; *"Thy wife shall be as a fruitful vine,"*—not "wives," Ps. 128:3; *"Rejoice with the wife of thy youth,"*—not "wives," Prov. 5:18; *"Even the husband with the wife,"*—not "wives," Jer. 6:11, and so on, throughout the Bible. These are strong bits of evidence against a Divine countenance of polygamy.

596. But the traditional assumption that the O. T. sanctions polygamy has led to careless and perverted translation, at this point. Deut. 21:15 should read: "*If a man* has had (past tense) *two wives,*" as proved *by* the tenses a little further along, "have borne" and "was hated." The Hebrew language has no proper tenses, as we understand them, so that the tense must be determined largely by other forms in the context. The verse begins, "If a man has had two wives," in the Septuagint Greek, the Latin Vulgate, the Syriac and the Arabic versions; and also in the Targum. The teaching is: If a man, whose first wife "was hated", remarries, after her death or divorcement, he may not transfer the birthright from the first wife's eldest son to the second wife's eldest son, as the second wife would naturally wish him to do.

597. We do not pretend that what is said in the Mosaic law concerning polygamy is ideal; but it was the best that could be said to a degraded people. The same can be said of polygamy that Jesus Christ said of divorce, in Matt. 19:8, "*Moses, because of the hardness of your hearts, suffered you to put away your wives,*" not because it was *right* so to do, but *because there was wrong in the men.* All that law, put into the hand of man to enforce, ever can accomplish is, (1) to find the transgressor on his own level; (1) give him a help against sinking lower, and (3)| protect others against his bad influence, or his abuse. "*The law could make nothing perfect,*" says Heb. 7:19. This is taught all through the N. T. Had Moses made his laws absolutely ideal, there would have been an open rebellion against him, and his entire following would have returned to Egypt and degradation. Practically, he could never have enforced *ideal* laws among a people just emerging from slavery. Spiritual and moral teaching must always accompany the enactment of laws, or a people cannot be elevated.

598. There are many instances in the O. T. where circumstances prove a closer tie between a child and its mother than between the same child and its father. These were all formerly explained on the basis of polygamy,—that is, in polygamous countries, and among such people, the father does not seem so close to his children as the mother. But since the discovery of the early matriarchy, such instances are not considered as

necessarily proof of an existing polygamy in the family, but rather as testimony in the direction of female kinship. Thus, the fact that Rebekah's father has less to do with her matrimonial affairs than her mother, is testimony to existing matriarchal customs. But on the other hand, the fact that Samuel's mother has more to do with Samuel than his father seems to be the natural result of his father having two wives. There are many other instances which will be found in illustration of these two customs, alike demonstrating a closer tie between mother and child than father and child.

(To be continued.)

LESSON 75.

THE OLD TESTAMENT AND POLYGAMY.

(Concluded.)

599. As now rendered into English, 2 Sam. 12:8 seems to give Divine countenance to polygamy, but that is only on superficial reading. Nathan, as translated, says to David: *"Thus saith the Lord God of Israel, I anointed thee over Israel, and I delivered thee out of the hand of Saul, and I gave thee thy master's house, and thy master's wives into thy bosom,"* etc. But Saul's wives did *not* become David's wives, and hence that comma should not have been placed after "house," and the word should have been translated "women," not "wives." It is predicated both of the "house" and the "women" that they were given into David's "bosom." The word might better have been translated "lap" as it is in Prov. 16:33, instead of "bosom;" it means here simply "possession." Saul's house and all his female court and domestics passed over into David's possession.

600. Three things prove this. (1) The only two wives Saul had were *"Ahinoam, the daughter of Ahimaaz"* (1 Sam. 14:50) and mother of Michal (David's wife); and *Rizpah* (2 Sam. 3:7). The penalty for marrying one's mother-in-law was to be burnt alive, Lev. 20:14, —so we may be sure David did not commit that crime. (2) As to Rizpah, David delivered her two sons, after the death of Saul, with five others, to be hanged (crucified) at Gibeah, on the demand of the Gibeonites. This woman has been famous in art, as guarding the seven bodies, for months, from the vultures. It is not

266

credible that David should have treated his own wife thus. [Note: In this account of Rizpah, 2 Sam. 21:8, the other five are spoken of as "the five sons of Michal .. which she bare to Adriel." It is thought that the word "sister" has been lost out of the text here—see Margin—for Adriel was brother-in-law, not the husband of Michal, 1 Sam. 18:19.] (3) David's wives are enumerated several times over (see 2 Sam. 2:2, 3:2-5; 1 Chron. 3:1-9, etc), and that after Saul's death, but Saul's wives are never in the list. David, to be sure, had also a wife by the name of Ahinoam, but she is distinguished from Saul's wife as "Ahinoam of Jezreel," and David had her as his wife during Saul's lifetime, 1 Sam. 27:3.

601. Please turn to Ex. 21:7-11, and give it careful study as the only passage seeming to provide for polygamy. But studied by a candid mind, in the original, the English translation will appear forced. (1) The expression, *"betrothed her to himself,"* (8) reads according *to the original Hebrew text,* not "to him (*low*) betrothed," but "not (*loa*) betrothed," but the rabbis read "w" for "a" as the vowel-letter, into the word (see par. 6). But the order of the words "to him betrothed" is unusual, and seems strained. "Not betrothed" is the rendering of the Samaritan, Syriac and Persian versions; of many manuscripts of the Greek Septuagint; of the Greek versions of Theodotion, Aquila and Symmachus, and it receives the support of the Latin Vulgate and the Arabic. The teaching is, then, if the master does *not* betroth the girl, either to himself or to his son, he must let her be redeemed. This is the first error to be corrected in this tangled passage. The rabbis have perverted the sense here.*

602. In verse 10 of this passage we find the second mistranslation: *"If he take unto him another"*—that is all the phrase says. The translators insert "wife." Not so; they should have inserted "as wife." The thought is, "If he take unto himself another woman for his wife, instead of taking this girl,"—not, "If he take unto himself another wife in addition to this girl, who has become his wife."

603. In verse 10 occurs that expression, *"her duty of marriage,"* which is explained by expositors after the

---

* "What you say here is certain."—Dr. A. Mingana.

unclean, polygamous manner of the rabbis as referring to intimate matrimonial relations. The single, short Hebrew word, *'onah* translated *"duty of marriage,"* occurs nowhere else in the Hebrew unless it be identical with a word translated "furrows" in Hos. 10:10. It has been the habit, quite too much, of Christian translators to adopt, without question or due investigation, the meaning put upon these ambiguous words which occur but once or twice by the Talmud, or Jewish works based on the teaching of the Talmud. But the Talmud, in some of its teachings, is scarcely above the level of an unclean parody on the Bible; thus some most objectionable expressions have crept into the English Bible, and this is one of them. Then this salacious sense has cast its shadow forward upon the N. T. page at 1 Cor. 7:3, and a special, sensual sense given to the word "due" there.

604. The noun, *'onah,* has been formed upon one of two Hebrew verbs. It is derived either from *'awun* "dwell," or from *'anah,* "afflict," in that form of the latter verb which means when applied to a woman, "to humble" that is, to outrage her—the *piel* form, as it is called. In this sense it is the word found in Deut. 21:14; 22:24,29; Judg. 20:5 ("forced"); 2 Sam. 13:12, 14, 22; Lam. 5:11; Ezek. 22:10, 11. The first verb, *'awun,* is obsolete, but it has one certain derived noun, *monah,* which means "dwelling place," Psa. 76:2, which occurs nine times. The letter "m," when prefixed to a noun, often, as here, signifies "place." But this "m" does not always occur when it is desired to transform an act into the place where an act is performed. For instance, *'ahal* means "to pitch a tent," and *'ohel* from the same root, means "tent" or dwelling-place," Psa. 91:10. So here, *monah* and *'onah* could both mean "dwelling-place."

605. There is no connection whatever between that original word, translated "duty of marriage" and any other word from which the idea of "marriage" could be derived. Some would derive the word from *'anah,* "to answer." But this is very far fetched in our opinion. The second verb, "outrage," speaks only of abuse, violence and crime, when connected at all with the idea of the relation of the sexes. Aside from that relation, its general sense is "affliction." The first word gives

no hint of the marriage relation; it simply means "to dwell."

606. Now the translators cannot amalgamate the two senses, and get cohabitation out of them. They cannot have it both ways, after any such fashion. This noun means "dwelling-place," pure and simple, or else it refers to indecent, God-defying wickedness. But what is more forced than to introduce the thought of "duty of marriage" along with a slave's food and clothing? And what is more natural than to mention "shelter" next after food and clothing, when speaking of one's obligations to a dependent? "Food, clothing and shelter" go so naturally together that one could have guessed what was said here, if no derivation could have been found for the word. The truth is, the other sense "duty of marriage," is only required, for this otherwise obsolete word, because it was the sense *desired* by the early rabbis. The whole passage, then, should read: *"If she please not her master, so that he hath not espoused her, then shall he let her be redeemed . . If he take another woman for his wife, her food and clothing and shelter he shall not diminish. And if he do not these three unto her, then she may go out free without money,"*— that is without paying for her freedom. And 1 Cor. 7:3, cleared of the shadow of this perversion, means "what is due" in a more general sense.

Note by Dr. A. Mingana.

" 'Her duty of marriage' is to say the least arbitrary. You should add in this connection that the Syriac version has **Mashkiva which means** 'place of resting, of sleeping, or of dwelling, and this corroborates your interpretation of the word."

LESSON 76.

WOMEN OF OLD, AND OF CONSEQUENCE.

607. When Jacob was dying (Gen. chap. 49) he called his twelve sons about him, saying, *"Gather yourselves together, that I may tell you that which shall befall you in the latter days."* Concerning Joseph, he is interpreted as saying: *"Joseph is a fruitful bough, even a fruitful bough by a well; whose branches run over the wall."* But this is quite far from the literal sense of the words employed, which is, "Joseph son of a bearing —, son of a bearing—, by a fountain; daughters ascend over a wall." The translators supply "tree" after "bear-

269

ing," a participle, making it "a bearing tree," i. e., "a fruitful tree" (see R. V.). But "bearing" is feminine in form, and "tree" is a masculine noun, so that the grammar is faulty. The word they translate "branches" is the very ordinary word for "daughters." "Daughters of a tree" might mean "branches of a tree," but it is assuming a good deal to allow a word *supplied* to a sentence, on the option of the translator, to determine a sense different from the ordinary one of a word *actually used*.

608. We are not satisfied with such an arbitrary rendering. Participles are in common use in the Hebrew language, without any associated noun, as describing a man or woman "working" or "worker," "sowing" or "sower" (or whatsoever the verbal form may describe), according to the gender of the participle employed. Therefore, the natural sense of the feminine participle "bearing," is "a bearing woman,—a fruitful woman," and we believe this is what Jacob saw in connection with Joseph. He saw Rachel, his dearly-beloved and only chosen wife, Joseph's mother, and speaks of her, as he did in the previous chapter, when blessing Joseph's children. She died a pathetic death, early, in child-bearing; and God comforts this old man who never ceased to mourn for his Rachel, in a way simliar to what found expression, centuries later, through the prophet Jeremiah (31:15, 16): *"A voice was heard in Ramah . . Rachel weeping for her children refused to be comforted for her children, because they were not. Thus saith the Lord: Refrain thy voice from weeping . . for thy work shall be rewarded."* Rachel had said: *"Give me children, or else I die."* Children were given her, and the second one caused her death. What a defeated life! But God comforted Jacob with a prophetic vision of Rachel as "a fruitful woman," as to progeny.

609. But he saw more: there would be daughters, and daughters who would surpass the restricted life of ordinary womanhood. Did this come to pass? Certainly. Please turn to Num. 26:33. There we read, *"Zelophehad, the son of Hepher had no sons."* Zelophehad was a grandson of Gilead, who was grandson of Manasseh, Joseph's son. His pedigree was Joseph, Manasseh, Machir, Gilead, Hepher, Zelophehad (Num. 27:1)!. When the Promised Land was apportioned out to the children of Israel, by tribes and families, the five daugh-

ters of Zelophehad were unwilling that their family should have no inheritance because they were all women. They called an assembly (Num. 27:1-7), to which Moses, all the princes of the twelve tribes, Eleazar the priest, and all the congregation of Israel came; in fact, every-one was there. And then they pleaded their "rights," and gained them. They became women of immense property.

610. Hershon (*A Talmudic Miscellany*, p. 282), tells us that the Talmud highly honours these women as *"sages," "expounders,"* and *"righteous women,"* and adds: "It stands to reason that if they had not been female expounders [of law] they could not have known the correct interpretation of law, which even Moses, the prime legislator himself, as we see from the context, was not aware of: while we have the Divine testimony to justify the conclusion that they were correct in their exposition, and, in the whole case, a warrant for the inference, which is inevitable, that education in the law was not forbidden to females by Moses. Only those who affected to 'sit in Moses' seat' have enacted the harsh dogma, 'Let the words of the law be burned, but let not the words of the law be imparted to women'" (a famous rabbinical decision).

611. But God said to Moses: *"The daughters of Zelophehad speak right: thou shalt give them a possession of an inheritance among their father's brethren; and thou shalt cause the inheritance of their father to pass unto them."* The God of the O. T., at any rate, did not disapprove of women speaking in public, and even "laying down the law" to Moses. How much was secured by the daughters of Zelophehad expounding the law, and claiming their "rights" under it, before this vast assembly may be inferred from the case of another descendant of Gilead of the same degree. Hezron, of the tribe of Judah (1 Chron. 2:3-5), married a sister of Gilead. He "went in unto her" (verse 21), that is, he became identified with the tribe of Manasseh,—so that his grandson Jair is called "the son of Manasseh" in Num. 32:41. Moses gave Machir a very fertile country, called "Gilead" by Machir, after his son Gilead (Numbers 32:40). Now, for greater clearness, let us put the ancestry of Jair and Zelophehad side by side

for comparison, remembering that the wealth of both came from Machir.

$$
\text{Machir}\begin{cases}
\text{His son Gilead . Hepher . Zelophehad .} \\
\qquad\qquad\qquad\qquad\qquad\text{5 daughters.} \\
\text{His daughter . . Segub . . Jair .} \\
\textit{Hezron's wife.}
\end{cases}
$$

612. We have no reason to infer that the daughters of Zelophehad inherited any less property than Jair did through Segub and Gilead's sister, for Zelophehad was of the same generation with Jair, and in the direct male line of the first-born, who according to custom would receive the double portion. Jair inherited *"three and twenty cities,"* and the opportunity to gain many more (1 Chron. 2:21-23). Canon Payne-Smith remarks: "Certainly what the daughters of Zelophehad were anxious about was not a miserable acre or two apiece, but some such princely territory as their cousin carried as dower to Hezron."

613. In connection with this we will examine another woman's inheritance. This Hezron, through whom Jair inherited so largely in Gilead, at last died in Caleb-Ephratah, that is, Bethlehem, and he was father of Caleb, chief of the tribe of Judah, by a former wife (1 Chron. 2:18-21.) Caleb married his daughter to his own younger brother,* her uncle Othniel (Josh. 15:16-17; Judg. 1; 13, 15). This Othniel succeeded Joshua, being the first to "judge Israel." He delivered them from the king of Mesopotamia, and judged them for about forty years, Judg. 3:8-11.

614. Hebron and the surrounding country became Caleb's, by lot and by conquest. Judah (that is, the *tribe* under Caleb, for Judah himself had been long dead) conquered certain lands in the south (Judg. 1:9-15), and on the occasion when Othniel, as a young man, married Caleb's daughter, she *"moved him to ask of her father a field."* Evidently Othniel was not willing to do this, so the young bride took matters into her own hand. She said to her father, *"Give me a present: for that thou hast set me in the land of the South; give me also springs of water."* (Josh. 15:19 R. V.). *"And*

---

* The English is obscure here, but expositors so understand it.

272

Caleb gave her the upper springs and the nether springs." Precisely how much this meant, and which springs are meant, we do not know; it was a princely portion, and Canon Payne-Smith remarks: "What good would the vast territories which Caleb gave his daughter Achsah, her southland, and her upper and nether springs, have done her, if neither she nor Othniel had had dependents to till them?" The possession of such vast estates implies the possession of a vast number of labourers to care for them.

615. This property was given to Achsah, not to Othniel. It probably never became his. At a much later date, Solomon married a daughter of Pharaoh. On this occasion Pharaoh gave his daughter, as dowry, the city of Gezer, 1 Kings 9:16, which he had seized from its Canaanite inhabitants, though it was in the land of Palestine. Solomon raised a levy, and repaired Gezer (verse 15), and one might readily suppose that Solomon would not have done this unless he regarded the property as his own. But we have positive proof that the property *never became his.* Gezer remained this wife's independent property. An Assyrian contract tablet was found at Gezer, (as told us by Stewart Macalister, Director of Excavations, Palestine Exploration Fund), which shows that the city was governed by an Egyptian, Hurwasi, as late as 651-649 B. C. This proves that the Egyptian heirs of King Solomon's wife were allowed to claim this property as theirs, after her death. The laws of the children of Israel did not, evidently, rob women of their property, to give it to their husbands, after marriage.

LESSON 77.

SEX BIAS INFLUENCES TRANSLATORS.

616. It is well known that when a man gets lost on the prairie, he begins to go round in a circle; it is suggested that one side (the right, generally), being stronger than the other, he pulls unconsciously with greater strength upon the corresponding guiding rein of his horse. Just so does the translator; he pulls unconsciously on the strong side of preconception or self-interest. This may not be intended, but it is none the less inevitable to the uninspired hand. For this reason, no class nor sex

should have an exclusive right to set forth the meaning of the original text. It is notorious that the Samaritan Hebrew *text*, even, has been manipulated to a considerable extent to suit Samaritan prejudices, so that that manuscript must be corrected by comparison with others before it can be trusted on points that involve Samaritan interests. The Alexandrian, or Septuagint version, shows traces of an attempt to meet the prejudices of Egyptians. What wonder that all versions, having for all time been made by men, should disclose the fact that, on the woman question, they all travel more or less in a circle, in accordance with sex bias, hindering the freedom and progress of women, since (in times past more than at present), the self interest of man led him to suppose that woman served God best as his own undeveloped subordinate?

617. Let us first note two cases, brought to light by the Revision Committee, by way of illustration of sex bias. In Genesis, 20th. chapter, we read the story of the exposure of Sarah, at Abraham's request, in Abimelech's harem (?). When the king discovered that she was a married woman (through the reproof of God), he sent for Abraham, reproved him, and then paid a thousand pieces of silver to him for the injury done her good name. The version of 1611 (A. V.) and the version of 1884 construe the language spoken by the king on this occasion quite differently.

A. V.—"He is to thee a covering of the eyes, unto all that are with thee;"

R. V.—"It* is to thee for a covering of the eyes, to all that are with thee;"

A. V.—"and with all other: thus she was reproved;"

R. V.—"and in respect of all thou art righted."

Abimelech did this so that all would understand that the wrong was his, not Sarah's; and she would be righted before all and ashamed before none, and would not need to cover her eyes (face) for shame. So the R. V. indicates; but the A. V. makes the blame fall upon Sarah, who is "reproved." Abraham was no "covering to her eyes,"—he was the primal cause of her shame and humiliation. It would seem as though the rendering of the A. V. was an attempt to fortify the supposed teaching of Paul that women should go veiled.

---

* Hebrew has no word for "it," which must be represented by either "he" or "she."

618. Another passage, bound to be corrected apace with the improvement of woman's social position, is Leviticus 19:20. This relates to wrong relations with a female slave, who is, *"not at all redeemed, nor freedom given her."* The R. V. shows progress here toward the light, which is yet obscured, however. The A. V. says:—*"She shall be scourged . . . and he shall bring his offering."* The R. V. says: *"They shall be punished . . . and he shall bring,"*—etc. But the literal sense is,—*"There shall be inquisition . . . and he shall bring."* That is, there shall be rigid inquiry made, and when it is ascertained that she is not in a state of freedom at all, then only he shall bring the offering.†

619. Luther once said: "No gown worse becomes a woman than to be wise." Luther only held the prevailing views of his day as regards women. Such men could not easily perceive when Scripture expressed a different thought on the subject. Prov. 14:1 says, in Hebrew, *"The wisdom of woman buildeth her house,"* but not being able to appreciate the advantages of female education, men rendered it: *"Every wise woman buildeth her house,"* that is, the woman who devotes herself to housewifely duties is pronounced "wise." But this is not the thought; rather, wisdom itself, in woman, will build her own (not her husband's) house,—elevate her to a place of honour. Every time there has been an opportunity for the use of *option* in translation, use has been made of that option, by this or that man of learning, to build up one sex and to depreciate the other, and so the result, through the ages, has been cumulative, and that without actual intention.

620. Again, *Cha-kam* חכם "wise", occurs (on a hasty count) 130 times in the Hebrew Bible. It is invariably translated "wise" excepting in the following places: in 2 Sam. 13:3 "subtil;" and in 10 instances "cunning," when used of skilful workmen, 1 Chron. 22:15; 2 Chron. 2:7 (twice); 13, and 14 (twice); Isaiah 3:3; 40:20; Jer. 10:9. But in Jer. 9:17 we read in our English, *"Thus saith the Lord of hosts, Consider ye, and call for the mourning women, that they may come; and send for* cunning *women that they may come, and let*

---

† "Your opinion that the sentence, 'they shall be punished' of the R. V. is erroneous, is in my judgment very correct. You should, however, add that the Syriac Version has . . . . [Syriac words] which means precisely, 'there shall be inquisition.' "

them make haste, and take up a wailing for us," etc.
The reference is to the low moral tone prevailing at
Jerusalem, which threatened the overthrow of the city.
Now here, surely, there is no reference to skilful work-
manship on the part of women, and moreover the A. V.
leaves out the rather importar.. article "the"—see R. V.
Here "the wise women" are called upon by Jehovah to
show their interest and concern in matters of State,—
the moral corruptness of the city; and "the wise
women" are further instructed to teach their daughters
to be concerned about such matters,—verse 20. Huldah
(2 Kgs. 22:14), admittedly the wisest prophet of the
times, may have been still living at this very time.

621.   I think we find another case of prejudiced translation in Isai. 3:12. The word translated "children" in
this verse in Isaiah, is a plural masculine participle of
the verb "to glean," "abuse," practice." It is translated
"glean" in Lev. 19:10, Deut. 24:21, Judg. 20:45, and
Jer. 6:9. The word has no translation such as "children" anywhere else in the Bible, and it occurs 21 times.
Another word altogether is used for "children," and
"child," in verses 4 and 5 of this same chapter; the
sense seems to have been fixed by the supposed context,
to correspond with "women." As to the word translated "women:" Two words, without the rabbinical
vowel "points," are exactly alike. One is pronounced
nosh-im and the other na-shim. In appearance the only
difference is a slight mark under the first letter of the
Hebrew word na-shim. The first word means "exactors;"
the one with a vowel mark under the initial letter means
"women." The entire decision, therefore, as to whether
the words means one or the other depends upon OP-
TION. Those who pointed the word, evidently thought
the nation could sink no lower than to pass under
women rulers, and then translated the other word "children" to match it. Commentators frequently call attention to the alternate reading. See Adam Clarke on the
passage. The Septuagint translates: *"As for my people, tax-gatherers* (praktores) *glean them, and exactors*
(apaitountes) *rule over them."*

622.   There seems little in the context to support the
translation "children" and "women." But study the
context as regards the other reading. After complaining of the "gleaners," (that is tax-gatherers) and
"extortioners," they are threatened in the following

language: *"The Lord standeth up to plead and standeth up to judge the people. The Lord will enter into judgement with the elders of His people, and the princes* ("rulers," masculine, not feminine gender), *thereof for ye have eaten up the vineyard* (the conduct of extortionate tax-gatherers), *and the spoil of the poor is in your houses. What mean ye that ye crush* (R. V.) *my people, and grind the faces of the poor?"* Because of this context, we believe that OPTION took the wrong turn when it decided to translate this verse as it stands in our English version; and that this translation would have had a strong showing up of its sophistries, had educated women been on the last Revision Committee.

These instances are trivial, when taken one by one, but many straws floating in one direction prove that the current runs that way strongly.

(To be continued.)

LESSON 78.

SEX BIAS INFLUENCES TRANSLATORS.

(Continued.)

623. Before we proceed to exhibit other places in the O. T. in which an unusual meaning has been put upon a word that would not have been put upon the same word had it not specially related to woman, we must explain: Words in the Hebrew language are more difficult to set forth after this fashion, to those who do not understand the language, because of the great variety of uses to which a word can be put. The same form may do duty as a noun, a verb, an adjective, an adverb and even a preposition.

624. Next we will consider the Hebrew word *cha-yil* (חיל), which occurs 242 times in the Old Testament. It is translated "army" and "war" 58 times; "host" and "forces" 43 times; "might" or "power" 16 times; "goods," "riches," "substance" and "wealth' in all 31 times; "band of soldiers," "band of men," "company," and "train" once each; "activity" once; "valour" 28 times; "strength" 11 times: these are all noun forms. The word is often translated as an adjective or adverb. It is translated "valiant" and "valiantly" 35 times; "strong" 6 times; "able" 4 times; "worthily" once and

"worthy" once. We have now given you the complete list of the various renderings of this word excepting four instances in which the word is used in describing a woman. Please review the list, and get the usage of the word clearly in mind before proceeding further.

625. Now we will take the first of these four remaining cases, relating to women: Ruth, the Moabitess, was a woman of courage and decision of character. In her loyalty to her dead husband's mother, she refused to turn back and re-marry in her own land, but forsook her country and kindred to accompany her mother-in-law to a (to her) foreign land, and undertook there, to keep them both from starvation by the labor of her hands. Boaz, who afterwards married her, said to her: *"All the city of my people doth know that thou art a woman of* cha-yil," (Ruth 3:11). Now considering the girl's courage and devotion, how should this word have been translated? You have the list of meanings before you, and are quite competent to form an opinion. How would *"thou art an able woman"* or *"thou art a woman of courage"* do? The Septuagint Greek says, *"Thou art a woman of power"* (*dunamis*).

626. But it almost looks as though our English translators took no care, as to the precise language here. The circumstances, when Boaz spoke the words, were peculiar, but not improper in Israel; but man was praising a woman, and "of course" here is a reference to her reputation for chastity, and so it is translated, *"thou art a virtuous woman."* But glance over the various meanings given to this word elsewhere. Not once has it reference to any other moral characteristic than that of strength or force. What courage this foreign girl had shown in supporting her mother-in-law!

627. Now for the next mistranslation of this word, because it relates to woman. The last chapter of Proverbs describes an ideal woman for a wife. The description is a mother's, to her son. It is quite different from the average man's ideal of woman at her best. But the Bible describes her, in the language of Lemuel's mother, as a woman whose "price is far above rubies." Here are some of her striking characteristics: *"She is like the merchants' ships, she bringeth her food from afar."* *"She considereth a field and buyeth it."* *"She girdeth her loins with strength, and strengtheneth her*

arms." "*Strength and honour are her clothing.*" Surely this must be a "strong-minded" woman who is praised here.

628. Three times over the "strength" of this woman of Proverbs is referred to. Each line of the description speaks of efficiency. She is praised in turn for general goodness and trustworthiness, energy, efficiency, enterprise, far-sightedness, early-rising, business capacity, gardening, muscular strength, weaving, benevolence, fore-thought, embroidery work, elegant clothes for herself, tailoring for her husband, honour, wisdom, kindness, piety. But, as it happens, no definite reference is made to her purity, or to her faithfulness to her husband in the marriage relation.

629. Now what one word would best sum up such a character? The precise original expression is the same as in the verse we have quoted from Ruth,—"*A woman of cha-yil.*" We must suppose that the translators hastily concluded that they knew, without looking closely at the original, what sort of a woman a mother *ought to recommend* to her son for a wife, and so they translated: "*Who can find a virtuous woman?*" That represents the undoubted sentiments of the translators; but it *does not represent* the teaching of the original text. "Virtue" is of priceless value to woman, to be sure; but her duty to her husband is not her *only* duty; all her life cannot be summed up in that *one* moral quality.

630. "But," someone will reply, "virtue is often used in the sense of a summing up of all moral characteristics." That may be; but it would not be so understood by the common folk, in this connection, and the Bible is supposed to be translated for them. The vast majority, reading this verse, would suppose the word "virtue" to refer to the woman's chastity. The Septuagint translates here ("*Tell it not in Gath, publish it not in Askelon,*" lest the study of the sacred tongues be prohibited to woman!), "*A* masculine *woman . . . more valuable is she than very costly stones.*"*

And finally, the description of this ideal woman is summed up in the 29th verse, in the words: "*Many daughters have done* cha-yil, *but thou excellest them all.*" "Worthily," "valiantly," are the only translations

* "Another point in your favour is that the Syriac text has actually a 'strong, powerful, virile woman,'"—Dr. Mingana.

279

that we have in any other part of the Bible for this word, when used as an adverb. But after the same careless manner, the word is here translated "virtuously." We suppose there was an instinctive distaste, disrelish, for showing that the Bible praised, in the inspired words of a woman writer, a "strong" woman, for doing "valiantly."

631. Now for the fourth instance of the mistranslation of this word: Proverbs 12:4 reads, in the original, *"A woman of* cha-yil *is a crown to her husband,"* and there is no doubt that she is here again praised for her strength of character. But the English reads, *"A virtuous woman is a crown to her husband."* Doubtless such a woman is a crown to her husband, but women prefer to know what the Bible *says,* rather than to be merely reminded of a favorite axiom among men. Here again, the Septuagint translates, "masculine."

632. "But," an objector will say " 'virtuous' comes from the Latin word *vir,* which *means* 'man,' and why is it not the proper word to use here,—in the sense of 'manly,' 'strong?' " Because "virtue," while it has this *literal* sense, is not used to describe "manliness" in English, but "morality" in general, among men: and when used of woman, it is understood to refer to morality of one sort, more particularly, which happens not to be referred to in these extended descriptions in the quotations from Proverbs. If the translator had thought that this word "virtue," or the word "virtuously" were likely to be understood in their literal sense by women, —"manly" and "manfully," who can believe that he would ever have employed those words here?

633. Virtue is a quality of great importance to women, and had they been more clearly taught from pulpit, and by a more careful translation of such passages as we have been considering the obligation laid upon them in the Bible, to be strong, in body, mind and spirit; if these theologians themselves had learned this from the Bible, women would have been far better equipped to guard their virtue,—since the ruin of girls is usually due to weak character and general unfitness to cope with the world. To sum up: This Hebrew word, *cha-yil,* used over 200 times in the Hebrew Bible, signifies "force," "strength," "ability." But in every instance where it relates to *women,* and nowhere else, it is translated "virtue,"—i. e., chastity.

LESSON 79.

SEX BIAS INFLUENCES TRANSLATORS.

(Concluded.)

634. One more instance of this sex bias in the O. T. translation, and then we will consider some cases in the N. T. that were not mentioned in our former lesson, "Divers Weights and Measures" (Lesson 48),—though, for that matter, almost every one of the Lessons brings out points on this subject.

1. Isaiah 2:9 reads, "*The mean man boweth down and the great man humbleth himself*".
2. Isaiah 5:15, "*The mean man shall be brought down, the mighty man shall be humbled.*"
3. Isaiah 31:8, "*Not of a mighty man, . not of a mean man.*"

Perhaps it will surprise the reader to be told that within these three short passages adjectives to the number of six have been added to the translation that do not exist in the original text, and no one but a Hebrew scholar can discover this for himself or herself.

635. We have been taught to believe that wherever words of importance are inserted into the English translation that do not exist in the original text, in order to convey the correct meaning to the English reader, those words are printed in *italics*, that all may understand that they are not in the original, and thus judge for themselves, by the help of the Spirit, as to their appropriateness. Thus, in verse 7 of this second chapter of Isaiah we read: "Neither *is there any* end of their chariots," and we know that the three words in italics, —"*is there any*,"—do not belong to the original.

Not so, in these three passages. No word in them is printed in italics, and yet, the adjectives "mean," "great," and "mighty" have been added in every instance. We will explain this presently.

636: 4. Again, Psalm 49:2 reads, "*Both low and high.*"

5. Psalm 62:9 reads, "*Surely men of low degree are vanity, and men of high degree are a lie.*"

Within these two short passages eight words are added to the text, and two words are left out, yet only a Hebrew scholar can discover it without aid, because the added words are not italicized as they should be, neither is there any indication of omitted words.

637. What does all this mean? We will explain: In most languages there are at least two words for "man," one indicating the adult male, and the other meaning "mankind." In Hebrew, as we have already explained, the adult male is indicated by the word *ish*; on the other hand, "mankind" is meant where *adham* (Adam) is used, when not of the person who first bore the name.

These passages should have been translated respectively something like this:

1. "Man boweth down (or mankind boweth down), and the men humble themselves."
2. "Man shall be brought down, and the men shall be humbled."
3. "Not of the men . . not of mankind."
4. "Both mankind and the men."
5. "Surely humanity (or mankind) is vanity, and the men are a lie."

638. The best we can do, it is a little difficult to express the thing smoothly in English, because it lacks words which can always be used elegantly to distinguish between the adult male and mankind generally. The word we translate "the men" to conform to English usage, *ish*, is in the singular number. But a marginal note could have made this clear, without a dishonest translation of the text. And who but a set of pedants, inflated with intellectual pride, would have agreed that men were "great" when their mothers and wives did not appear in the same category, and "mighty," "of high degree," and "high;" but if the female sex and children get mixed with them, they must then be described as "mean," and "low," and "of low degree?" These are not instances of faulty translations, but of unwarranted corruption of the meaning of the original text. The Hebrew has words for "high" and "low;" "mighty" and "mean," if those were the ideas to be expressed; while *ish* is such a common word to be given these exalted meanings, that it is often rendered "each," "everyone," "whoso," and "whosoever,"—referring to both sexes, sometimes to inanimate things, but mainly to the male.

639. A few instances from the N. T. now: *Sophron* is an adjective which occurs four times, and is translated "sober" twice, "temperate" once. In the fourth place it refers to women only, and is rendered "discreet" (Titus 2:5). That this different meaning is

282

given to it purposely because it refers to women, will be made plain by the learned Dean Alford's note in his commentary. Having first established the sense of the word as "self-restraint," in its noun form, he says, concerning the rendering "discreet," "This term certainly applies better to women than 'self-restraint:' there is in this latter [in "self-restraint"] in their case, an implication of effort, which destroys the spontaneity, and brushes off, so to speak, the bloom of this best of female graces." We thank Dean Alford for thinking that women can practice self-restraint without effort, but when we are reading our Bibles we prefer to know *precisely* what the Holy Ghost addresses to us, instead of finding between its pages the opinion of even the most excellent uninspired man.

640. The Greek noun *sophrosune* is built up on the adjective *sophron,*—as we add "ness" to "good" to transform it into "goodness." A book of the Apocrypha, 4 Maccabees (1:31), defines the word correctly, where it says it means "the mastery of the lusts." In the one instance in which the word is used of women it is rendered "sobriety" (1 Tim. 2:15) which is not bad. But I hunt up the word in my Green's small lexicon to the N. T., and read there that the *female* meaning of the word is "modesty," which precisely accords with what we are pointing out,—that these men seem to imagine that the same word has two meanings according to whether it refers to men or to women,—in the Bible, at least.

641. Then take the word "power." *Exousia* occurs 103 times in the N. T. It is rendered "authority" 29 times; "power" 69 times; "right" twice; and once each "liberty," "jurisdiction," and "strength." Its meaning is patent; there is no mystery about the word. But in one single instance it happens to be used exclusively of woman's power. Here at once its sense is called into question (see par. 217, etc.). It cannot be possible that women should have power! In the margin the translators write the longest note to be found in all the Bible (see A. V.) to explain how Paul means that this "power" must be abdicated by woman, in order that her *husband* may assume it instead.

642. *Episemos* occurs in only two places in the N. T. In Matt. 27:16 we read of "*a notable prisoner called*

Barabbas;" and in Rom. 16:7, St. Paul mentions *"Andronicus and Junia, who are of note among the apostles."* Two disputes have been provoked by this passage: (1) Should we read, here, Junia, a woman, or Junias, a man? (2) Does the word *episemos* in this passage mean "of note among," or "well known to?" The name is in the accusative, *Janian,* and admits of either construction as to gender. The R. V. has decided for the male form. But the masculine form cannot be found (at least, I could not find it) in any biographical dictionary of Greek names, while the feminine form occurs several times. Chrysostom, himself a Greek, born at Antioch, Syria, about 350 A. D., understood this person to be a woman, and also an apostle, exclaiming, in his Homilies, "Oh, how great is the devotion of this woman, that she should even be counted worthy of the appellation of apostle!"

643. Not so, our present-day commentators, Jamieson, Faussett and Brown, but at one stroke they seize the preeminence for the male, whichever way the decision, arguing that if it be "Junia" a woman, then we must read "well known to the apostles;" on the other hand, if it be "Junias," a man, then the meaning may be a "well known apostle." We are reminded of the legend of a man who got into a crocodiles' nest, and saved himself by ramming "the head of one down the throat of another;" until he dispatched them all, pair by pair.

644. *Kosmios* means properly "well ordered, in both outward deportment and inner life." It occurs twice. It is translated "modest" where it refers to woman's dress, 1 Tim. 2:9, and perhaps it could not be improved upon. But why not say that *"a bishop then, must be . . modest"* for *"of good behaviour,"* since the latter statement is so obvious as to be inane? (1 Tim. 3:2).

Hagnos means "holy." It occurs 8 times, and is translated "pure" four times; "clear" once, and "chaste" three times. Every time that it is translated "chaste" it qualifies a noun of the feminine gender. But why should not men be taught chastity too?

These may be straws. Yet they all point in the same direction.

LESSON 80.

"BLESSED BE JAEL."

645. In the 4th, and 5th, chapters of Judges we have an account of a terrible man, Sisera, who, besides oppressing Israel generally, was like a sleuth-hound in pursuing and capturing Israel's maidens, to despoil them of their beautiful, double-embroidered garments (5:30), and deliver them over, "*to every soldier a damsel or two.*" Deborah arose, "*a mother in Israel,*" stirred up Barak, and together they went forth to war. But another woman, an alien to Israel, but living in the midst of it, had likewise been fired with indignation at the depredations upon her sex. The war that Deborah began Jael finished, for God sold Sisera into the hands of the woman (4:9). Deborah celebrates this victory of two women over a capturer of women, in a song which knows no rival for beauty in Hebrew literature. The opening line of that Song of Deborah, Judges 5:1, has caused much labour to translators, who can never agree as to its meaning. Here are some renderings:

"*A revelation was revealed in Israel,*" Vatican Code Septuagint.

"*In the leading of the leaders of Israel,*" Alexandrian Code, Septuagint.

"*In the vengeance with which Israel was avenged,*" Syriac Version.

"*For the avenging of Israel,*" English, A. V.

"*For that the leaders took the lead,*" English, R. V.

"*In the breaking forth of the breakers,*" Cambridge Bible.

"*That the strong in Israel showed themselves strong,*" Keil and Delitzsch.

"*For those whose hair was let flow loose,*" Cooke.

"*That the hair waved wildly in Israel,*" Cassel.

646. The subject of this sentence is a feminine form, being the plural participle of the same verb as the predicate. This verb is *para* (פרע), and Gesenius' Lexicon informs us that it means "to loose, to let go," and it is so translated in Ex. 5:4, (R. V.): "*Wherefore do ye . . . loose the people from their works?*" It appears, therefore, that the most natural sense of the words would be: "*For that freeing women freed Israel, . . . Praise ye the Lord.*" What better would suit the context? This has always been known as "Deborah's

Song," and rightly, for the announcement is: *"Then sang* (feminine singular) *Deborah—and Barak,"* his name coming in as a sort of afterthought, showing that she was the proper renderer of it. The song is composed by a woman, to celebrate the deliverance, by two women, of both Israel as a whole, and also the maidens of Israel, from an oppressor. Although no Hebrew scholar could be ignorant of the fact that this is a feminine form, no one in translating the verse, so far as we can learn, has ever indicated this in his translation.

647. Deborah means "a bee," and there was something of a sting in this woman, for evil-doers. She may have had this name given her as a title during her public services to her people. The wars Sisera conducted seem to have been for two purposes, conquest and women. Israel submitted to his depredations for some time, and then two women became thoroughly aroused with indignation for the unavenged wrongs of their sex Deborah began the war, and Jael finished it, and that is why Deborah's song begins,

> *"For women-deliverers freeing Israel,*
> *For the people volunteering,*
> *Praise ye the Lord."*

The song continues, according to the translation, v. 6. *"The highways were unoccupied, and the travellers walked through* [crooked] *byways.* But the word translated "unoccupied" means "to cease," and has never been translated "unoccupied" anywhere else in the Bible, while "highways" is the feminine plural of the participle "wandering"—meaning, literally, "the female wanderers." This leads the R. V. to suggest, in the margin, "caravans ceased." But since this is a woman's song, nothing is more natural than for Deborah to note that women had ceased altogether from going about, and men "travellers" (masculine) went only in the "crooked bypaths," where they would be unobserved. (See Additional Note.)

648. Deborah continues: *"The rulers* [R. V.] *ceased in Israel, they ceased, until that I Deborah arose, that I arose a mother in Israel."* This word "mother" means, according to Semitic usage, in this connection, " female chief," a female ruler,—of the tribe of Israel. Not only was there no one to rule, until she took the reins of government, but Deborah goes on to complain (verse 8) that whereas, when Israel entered the Promised Land, forty-thousand armed men marched before them

(Josh. 4:12, 13), now not a spear or a shield had been lifted to defend Israel against Sisera.

649. When the children of Israel entered the Promised Land, the children of the Kenite, Moses' Midianite father-in-law, went with them from Jericho into the land of Judah, at the south, and settled there, Judg. 1:16. But Heber removed his tent from there, and was living far to the north, near the southern extremity of (what was later called) the sea of Galilee (Judg. 4:11). The encounter with Sisera took pace at the western part of the plain of Jezreel, by the river Kishon, and Sisera fled north-eastward to the tent of Jael for shelter and protection, arriving perhaps three days after the battle. The effrontery of it! A man out capturing women is in danger of being captured, and runs to a woman for protection!

650. He would probably have captured Jael, herself, at another time, if he could. She knew this very well. The house of Heber was at peace with Jabin, Sisera's king. But that is not saying Jael was at peace with Jabin or Sisera, for women were very independent in those days, and only a treacherous woman loses the sense of loyalty towards her own sex. Sisera stood a suppliant at the door of Jael's tent, while Barak was in hot pursuit. It is not likely that Jael recognized him at this moment, but she would under the circumstances be filled with fear lest an armed warrior meant mischief to herself; and realizing that the giving of the hospitality he desired meant her own safety, while the refusal of that hospitality meant peril, she bade him welcome, and when he asked for water gave him milk.

651. Once inside, his quick request for her to stand guard at the door, and tell a lie when his enemy came,— she an unarmed woman, and he a warrior, armed to the teeth—(while he showed no sign of going again, but lay down exhausted), would arouse her suspicions. She probably then realized for the first who this man was. Sisera, the despoiler of the women of Israel,—Israel with whom the Kenites, from the days of Moses, had had a most sacred covenant (Ex. 18:12): among whom, in fact, the Kenites dwelt as guests (1 Sam. 15:6).

652. She hesitated no longer. He had thought to entrap her by the Arab custom of desert hospitality, which carries the promise of protection with the giving of

food. Fired with indignation, at once she dispatched him by the only means she had at hand (4:21). Barak now stands at the tent door, but too late. Jael has the honour of slaying the enemy, and Deborah sings: *"Blessed above women shall Jael be . . Blessed shall she be above women in the tent."* And a few miles away, a woman of fashion and of folly is saying to the women of her train, *"Have they not found, have they not divided the spoil? A damsel, two damsels to every man"* (5:30). Commentators have wrangled over the question whether Jael ought not to have obeyed that custom of Arab hospitality, and spared Sisera. Jael knew better than to transgress a covenant with God's people (Num. 10:29-32), for the sake of man-made custom. And let us hope she realized, too, that no compact should be held so sacred among women as that which binds them in a common defense of their virtue Many Biblical scholars hold that Deborah was of the tribe of Ephraim. If so, we may be sure Jacob saw her also among those daughters of Rachel who could "ascend over a wall" and blessed Jael for doing the same (pars. 607, 608).

653. The entire Song of Deborah is pronounced by scholars the most remarkable specimen of Hebrew poetry in the Bible; but "The closing part of Deborah's Song has justly been regarded as a specimen of poetical representation that cannot be surpassed" (Cassell, in Lange's Commentary).

ADDITIONAL NOTE: "Your new translation of the Song of Deborah is in my judgment somewhat arbitary and unconvincing, but I must own that the Hebrew text is very difficult,"—**Dr. A. Mingana.**. But are the other renderings any less "arbitrary and unconvincing?"

LESSON 81.

"NO WORD OF GOD IS VOID OF POWER."

654. We quote from a valuable book on *"Lines of Defense of the Biblical Revelation,* by Prof. D. S. Margoliouth, M. A. of Oxford, some words of special interest to women. He says: "The whole of the modern theory of the Pentateuch is liable to be wrecked on a verse of 1 Samuel, where it is stated that the sons of Eli misused the women who assembled (A. V.) at the door of the Tabernacle of the Congregation" 2:22.

655. We are interested at once, as women, to know what all this means. First, what is the "modern theory,"—for some may not know? The Higher Criticism teaches that the rules relating to worship set forth in Leviticus, and to some extent in Exodus and Numbers, did not take shape, and were not promulgated in full until somewhere about the time when Ezra makes his appearance in Scripture history,—just before or after the Babylonian exile was past. In fact, some claim that Ezra himself promulgated them. For, denying revelation (in the sense that we generally understand it), and substituting evolution in its place, *time* must be allowed for the evolution of such an elaborate and intelligent as well as monotheistic system of worship.

656. When I was a missionary in China, I knew of a Chinese mother who was so provoked because her daughter's bound foot was too large for the tiny shoe she had embroidered for it, that she seized the shears and attempted to cut the foot to the size of the shoe. Revelation is too great and wonderful a fact to be fitted into the narrow theory of evolution; so the destructive critics attempt to hew away the Living Word to fit it into their theory. They would cut the foot to fit the shoe.

657. Now it is not so difficult to declare a very ancient book centuries newer than it happens to be. But other things are involved, in this particular case. For instance, what about the Tabernacle itself, for which these regulations regarding worship were made? Solomon's Temple was built some 500 years before Ezra's day. Was the Tabernacle built 500 years *after* the Temple? The Bible declares it was built about 500 years *before* the Temple. The Tabernacle dates (in round numbers); 1500, Solomon's Temple 1000, and Ezra 500 B. C. Can we date the Tabernacle 1000 years later than we have been accustomed to date it? The Higher Criticism theory does so. Wellhausen, the chief exponent of the Higher Criticism says, "The Tabernacle is a copy of the Temple at Jerusalem." This looks to most of us like childish nonsense. For what object was the *portable* structure called the Tabernacle built, if not for meeting the conditions of the wilderness life of *wandering* Israelites?

658. And how could Ezra, or anyone else, invent the entire ritual law, and then convince the Jews that the

law was revealed to Moses, and had been in use among their own people for long centuries? And yet, this is what is claimed; this is that "modern theory." The children of Israel must be convinced that this newly invented system of laws is centuries old, to secure veneration for it! Abraham Lincoln once said, in his own homely way: "You can fool all the people some of the time; and some of the people all of the time; but you can *never* fool ALL of the people ALL of the time." We all know this is true. The Higher Critics would have us believe, "All the Jews and all the Christians, from Ezra's day until now—including even the Apostles and Jesus Christ—have been fooled ALL THIS TIME, until our brilliant intellects have discovered the fraud for you." But this is something more difficult to believe than to believe that it is the Higher Critics themselves who are perpetrating the fraud for us to accept. If Ezra could do so badly, why not they?

659. One passage in the Bible ought to be regarded as sufficient to explode this "modern theory,"—1 Kings 8:4-9. The Ark and all the furniture of the Tabernacle —including, by inference, the Tabernacle itself—were stored away in Solomon's Temple, when it was dedicated. Thus, Lange's Commentary (Bähr) says: "Not only the Ark, but the Tabernacle which had hitherto stood at Gibeon, with all its vessels, was brought . . into Solomon's Temple." The Tabernacle could not very well have been put into Solomon's Temple, if it was not built until a long time after that Temple had been destroyed. How do these critics get around this statement? Wellhausen declares that the words "Tabernacle of the Congregation" have been interpolated into this particular passage. This is an easy thing to say; the proof is a different matter altogether.

Now this is not primarily a lesson on Biblical criticism, but on women. Therefore we will not stop to discuss this claim of Wellhausen's, further than to say that feeble as it is, it satisfies those who wish to believe in it. Having laid our foundation, we will turn to the passage about women of which Prof. Margoliouth speaks,—about "the women who assembled (A. V.) at the door of the Tabernacle of the Congregation." We wish to know how this verse in 1 Samuel 2:22 is "likely to wreck" this "modern theory" that the Tabernacle was a copy of the Temple, and built 500 years, more or less after the Temple.

660. It is, of course, not logically proper to bring the Pentateuch, or the "Hexateuch" (the first six books of the Bible), into the argument against this "modern theory," since they are the books whose date is called into question. These books mention the Tabernacle some eighty times. For *logical* purposes we must search for a mention of the Tabernacle in books of the Bible that these critics will admit are older than the Hexateuch. The books of 1st and 2nd Samuel, 1st and 2nd Kings and 1st and 2nd Chronicles can be admitted as proof, in the argument against this "modern theory," because the critics claim (not we) that these books *are older* than the Hexateuch,—that is, their date is older than the date when the Tabernacle was built. The Tabernacle is mentioned in these books many times— certainly very clearly some fourteen times, according to Bishop Hervey.

661. But the destructive critic is very fastidious as to terms. He will only accept one expression as clearly designating the Tabernacle,—the Hebrew *'ohel moed,* "tent of meeting," and against every one of these four- teen cases he finds some objection which causes him to doubt the proof. Now it happens that the verse in 1 Sam. 2:22 is the strongest instance among these four- teen, so the argument against the "modern theory" centres here, and the verse is being given increased study. The verse employs the accepted Hebrew expres- sion *'ohed moed,* and it relates to a period of time prior by about 200 years to Solomon's day; and the reliability of this book of Samuel has not been seriously called into question by the destructive critics.

662. But those critics thought *that* particular verse could be dismissed with scarcely a thought, because the part that relates to women does not appear in the manu- scripts of the Septuagint Greek version (which was made by the Jews nearly 300 years before Christ.) So they declared the verse to be an interpolation into the Hebrew text, and not genuine. But here is a difficulty, as pointed out by Dr. Orr: Why should the Jewish translators of the Septuagint make mention *of the same women* in Exodus 38:8? And why should Ezra, or whoever (according to the modern theory) concocted

the Pentateuch, mention these women in the Pentateuch, *at a* later *time* (if the Pentateuch is indeed a comparatively late production), in a period when women were known to have been held in contempt, unless there was a strong tradition, at least, that women had served in the Tabernacle, and what more likely than that the statement lay before him in 1 Sam. 2:22?

(To be continued.)

LESSON 82.

"NO WORD OF GOD IS VOID OF POWER."

(Concluded.)

663. It is possible to demonstrate that this clause which is omitted from the Greek Septuagint rendering of 1 Sam. 2:22, existed in the original Hebrew, and was intentionally omitted from the Greek,—so that it is futile for the Higher Critics to shelter their "modern theory" under the pretext that it is an interpolation into the Hebrew.

664. Prof. Margoliouth has worked out the demonstration, but it will require very close attention for the student to appreciate its full value. Rather than hazard an attempt to represent him, we will quote his proof: "The whole of the modern theory of the Pentateuch is liable to be wrecked on a verse of 1 Samuel [2:22], where it is stated that the sons of Eli misused the women who assembled (A. V.) at the door of the Tabernacle of the congregation.' That clause is omitted by the Septuagint translator. . .

665. "Either the editor of the Hebrew interpolated the clause [as the Higher Critics claim], or the Septuagint omitted it. Omission can happen accidentally, whereas addition in such a case must be intentional; whence the supposition that it can have got accidentally into the Hebrew may be dismissed, whereas the possibility that it may have been accidentally omitted by the translator [of the Septuagint] must be allowed."

666. "Was there then, any motive for omitting it, supposing the omission to be intentional? One has but to glance at the rabbinical commentaries to see: the rabbis do their utmost to clear Eli's sons from this ter-

rible charge. The oldest exegesis made the words allegorical; the crime of Eli's sons was so bad that the text is supposed to *compare* it to the crime with which it really charges them. The later exegesis gives the words senses which they certainly do not possess. Hence it is clear that there was a motive for the omission of the words from the Septuagint." (It must be remembered that Jews made this translation).

667. Next the writer questions whether there was an equally strong motive for adding them to the Hebrew text, an addition of this sort must be by intention, as he has said, *after the Septuagint was. made,*—for it must have been after that time (nearly 300 years before Christ, or the translators would have had the words before them to translate. At this point the subject has special interest for women. Prof. Margoliouth says that against the view that the clause was interpolated into the Hebrews after 300 B. C., "It is to be observed that there is a second difficulty in the clause, which the Jewish exegesis has to overcome. Who were the *women* that served at the door of the Tabernacle? The word translated 'assembled,' but really meaning 'served,' is of great antiquity, and corresponds with the word 'served' in being specialized in certain contexts. 'One who has served' means, if used of a man, one who has been a soldier; and the word used in Hebrew for 'the army' means literally 'the service.' But just as the word 'service' in other contexts means religious service, so this Hebrew word used of something done at the door of the Tabernacle of the Covenant means some religious performance done by these women as *functionaries* . . . But the idea of *women in attendance* at the Tabernacle is so odious that it has to be got rid of."

668. He next proceeds to show that just as the rabbinical commentaries prove that there existed, in the desire to "whitewash" the character of the sons of Eli, a motive for omitting the clause, and it was intentionally omitted, so there appears, in the various versions of ancient times, proof that the strongest prejudices of Jewish men would have been violated by interpolating such a clause, at this time, into the Hebrew text of Samuel, and hence it could not have been done: "The Peshitta [a Syriac version of the early part of the 2nd century,—see par. 131] renders 'the women who *prayed*' there; and this the Targum [see par. 134] adopts. The

rabbis, followed by our Authorised Version [margin] renders it 'the women who *thronged*." He next turns to the passage in Exodus.

669. "In Exod. 38:8 . . the same objection is felt [an objection to admitting that women had a share in the Tabernacle ritual service]. The Aramaic [Peshitta and Targum] translators make them women who *prayed*, the Septuagint, women who *fasted*. Thus it is evident that by the time when the Septuagint translation of the Pentateuch was made, the idea of women ministering at the door of the Tabernacle had become so odious that it was wilfully mistranslated. What chance is there, then that anyone would have wilfully added an allusion to them after that date?"

670. "This, then, is a case in which an argument, at first sight powerful, if steadily glanced at, vanishes. The Septuagint rendering of Exodus is most likely earlier (certainy not later) than that of 1 Samuel. From that rendering, coupled with those of other authorities, we learn that a certain phrase had become odious by the time when the translation was made. What we infer thence is surely that no one would have wilfully inserted the same phrase [in 1 Samuel] where it did not occur."

671. The omission, he declares, is fully accounted for. The crime of Eli's sons was bad enough. They corrupted some of the women they were in daily association with; and the context, in that God visited them with judgment, shows the sons of Eli were the chief offenders, not the women. But when, to escape admitting that women served at the door of the Tabernacle, the word was mistranslated "*prayed*" and "*fasted*," such terms acquitted the women altogether, and left the inference that Eli's sons committed violence towards pious women bent only upon worship, and when they were in the act of worship. But when others translated "assembled" (or "assembled in troops") the inference is that women "thronged" to these two evil men,—indeed the rabbis and our A. V. margin so render.

672. Such misinterpretations as these might pass at home in Palestine—particularly after women were "silenced" in the synagogues and churches, and could not defend themselves from such slander. But when the Jews sat down at Alexandria to the task of translating their Bible for the foreign Egyptian king, would

they admit that their priesthood ever sank so low?
Would they wish to admit that their *women* ever sank
so low, to a foreign nation? Prof. Margoliouth says:
"When faced with such difficulties, many persons think
the wisest course is to flee. And this is what the Septuagint translator has done." In a word, they omitted
the clause intentionally from 1 Sam. 2:22.

673. Thus, the effort to defend the reliability of the
Mosaic literature involves the defender in the duty to
uphold the ancient right of women to serve at the Temple
of the Lord either as priests or as Levites. "No word
of God is void of power," not even such a word as certain men, because of preconceptions as to "woman's
place," wish to alter or reject. In due course, the male
translator discovers that he must retrace his steps, and
pick up again the genuine meaning of a word which he
has corrupted in the translation, unless he is willing to
weaken the credibility of the entire Pentateuch, and
probably, it will be found in the end, of the entire Bible.

This honour put upon women of the Old Testament
is in marked contrast to the decision of the ecclesiastical Council of Laodicea, of the 4th century, and by
which the Church abides to this day: "Women may
not go to the altar." This was explained by Zonaras,
and by other "Fathers" as due to the fact that women
are "unwillingly indeed," at times ceremonially "unclean." As though men priest were not sometimes
"ceremonially unclean,"—yes, and even *morally* unclean!

We may be accused of sex bias if we charge translators of the Word with lack of candour in dealing with
the position of women in God's economy. But we ask,
Have women ever used stronger language than Prof.
Margoliouth has used in this connection—*"wilfully mistranslated"*—to drive the accusation home? And we
must remember that that same wilful mistranslation
stands in the text of our Authorised Version to this day.
It has been corrected in the Revised Version.

LESSON 83.

THE PERICOPE DE ADULTERA.

674. Misinterpretations of Scripture are bad enough;
mistranslations worse. We have dealt with both of
these as they concerned woman's place in the Divine
economy. But worse than either misinterpretations and

mistranslations are mutilations. God has pronounced a solemn curse upon those who are guilty of such manipulations,—at least as far as the last book of the Bible is concerned, and it may apply to all the other books as well, for Prov. 30:5, 6 reads: *"Every word of God is tried: . . add not thou unto His words, lest He reprove thee, and thou be found a liar."* The curse in Rev. 22:18, 19 reads: *"I testify unto everyone that heareth the words of the prophecy of this book, If anyone shall add unto these things, God shall add unto him the plagues that are written in this book: and if anyone shall take away from the words of the book of this prophecy, God shall take away his part out of the book of life, and out of the holy city, and from the things that are written in this book."*

675. If we will look in a Revised Version of the English Bible we will discover that a certain section,— St. John 7:53 to 8:11,—has been placed within brackets and spaced off from the rest of the text of the Gospel; and this marginal note has been added in explanation: *"Most of the ancient authorities omit John 7:53—8:11. Those which contain it vary much from each other."* Now we must examine the exact facts of the case; and, thanks to the careful investigations of the late learned Dean Burgon of Chichester, our task is not so difficult.* The story recorded in John, 8th chapter, is but consistent with Jesus Christ's entire human history in His treatment of women. Because of this fact, it will never be blotted out of the Book, but will be the "word" by which men will be judged, as to their treatment of the social evil, in that Last Day of Judgment (Jno. 12:48).

676. First, let us explain: The ancient manuscripts of the N. T., none of which are older than 400 A. D. (though, of course, they may in some cases be direct copies of the original autographs), are divided into Uncials and Cursives. The former term means that they are written wholly in CAPITAL LETTERS, the latter term implies that they are written in a *running hand*, something like handwriting. There are about sixty uncials of the Gospels, and a thousand or so cursives. It is generally assumed that the uncials are older than the cursives, but this is not always the case; certain cursives are a century older than the uncials. Tischendorf, in 1859, made the latest discovery of an entire Bible of

---

*Causes of Corruption in the Traditional Text.—Appendix 1.

ancient date, in the Greek tongue. This particular uncial is certainly very old, and it did not contain the story of the woman taken in adultery; and this fact, it has been claimed, clenches the proof that the story does not belong to the original text; for seven other uncials, it is claimed by Tischendorf, omit this portion. This has led to the marginal note in the R. V. The portion has been called the *Pericope de Adultera*, meaning an excerpt,—a portion selected for the Church readings, relating to an adulteress. For short, we will call it by this name in these Lessons.

677. Whether the marginal note in the R. V. is correct or not, those who hold Tischendorf's manuscript in high esteem are likely to contend that "most ancient authorities" are against the *pericope;* but that is largely a mere opinion that those that contain it prove thereby their own lack of authority. Dean Burgon says of Tischendorf's claim that eight uncials in all omit the *pericope:* "*No sincere inquirer after truth could so state the evidence,*" and then shows that several of these manuscripts happen to omit the *pericope* for the simple reason that they are lacking at this place,—that is, a page or two is lost out. This sort of "evidence" is as though I claimed that "*All hail the power of Jesus' name*" was not in the Church Hymnal, because my copy of it had two or three pages torn out at the very place where one would be guided by the Index to look for it. After weighing the claims as to the omission of the *pericope*, Dean Burgon asserts that only *three* uncials ("ancient authorities") actually omit the portion; and two of these are demonstrably copies of a common original. That seventy out of a thousand or so cursives omit it is a matter of small moment, of which Dean Burgon gives satisfactory explanation,—as also for its omission from the three uncials, at the same time.

678. It happens that the Eastern section of the early Church appointed that Christ's discourse at the Feast of Tabernacles, given in the 7th chapter of John's Gospel, should constitute the church reading portion on the day of the Festival of Pentecost (Whitsunday); and to this section was added, not unnaturally, the 12th verse of chapter eight. But the verses immediately concerned in recounting the story of the woman taken in adultery were reserved for another day,—St. Pelagia's Day, October 8th. In order to join up well the verses for

Whitsunday, the following were omitted altogether: *"And every man went unto his own house. Jesus went unto the mount of Olives. And early in the morning He came again into the temple, and all the people came unto Him: and He sat down and taught them,"*—7:53 and 8:1,2. Thus, by the entire omission of three verses, two Lessons were made, one for the Festival of Pentecost, and the other for St. Pelagia's Day.

679. St. Pelagia is a name applied to at least three persons, but undoubtedly the one to whom this section finally referred was the one sometimes called "the sinner." She lived at Antioch (as did a virgin "St. Pelagia"), and was a courtesan and dancer. She was suddenly converted under the preaching of Bishop Nonnus, some time in the very beginning of the fifth century. After conversion, she retired to the Mount of Olives, and died three years later of strict penance. Some of the cursives, as we have said, and an uncial or two have omitted the *pericope* altogether. Now, it appears why; they were either manuscripts prepared for Church lessons, or copies of such,—or at any rate, copies of John's Gospel which had been influenced by the Lectionaries of the Church.

680. The proof that such was the case is given by Dean Burgon: Some of the ancient manuscripts of the Gospels are so marked on the margin as to indicate the portions to be used in church. At the beginning of such a portion, the Greek word for "beginning" (*arche*) is written, and at the end, the Greek word for "end," (*telos*). But for the reading for Whitsunday, another Greek word is written at the margin of John 7:53, namely *hyperba*, "overleap, skip;" and at 8:12 a second Greek word signifying "recommence" (*archai*), and lastly the usual *telos* at the end of the lesson. Now Dean Burgon claims that it is impossible that this section, if actually without authenticity, should ever have got so imbedded in the ancient Church readings, into the middle of the lesson for Pentecost, that the ancient Church authorities should invariably have written these directions,—for the Church reading must have been fixed before any of the present-day uncials had come into existence, being very old. All the manuscripts having these markings for Church lessons on their margin, have these special directions for the reading for the Festival of Pentecost. In a word, the Reader of the Scripture

Lesson at Church would not have been directed to "skip" something that had not previously existed there.

681. To use Dean Burgon's own words: "By the very construction of her Lectionary, the Church, in her corporate capacity and official character, has solemnly recognized the narrative in question as an integral part of St. John's Gospel, and as standing in its traditional place, from an exceedingly remote time." . . "In this way then it is that the testimony borne to these verses by the Lectionary of the East proves to be of the most opportune and convincing character. The careful provision made for passing by the twelve verses in dispute: —the minute directions which fence off twelve verses on this side and on that, directions issued, we may be sure, by the highest Ecclesiastical authority, because recognized in every part of the ancient Church,—not only establish them effectually in their rightful place. . . but fully explain the adverse phenomena which are ostentatiously paraded by adverse critics."

(To be continued.)

LESSON 84.

THE AUTHENTICITY OF THE PERICOPE.

682. That this narrative of the woman taken in adultery has the living truth of God in it is proved by its amazing vitality. What but truth could hold its own and progress through the ages with such adverse winds against it? For all through the ages, particularly since the supplanting of female kinship by male kinship, men have held that woman must be more chaste than man, as otherwise man might have more children than his own reckoned in among his progeny; in female kinship no such danger must be guarded against, in genealogical tables. Herein is the chief cause of the persistent maintenance of two standards of chastity, one for men and one for women. But the teaching of Jesus Christ is that man must first show himself to be chaste before dealing with woman's unchastity.

683. The Talmud, for instance, during a discussion between rabbi and scholars, reproduces words incidentally which show that some of the most honoured among them,—married men—expected women to be furnished them when away from home in the performance of

their duties as religious leaders; and yet the Talmud teaches that a man should repudiate his wife *as a proved adulteress,* if merely found abroad with her head uncovered. And we know of pagan customs dealing no less cruelly with women guilty of the least indiscretion. Further, we have only to read the discourses of some of the "Church Fathers," as Tertullian, particularly on the veiling of women, to see exhibited the same spirit of injustice to women. And surely, no one can pretend that anything more than lip-homage to the teaching of the *pericope* has ever been exhibited in the Church up to the present day, excepting in rare instances.

684. Where ever has existed the man, in ancient times or modern, so jealous for the rights of women, so skilful in drawing a picture of *absolute justice,* and yet so unscrupulous in character, and so influential, as to have foisted this story upon the credulity of the Church, so that the ecclesiastical authorities, who live so far beneath its principles of justice in dealing with fallen women, are compelled to let the story persist, and dare not wipe it out of existence? No stronger proof than this is needed that it is a true incident in the life of our Saviour. That we should find that a few attempts have been made to discredit it (such as the Revisers'), is no more than we should expect. The textual critics, Westcott and Hort, are the chief ones in England to cast doubt upon its authenticity, and yet they say: "The argument that has always told most in its favor in modern times is its own internal character. The story itself has justly seemed to vouch for its substantial truth."

685. Besides the oppressive measures instituted by the male in order to maintain male kinship making it necessary to see to it that women are chaste, whatever men may be, another factor has worked prejudicially against the authenticity of this story. This is well expressed in the words of Dr. Philip Schaff: "The story could not have been invented, the less so as it runs contrary to the ascetic and legalistic tendency of the ancient Church which could not appreciate it." We have only to think of the days when monks fled to the wilderness, that they might never be defiled by looking upon the face of a woman; and when celibacy was so exalted that marriage was looked upon as a mild sort of adultery (Tertullian spoke of married women as "women of the

second degree [of modesty] who have *fallen* into wedlock"), to understand these difficulties in the way of a preservation of the *pericope*. Augustine tells us (died about 430, A. D.) that men "from fear lest their wives should gain impunity in sin, removed from their manuscripts the Lord's act of indulgence to the adulteress." Ambrose, twenty-five years earlier, intimated that danger was popularly apprehended from the story; "while Nicon, five centuries later, states plainly that the mischievous tendency of the narrative was the cause why it had been expunged from the Armenian versions."

686. Furthermore, to quote Dean Burgon again, "In the earliest age of all,—the age which was familiar with the universal decay of heathen virtue, but which had not yet witnessed the power of the Gospel to fashion society afresh, and to build up domestic life on a new and more enduring basis;—at a time when the greatest laxity of morals prevailed, and the enemies of the Gospel were known to be on the lookout for grounds of cavil against Christianity and its Author,—what wonder if some were found to remove the *pericope de adultera* from their copies, lest it should be pleaded in extenuation of breaches of the seventh commandment? The very subject-matter, I say, of St. John 8:3-11 would sufficiently account for the occasional omission of those nine verses."

687. We need not fear, however, that this story has ever done any mischief, or ever will. The story does not suit the views of men who are over-careful as to the prudent conduct of their wives, while loose in their own morals. Christ's blow was aimed at two standards of morality; at injustice; at hypocrisy. It was not a blow in defense of adultery in either man or woman. Those who have made use of the narrative, or its principle of justice, in dealing with fallen women, have discovered how it encourages the victim of society's cruel injustices to try again, in the strength of Him whose sceptre is *"absolute justice."* We have known the story to bring a hardened woman sinner to instant repentance,—for the reckless immorality of a fallen girl is generally to be accounted for in the words of Jeremiah, which so vividly describe the effect of hopelessness upon women: *"And they said, There is no hope; but we will walk after our own devices, and we will every one do the imagination of his evil heart. Therefore thus saith the Lord: Ask ye now among the*

heathen, who hath heard such things: the virgin of Israel hath done a very horrible thing" (Jer. 18:12, 13).

688.   There is absolutely nothing which destroys morality out of the human heart so effectually and quickly as injustice, and there is nothing which so quickly lights the Divine flame of penitence and aspiration for holiness, in the heart of the fallen, as the hope of justice. Justice is the kindest thing in the world; injustice is the cruelest and the most depressing. We have seen, repeatedly, the softening effect of this story upon the dark, pagan hearts of women of shame in the Orient,— "Our gods have taught nothing so wonderful as this," they have said, "yours *must* be the true God."

689.   Jesus Christ would not have said to the woman, *"Neither do I condemn thee,"* had she remained impenitent,—so no harm was done. If the effect of the story upon the fallen is so marked, we do not infer too much when we say that the Saviour's sentence of justice was quite enough to bring the woman to instant repentence. His kindness was such a tremendous contrast to the Pharisees who had dragged her into publicity while they let her male partner go free,—for the details of the story convict them of having had the man in their power, had they cared to make an example of him. Thus they had come, redhanded in compromise with male adultery, to make a chance to strike at the Holy One. What cared they if a woman must be made to suffer, too, with the Christ,—if only they could entangle Him!

690.   The truth is, no quality, whatever it happens to be, has anything of use or morality in it unless it be founded upon the basic principle of all morality,— justice.   The lack of justice vitiates any moral quality which we may seek to exercise apart from justice. Hence, no good was ever done, and no good can ever be done, by legal enactments for the benefit of society, which, for reasons of "prudence" omit principles of justice.   Here is where the great mistake is being made on the "woman question."   Is it "prudent" to allow women to do thus and so?—men ask themselves at every step of woman's progress.   The only question that should be asked is, Does justice demand this?   If so, "let justice be done though the heavens fall;" anything short of justice is mere mischief-making.

(To be continued).

302

LESSON 85.

"RAGGED ENDS."

691. We have now considered the principal weak arguments against the *pericope,* and the strong arguments in favour of it, in internal evidence. Other arguments against it must be briefly considered. Many of the Church Fathers do not mention the *pericope* in their commentaries. This objection is not serious. The lesson of the incident was not palatable, as we have shown, because of the ascetic views of the early Church, teaching that the very face of the chastest woman was a cause of corruption. How much more the presence of an adulteress, brought to the thought of a congregation by discussing her case! How *could* the leniency of the Lord be accounted for by men who harshly put away from their midst the purest of women as a source of defilement of their imagination? Then, if husbands and brothers, they did not care to teach that a fall in a woman was no worse than a fall in a man,—especially as they believed that every fall in man was due to some woman. They could understand that the integrity of family life (at least, a man's ability to know his own children), depended upon the chastity of women; but they could not understand that in the remoter sense it depended even more upon the chastity of men. In fact, few men understand this up to the present hour. Again, many of these Fathers' writings are comments on the Church lessons, and as the *pericope* was for a special occasion, and not so well suited to a public address, in their opinion, it would naturally be passed over.

692. Other modern expositors declare that the chief difficulties in the way of crediting the *pericope* are textual. The story contains words that John uses nowhere else in his Gospel. This is true; but, on the other hand, the style of the writing is also much like John's. Supposing, then, that John wrote this portion when the event occurred, and while it was fresh in mind? He did not write his Gospel until fifty or eighty years afterwards, when he was living in Ephesus. This would explain a change of words. Or, supposing the woman herself wrote the account down for him, and allowed him, long after the event when none could identify her, to put it in his Gospel, for the encouragement to repentance of other sinning women; then the *pericope* would,

as the woman's account brushed up by John, exhibit precisely that mixed character which it does. As for its containing several unusual words and expressions, the entire nine verses contain scarcely any more than the first two verses of John 19; and no one has ever questioned the authenticity of the latter, where nine unusual words (for John) occur.

693. On the other hand, note how characteristic, for John, is the expression, *"This they said tempting Him, that they might have to accuse Him."* Compare it with John 6:6; 6:71; 7:39; 11:13, 51; 12:6, 33; 13:11, 28; 21:19. We pass over many other points of similarity to John's own style, in the *pericope,* because they could only be appreciated by those acquainted with the original Greek, for the most part.

Then there are other doubters who have claimed that this incident is an interruption in the text; that the story of Christ at the Feast of Tabernacles runs more smoothly if it is left out; but Dean Burgon contends that the exact truth lies quite at the other extreme: If this *pericope* is torn out of this place, either to be put elsewhere (some would place it at the end of the Gospel of John, others after Luke 21,—in accordance with a few ancient manuscripts), or to be thrown aside as discarded, then "ragged ends," he maintains, show where the violence has been done. Let us see: Let us join up 8:12 next to 7:52, dropping out all between, and study the result,—holding in mind all the time, of course, that this mutilation represents the wishes of certain critics, not our own view as to events.

694. But, let us first pause to consider the fact that no other *place* or *time* could better suit such a story of moral corruption. According to John, the Feast of Tabernacles was on, and hundreds of thousands of people were living in tents all about Jerusalem. Life was very irregular, and afforded opportunities for such a deed. As for the rest, Jesus had been speaking to the common people, in the temple precincts, in the informal way which was allowed to religious instructors. The rulers of the people were angry, but doubtless as on other occasions feared to arrest Him openly (Matt. 21:46). They were angry because they knew He was making great claims for Himself, by such expressions as, *"If anyone thirst, let him come unto Me and drink."* So the Pharisees and chief priests held a council and

concluded to arrest Him,—probably when He ceased to speak, and the people dispersed. They sent officers to fetch Him (7:32), as they had opportunity to do so, quietly.

695. Finally the last day of the Feast comes (7:37), and at its close the Pharisees and priests assemble, confident that surely, at last, He will be brought. But their officers return to them without Him, and all they can say regarding their failure to bring Him is *"Never man spake like this man."* (verse 46). The Pharisees enquire of the officers, *"Have any of the rulers or Pharisees believed on Him?"*—both in derision at the very idea of it, and yet, perhaps, because they wished to really know whether the officers had spied any of their own class and caste in the crowd about Him. It is to be noted that these Pharisees had disdained to go and listen to Him for themselves.* Then Nicodemus, who had gone to Him by night, and felt the force of the officers' testimony that *"Never man spake like this man,"* remonstrated with them, to the effect that it was contrary to their own principles of justice to condemn a man wholesale to whom they had never listened, to know what he had to say for himself. His feeble defence of the Master in whom he secretly believed, acted like the "apple of discord" in the meeting, and *"every man went unto his own house."*

696. But according to the theory, after all the assembly did *not* break up,—for verse 53 must drop out, and all as far as verse 12 of the next chapter; and we must read to the effect that immediately after the words of Nicodemus, and the retort of the others of that council to him, *"Then spake Jesus* again [note the word] *unto them"* (verse 12 chapter 8); and (verse 13) "the *Pharisees"* replied to His words. Now when had He spoken to the *Pharisees* at this Feast, that it can be said that He spoke "again" to them? Had not Nicodemus just declared that they had refused to give Him a hearing, but were in ignorance of His exact representation of His case condemning Him? We must account for that "again" somehow; and those who rule out the story of the woman cannot do it. But put that story back in its proper place and all becomes clear.

* See verse 32.

697. Convicted by the words of Nicodemus that they must hear something from His own lips that will be His own condemnation,—"hear Him for themselves," to make the testimony sure, the Pharisees take with them some experts as to points of law—scribes—and dragging a wretched woman into His presence, demand His decision as to what should be done to her Thus they accept the challenge of Nicodemus.

698. This is on the day following the last day of the Feast, when Jesus is teaching those who have not yet returned to their country homes. If Jesus rendered a decision contrary to the Mosaic law, they would have something of which to accuse Him; if He condemned the woman to die, they might entangle Him with the Roman law. How truly they were to experience the fact that *"Never man spake like this man!"* They became, in His presence, as useless as the officers; they *"went out one by one."* Instead of succeeding in bringing Him to judgment, He had brought them to their own judgment of themselves. The effect of hearing Him for themselves was what Nicodemus had anticipated; they could not bring Him to the bar of their judgment and condemnation. But their Judge did not let them escape so easily. He followed them, still, in His mercy, offering them light and life: *"Again* [later] *He spake unto them,"* and a long argument followed, in which they resisted all His efforts to enlighten their darkness, until at last, in a rage, they took up stones to cast at the Judge who would not allow them to be cast at the sinful woman. This discourse must have occurred later in the day.

ADDITIONAL NOTE: This decision of the Lord, as regards the adulteress, is well-founded in O. T. Scripture, as the scribes and Pharises must have recognized. Hosea 4:14 (R. V.) reads: **"I will not punish your daughters when they play the harlot, nor your brides when they commit adultery, for the men themselves go apart with harlots, and they sacrifice with prostitutes."** Rabbi Yochanan ben Zachi ordered the discontinuance of the trial of jealousy, on the authority of this word, saying, "If you follow fornication yourselves, the bitter waters will not try your wives." Indeed the Sanhedrin had abrogated the ceremony of trial of jealousy, on this word,—since the second Temple, B. C. 520, it is said. But there are evidences of its use in later times.

LESSON 86.

"CAN NOT" FOR "DO NOT."

699. The Greek noun, *chora*, means literally, "the space or room which a thing occupies." The word is variously translated in the N. T. as "country," "land," "field," "coast," and "region." The verb corresponding to it is *choreo*, and it means literally, "to make room or space." It is used in two senses in the N. T. One makes room for a thing or a person, by retreating, or withdrawing; hence it comes to mean "to pass on." Again, one makes room beside or within oneself to receive the thing; hence it comes to mean, "to receive, to contain."

700. The word is used in Matt. 15:17, "*Whatsoever entereth in at the mouth* passeth on,"—see R. V. The word is used likewise in this sense, Dean Alford (rightly) holds, in 2 Peter 3:9, "*Not wishing any to perish, but all* to pass on *to repentance.*" The verbs are infinitives here, and we translate them accordingly. Paul used the verb in another sense, 2 Cor. 7:2, "Receive *us; we have wronged no man.*" The verb occurs in Mark 2:2: "*There* was *no longer* room *for them*" (R. V.). John 2:6 tells us of water-jars "containing *two or three firkins apiece;*" John 8:37, reads, "*Ye seek to kill me, because my word* hath *no* place *in you,*" (i. e., they have not given room to it). John 21:25 again uses this same word in its infinitive form, and we translate literally, "*I suppose even the world not* to contain *the books that should be written.*" In each case the word, or words, not italicized represent *choreo* in the text.

701. This word *choreo* occurs ten times in the N. T. We have quoted seven instances, and the remaining three are all found in the 19th chapter of Matthew. At the 11th verse we read, "*All men* can not receive *this saying* [*logos*, "word, teaching"] *save they to whom it is given,*" both in the A. V. and R. V. But the form of the verb here is the simple indicative case, third person, plural of the present active, and there is no such word as "can" in the sentence. It should therefore have been translated (as the International Commentary renders), "*All men* do not receive *this saying,*" or "teaching,"— i. e., many reject it. The meaning is the same as expressed in John 8:37, "*Ye seek to kill me because My word* [*logos*] hath *no* place *in you.*" The form of the verb

is precisely the same in the two passages, excepting in the latter it is in the singular number. In John it is declared that the *logos* has no place in them; in Mathew, that men give no place to the *logos*... The result is, in the first case, murder; in the second adultery, at heart.

702. Yet upon this misconstruction of Christ's language —by the adroit insertion of "can"—is built up fallacious teaching, about "a gift of continence" being necessary to enable a single man to lead a pure life,—a teaching which places the standard of purity for man as much below the actual standard for man and woman both, set forth in Scripture, as immorality is below morality.

703. But what is this teaching as to a "gift" for men? Says the commentary of Patrick, Lowth, etc.: *"They only can lead a pure single life, who by a special gift of God are enabled so to do."* Calvin's Commentary says: *"The gift of continence is a special gift."* Burkit, *"All men, without sinning against God, cannot abstain from marriage, but those only to whom God has given the gift of continency and grace of chastity."* Bishop Wordsworth (in a book published in 1901,) declares, *"Continenec is as much a special* charisma [gift of grace. spiritual gift] *as the gift of tongues, or prophecy, or working miracles of any kind."* This covert apology for the sin of uncleanness among men, in spite of God's stern commandments to the contrary, can be found in almost every commentary of the Protestant Church.

704. The passage is falsely applied as though referring only to the adult *male.* These very commentators would have been scandalized by the teaching that their wives, sisters, or daughters could not keep moral except by a special *"gift."* *Christ* is not remarking here on the difficulty of men living chastely, as we shall show:

He has used the same sort of expression repeatedly elsewhere, as to its being "given" to some to receive His teaching, to others, not. Matt. 13:11, 12 is an instance. His own teaching, not the disciples' remarks, is the *logos* which the men do not receive. The Lord even plainly declares the precise contrary to the view that men *"can not receive"* by saying that some are born with a natural self-control over sensual tendencies; others have not been trusted to be self-controlled, but have been mutilated; others again practice continence "for the kingdom of heaven's sake." We could have no clearer demonstration that *"All men DO NOT RECEIVE"* this teaching of the Lord, than in the fact that theologians deny His plain statements here, by building upon them a teaching that men *cannot* practice self-control apart from a special, miraculous "gift" of grace.

705. The argument on which this vicious teaching of a need of a special "gift" rests is, that the Greek word *choreo signifies* "capacity." So it does; but not *limited capacity.* Whether the capacity be limited, expansive, or abundant depends entirely upon conditions external to the scope of meaning of the word. To illustrate: In John 21:25, it is, practically speaking, immaterial to the sense conveyed, whether we say, with the A. V., *"the world could not contain the books,"* or, more correctly, with the R. V., *"the world would not contain the books."* And why? Because the world is inanimate, and its size arbitrarily fixed. Not because this verb *means* equally "could contain" or "would contain;" the latter is the proper sense here, on the evidence of the R. V. So as to the water-pots, at the Marriage Feast in Cana: Being of the limits they are, they both "contained" and "could contain" only so much; they had *limited* capacity. But this is proved *by the nature of the vessel,* not by the use of the word *choreo.* But *moral* capacity is not limited after this fashion. No man, no matter how excellently born, is bound to live within the moral limits of his natural birth. These very theologians have no object in preaching the Gospel if they do not include the teaching that the atonement and redemption of Jesus Christ is the precise remedy for the enlargement of moral capacity,—or, at the very least, that humanity is capable of such development, since otherwise there is no need for preaching righteousness.

706. But does it not say in verse 12, *"He that is ABLE to receive it, let him receive it?"* Yes, and here, in the verb "receive" we have the remaining two uses of the verb *choreo.* But what of it? Is that any more than to say as Jesus did, a dozen times, *"He that hath ears to hear, let him hear?"* Does the latter signify *incapacity* of a natural sort, or indifference of a *moral* sort? Jesus said, John 6:65, *"No one CAN* [using the word translated "able" in our Lesson] *come unto Me, excepting it were given unto him of my Father."* Does that shut all out excepting those who receive a special and miracu-

lous "gift of coming?" We know very well that all may come that *"will come,* and we know, too, that all who stand about waiting until a special "gift of coming" is bestowed will be left outside. And so, as to this fabricated "gift of continence;" no such special "gift" has been bestowed, or ever will be bestowed, excepting in the ordinary way that all morality comes; all morality is a "gift" from God. Jesus Christ exclaims in another place, John 8:43, *"Why do ye not understand My speech? even because ye CANNOT hear My word."* Does this excuse those who do not hear? Not at all, for He says again, John 12:48, *"He that . . receiveth not My words hath one that judgeth him: the word that I have spoken, the same shall judge him in the last day."* More to the same import will be found in Mark 4:11, 12, 23-25; Luke 8:10; John 3:27; 12:37-40.

707. A precisely similar manipulation of Scripture, excusing that sin which Jesus Christ condemned as heart adultery, in Matt. 5:28,—and concerning which He plainly taught there, man must rid himself, if even at the cost of a right hand or right eye, or else go into hell fire,—is to be found in 1 Cor. 7:9, which reads, *"If they can not contain,"* whereas the original says "do not." The meaning is perfectly obvious when the Apostle is so read,—"If they do not behave themselves with self-control, they would better marry,"—is the thought expressed.

LESSON 87.

ADVICE FOR EMERGENCY.

708. Turn to 1 Corinthians, Ch. 7. This chapter has been used by the Church to combat the false teaching of the superior holiness of celibacy, to that extent that its natural sense is difficult to grasp. Paul did not have sacredotal celibacy in mind when he wrote it, but he did have a tribulation in mind, as verses 29-31 and other verses prove.

Three of the Gospels (Matt. 24:19, Mk. 13:17, Lk. 21:23), record a warning of Christ's, that no woman should be found pregnant or with little children when that Day came; and the fact that every account of Christ's prophecy of this period repeats this "woe," proves that the warning had taken deep hold on the hearts of the disciples. Nothing could be more natural to suppose than that the Corinthians had asked Paul in their letter some question like this: "If our wives are not to bear children, in view of the coming tribulation, shall we not separate altogether, husbands from wives?" (Read par. 111).

709. Paul's advice is suited to an emergency, but not intended for permanent conditions. This letter was written in A. D. 57, and sore tribulation began in A. D. 64 by the martyrdom of the Roman church (see Lessons 41, 42), and persecutions throughout the Roman empire; and in the destruction of Jerusalem in A. D. 70. (See also Lk. 23:29). Expecting this tribulation under Rome, who knew but that it might prove to be the great tribulation?

Verse 1. Paul's answer to this unrecorded question is, that it is well for a person to have no intimate relations with his wife (the word translated "woman" is also the ordinary word for wife).

Verse 2. But he does not recommend an actual separation, "because of fornications." The A. V. does not render this accurately. There is no such word as "avoid" here. Corinth was an exceedingly wicked city. Profane history says that every other house was one for prostitution. There were over a thousand "religious" slave-prostitutes kept at the Temple of Venus in that city. Pagan religion and fornication went together, in worship. Men recently converted from a paganism which made a virtue of fornication, if thrown out of homes by the break-up of their domestic relations, from very loneliness might backslide into these corrupt conditions. So each man should keep his home and wife, each woman her husband. Or, if this did not happen, separated wives and husbands might become estranged, and remarry without Scriptural grounds for divorce; and this would amount to fornication.

710. Verse 3. The expression "due benevolence" has been given the same vile translation, "duty of marriage", of Exod. 21:10. See our notes, pars. 603-606 in refutation of any such sense. Such a meaning, here, would make Paul teach, between these two verses, "It is good not to do so, but nevertheless be sure to do so." It would not only put verse one at variance with verse 2, but also at variance more or less, in spirit at least, with the teachings of verses 5 (as we shall presently explain), 7, 8, 11, 26, 27, 29, 32, 34, 37, 38, and 40. In fact, it makes

of the chapter a mass of contradictions. All Paul means by this verse is that the husband should continue to minister to his wife by performing his usual duties of support, protection, and heavy tasks about the home; and that the wife should continue her domestic ministrations. This is "due" from each to the other. It is doubtful whether "benevolence" belongs to the original text.

Verse 4. Speaks of the power of restraint, not of self-indulgence, in view of the teaching of continence for an emergency, of verse one. The one can exert this over the other.

711. Verse 5. Dean Alford, in another passage (Mark 10:19), shows that the word rendered "defraud" is equivalent to "covet." This "coveting" in the marriage relation brings about the defrauding of time that should go to prayer, and the "incontinency" spoken of at the end of the verse. Sex union must be of mutual consent "as to time." The expositors who make out that Paul is speaking of incontinent continence, lend themselves to cheap sophistry. The word "fasting," here is probably an unauthorized addition to the original text.

Verse 7.—"his proper gift." If this meant, as is taught, "the gift of continence," then we must believe that Paul taught that other men had from the Lord "the proper gift of incontinence!"((See par. 703).

Verse 9. See Lesson 86. "Cannot," here, is a corrupt rendering; the original says "do not." Guilty couples should get married.

712. Verses 12-16 teach that the matter of absolute avoidance of the matrimonial relation, in case one is married to an unbeliever, or else divorce, is not to be enjoined. There is but one cause for divorce, at least, as Christ taught; and the date of the approaching tribulation was too uncertain to found such rigid teaching as this upon it. This was emergency advice to believing couples expecting at any moment, what however might not occur for many years,—the close of the age and its attendant tribulation.

Verses 20, 24. The teaching of these verses has been much abused,—for instance, to teach a slave that he should not struggle for his freedom. There is excellent reason for believing rather that Paul would direct attention to our one calling of eminence, our "high calling in Christ Jesus," and teach us at all cost to abide in that calling, and do nothing which would mar our title to that high calling. Verses 21, 23 show that Paul did not instruct slaves to be contented with slavery.

Verses 25. Answers to another question from Corinth begin here, and the answers are somewhat obscure. Evidently the question relates to virgin persons of both sexes, as shown by verses 26, 27; the word "virgin" is applied to males in Rev. 14:4. In verse 28 the word is used in its more common female sense.

Verses 26-35. Paul makes it clear that he is not talking of what is "right" and "wrong" in the ordinary sense, but what is wise, or less wise, in the emergencies of the time.

713. Verse 36. The sense is obscure. Most expositors think it refers to fathers disposing of their virgin daughters. Others think that it refers to a man disposing of his virginity in marriage, because he is getting older, than the usual time for marriage. My own belief is that Paul is speaking of affianced young men, and their duty towards their betrothed virgins. If marriage is delayed so long that he feels he is not treating her right in the matter (in those days it was a reproach to a maiden to remain long unmarried), then "let them marry."

Verse 37. The word "nevertheless" is misleading, as though showing a contrast. The Greek word should have been given its usual rendering—"*But* the young man who has deliberately made up his mind not to marry, and with whom there is no (such) need to marry (as spoken of in the pervious verse,—on account of his betrothed), and has decided to keep his virginity (under the present stress of the times), does well not to marry." This I believe to be Paul's teaching.

Verse 38. Dr. Adam Clarke calls attention to the many ancient authorities who read, here, not "giveth her in marriage," but merely "marries," and "does not marry." Note that the word "her" in the Bible is italicized; it does not occur in the original. "He that marries doeth well, and he that marries not doeth better."

714. As to that expression "giveth" in relation to the marriage of a woman: Such an expression occurs nowhere in the entire Greek N. T. The O. T. sometimes uses the word "give" of a woman's marriage. She is often "given" or "sold" to a husband in the O. T., but

no such idea is conveyed by any expression used of the marriage of a woman in the N. T. This is an English importation into both the A. V. and the R. V., because we have not two words which distinguish between the male and the female part in marriage, such as the Greek has.

LESSON 88.

WOMEN PROPHETS OF THE O. T.

715. When Jeremiah uttered those words, *"Send for the wise women* [the literal rendering] *that they may come"* (see par. 620), he probably recalled how his father Hilkiah the priest had gone with others to Huldah, the prophetess, to learn whether the roll they had found in the Temple, when cleaning it up, was really the law of God; and how her wisdom and the revelation God gave her for the benefit of the nation, had led to national reform and revival of religion. We read of women prophets in the O. T., Ex. 15:20, Judg. 4:4; I Chron. 25:8 (compare verse 4) ; Neh. 6:14; Isai. 8:3, and Ezek. 13:17, besides the instance of Huldah recorded in 2 Chron. 34:22.

716. There is no reason to assume, as the average commentator does, that the wife of a prophet is called a "prophetess." Even of Isaiah's wife, Nägelsbach, remarks, "Isaiah's wife is hardly called 'prophetess' because she was the wife of a prophet." Nor is there any reason to assume that women were usually false prophets because such are spoken of or reproved. The fact that they are mentioned and rebuked because *false,* and never because they prophesied, goes a long way towards proving that women prophets were recognized as a matter of course. On the passage in Ezekiel, Schroeder remarks in his commentary, "Prophecy in Israel was a gift of the Spirit, and already, as being so, had no restriction as to sex. But when it came to be upheld by the Spirit of Christ, in whom there is neither male nor female, this overlooking of all sexual distinctions of necessity still more characterized it."

717. We have already (pars. 206-215) treated of the prophesying of women, as predicted in Psalm 68, Isaiah 40, and Joel 2. Now let us turn our attention to a lesson taught in Isaiah chs. 31, 32.

This was a time when Assyria, the first great world power, threatened Palestine. The ten tribes of Israel had been already carried away into captivity (2 Kings 17:6). Isaiah, chs. 36 and 37 describe the political situation:—

31:1-3 show Judah as warned against appealing to Egypt.

31:4. God is represented, in figure, as a lion and a young lion, holding His prey, Jerusalem, under His paw for judgment (Hos. 5:14), and the "multitude of shepherds," Assyria and other nations, cannot take the prey from the fearless Lion. But at a future time, it is promised, *"the Lord of hosts shall come down to deliver."* The immediate and partial realization of this promise is related in Ch. 37:7, 8.

718. 31:5. But here the prophet's eye is centered, in wonder, upon a deliverance which relates to the far future. This promise had only a partial fulfilment in that age.

"Like as flying-birds so will the Lord of hosts cover [protect] *Jerusalem; defending also He will deliver it. Passing over, He will preserve it."* This seems to be the literal meaning.

Never but once in the history of Jerusalem Dec. 9th, 1917, has this promise been completely fulfilled. Think for a moment of the tremendous efforts that were put forth to deliver Jerusalem from the Mohammedan. The crusades lasted for 177 years, and involved nearly all Europe in the effort. Hundreds of thousands of lives, of men, women and children, were lost in the task, and then it had to be abandoned.

719. But why has the Mohammedan had such tremendous power? He has not had it. We think that God, the Lion, has kept Jerusalem under His own power, through all these centuries; and mainly because He would not allow Jerusalem to pass under the rule of any people given to idolatry, He has allowed Mohammedans to rule there. One had only to go to Jerusalem and watch the genuflections to images of so-called "Christian" sects, to see that idols would have filled the place, had the crusades succeeded. God has caused a people who did not make idols to rule there.

But when the Lion lifted His paw, how easily deliverance came! "General Allenby's report show that the flying men took a prominent part in delivering Jerusalem], and its deliverance came largely from the air. The promise *'passing over He will preserve it'* accounts for such a strong position being taken without any injury to any of the sacred places in the city." (*The London Christian,* Jan 10th, 1918).

720. Judging from the connection, soon after this event, the reign of Christ in righteousness begins, see the opening verses of chapter 32. (Yet we must not be too certain on this point).

32:8. But note the abrupt breaking off, at the end of this verse, in the description of that blessed reign, and that it is resumed at verse 16.,

32:9-16. We have introduced these chapters because of the great importance to women of this passage. It was necessary to get its historical setting, to show that the admonition and the warning relate to our time. Will we women cast aside our careless indifference to responsibility, clothe ourselves in the sackcloth of deep repentance, and seek God with all our hearts? This is what the prophet Isaiah demands of us. And the fearful judgments which are impending, he makes it clear, will descend upon those women who do not.

721. There is an obstruction to Christ's coming. Joel had before this declared that God's Spirit was to be poured out upon "all flesh," bond and free, young and old, women as well as men; and Peter has made it perfectly clear that his prophecy belongs to the present age (Acts 2:16-18). But the Church has contrived, in its sex prejudice, to find reasons why this prophesying is to be done by men alone, and that the world is "to be saved by the foolishness of preaching" by men only.

Such is not the case. The diffculty with the teachings of St. Paul exists in the minds of men, not in the Word of God. It is a difficulty, largely, of prejudice and egotism; and women must not fear to brook the displeasure of men by an attempt to open their eyes to the fact that their difficulty is with God, rather than with women,—though few men are willing to admit this, or even to perceive it. They are not so candid as the Rev. James B. Finley, who, in his Autobiography says, concerning the offence of a woman speaking in church, "I . . quoted the language of St. Paul in regard to women teaching in the Church, and expressed a hope that the Spirit (!) would not move any more to speak on such occasions." But the Spirit *will* move women, in spite of the hopes to the contrary.

722. 32:15. The prophet calls upon the women to get ready, *"so that* [as it might be rendered, in place of "until"] *the Spirit may be poured upon us from on high,"* and the way made ready for the return of the Lord. That Spirit will not be poured out in fullness until women are ready.

Women had their share of the "former rain" at Pentecost: but soon pagan influence within the Church wrested Paul's word (2 Pet. 3:16), and excluded women from their portion of this witnessing, within the Church. Women have too readily taken advantage of this excusing of women from such service,—too often because they *"loved the praise of men more than the praise of God"* (John 12:43).

This prophecy of Isaiah shows that God has not excused where man has, but rather, that a fearful judgment awaits those women who do not hasten to bring about that FULL-filment of Joel's prophecy regarding "daughters" and "handmaidens," and thus make way for that "latter rain" which opens the door for the Lord's second coming. May God's own Spirit convict women of their negligence!

LESSON 89.

WOMEN MAY PREACH.

723 The Church has often told woman—we might say very loudly—that Paul commanded her to "keep silence in the churches." The Church has told woman very softly, or not at all, that Jesus Christ obliged one woman to *not keep silence,* but to proclaim before a great multitude, made up largely of men, that Christ had redeemed her from that very "curse," as it has been called, which is supposed by some to lie at the base of the doctrine of silence and subordination for women, and which was the pretext for her original exclusion from service at the altar,—see par. 673.

724. The account of this woman's case will be found in Luke 8:43-48. Zechariah had proclaimed, 500 years before this incident, that there was to be a *"fountain opened for sin and uncleanness"* (13:1), referring to the coming Christ, and using the very word for "unclean-

ness" which, according to Levitical law, separated a woman from the congregation of Israel (Lev. 15:19). Men straight from a battle; from stumbling over a grave in the churchyard; from administering comfort in the home of the dead, and from many other conditions producing that same state called "separation," (or "uncleanness," as translated), for which exclusion from the congregation of Israel was prescribed, have never thought of excluding themselves, even temporarily, from the altar of the Church. In a word, men found that *"fountain for sin and uncleanness"* when Christ came and took full advantage of it; but presently they excluded women from its benefits, and placed her back under Levitical disabilities.

725. We have a lesson to learn from Christ's bringing the woman to the front to declare her own redemption from an infirmity, instead of His merely declaring it for her. It is not enough that Christ's teaching is plain on this subject, *we women must proclaim this.* It is not enough for women to modestly and quietly seek their own redemption, they must proclaim it, even when that proclamation lays them open to the false charge of immodesty.

726. This brings us to another lesson that Christ taught, when he caused yet another woman *not to keep silence.* This case is recorded in Luke 13:11-13. We can easily picture this poor deformed creature making her way wearily to the synagogue, to hear the great Prophet; climbing the steps to the stuffy little compartment behind a lattice, usually up in the gallery under the roof. How amazed she must have been to have the great Prophet call out suddenly, "Mary, come here to me." The other women help her to descend as quickly as possible, and she walks up the aisle to the platform with trembling feet, and stands in a most unusual position,—out in public, among all the men! Gently He spoke to her and *"laid His hands on her,"* and behold! not only is she *"loosed from her infirmity"* of a bowed back, but also of a silenced tongue; *"she was made straight and glorified God."* This means, of course, that she broke the silence with her hallelujahs, and with rapid tongue began to tell eagerly all about her former suffering, and healing, to all in the synagogue.

727. Of course it angered the Rabbi in charge, and he forbade the people coming to be healed any more on the Sabbath day. Christ first answers him effectually on this "Sabbath question," and then He takes up the "woman question." This act of the *"laying on of hands"* afterwards came into use among the Apostles as the ceremony which fitted men for preaching the Gospel and to this day men boast that they are in the "Apostolic Succession," which means that someone laid hands on them, who had had hands laid upon him, of one who had had hands laid upon him, of one, etc., etc., all the way back to an Apostle. They forget that this "laying on of hands" goes farther back than to the Apostles, to a certain woman, who had *Christ's* hands laid upon her ; and she immediately responded by publicly glorifying God, in spite of the prohibitions of man. Men might have been not merely in the "Apostolic succession," but in the Divine succession, had they not despised the ministry of women. They should have sought of this woman the "laying on of hands," if there be any virtue in "succession.

728. After answering the Rabbi on the Sabbath question, Jesus uttered two parables. That the incident of the healing led to the utterance of the parables is not made clear in the A. V. which translates, *"Then said He, Unto what is the kingdom of God like?"* The R. V. is more correct, rendering, *"He said, therefore,"* etc. But Weymouth's Modern English translation brings out the full force of the connection, rendering, "This prompted Him to say." He was prompted to say that man took the seed of the kingdom and planted it in his own garden. That planting has done a vast deal of good to all mankind, including women. But yet it is true, that in teaching woman to forever do penance for the sin of Eve, while Adam was to be exalted to government over woman (something he did not have previously), by the sin in Eden, there has been something very self interested and selfish in the way man has preached the Gospel of the kingdom.

729. But Christ's parable prophesies that one day the kingdom will be like leaven in woman's hand. Oh, I know they tell us that this leaven "always means something evil." Do not believe it! This was supposed to be a necessary invention to combat the teaching that the world will gradually grow better and better till the end

319

This is not the first instance of well-intentioned men getting so nervous lest true doctrines are not sufficiently forcefully taught in Scripture, that they have unwarrantably twisted the truth. Christ said, of the "kingdom of God," *"it is like a grain of mustard seed."* Again He said, *"Whereunto shall I liken the kingdom of God? It is like leaven."* Scripture has no sense, if this plain statement is not sufficient to prove that leaven is *not* always something evil,—since the kingdom is not evil. And besides, things that are equal to the same things are equal to each other; and so long as men teach that the "mustard seed" is something good, do they prove that leaven is, in this parable, something good also. "Like" does not mean like, if leaven is "something evil" here.

730. God never directed man to put "something evil" in his offerings to God. Read Lev. 7:13 and 23:17. To be sure, leaven was not to be burned in sacrifice, but that was because the odor was not pleasant (Lev. 2:11 12). And no leaven was allowed at the passover time. and we are expressly told that this was because unleavened bread was *"the bread of affliction,"* and to commemorate the haste of the departure from Egypt (Deut. 16:3). Whether leaven refers to something good or something evil, depends upon the context. It signifies merely an all-pervading influence.

We may be sure that our mothers will never preach the Gospel in such a manner as to exalt one sex above the other. And when that mournful time comes of which Paul prophesies, the "falling away" of the Church, and the banner of the Cross is trailed in the dust, we may expect to see our mothers seize the precious standard, and raise it aloft, for, as Payne-Smith says, "God has never given to any body of men whatsoever a chartered right to lock up heaven, and let His people perish for lack of knowledge." We are coming very close to such times, if we may judge from the rationalistic utterances from our present-day pulpits. *"Three measures of meal"* does not mean the whole world. This was the usual quantity used to supply bread for a family. The meaning is that the whole family of God will each have his or her share.

731. On a third occasion the Master's words so stirred a woman's heart that she began to pour out blessings on His head; she "preached Christ" after her own

fashion, interrupting Him in His discourse to do so.
Did Christ silence the woman? Not at all. He said
"Amen" to what she uttered, and added to her teaching.
(Luke 11:27). Yet apparently not one of these three
incidents of unrebuked women speaking in public in
Christ's presence has ever been sufficient to arrest the
attention of expositors to the degree that they would
consider whether Paul's one utterance, *"Let the women
keep silence,"* could not be brought into conformity with
the precedent set by Jesus, and with the Apostle's own
words elsewhere. But if one such saying is pronounced
sufficient to silence one half—yes, more than one half—
the Church membership, why are not other sayings sufficient to silence the other half?

LESSON 90.

WOMEN MUST PREACH AND TEACH.

732. Penance has no purpose excepting to expiate
guilt. When women are taught that they must take a
specially lowly position; that they must meet their husbands' sensual demands with unquestioning obedience
(see Lesson 14); that they must be silent in Church;
that they must go veiled; must not teach or preach; that
they must have no part in Church government,—and all
because Eve sinned, they are taught to do penance, and
they are taught thereby that in some sense guilt adheres
to them. The teaching of all these things (whether
acknowledged or not), is precisely what Tertullian dared
to say, namely,—"God's verdict on the sex still holds
good, and the sex's *guilt* must still hold also."

733. Now the question is, Will enlightened women
accept this as "the gospel" men should preach to them?
They will not, of course, if they honour their Saviour
as One who made a full and sufficient atonement for
the sins of the whole world.* Nor will they pass under
the control of the incompetent or unworthy simply
because such may be *males.* And so long as the Church
endorses such teachings, by practicing the custom of the
male management of all its affairs, just so long will it
see its more enlightened female membership diminishing,

734. There was a time when in civil government and
every department of life men governed, but that day is

*I John 2:2.

321

passing everywhere excepting where its existence is most incongruous,—in the Church; for long ago it was written, *"If ye have respect of persons, ye commit sin, and are convinced* [i. e., convicted] *of the law as transgressors"* (Jas. 2:9). When the rule of the male was universal, woman could accept membership in a Church without change of status. She cannot, today. An invitation to identify herself with any religious society which carries with it the inference that she will turn backward into servitude will be declined with increasing frequency, in days to come. And this attitude on the part of Christian women may not be justly ascribed to pride and want of sanctity. No mature human being has a right to yield unquestioning obedience to other than God Himself. The competent have no right to accept the leadership of the relatively incompetent,—and women have fully demonstrated the fact that they cannot all be reckoned as less competent than men. Nor must the more righteous accept control by the less righteous.

735. But far and above all this, *NO CHRISTIAN* SHOULD EVER DISHONOUR THE ATONEMENT *OF JESUS CHRIST,* nor can a Christian do this without sin. There is no place in this whole world for a Christian to seek to please God by doing penance. The acceptance of penance is *a denial* of the *sufficiency of the atonement* for our sins. We women refuse that attitude towards Jesus Christ. Jesus Christ's atonement did not fall short of reaching Eve, by any means.

736. But again the question, "Why should Eve's female offspring suffer for the sin of Eve more than her male offspring? every human being is the child of Eve." No possible answer is forthcoming excepting that in some obscure sense the *female* is Eve's *special* offspring, or seed, or at least so reckoned by God and man.

Ah, now we are getting to the point. Who else is the *special* Seed of the woman? Jesus Christ. We women are put in a class by ourselves because we are specially related to the first woman; and we find Jesus Christ in that same class with us. But if the class to which Jesus Christ belongs—the special Seed of woman—is to be in perpetual dishonour, there can be no doubt as to what *spirit* teaches this,—not the Holy Spirit, the real teacher of the Word and Expounder of it, but the spirit of Anti-christ,—for *"even now are there many anti-*

christs" (I John 2:18). And is it not worth while, sisters, for us to rise up and challenge this lying spirit which has gone forth into the world,—this denial to woman of the full benefits of the Atonement?

Nay more: It is not enough to say this is worth while,—*"Woe be it unto* [us women] *if we preach not the gospel,"* for just to the extent that these other matters are taught Christ, more than woman, *is dishonoured;* and the world may perish for want of a knowledge of the fullness and sufficiency of the atonement of Jesus Christ unless we women challenge this false doctrine, by exhibiting in our lives the results of an atonement with *no sex limits on it.*

737. Again we ask, If one only expression, *"Let the women keep silence"* (I Cor. 14:34), which readily admits of a qualifying interpretation, is allowed to pass **as** forbidding one half of the human family forever from proclaiming the gospel of Jesus Christ, why may not other like expressions silence the other half forever? As samples we cite Habakkuk 2:20, *"Let all the earth keep silence before Him;"* Jeremiah 8:14, *"Let us enter into the defenced cities, and let us be silent there: for the Lord our God hath put us to silence . . because we have sinned against God;"* Zechariah 2:13, *"Be silent, O all flesh, before the Lord,"*—etc.

738. There is such an offence as handling the Word of God deceitfully,—as distorting it out of semblance to commonsense. This is precisely what is being done by those who, in the face of a world perishing for the lack of the gospel of Jesus Christ, and in an age when it is clearly to be seen that the present state of Christendom is a disgrace, because of its utter failure to meet the requirements of Christian life; when the world is mangled and bleeding to death, starving and rotting in its social corruption, while male ministers of the gospel are as frequently discrediting Christ, in their pulpits, as honouring Him, as frequently attacking the Bible as explaining it,—in such an age as this it is pertinent to ask the question whether women have any right to keep silent?

"But Eve was *deceived* when she dealt with the Serpent, in Eden, and can women ever be *safe* religious teachers?" Review the past: The Sanhedrin that compassed the death of Christ, over the protest of the "daughters of Jerusalem" and Pilate's wife; the sects of

Nicolaitanes, Ebionites, Gnostics, Ophites, Manichaeans, Predestinarians, extreme Antinomians, Irvingites, Agapoemonians, Mormons, and scores more, led by men; the ignorant and stupid ecclesiastics who resorted to imprisonments, torture, massacres, inquisitions, and burnings at the stake, to compel men and women to renounce the truth and accept spiritual darkness instead,—then tell us on what historical authority it can be assumed that *men* are safe religious leaders. And why the mere fact that Eve was "deceived" and women have led in Christian Science, Theosophy, and modern (not ancient) Spiritism, proves that all women are unsafe as religious leaders? This claim lacks candour, in view of the fact that few women have ever been allowed to try if they could lead; it is born of ignorance and prejudice. On the other hand, think of the millions of women who have trusted the "authority" of male leadership in religious matters, to be hurried forward into the ditch of spiritual darkness or unrestrained license, to their eternal loss.

739. The statement has been made on very high authority, in a recent pamphlet published in England,* that of 4,000 missionaries in India, Burmah and Ceylon today, not more than 2,000 believe in the Bible as the inerrant and infallible Word of God. Are we women going to keep quiet in the face of such facts,—2,000 foreign missionaries *weakening* the faith of the natives of India in the Word of God, rather than strengthening it? "God has never given to any body of men whatsoever a chartered right to lock up heaven, and let the people perish for lack of knowledge," says Dean Payne-Smith. Those who oppose the preaching of women, and the teaching of women, are committing precisely this offence. It is wicked for any human being to shut the mouth of anyone, male or female, who will sound forth a *testimony to the truth* in these days of apostasy.

740. I recall an incident which my mother used to relate, of early days in New York city,—quite close to Colonial times. She was, as usual, on the Sabbath sitting in the old Dutch Church, in a pew with her parents. The cry of "Fire, Fire!" broke into the calm discourse of the minister, and a large number of men

* "The Ravages of Higher Criticism in the Indian Mission Field", by W. R. Roberts: Foreward by Prebendary H. E. Fox. Published by the Protestant Truth Society, London, price four pence.

quietly withdrew, knowing that help was needed, otherwise sacred services would not have been interrupted. Later, a second cry of "Fire!" was sounded, and more men withdrew. A third cry came, and all the men withdrew. At last an urgent cry came, "Fire, Fire!—and if there are no more men the women must come!" Then the meeting broke up, and all rushed forth to save the whole city, for it seemed doomed.

741. A very fire of hell is raging all about us, even though largely unrecognized, in modern rationalism. Its crudest features have, perhaps, found expression in Russia; its most pervasive sulphurous fumes are stifling the youths of our schools; its most consummately treacherous havoc prevails in the pulpit. We women have no alternative but to help extinguish the fire or be scorched by it, and see our children perish in its flames. Shall we women, at such a time as this, sit still, and *remember our sex?* Never! We will brush aside the opposition of those who can think only in terms of *sex,* and go up *"to the help of the Lord against the mighty."*

And what must women preach? Review the history of the past few years, and the answer must be plain to every Christian. Women must preach that "religion of blood" which the fastidious have affected to find so offensive to their aesthetic taste,—the "blood of the Cross" of the Only One, whose blood would have sufficed to spare that of millions of their sons who have been offered up as human sacrifices to Mars, had its flow of "sorrow and love" been accepted on earth as an atonement and remedy for sin before sin begot its bloodthirsty brood. There is no alternative. It must be the "blood of the Cross" and self-immolation, or else bloody wars for self-deification. Antichrist is at hand. Which shall it be?

LESSON 91.

WOMEN WERE WITNESSES, TOO.

742. Please center your thoughts on a little group of women who came out of Galilee with our Lord, and followed Him from place to place in His ministry. They are first mentioned clearly in Luke 8:2, 3, as *"Mary called Magdalene, . . . Joanna the wife of Chuza, Herod's steward, Susanna, and many others."* Those

that are mentioned by name here are probably the women of comfortable means, *"who ministered unto Him of their substance."* Three of the "many others" can be identified: *"Mary the mother of James and Joses; and the mother of Zebedee's children"* (whose children were James and John, and the mother's name Salome, Matt. 27:56, Mark 15:40); and the mother of Jesus, frequently mentioned.

743. Now let us recapitulate: (1), Mary of Magdala, probably a woman of wealth who had been insane; her name stands as security, so to speak, for every penitent "Magdalen" (though there is no proof that she was ever impure in life), because of the words,—*"out of whom went seven demons."* (2), Joanna, wife of the steward of Herod Antipas, tetrarch of Galilee, a woman of the higher social caste. (3), Susanna, of whom we know nothing but her name, but probably a person of means, (4), Mary, the Lord's own mother. (5), Mary, the wife of Cleophas (Alphaeus), described also as "the mother of James and Joses." Very reliable tradition declares Cleophas was Joseph's brother. (6), Salome, wife of Zebedee, mother of James and John, a sister of Jesus' mother. From the expression *"many others,"* we infer that the number of women who accompanied Jesus in His three years' ministry, was not inconsiderable.

744. They must have witnessed most of His miracles; heard most of His discourses; seen His sufferings, and known His claims,—that He was the Messiah. These women had no more lofty ambition for themselves than to minister unto their Lord. To be sure, the mother of Zebedee's children, the aunt of Jesus Christ, is shown as asking for a high place for her sons in Christ's kingdom (in Matt. 20:21); but it is evident she was pressed into this service by her sons,—since the Lord answers, not her, but the sons: *"Ye know not what ye ask;"* and *"When the ten heard it, they were moved with indignation against the brethren."* This shows that they did not hold the mother culpable. Mark does not even mention the mother, as voicing the request of the sons (Mark 10:35). No, these women who followed the Lord had no wishes of their own to be gratified. Their service was a disinterested one.

745. When Jesus was about to be received up into heaven, He gave His disciples a strict injunction *not* to

go forth to witness for Him, until they received the spirit of prophecy (Acts 1: 4, 5, 8). It was to be given to them (1) Because they had witnessed His life on earth; (2) To enable them to give forth a recital of all they had witnessed, with "power," and (3) The possession of that Holy Spirit was proof to others, that they were witnesses chosen of God to give testimony. For these reasons is it said that *"the testimony of Jesus is the spirit of prophecy,"* Rev. 19:10. That Holy Spirit was not poured out upon any, on that day of Pentecost, save Christ's own chosen witnesses to His birth, life on earth, death, resurrection and ascension. These numbered one hundred and twenty persons (Acts 1:15, 2:3). Not each one was a witness of all these events, but each had a part to tell.

746. A witness has no other business, as a witness, but to give a simple recital of what the witness has seen. Jesus Christ would not, in fact could not, choose *as witnesses* for certain events in His career on earth, those who had not witnessed those events. Imagine the anger of a judge, who calls up a case in court, to find that the complaining parties have not brought a single witness of that which had been complained of,—only a lot of eloquent pleaders. He would say, "Away with these! One intelligent child is of more value to me than a hundred eloquent men, if that child *saw something,* or *heard something.* You cannot *witness* to what you never saw or heard. I want evidence; I do not want talk." Jesus Christ could not make use of any as His witnesses, save as they witnessed concerning what *they saw.* Even He had no choice at this point; the witness to an incident must have *seen* that incident, and *heard* what was said.

747. We proceed at once to show what the women who accompanied Him out of Galilee *saw* and *heard,* which His male disciples did not see and hear. (1), The Virgin Mary *"went with haste"* far away from Nazareth, when she knew she was to become a mother; and many, therefore, especially Elisabeth and Zacharias, would *know* that her child was not Joseph's, as well as of her chaste reputation. But who save the Virgin herself could give "the testimony of Jesus," as regarded the appearance of the Angel Gabriel, to talk with her face to face, and as to Christ's incarnation as the very Son of God, having no human father, but "conceived of

the Holy Ghost?" The doctrine of the Incarnation, as fulfilled (it was prophesied of) rests, for human testimony, wholly on the word of the Virgin, corroborated by the dream of Joseph (Matt. 1:20).

748. (2), Passing by the fact of the women from Galilee witnessing a large share of the miracles which Christ wrought, hearing His discourses, so as to be able to repeat them, and His claims to be the Messiah (the account of much of which, as given by women, must have found its place in the writings of the Gospel),* we come to the incidents of the crucifixion. We are plainly told that when Christ was arrested, in company with the eleven, all *"forsook Him and fled"* (Matt. 26:56); and it is certain they were so afraid for their own lives that none of them summoned courage sufficient to appear at the crucifixion, save John. He was there a part of the time. But John withdrew when Jesus committed His mother to John's care, taking her away from the dreadful sight. He returned later.

749. What John did not see, he does not tell; therefore, the events of importance described by the three Evangelists, Matthew, Mark and Luke, that are not found in John's Gospel, rest upon the testimony of the women,—for it is certain that only John was an eye witness of the crucifixion. Matt. 27:56 speaks of Mary Magdalene, the other Mary and Salome as *"beholding afar off,"* but when Jesus spoke to His mother and John, Mary Magdalene and the other Mary with the mother had drawn nigh in the darkness, and *"stood by"* the cross (John 19:25). John then withdrew with the mother.

750. Of the Seven Words uttered by the dying Lord, John records but three. These two women, both named Mary, must have had "the testimony of Jesus" as regards the other four: the prayer, *"Father, forgive them, for they know not what they do"* (Luke 23:34); the promise to the thief, *"Today thou shalt be with Me in Paradise,"* (Luke 23:43); the cry, *"My God, My God, why hast Thou forsaken Me?"* (Matt. 27:46; Mark 15: 34); and the prayer, *"Father, into Thy hands I commend My spirit"* (Luke 23:46). And of the events in connection with the crucifixion, the women

---

* There is credible tradition that St. Luke got much information for his Gospel from the daughters of Philip.

alone must have testified how the passers-by railed on Him (not recorded by John); how one thief on the cross addressed Him in penitence, the other one mocking; and the giving of the vinegar to Him. After these events, John returns, and after His death Joseph and Nicodemus also appear in connection with Christ's burial. Bear in mind, therefore, that of the Seven Words of the Lord on the cross, four secured their place in the Gospels and in the teaching of the Church on the witness of women only.

751. Yet the women linger; and when the body is laid away in the tomb, *"The women also, which came with Him from Galilee, followed after, and beheld the sepulchre, and HOW HIS BODY WAS LAID"* (Luke 23:55). Evening came on (Matt. 27:57); the last service to the dead body was performed; the stone closed over the tomb, but yet *"There was Mary Magdalene, and the other Mary, sitting over against the sepulchre"* (Matt. 27:61).

LESSON 92.

WOMEN WERE WITNESSES, TOO

(Concluded)

752. We have brought out many striking points, as regards the incidents relating to the Incarnation and Crucifixion, which we know on the testimony of women only. As to the events connected with the latter, the *written record* in the Bible depends wholly on the word of the women coupled with John's; no other witnesses are cited. It is more than likely that some unbelievers who witnessed the crucifixion became believers afterwards, and testified orally to the events; but these are not cited in the written record.

753. It was a fixed law, in the Bible, that one witness was not sufficient to establish testimony (Deut. 19:15), but, as twice taught in the Gospels also, *"In the mouth of two or three witnesses every word may be established."* (Matt. 18:16; see Jno. 8:17). Hence, since John alone witnessed the Crucifixion, and the testimony of one is not to be accepted; and all the Gospels cite "the women from Galilee," and no others as their other witnesses to these events, we discover that the written record of the events connected with the Lord's Cruci-

fixion rests, in its major part, upon the testimony of women.

754. The Resurrection: We must be ready for yet more surprises, as regards the women's testimony to the incidents connected with the Resurrection, the earliest events of which, told by Matthew, are as follows: *"As it began to dawn towards the first day of the week, came Mary Magdalene and the other Mary to see the sepulchre. And behold there was a great earthquake: for the angel of the Lord descended from heaven, and came and rolled back the stone,"*—and so the incident proceeds (Matt. 28:1, 2).

755. Most of us read this as though written: "And, behold there *had been* a great earthquake: for the angel of the Lord had descended,"—before the women arrived. But this is not as stated, and Dean Alford declares: "This must not be taken as pluperfect, which would be altogether inconsistent with the text. . . . [It] must mean that the women were *witnesses of the earthquake,* and *that which happened* . . . was not *properly* an earthquake, but was the sudden opening of the tomb by the descending Angel, as the *gar* [word "for"] shows. . . It was not *for Him,* to whom (see John 20:19,26) the stone was no *hindrance,* but *for the women and His disciples,* that this was rolled away. All attempts to *deny* the angelic appearances, or *ascribe them to later tradition,* are dishonest and absurd. That related in John is as definite as either of the others, and he certainly had it from Mary Magdalene herself."

756. To recapitulate: That which we know about an earthquake; of the appearance of an angel; of the rolling away of the great stone; of the "keepers" falling as dead men, from fear; of the announcement *"He is risen";* all this, told by Matthew, the two Marys alone were witnesses to. From Mark we learn that the women saw a young man (angel)l *sitting on the right side, clothed in a long, white garment."* Luke says they saw "two men in shining garments." At any rate, on that Resurrection morning two angels were seen, and by women alone. Not by Peter, nor by John. The guards felt the earthquake, and fell. It is not likely they saw the angels. If perchance they did, they were not fit witnesses. The testimony of women alone is cited here, in the Bible record. Providence saw to it that the earth-

quake did not take place, nor the angels descend, until the two Marys were brought there to witness and to record the events.

757. The question is, Did Jesus have no higher choice for the women who came with Him out of Galilee, and accompanied Him throughout His three years' ministry, —the women who were "last at the cross, and first at the tomb," on the Resurrection morn—than to let them feed and clothe Him? Were they not, all unconsciously to themselves, likewise in a school of training as His witnesses? Nay more, twelve were called for this special work; all failed Him, when danger was at hand, but one. But He had His chosen witnesses; the Marys were at hand. Did He never think ahead of how this should come to pass, when He said, so often, *"There are first that shall be last, and last first, for many are called, but few chosen?"*

758. The twelve who had indeed forsaken much to follow Him, were not always actuated by the highest motives. Judging from the conversations among themselves which have been recorded, they thought largely of an exalted position to be given them, when their Master should come into a kingdom of earthly glory. But the women followed with no other motive than to make themselves of use to Jesus, and to His disciples. Could it be possible that the One who was teaching His disciples such lessons as, *"He that is greatest among you, let him be as the younger; and he that is chief, as he that doth serve,"* and *"Whosoever will be chief among you, let him be your servant: even as the Son of Man came not to be ministered unto, but to minister,"* and who declared, *"Whosoever shall exalt himself shall be abased: and he that shall humble himself shall be exalted,"* intended to show, in His treatment of those who had humbled themselves and served (while the twelve exalted themselves, and discussed which should be the greatest of them), that His practice was inconsistent with His teaching? Nay, verily; this could not be. It did not *happen* that the women knew these incidents, and saw that they were recorded for future ages. They had humbled themselves; Christ exalted them. He gave them visions on the Resurrection morning that no one else had. *He made the witness of women the very meat and marrow of His Gospel.*

759. Then how did the male disciples receive the women's testimony? *"Mary Magdalene . . went and told them . . And they, when they had heard that He was alive, and had been seen of her, believed not."* (Mark 16:9-11)|; and Luke says: *"Their words seemed to them as idle tales, and they believed them not."* When He met the two, later, on their way to Emmaus, they said *"Certain women of our company made us astonished, which were early at the sepulchre . . . saying, that they had also seen a vision of angels, which said He was alive."* Jesus replied, *"O fools and slow of heart to believe all that the prophets have spoken."* Then He opened their understanding, expounding the Scriptures to them; and they knew that what the women had seen was true (Luke 24:22-27).

760. It was not so strange that they did not receive the testimony of the women (for Mark records that these two also did not believe), for we know, from Josephus, that the Jews had added to the word of the law (which says that on the testimony of two or three only can anything be established), these words: "But let not the testimony of women be received, because of the frivolity of the sex." The rabbinical teaching was that the testimony of one hundred women was not sufficient to refute that of one man. But Jesus Christ entrusted to women the part of witnesses (and often the sole witnesses) to the most tremendous facts in His life. He could well take this risk, since it was never the Divine purpose that testimony to the truths of the Gospel should rest wholly, or even principally upon a human foundation. Those who are His chosen witnesses will always have the convicting power of the Holy Spirit to enforce the truth of all that is said upon the hearts of those willing to receive it. But as to testimony to the average prejudiced Jew steeped in rabbinical contempt for the testimony of *mere women,* there was no hope of getting an entering wedge into these hearts but through the testimony of *men.* This fully accounts for the fact that there were no women among the Twelve Apostles.

LESSON 93.

PREPARING WOMEN WITNESSES.

761. The Lord was certainly preparing these women from Galilee to receive that "testimony of Jesus" which is the "spirit of prophecy." Bishop Westcott, in his commentary on the Gospel of John, gives the following order of events connected with the Resurrection:

Just before 6 p. m. Saturday, Mary Magdalene and the "other Mary" (not the Mother) go to view the sepulchre (Matt. 28:1).

After 6 p. m., Saturday, The two Marys and Salome purchase spices (Mark 16:1).

Very early Sunday, The Resurrection occurs, then the earthquake, descent of an angel, opening of the tomb, and fall of the guards. [Bishop Westcott does not so state, but we have quoted Alford as showing that the women witnessed these things. It is clear, by comparison with Mark's account, that Salome was with the two Marys, and, excepting Mary Magdalene, the women were too frightened to do anything, or see anything clearly. Mary Magdalene grasped the situation more clearly, and ran for Peter and John].

762. Bishop Westcott's arrangement of events continues thus:

5 a. m., The two Marys, Salome, and probably other women, start for the sepulchre in the twilight. Mary Magdalene goes before, and returns at once to Peter and John (John 20:1-2).

5:30 a. m., Her companions reach the sepulchre when the sun had risen (Mark 16:2).—A vision of an angel. Message to the disciples (Matt. 28:5-7. Mark 16:5-7).

6 a. m., Another party, among whom is Joanna, come a little later, but still early morning (Luke 24:1 compare Mark 16:1). A vision of "two young men," words of comfort and instruction (Luke 24:4).

6:30 a. m., The visit of Peter and John (John 20:3-10). After they *"went away again"* Mary Magdalene sees two angels (John 20:11-13). About this time, the company of women carry their tidings to the Apostles (Luke 24:10).

7 a. m., THE LORD reveals Himself to Mary, Magdalene (John, 20:14-18; Mark 16:9). Not long after, He reveals Himself, as it appears, to the company of women who are returning to the sepulchre again, and gives them a charge to the brethren to go to Galilee (Matt. 28:9). [But this charge included also the 'women. Alford says: "Not spoken to the women directly, but certainly indirectly including them. The idea of their being *merely* messengers to the Apostles, without bearing any share in the promise ("—*there shall they see Me*"), is against the spirit of the context"].

763. The Apostles Peter and John had seen the tomb, but nothing more than that.

After 4 p. m., Christ appears to Peter (Luke 24:34; compare 1 Cor. 15:5).

From 4-6 p. m., Appears to the two disciples on the way to Emmaus (Luke 24:13-32. Mark 16:12).

8 p. m., Christ's appearance to the eleven, and others (Luke 24:36; Mark 16:14; John 20:19).

764. We see, therefore, that all the events of the morning of the Resurrection were seen *by women disciples only*. Two evidential points of tremendous importance were lodged with them. Matthew tells us with particularlty that the two Marys were *"sitting over against the sepulchre,"* after Christ was buried, and the stone rolled against its door. *"The chief priests and Pharisees"* went that night and demanded that the tomb be sealed, and a watch set before it. Pilate assented: *"So they went, and made the sepulchre sure, sealing the stone and setting a watch."* Who saw this done? Not John; he does not speak of the matter. The two Marys saw it, being the last at the tomb.

765. On the next morning, the angel said to the Marys: *"Come and see the place where the Lord lay."* It was not, certainly, to satisfy their curiosity he said this; it was not even to put them at ease, and gratify their tender interest. No, not all; it was these two who had seen *"where"* and *"how"* His body was laid away (Mark 15:47, Luke 23:55), who are now called to see *where* and *how* the wrappings of the body yet lay. Mary Magdalene runs to call Peter and John to see. And John tells us that he outran Peter, and came and looked in and *"saw the linen cloths. Then cometh Simon Peter following him, and went into the sepulchre, and seeth the linen cloths* [not "clothes" —see R. V.—the wrappings of a dead body] lie, *and the napkin that was about His head, not lying with the linen cloths, but wrapped together in a place by itself. Then went in that*

other disicple, which came first to the sepulchre [John], *and he saw and believed"* (John 20:5-8).

766. What did they see? They saw plain evidences to refute what the guards told. For the guards, when they recovered, rushed off to the chief priests, and told what had happened. "A great earthquake, and a *something,* that frightened us horribly; when we collected our senses, the great stone was completely off the tomb's mouth; and yet we *know* no human hand did it. We were wide awake; we saw everything. No human being was anywhere in sight, save two or three women. But they did not come near, so long as we were there. We looked into the tomb, and are absolutely *sure* the body is not there; but the grave-cloths lie there empty."

767. The Sanhedrin, in part or whole, was called together, and the guards most carefully questioned on every point. At the end, all they could do was to believe the guards. So they bribed them heavily to tell a falsehood: *"His disciples came by night, and stole Him away while we slept"* (Matt. 28:11-13). But what the women witnessed—the earthquake and all, with Mary's quick obedience had preserved strong counter-testimony to that. Could anybody have snatched up a dead body and carried it away—either the Jews or the Apostles— and left the grave-cloths not even disturbed? The head cloth at the head; the lower-limb cloths extending along towards the feet; just in the position in which they had placed the body the night before? "It was clear, therefore," says Bishop Westcott, "that the body had not been stolen by enemies; it was scarcely less clear that it had not been taken away by friends." "The undisturbed grave-cloths show that the Lord had risen through and out of them;" as someone has expressed it, Christ "passed through the heavy wrappings as He later passed through doors" (John 20:7, 19).

768. And John says that when he and Peter fully grasped what Mary showed them—what the angel had pointed out to her,—then they believed: *"For as yet* [after all that Jesus had plainly told Peter and John] *they knew not the Scripture, that He must rise again from the dead."* Mary herself had not seen the importance of this evidence,—the impossibility that human hands could have removed the body and left the grave-cloths undisturbed. Then, as she stood without, weeping,

the Lord Himself appeared to her and *"She, supposing Him to be the gardener, saith unto Him, Sir, if thou have borne Him hence, tell me where thou hast laid Him, and I will take Him away."*—John 20:15.

769.　Now we understand better that Jesus entrusted to those women who followed Him out of Galilee the most important items of evidence connected with the events of the Resurrection.　They saw where and how the body lay; they saw the sealing of the tomb; they saw the bursting of the seal, and rolling away of the stone by the angel; they saw the guards fall as dead, and could testify that the guards were *not asleep* when the tomb was opened; and they saw the evidences that the body had come through the grave-cloths, leaving them undisturbed, just where they were the night before, about the body, which had now departed.　In the evening, *"the eleven gathered together, and them that were with them"* (Luke 24:33-48), which would mean the women particularly, and Jesus appeared in their midst, and said: *"Thus it is written, and thus it behoved Christ to suffer, and to rise from the dead the third day. . . And ye are witnesses of these things."* But He could not, by these mere words, make Peter, or John, or James, a witness of things they had *not seen.* He spoke this of those who had *witnessed* these events,—particularly, therefore of the women, who had witnessed far more than any of the Twelve.

LESSON 94.

THE ANOINTING OF WOMEN WITNESSES.

770.　There is some difference of opinion as regards whether Jesus said those words, *"Ye are witnesses of these things,"* as recorded in Luke 24:48, on the evening of the resurrection, an interview at which others besides the Apostles are distinctly mentioned as present, or on a subsequent occasion to the Apostles alone.　We merely mention the matter to call attention to the fact that it does not materially affect the argument, though someone might attempt to use it for the purpose.　The women themselves stood in a better position to understand the Lord's wishes than anyone else, either then or now, and we know *they believed* He wished them to tarry and get that power for witnessing, for they tarried for it.　Nay, more, *they got that power*, which is the strongest possible proof that they were doing precisely what Jesus Christ wished them to do,—had required of them.

771. We have proved that they were able to witness concerning the most important points which would be disputed regarding His resurrection; that they alone had witnessed those many important things concerning His crucifixion; and His mother alone was the repository of certain testimony regarding His being the very Son of God, incarnated in human flesh. In other words, these women were Jesus Christ's *most important witnesses.* When He said, *"Ye are witnesses of these things,"* the God of all truth could but state *facts.* He did not *create* or *ordain,* as witnesses of certain events, those who had not witnessed those events,—else had He been guilty of a fraud. Rather, those who have imagined that Jesus Christ appointed *men only* as His witnesses, and have taught others this, have practiced a fraud upon themselves as well as upon others. Jesus said again, as He was about to be taken up into heaven, *"Ye shall receive power, after that the Holy Ghost is come upon you: and ye shall be witnesses unto Me both in Jerusalem, and in all Judaea, and in Samaria, and unto the uttermost part of the earth"* (Acts 1:8). The women believed that the commandment to tarry and receive that power included themselves. One hundred and twenty persons tarried for the power; and among them, the mother of Jesus *"with the women"* (Acts 1:14, 15)!

772. Had there been a man present among that company of one hundred and twenty who had doubted whether these women were to become qualified witnesses (or to be veiled, subdued and silenced creatures, because Eve sinned), the last remnant of such a delusion must have been swept away, when *"there appeared unto them cloven tongues, like as of fire, and sat upon each one* [R. V.] *of them: And they were all filled with the Holy Ghost, and began to speak with other tongues, as the Spirit gave them utterance,"* Acts 2:3. But a man can be convinced, and recoil again to his position of past bigotry. If such a thing happened to one present at that assembly, he must have been again shaken to the foundation, out of his prepossessions, when he listened to Peter, sweeping all prejudices before him, saying, in the power, and by the authority of the Holy Spirit: *"This is that which was spoken by the prophet Joel: . . Your daughters shall*

prophesy . . and on my handmaidens I will pour out, in those days, of My Spirit, and they shall prophesy" (Acts 2:16, 18).

773. These women were now prepared to do in type what the Holy Spirit through the prophet Isaiah (40:9), has commanded women to do, near the close of the Gospel dispensation in full: *"Oh thou woman, that bringest good tidings to Zion, get thee up into the high mountain; Oh thou woman, that bringest good tidings to Jerusalem, lift up thy voice with strength; lift it up, be not afraid; say unto the cities of Judah, Behold your God!"** They knew the story of the Incarnation, Crucifixion and Resurrection, with a completeness of detail such as none of the Apostles had. It is not likely, however, that they, being women, could speak in the Jewish synagogues of Palestine. The men disciples must have been the spokesmen here. The women could speak to those who came to their home to hear their story. And after all but the twelve Apostles were driven out of Jerusalem (Acts 8:1), the women would find many opportunies in the Gentile world to give their message. At any rate, we may be. sure that the women, even at Jerusalem, before they were driven out, had made their message heard in Christian meetings for both sexes in private homes. They gave their witness with power and to good effect, and the first Christian Church was in the home of the mother of Mark, who was persumedly a widow, Acts 12:12.

774. How do we know that women were active witnesses? Listen to Saul, one of the persecutors of the Christians of these days: *"I persecuted this way* [Christianity] *unto the death, binding both men and WO-MEN* (Acts 22:4). And listen to this testimony against Saul: *"As for Saul, he made great havoc of the Church, entering every house and haling men and WOMEN, committed them to prison"* (Acts 8:3). Again, *"Saul, yet breathing out threatenings and slaughter against the disciples of the Lord, went unto the high priest, and desired letters to Damascus to the synagogues, that if he found any of the way, whether they were men or WO-MEN, he might bring them bound to Jerusalem"* (Acts 9:1, 2).

---

* See par. 209, and our leaflet, "Women Preachers."

775. Now we submit: Had these women been veiled and silenced creatures, who would not presume to teach anyone, who would have persecuted them? Men *could not*, for lack of proof against their teaching, if they had not taught. At a later date in the history of the Church, it was only necessary to raise the cry, "A Christian!" to get one punished. But in these days of ignorance as to what Christians taught, some sort of *proof* on that score must have been brought forward to secure conviction. The fact that women were prosecuted, in these very early days, proves that women were giving their testimony,—witnessing as to what they had seen and heard—and this witness of theirs was heard by men, who reported the same, and conviction was had thereon. It is not enough to say they were giving this witness to *women only,* and that other women testified against them. The testimony of women was very lightly esteemed in Jewish courts,—would not have been accepted, in fact. No, Paul, or Paul's spies, were in meetings attended by both sexes, and heard women give their testimony in "power" to the death and resurrection of Jesus Christ, and because of this testimony which women gave, women were punished All must agree to this excepting those willing to sin against their reasoning faculties.

776. The conquests made by the Pentecostal Christians were marvellous. On the first day, 3,000 were converted; a little later, 5,000 more, and so they progressed. Most of the first converts lived about Jerusalem, and many of them must have witnessed, as unbelievers, some of those events, which, at first, the women disciples alone knew. Now they could give their testimony too. Perhaps of this number of new converts were Stephen and Philip. To the testimony of the former, God added *"great wonders and miracles"* (Acts 6:8), and from the time these began to appear, to attest the genuineness of the first witnesses, the earlier testimony as to particular incidents in the life of Christ would become less important because well known.

777. The *necessity* for the testimony of the women, in the region of Jerusalem, soon passed. Their testimony in other cities, like Damascus, to which Paul starts in pursuit of them, was given; then in more distant places. Finally, that persecuting fury of Satan, which is always visited upon women with special malignity, was the occa-

sion of a Divine interposition, and we have the Apostle Paul, under Nero, at a much later date, because of the special attacks upon the virtue of women Christians, and upon the reputation of the churches as to chastity, advising as a matter of prudence, something of a separation of the sexes, and a quieter part for women (see Lessons 40, 41).

LESSON 95.

WOMAN'S GREAT DESTINY.

778. That we might make no mistake as to God's own approval upon women of old who broke the silence of public assemblies, we have it expressly told us that Miriam, Deborah, Huldah and Anna were all "prophetesses,"— for they are so called where their names are mentioned. It behooves us to ask, What is it to prophesy, in the Biblical use of the word? Scholars will agree that the primal thought of the word is that of one who is acting as spokesman for another. The idea of prediction is not necessarily implied. But as a true prophet in the Bible is one who speaks for God, and as God does not live, nor necessarily speak, within the limits of time, by which mortals are bound (but, to Him, yesterday, today and tomorrow are all present), therefore it follows that what He causes mortals to say for Him often relates to a future as yet not experienced by them; hence we use this verb in a secondary sense, "to foretell." But let us keep in mind its proper meaning,—to speak for God.

779. It is certain that women were not, as theology has claimed, subordinated to men from the day Eve sinned. History proves that that subordination was gradually brought about by men themselves, and was not accomplished for hundreds of years. It is as certain that not one syllable can be found in the Old Testament ordering women to "keep silence" in the Jewish public assemblies; and it would be astounding, since women were NOT silenced under the Old Covenant, if it were true that they were silenced for the sin of Eve under the New, the very heart of the teaching of which is, *"There is therefore NOW no condemnation to those who are in Christ Jesus"* (Rom. 8:1).

780. The congregation of Israel, a religious body called by God out of bondage and into the wilderness, was

certainly a "church." Indeed, Stephen spoke of it as *"the church in the wilderness,"* Acts 7:38. The very first note of praise raised to God in that "church," was responded to by Miriam and her women, with timbrel and dance,—*"Miriam the prophetess"* (Ex. 15:20). And why should she have been called by the inspired Word *"the prophetess,"* if God had never, and did never use her voice to declare His will to Israel? God gives no empty (lying) titles. And this woman prophetess, was one of three great leaders of whom God said: *"I brought thee up out of the land of Egypt . . and I sent before thee Moses, Aaron and Miriam"* (Micah 6:4).

781. And women were not silent in the Tabernacle, after the children of Israel became a settled people in the Promised Land. Where else did Hannah sing that wonderful psalm of praise she composed for the dedication of Samuel to the Lord's service at the Tabernacle? All the context here goes to show she *"prayed"* it (1 Sam. 2:1) in public (compare 1:28 and 2:11); and it became public property, preserved to us to the present day, and its comforting words re-echoed in a dozen Psalms, composed in later days, like this, for the service of the Temple.

782. And women were not silent in the Temple: We have high authority for believing that two Psalms, at least, were meant for women's voices alone (Psalms 8 and 45). Hannah must have been gifted in music. Her Song proved this; and her son Samuel, as can be gleaned from many incidental statements in the Bible (and as has been so well brought out in a book by Dean Payne-Smith. *"Prophecy a Preparation for Christ"*), taught his young prophets, whom he had in training, to praise the Lord in song.

783. This writer says: "One of that choir [of the prophet Samuel] was Heman, the son of Joel, Samuel's first-born (1. Chron. 6:33; 1 Sam. 8:2), who there acquired that mastery of music which made him one of the three singers selected by David . . to arrange and preside over the Temple service (1 Chron. 25). Blessed with a numerous family, who all seem to have inherited Samuel's musical ability, he trained them all for song in the house of Jehovah, with cymbals, psalteries and harps (1 Chron. 25:6), and it is remarkable that no less than fourteen of the twenty-four courses of singers were

341

Samuel's own descendants, and that as long as the first Temple stood they were the chief performers of that Psalmody which he had instituted."

784. *"God gave Heman fourteen sons and three daughters. All these were under the hands of their father for song in the house of the Lord."* This certainly proves that women did not "keep silence" in the Temple. We know this also from the mention of the "women-singers" in Ezra 2:65, and Neh. 7:67. The same thing is made clear by the description of a religious procession, Psalm 68:25. If, as Dean Payne-Smith says, "Psalmody commenced with that hymn of triumph sung by Miriam and the women on the shores of the Red Sea, with timbrel and dance," surely psalmody was introduced into the Temple service by the Song of Hannah, taken up by Samuel and his female as well as male descendants, through Heman, and extended through the days of Ezra and Nehemiah, by both women and men. There is no just reason for supposing that women ever ceased to have their part in prophecy with song, up to the days of Anna, the aged prophetess, who never left the Temple, but preached there, to the worshippers, that Messiah had come (Luke 2:36, 38).

785. It was not until after woman had brought the Redeemer into the world,—not until after she had given her testimony to the most important facts in the Christian's faith, and convinced the early disciples of their truth; not until long after Paul's days, when *"grievous wolves"* had entered the flock, as Paul said they would do (Acts 20:29); and wrested Paul's language, as Peter said they did (2 Pet. 3:15-16), that the teaching arose that Paul had silenced women, veiled them, and subordinated them to men. We have shown that his language is capable of more consistent interpretation.

786. Woman has the honour of being the subject of a GREAT PROPHECY. That prophecy is, that the Seed of the woman shall bruise the Serpent's head; and, as we have shown, that prophecy was only fulfilled in part by the advent of Jesus Christ into this world. He has not yet come in power, to bruise the Serpent's head; and when He does come the second time, women will have prepared the way by preaching that second coming. Woman is to have a special part with Him in this late

war upon Satan; for not only is Christ the enemy of Satan, but we know, by the express word of God, that woman is destined to be the same,—*"I will put enmity between thee and the woman,"* is said quite as plainly as, *"—between thy seed and her Seed."*

787. God revealed to Satan, by this saying, not merely what woman was, not even what she now is, *but what woman is to become.* And this is the meaning of her sufferings, which were predicted Gen. 3:16, all through the ages. This is why she corresponds, in shadow, to the substance,—*"A woman of sorrows, and acquainted with grief,"* Isai. 53:3; that all the thousands of millions of human beings who have entered this world, came along the pathway of woman's agony. This is why every woman should have an unutterable horror of godlessness and atheism. Without God, man is Satan's slave, and woman is the slave of Satan's slave.

788. As God revealed to Jacob (even while he was yet a most unworthy man, fleeing from the wrath of his brother), his future destiny, and the providence of God that overshadowed him (Gen. 28:12-15), in order to arouse in Jacob those aspirations which would eventually seal his destiny to him; so has God revealed to woman, even while yet very unworthy, her destiny, so that she may be able to seal it to herself by exalted aspiration. She will yet appear as God's ally, in a tremendous conflict with evil, which will end in the binding of Satan for a thousand years, and the complete crushing of his head.

LESSON 96.
ANOTHER ANOINTING OF WOMEN.

789. The Jews observed three great festivals of Divine appointment, at which the presence of males was required, the Passover, Pentecost, and the Feast of Tabernacles. We can readily see that these requirements could not be laid upon the sex which bore and nursed the children, without great hardship. But it was *specially provided,* Deut. 16:11, that women attend the Pentecostal feasts,— hence the Jews did not exclude them. This is very significant, in view of that Great Day of Pentecost, when women as well as men received power to bear witness to the death, resurrection and ascension of Christ Jesus (Acts 2:4).

790. We have shown that women were Christ's most important witnesses, in the earliest days of the Church. They were also the martyrs who suffered the greatest inhumanity (pars. 321-325). Their work was soon over, for it was too costly, unless absolutely neecssary, when it meant to be immured in dens of infamy as a punishment. But when the church made compromise with paganism, under Constantine—in fact, even further back, when it organized itself into The Catholic Church, in the very beginning of its pagan corruption (see par. 362), the Church recoiled from its former esteem for women, and later taught the pagan and rabbinical doctrines of contempt for woman as the source of evil (see Lesson 11). St. Paul has been interpreted to give countenance to this pagan view, though his Epistles bristle with the names of women who *"laboured with him in the Gospel,"* an expression which, only by forced interpretation, can be made to imply that women laboured with Paul in other ways *excepting in the Gospel.*

791. But woman will emerge—in fact, is now emerging —from obscurity. It is amazing that certain men most insistent on the doctrine that Christ is coming soon, are blindly zealous in delaying that coming as much as possible, by hindering the emancipation of woman, and her ministry in the Gospel. They refuse to see that the *express order* of development in Christ's kingdom on earth was given by Christ Himself in the two parables of the Kingdom; and by the Apostle Paul in the symbol, *"Adam was first formed, then Eve"* (1 Tim. 2:13).

792. When Jesus Christ preached in the synagogue in Nazareth, he read: *"The Spirit of the Lord is upon Me, because He hath anointed Me to preach the Gospel to the poor,"* and on through the passage past the words, *"to proclaim the acceptable year of the Lord"* (Luke 4:18-19), and there He paused, for His time had not yet come to fulfill the other portion of the passage, and proclaim, *"the day of vengeance of our God"* (Isa. 61:1, 2). Precisely parallel is the order laid down in Isa. 40:9, 10, for the "woman evangelist" (for that is the precise meaning of the word applied to those addressed here): *"Oh thou woman that bringest good tidings to Zion . . to Jerusalem . . say unto the cities of Judah, Behold your God"* (par. 209). The women of the early church obeyed this, from Anna onward (Luke 2:38), as the good news came to them. They did not announce Christ's first coming,—

John the Baptist did that—but they announced His *arrival,*—that He had come, and that He was God incarnate.

793. The remaining portion of this passage is now to be proclaimed by women: *"Behold, the Lord God will come as a mighty One* [R. V.—not in the form of a humble, suffering servant now], *and His arm shall rule for Him; behold His reward is with Him, and His recompence* [R. V.] *before Him."* This speaks of Christ as coming to judge this world; this is His second coming, which women are commanded to proclaim. It is to this present time that the prophecy applies, *"God giveth the Word: the women that publish the tidings are a great host* (Psalm 68:11), and God has now seen to it that these verses should no longer lie in the obscurity of a perverted translation (as they do in the A. V.), but should be known by women.

794. On the day of Pentecost Peter said: *"This is that which was spoken by the prophet Joel . . I will pour out of My Spirit upon all flesh: and your . . daughters shall prophesy . . and on My handmaidens I will pour out in those days of My Spirit,* Acts 2:17-20. That prophecy has, as yet, been only partially fulfilled. It is yet to be filled out to the full. The sun has not yet been turned into darkness, and the moon into blood, nor has the great and notable day of the Lord yet come. Only a handful of women, as compared with "all flesh," has, as yet, prophesied. That prophecy must be *filled out to the full* before *"that great and notable day,"* and those who stupidly hinder that prophesying on the part of women are placing themselves, as it were, across the path of the fulfilment of God's Word. Instead of *"hasting the coming of the day of God"* (2 Pet. 3:12, margin), they are hindering the preparation for that coming.

795. When Christ laid His hands upon the bowed back of the woman, that Sabbath (see Lesson 89), and ordained her to glorify God in the synagogue, it was not precisely to heal her of her bent back. Before that, He had told her, *"Woman, thou art loosed from thine infirmity,"* but she could not grasp the full import of His words. She was bound in spirit, as well as in body. She had had *"a spirit of infirmity eighteen years,"* we are told. She could not dispel that *spirit* of infirmity without Divine aid. After His laying hands on her, however, then she could straighten up and glorify God.

796. *"Where the Spirit of the Lord is there is liberty."*
Was ever anyone able to change his or her delusions
short of aid from without? We doubt it. A cure of the
spirit demands the aid of the Spirit. Who does not understand that the chief difficulty that God and Moses had
in delivering the children of Israel from the bondage of
Egypt was not the Egyptians, but the *spirit of slavery*
and the *spirit of bondage to pagan gods,* to which those
Israelites were likewise enslaved? God easily disposed
of the Egyptians in the Red Sea, but He could not, in the
same easy fashion, drown the spirit of bondage in the
Israelites which they had acquired under slavery. Just
so with women of today. Except for a mere handful of
mistaken men, who could easily be put aside, the men of
Christian countries constitute no longer an obstacle to
womans' freedom and preaching of the Gospel.

797. The vast majority of men would welcome woman's
freedom in everything worth the name. In the past such
was not the case, and, as a consequence woman has
acquired that *spirit of infirmity* of which God prophesied
when He pointed out to Eve that her "turning" would be
to her husband,—in other words, she would turn away
from God to him, placing herself in dependent relations
to him such as she ought to hold toward God alone. This
tendency Eve bequeathed to womankind and it has been
fostered throughout past ages, and only Christ can cure
the spirit. Pagan and godless women, as such, with all
their struggles and often offensive efforts towards emancipation, will never get free. There is no freedom for
women excepting escape into Christ the Emancipator;
because the bondage is not really of the male's creation,
but of Satan's; and the reason of that bondage is because
Satan knows that *"the seed of the woman"* will yet completely destroy his seed.

798. And when will the Church come out into that
"glorious liberty of the children of God" (Rom. 8:21),
which is its rightful inheritance? When the free Spirit
of God descends upon it again as on the day of Pentecost.
And when will that time come? If I read aright, *when
the women of the Church become free,* or not at all,—
for the prophet Isaiah has said: *"Rise up, ye women that
are at ease; hear my voice, ye careless daughters; give
ear unto my speech . . . Tremble, ye women that are at
ease: be troubled, ye careless ones . . . Upon the land of
my people shall come thorns and briars; yea, upon all the*

*houses of joy in the joyous city. Because the palaces
shall be forsaken; the multitude of the city shall be left;
the forts and towers shall be dens for ever, a joy of wild
asses, a pasture of flocks; Until the Spirit is poured out
upon us from on high"* (32:9-15). Thus does the prophet of old call upon women to leave their careless ease,
and come and wait on God with all the rest, for the outpouring of His Spirit upon *them,* as well as upon men,
that the way may be opened for the restoration of Jerusalem, and for *"the times of restitution of all things,
which God hath spoken by the mouth of all His holy
prophets since the world began"* (Acts 3:21). Let us
women, then, hasten to our Lord, and beseech Him to
lay His hand upon us, dispel this *"spirit of infirmity"*
with which Satan has bound us, "lo these eighteen" centuries, and then lift our voices in the synagogues and
churches, and glorify our God.

LESSON 97.

THE NATURE OF SCRIPTURE PREDICTION.

799. Scripture prediction, or prophecy, as it is popularly
called, is not merely sacred history written beforehand.
That which is prophesied generally relates to events
which take place with increasing accuracy as to the
details described in the prophecy, in succeeding epochs
of human history, until the details are filled out to the
full. Providence designs that we shall only grasp the
chief features of the description before the fulfilment,—
and that, for two main purposes: 1st, That we may
recognise, as the events take place, that the Bible prophecy is inspired,—is the promulgation of One who knows
the future as well as the past, and so our faith in Him be
cultivated (John 14:29) ; and 2nd, That when we see
the event predicted about to come to pass, we may regu-
late our conduct to suit it (Luke 21:20, 21), and prepare
for what is coming.

800. Before ever visiting Jerusalem, we made a study
in certain books of its general features. But when we
visited the place, we recognised that our imagination had
failed to form a correct picture of it. Nevertheless that
previous study proved most useful, for it enabled us to
understand much that we saw, without explanation. After
we saw, we recognised the accuracy of the descriptions;
and we were able to understand where we were, without

a guide. So with prophecy: It has been given to us to study *in the present* and put to use *in the future*. Therefore we need not understand it fully until it is fulfilled, though it is a matter of no small importance that we study it. Someone has said, "The only certain interpretation of Scripture prophecy is its fulfilment."

801. The voice of God is, in its very nature, prophetic. He is not conditioned by time and space, like ourselves. Yet when He speaks we scarcely know how to understand His meaning until we have replies to questions relating to time and space. *When* will this occur, *where* will it occur, and *how long time* will it occupy?—and kindred questions at once spring to our lips. Take as an illustration the Lord's great prophecy of the 24th of Matthew. His disciples asked three questions: (1) *"Tell us when these things shall be,"* (2) *"What shall be the sign of Thy coming,* and (3) *of the end of the world?"* As to the Lord's answer, many have professed to be able to dissect it into three sets of answers, as relating to the three questions asked. But who is satisfied with the dissection? The Lord's reply to the questions is prophetic; and since such predictions relate to events due, with increasing accuracy, at stated periods of time, and not generally to one period, the prediction baffles dissection after this manner. Expositors talk of this as the "pregnant" nature of prophecy. Each fulfilment is but a type of a yet future and more accurate fulfilment, until the prophecy has been, in very truth, filled out to the full.

802. Let us seek for a clearer understanding of this matter: All Scripture is, in one sense or another, the account of a great struggle between right and wrong, or, more properly speaking, between beings arrayed on the side of right and of wrong. We are to be instructed which is the right and which is the wrong side. Let us go back, then, to the time when there was no such struggle involving the human family. In imagination we stand, now, on the very edge of human history, in God's great calm, when He had just made the world, and pronounced all His creatures "very good." Presently the calm is broken, first by a mere ripple on God's great ocean of calm, at the edge where we stand. Then occurs the entrance of Satan into the Garden. Then comes sin in humanity (Gen. 3:6), and now it is more than a ripple. Next, an opposing force of good strikes against the wave, tossing it yet higher,—*that* is Eve's confession, and

denunciation of the Deceiver. Thus the war begins,—for God puts enmity between Satan and the woman, and between the "seed" of each. Like a great billow, rushing in an ever-widening circle, onward to the end of time, ever with increasing violence, the strife rages, social right and social wrong in fierce conflict. This was in Christ's mind that day that the disciples asked Him these questions.

803. Like a great stone into a calm sea, Satan hurled his social disorder into this world. A billow of the sea does not push the water from one shore to the other; it merely lends its *motion* to the water just in front of its progress. And a wave, if uninterrupted, does not change its general features. So with the billow of social disorder. It did not die with the individuals who first felt its force. They died, but it rolled on to succeeding generations, carrying ever with it the same social characteristics. God and His prophets have been watching the course of that billow from the first, and from time to time telling us about it and opposing fresh obstacles to its progress; but ever it is the same old billow, yet acting upon fresh individuals.

804. The eye of Jesus was centered on that great billow, that day He talked with His disciples. It made havoc in the Garden; it created in man the desire to be "as god," which erected the Tower of Babel, and caused the scattering of mankind. Just before, Noah had taken warning of its coming,—for it was the means of bringing the great flood, to oppose its destructive course. In time that billow annihilated the ten tribes of Israel from the pages of human history for a while, and swept Judah all the way from Jerusalem to Babylon. But a great Rock was in its way; and Jesus knew that the greatest of all social upheavals, up to that time, would center about His cross. Next, all Jersusalem is wrecked, and the Jews scattered to the ends of the earth.

805. Jesus spoke, that day, to tell His immediate disciples how to escape the destructive billow, and to warn all Christians of it, likewise. What features it bore, by means of which it could be recognised, and how to avoid being caught in its wrecking path, as it swept onward to the end of the age. What need, then, for us to dissect His answer to the disciples into particulars concerning each point? The billow is one; its features are one; the method of escape has been similar, from the days of Noah until now, and will be to the end of tife.

806. We have described the billow as a wrecking force of evil. But with it is its enemy, the contending force of good,—the seed of the woman,—pre-eminently, her great Seed, Jesus Christ. But not only is it prophesied that her seed should be at enmity with Satan, but WOMAN HERSELF shall wage war with Satan. So from the beginning of evil we have the promise of good; even that greatest of all promises, *"I will put enmity between thee and the woman, and between thy seed and her seed; it shall bruise thy head, and thou shalt bruise his heel."*

807. Dean Payne-Smith speaks of this wonderful passage, Gen. 3:15, as "that promise, of which the whole of the rest of Scripture is but the record of the gradual stages of its fulfilment." But though Jesus Christ has conquered death, by rising from the grave, the enmity still continues; the conflict is still on. Christ is seated at the right hand of God; nevertheless *"we see* not yet *all things put under His feet"* (Heb. 2:8), for He sits *"on the right hand of God; from henceforth expecting* till *His enemies be made His footstool"* (Heb. 10:12, 13).

808. The same writer speaks thus concerning this "primeval promise made to the woman in the hour of the first great earthly sorrow: From that day onward one purpose, and one only, is ever kept in view in God's dealings with His fallen creatures. The promise was that man, worsted in his first encounter with his spiritual adversary, should crush the adversary's head by means of one of the same nature as himself, *emphatically the woman's seed*. That promise contained in outline the whole of prophecy. Of that promise the Gospel is the one fulfilment. From the day on which Eve was comforted by it, all God's dealings in grace;— for the Bible has nothing to do with God's dealings except as they belong to the covenant of grace; it is not a book of natural religion, but of supernatural;—but all God's dealings with man in grace, which are the proper object-matter of the Bible, relate to the performance of that promise."

809. Such being the facts—and who can dispute them?—have we not every reason for thinking that God would provide, in prophecy, some vision which would exhibit not a partial, a typical, but a final, *complete* fulfilment of that Great Promise that He had made regarding woman and her seed?

LESSON 98.

THE "GREAT SIGN."

810. The student will now be prepared for an exhibition of the complete fulfilment of God's promise that the seed of the woman should crush the Serpent's head. The revelation of that greater fulfilment will be found in St. John's vision of events attendant upon the Lord's second coming, —chapter twelve of the Revelation. But the last verse of chapter eleven should be joined up with it. John saw that the Temple of God was opened in heaven, *"And there was seen in His temple the ark of His testament."* This last word is the same one which is translated in other places "covenant;" so we will read it "covenant" here,— *"The ark of His covenant."* God wishes all in heaven to witness that He remembers His covenant; He opens the temple in heaven,—that is, the inner sanctuary of it,—so that all can see into the very "holy of holies," see the ark in it, to be reminded of a certain covenant. The twelfth chapter must, then, show the fulfilment of that certain covenant,—or, at least, the beginning of its fulfilment.

811. We must discover what, precisely, that covenant means.

(1). The first thing mentioned in chapter twelve is *"a great sign"* (R. V.),—so we decide that the covenant it represents must be some "great covenant," or promise (verse 1).

(2). The principal figure in the "sign" is a woman.

(3). The chapter tells us about *"that old Serpent, called the devil and Satan"* (verse 9).

(4)¦. Whose chief characteristics are that he is a "deceiver," and a persecutor of both the "woman" and the "seed" of the woman (verses 9, 13, 17).

(5). We are told, also, that she bore a *"a man child"* (part of her seed) who was caught up to God and His throne (verse 5); and Satan, *"was cast out into the earth,"* and after persecuting the woman until she was rescued from him (verses 6, 14), he turned upon *"the remnant of her seed"* (verse 17).

812. Now need we call attention to how vividly this "great sign" portrays a fulfilment, in outline, of that greatest covenant promise God ever made, in words He addressed neither to man nor woman directly, but to that same "old Serpent" the devil and Satan, the last time but this that he was mentioned in Scripture as the "Serpent"

when He said,—"*I will put enmity between thee and the woman; and between thy seed and her seed; it shall bruise thy head, and thou shalt bruise his heel*" (Gen. 3:15)? Furthermore, God said to that "old Serpent" at that time: "*Upon thy belly shalt thou go, and dust shalt thou eat all the days of thy life.*" In Eph. 2:2 Satan is called "*the prince of the power of the air,*" but from the time this war takes place "in heaven" he holds that place of exaltation, or erection, no longer. He is "*cast down to the earth,*" or ground, never to rise again (verse 9). Here we see, then, an outline of the fulfilment of "that promise, of which the whole of the rest of Scripture is but the record of the gradual stages of its fulfilment," —a fulfilment which, when these events of the closing chapters of the Revelation take place, will leave nothing undone that can give it greater fulfilment.

813. How completely the terms of the sign meet those of the covenant! We have the "woman;" the "enmity;" the "deceiver;" the "Serpent;" his head bruised in war; himself driven down to "eat the dust of the earth," and the seed which was snatched up to heaven, with the "remnant," or remainder of her seed suffering still from the Serpent's enmity; and then follows in the succeeding chapters a description of that time of the Great Tribulation, "*as travail upon a woman with child*" (1 Thess. 5:3)— filling out to the full, even in its spiritual completion, the words, "*In sorrow thou shalt bring forth children*" (Gen. 3:16).

814. Some would hold that the promise of Gen. 3:15 was completely fulfilled in the birth, death and resurrection of Christ, followed by His ascent to sit "on the right hand of God," on His throne. But like all prophecy which has had, as yet, only partial fulfilment, the details do not fit, in all particulars, to the complete prophecy. The head of Satan, as we have already said, was not at once crushed at the time Christ rose, victorious. Christ is still "expecting till *His enemies be made His footstool.*" This chapter twelve, then, tells about the enmity between the Serpent and the woman; of a victory won 1900 years ago by Christ, her Seed, "caught up to God and His throne," yet typical of the woman's seed that is yet to be caught up to God and His throne; and her persecution, and that of the "remnant of her seed," by that same Serpent. Chapter thirteen tells us more details about the enmity between the Serpent and "the remnant" of the woman's

seed, the persecution of her seed by Satan's seed—Antichrist and the False Prophet. Chapter fifteen shows us further details of the womans' seed escaped to heaven, and standing on the "sea mingled with fire."

815. Many affect not to believe, in these days, in the existence of the devil. Such do not believe in their Bible, for it is very explicit on this point. This one chapter in the Revelation is sufficient to prove the fact. Such people also talk of all human beings as the sons of God. But God does not so teach in His Book. Christ says: *"The good seed are the children of the kingdom; but the tares are the children of the wicked one,"*—that is, of the devil, or that old Serpent; and the apostle John says *"In this the children of God are manifest and the children of the devil."* Jesus Christ often spoke of wicked men as a "generation of vipers,"—that is, "that old Serpent," the devil, was their father, not God. He said to the Pharisees: *"Ye are of your father the devil."* The children of God are, by faith in Jesus Christ, also called *the children* of Christ,—Heb. 2:13: and *the seed* of Christ in Isa. 53:10. But since Christ is the Seed of the woman, so all believers are, through Christ, the seed of the woman also.

816. We believe the word "woman" is used in Rev. ch. 12 in precisely the same sense as in Gen. 3:15, 16. On the contrary, most expositors teach that the woman is the visible Church; and the man child is the *invisible*, real, or spiritual Church; so we will examine this teaching: This vision of John's—of the woman—is followed by chapters that relate to the Lord's second coming. But St. Paul tells us that Christ will not come *"except there come a falling away first* (2 Thess. 2:3). This means that the visible Church will be fallen away from Christ, it will be in spiritual *darkness.* But this woman is represented as *"clothed with the sun,"* and that, just about the time of the Lord's return. She surely does not represent that fallen Laodicean Church, which is *"wretched, and miserable, and poor, and blind, and naked"* (Rev. 3:17). *"Clothed with the sun,"* means clothed with Christ, *"the sun of righteousness."*

817. But if this woman, in the Revelation, be Womanhood, why is she represented as having twelve stars in her crown, the moon under her feet, and clothed with the sun? She is clothed with the sun, in that she is in Christ

Jesus, the Sun of Righteousness,—she has become Christian; the moon is under her feet, in that she has risen above Judaism, with its types and ceremonies,—"*a shadow* [or outline] *of good things to come, and not the very image,*" or thing itself (Heb. 10:1). The twelve apostles are the brightest gems in her diadem, in that all believers are comprehended as "the seed of the woman," just as they are "the seed of Abraham" (par. 83). And then this Woman is in the greatest agonizing toil, trying to accomplish the birth of the man child. This, some say, represents the translation of the invisible Church out of the midst of the visible Church. But we ask, will the visible, fallen Church ever agonize to accomplish that marvellous work? Never! That which is born of the flesh will ever persecute that which is born of the Spirit (Gal. 4:29). Like can only bring forth like. The visible Church can never produce anything but another visible body of its own quality. The carnal never yet brought forth the spiritual. "*That which is born of the flesh is flesh,*" always and always to the end of all time.

818. Others say that the Woman represents the Virgin Mary; the dragon means Herod who sought to kill the child Jesus; the flight into the wilderness is Mary's flight into Egypt. But Jesus was *not* caught up to heaven as soon as He was born, as is inferred in Rev. 12:4. Those events typified the events of this great sign, but there is only resemblance in some outlines between the two. Others think the man child is Christ because it is "to rule all nations with a rod of iron." But the same is the destiny of "overcomers" also (Rev. 2:26, 27), who carry out Christ's will in this regard. As we have said before, until the complete fulfilment comes, there will be only resemblances, not identity, between the type, or types, and the antitype.

(To be continued.)

LESSON 99.

WHO IS "THE WOMAN?"

819. The Woman is not the Virgin Mary merely, nor the man child Jesus, whom Herod sought to slay. These typify, but do not fill out full the vision of John. He saw the Dragon watching for the child *before* it was born, while Herod knew not of the child Jesus until *after* its birth, nor could he guess the time of the birth but

within a space of two years. And then, the child Jesus was not, as John saw, *"caught up"* when born, but long afterwards. Nor did Mary and her babe part company, when she fled, but she fled with the babe in her arms; and Egypt was not a "wilderness," anyway.

820. Others believe that the Woman is the Jewish church, which gave birth to Christ; or which gave birth to the Christian church. But according to these views what does the Dragon mean? The devil, certainly, remotely, who instigates Herod's attempt to "devour" the man child. The devil instigates the attempt whatever interpretation we put upon this Great Sign; it is, therefore, too vague. But can we be sure that "to devour" means "to slay," merely? It was the Jewish Sanhedrin that compassed Christ's death; and that is close to saying it was the Jewish church. In other words, if the Woman represents the Jewish church and her child is Jesus, then the *woman*, not the Dragon, "devours" her child; and certainly that Jewish church, any way we look at the case, never agonized to bring forth Jesus Christ. Therefore we refuse to accept any of these vague interpretations of this Great Sign, excepting in the sense that some of them are types of the events pictured by this Great Sign.

821. Now we ask, How did God *begin* to fulfil that Great Promise of Gen. 3:15 about the victory of woman's seed? Did He look about for some *body of people*, visible or invisible, who bore a name, appropriate, or inappropriate, of the *feminine gender*, and begin to fulfil that promise to them because of the *gender* of their name, when He had promised to fulfil it to *woman?* Did he think it sufficient, after He had made the promise concerning very real and very literal woman, in the presence of Eve, a woman, to fulfil that promise to a *sect?* Verily, He did not: that is not God's way of doing. He made that promise to woman, in the presence of a woman, Eve; and He began the fulfilment of that promise *to a woman,* —the Virgin Mary; and as He has begun so will He, in faithfulness to His word, continue.

822. God will not be satisfied to send an offspring to the apostate Christian church, merely because the word "church" (*ecclesia*) is of feminine gender. That offspring will be sent to a feminine *person* (or company of feminine persons), not to a feminine *word*, describing a masculine body,—for the visible church on earth, which

excludes women, for the most part, from ministry at its altar, and shuts them out of its councils, and out of the fullness of Christ's atonement, cannot appropriate such a Great Promise as this, by merely masquerading in the garb of a female. God deals with realities, not with shams. Women belong, in large numbers, to the *mystical* Body of Christ, the *true* church; they do not actually belong to that body—the visible church—which merely enrolls their names on a list while it makes them irresponsible as regards its entire polity. Therefore this visible church will never grasp this Great Promise.

823. We are driven to the conclusion that, just as the covenant promise of Gen. 3:15 was fulfilled to a literal woman, up to a certain extent, in the birth of Jesus Christ of a virgin (no human male having any part in its realization), so will it be *to the end*. As Christ was born of a literal woman, so will this man child be born of that sex. The beginning of the fulfilment was to one woman; but it seems more likely that the filling out to the full of the terms of that great covenant will be to many of that sex,—a body of women.

824. Since the only actual interpretation of prophecy must come after, not before its fulfilment, we can only form a conjecture as to the meaning of these things. Since the sign John saw was "in heaven," the events seem to refer to the spiritual world. The agony and travail of the Woman seem to signify some great spiritual travail of soul into which women will be plunged just before the Lord's second coming; and as a result a large body of men (the man child), of exceptional holiness and devotion will rise; this will be that bringing forth of a man child. The entire sign relates to spiritual transactions; and the man child will be the spiritual, not the physical, seed of the woman.

825. Again let us cover these points: A work of women has been prophesied of in Psalm 68:11: *"The Lord giveth the word: the women that publish the tidings are a great host"* (R. V.). It was prophesied by Joel, and St. Peter repeated his words on the day of Pentecost: *"I will pour out of My Spirit upon all flesh: and your sons* [first] *and your daughters* [second] *shall prophesy."* . . . This much seems to refer to the sons and daughters of the Jews. . . . *"And on My bondsmen* [first] *and on My bondmaidens* [second],"* this to Gentile servants of God.

St. Paul maintains this same order (as to gender), when he says, *"Adam was first formed [not "created"], then Eve."* As in the natural world, Adam was a more rapid development than Eve, as shown in the second chapter of Genesis (see pars. 24-43), so has God first fashioned man for His purposes in the Church. But as the masculine church falls away into the apostasy of the "last days," God will put His hands upon Woman, who will, by proclaiming the Gospel,—more especially the Lord's speedy coming—rescue the situation, through her seed, the overcomers of 12:11, the man child.

826. The Prophet Isaiah saw the day of the Lord's second coming, when scattered Israel would be gathered together, and led back to their own land, by the hand of Jehovah (Isa. 40:10, 11). The prophet represents God as calling: *"O thou [woman] that bringest good tidings to Zion, get thee up into the high mountain: O thou [woman] that bringest good tidings to Jerusalem, lift up thy voice with strength; lift it up, be not afraid; say unto the cities of Judah, Behold your God!"* (R. V.) There is precisely the same warrant, from the original Hebrew, for inserting "woman" in this passage in Isaiah, as there is for inserting "woman," as the Revision does in Psalm 68:11. The "woman" has received tardy justice in the latter passage by the translators; and such will one day be the case in the former one (see pars. 209, 773).

827. This in Revelation 12th chapter is that same *"childbearing"* of 1 Tim. 2:15, of which the Apostle Paul speaks prophetically, in connection with those words about the formation of woman after man, in the spiritual sense. He says of woman: *"She shall be saved through the childbearing [R. V.], if they continue in charity and holiness with sobriety."* We have elsewhere spoken of the partial fulfilments of this prophecy (par. 209), but now we come to its completion, in the special protection and care of Almighty God, when the world is in the throes of the Great Tribulation. Because Woman has brought forth that man child who will, with Michael's help, cast Satan down to the earth (12:13), Woman will be borne away into "the wilderness" beyond his power of avenging himself further on her.

828. God Himself, that Great Eagle who led and sustained the children of Israel during their forty years of

wilderness life (Deut. 32:10-12), will bear this company of women—Christian women—on the wings of "THE Great Eagle" (not *a great eagle*," as the A. V. translates) off "into the wilderness" where they will be protected and fed until the general rapture of the saints will occur for their rescue (14:14-16). Where that "wilderness" is, we will not attempt to say. What some of these things mean we shall not know until the time comes. We are inclined to the view that the man child of the Woman are the 144,000, a sealed, special Body-guard of the Lord, —see Rev. 7:4 and 14:1. We use the expression "bodyguard," incorrectly, however,—for the Lord needs no guard,—merely in the sense of attendants, 14:4.

LESSON 100.

A BIRTHRIGHT OR A MESS OF POTTAGE?

829. That false teaching derived from the Talmudic "Ten Curses of Eve," (see par. 106), that God is punishing women, at certain times of anguish, for the sin of Eve, is a wicked and cruel superstition which has no support in Scripture and is unworthy of our intelligence. Gen. 3:16 furnishes a cloak for masculine selfish and hypocritical sensuality within the marriage relation, as perverted and read, "*Thy desire shall be to thy husband.*" The teaching is, moreover, a travesty on Divine Justice, for are not men as much the offspring of Eve as women? The punishment does not fall upon *sin,* but upon *sex;* and God Himself is alone responsible for the sex of an individual.

830. Furthermore, the teaching that woman must perpetually "keep silence" in the Church, be obedient to her husband, and never presume to teach or preach, because Eve sinned, blights the doctrine of the atonement, and robs Christ of glory, in that His death atoned for all sin, including Eve's of course. It is entirely contrary to the spirit of Protestantism. Luther says: "It is a great error to seek ourselves to satisfy God's justice for our sins, for God ever pardons them freely by an inestimable grace."

831. And yet, amazing as it seems, Luther, as well as others, seems never to have grasped the idea of "free grace" for women. It is recorded of him that he said: "If a woman becomes weary and at last dead from bearing, that matters not. Let her only die from bearing; she is there to do it." Luther made much of "liberty of

358

358

conscience," yet as regards women he said: "She must neither begin nor complete anything without man: where he is, there she must be, and bend before him as before a master, whom she shall fear and to whom she shall be subject and obedient." He left no place for "liberty of conscience" for women.

832.   Luther is not an exception to the general run of Bible expositors. He may be a little more vivid in his utterances than some others.   Fortunately for women, when they have heard "free grace" heralded by ministers, they have taken it to themselves.   And contrary to the supposed teaching of St. Paul, women have of late years been encouraged to take part in public meetings in the churches, since it was discovered that the meetings were dull without their participation.   But what right has the Church to endorse a line of doctrine which by its own practices it sets at defiance?   Is it not time for the Church to either change its practice or expunge these teachings from its commentaries, making them consistent one with the other?   The duty is laid specially upon women to bring about this reconciliation between their own practice, in taking part in public meetings, and the popularly *supposed* teachings of the Bible.

833.   But if we banish from our belief and from our teaching, that God has laid a blighting hand upon the entire sex to which Eve belonged, because of Eve's sin, then what will become of the teaching that the promise that the seed of the woman shall bruise the Serpent's head. belongs to all women?   The difference is here: The sad prophecy of Gen. 3:16 has been abundantly fulfilled in the *physically inherited* sorrow and suffering of women. The glorious prophecy of Gen. 3:15 will be abundantly fulfilled also, *not* by a physical inheritance at all, but by a voluntary *choice*.

834.   Prophecy is not fate.   No woman is fated for the glorious destiny of fulfilling this prophecy, that the seed of the woman will bruise the serpent's head.   This will not come to me, in spite of myself,—so that I can glory in what is coming, whatever I do.   We are merely told that *some women* will grasp this prize of a high calling in Christ Jesus; and if I do not take my place with such, my humiliation, and my eventual punishment will be the greater, because the prize was set before me, and I despised it.

835.   As we have said before, in all the Bible no sin is held up to human contempt more than Esau's. He had a birthright in prospect, and a father's prophetical blessing to follow that birthright.   But these were things for the future, and might be long delayed in coming, while there was on him the urgent necessity of physical appetite. He might have stood in the line of ancestry through which Christ came into the world: but Christ was not coming for a long time,—did not, in fact, come for about seventeen hundred years. He sold his birthright for a mess of pottage.

836.   The New Testament pronounces him a *"profane person.. who for one morsel of meat sold his birthright,"* and adds, *"Ye know how that afterwards, when he would have inherited the blessing, he was rejected"*. (Heb. 12: 16:17).   His father's blessing on him as inheritor of the birthright, would have added much to his temporal advantage; but having sold that birthright, he could not inherit that blessing.   The deed had been done long before. There was no place left for a change.   He got a mess of pottage but he lost a double portion of his father's estate, and the place of honour in the family.   Isaac would not transfer the birthright-blessing he had uttered on Jacob back to Esau.   He had perceived, as we think, that it was only the *temporal* advantages that Esau was after.

837.   No greater contrast could be drawn than that between the case of Esau, and the case of Moses, of whom this same author of the Epistle to the Hebrews writes: *"By faith Moses, when he was come to years, refused to be called the son of Pharaoh's daughter. . . Esteeming the reproach of Christ greater riches than the treasures of Egypt,"* which were all laid at his feet for self-indulgence (Heb. 11:24-26).   Think of it!   This fine Moses, learned in all the wisdom of the Egyptians; son of the daughter of the king!   He turns away from it all, and joins himself *to slaves of the Egyptians!*   What a fanatic! Looking for a Christ, and sacrificing all the world for that Christ, fifteen hundred years before Christ ever came!

838.   And what will the women of our day do?   Will they say: "The prospect is too remote to be attractive to me. If I could see that by much effort, and by practising a great deal of self-denial, anything could be accomplished worth while, *in my day*, the case would be different. But

the little that I can do to hasten the evangelization of the world, and the coming of Christ will make no difference. I do not care to teach, or preach, or pray in public. I do not wish to be among those who are all the time proclaiming that Christ is coming again, and He never comes. They are a laughing-stock. I cannot join them." Such do not *"esteem the reproach of Christ greater riches than the treasures of Egypt."*

839. To which body will we belong? That is the question for each woman of us to answer to herself. This is not a matter concerning which indecision is of any avail. A great promise and prophecy—the very greatest in all the Bible—lies before us women. We cannot escape; we must either choose the best that could be, from the highest standpoint, or by failing to choose prove ourselves Esaus. God has given the challenge to our faith. Shall we despise our birthright? God forbid!

Katharine C. Bushnell

361

INDEX OF SCRIPTURE TEXTS

(Quoted, discussed, or referred to in the Lessons).

These texts embody a message from God to women. It would be well to read the principal ones over and over, together with the remarks on them in the indicated paragraphs of the Lessons.

NOTE: The letter f directs the attention farther on than the paragraph indicated; ff directs the attention on to a considerable distance. The letter n signifies that the passage will be found in a footnote; Adn, that the passage cited will be found in an Additional Note at the end of the Lesson.

THE OLD TESTAMENT.

INDEX OF SCRIPTURE TEXTS (Continued)

366

INDEX OF SCRIPTURE TEXTS (Concluded)

A DICTIONARY-INDEX OF BIBLE LESSONS.

SERIES 1.

We women have had so few opportunities to become acquainted with the theological world, that it has seemed well to add a few explanatory notes to our Index, making it, rather, a dictionary-index.

Paragraph

Abigail, wife of Nabal, then of David, 150.

Abimelech, 56, 59, 530, 542, 546, 617.

Abraham, seeks a wife for Isaac, 57, 464; commanded to obey Sarah, 110, 150, 301; name changed from Abram to Abraham, 277, respect a n d obedience mutual with him and Sarah, 301; married his half-sister, 474; of idolatrous parentage, 56, 521; 557; preparation for fatherhood, 521ff; has a child by Hagar, 539; sends Hagar and child away, 544.

"Acamoth," 253f.

Achsah, her great possessions, 613f.

"Acts of Pilate" cited 503.

Adam, perhaps originally bisexual, 23 f, 39 f; his gradual decline, 31 f, 35, 168 ff; his two duties, 36; fails to "keep" the garden, 37; a "help" for him, 34; his bad choice, 68ff, 90 ff; his treatment of Eve, 377; caused the Fall, 85, 90 ff; the O. T. and Paul on his conduct, 90ff; cast out of the garden, 95.

Addis, William E., born 1844 at Edinburgh, Prof. O. T. criticism at Manchester College, Oxford, 107.

"Adelphos," meaning of the Greek word, 62, 470.

Adultery, punished by death; 572; woman taken in, 675ff.

Afghanistan, capture of brides in, 428; symbolic capture in, 432.

Paragraph

African tribes, heads of, not exogamous, 440; symbolic capture of brides in, 427.

Agassiz, Prof. Louis, b. in Switzerland, 1807—d. 187; Prof. Zoology and Geology at Harvard University, U. S. A., 40.

Agnation described, 491.

Akkadia, Akked, see Sumer.

Alexander the Great, a celebrated Macedonian conqueror, born at Pella, B. C., 356, died in Babylon, 323 B. C., 505.

Alexander of Ephesus, 324.

Alford, Henry, Dean of Canterbury, poet and divine; b. London 1910; .d 1871; published a n excellent edition of the Greek N. T., with comments: wrote commentaries on books of O. and N. T.; author of many works, 75adn, 103, 105, 107, 195, 235, 238, 244, 285, 330, 639, 711, 755, 761f.

Amarna, Tell el, Tablets of, 448.

Ambrose, a Latin Ch. Father, b. about 340 A. D. in Gaul, d. 397, A. D., 144adn, 685.

American Indians, capture of brides among, 428; symbolic capture, 427; female kinship among, 473

Amram marries his aunt,—its import, 474.

Amraphel,—see Hammurabi.

Androgynous, 24, 41; i t s meaning, 24adn.

Andronicus and **Junia,** 642.

"Angels," of I Cor. 11:10, 237, 248, 253ff.

A DICTIONARY-INDEX OF BIBLE LESSONS.
(Continued).

Paragraph

Childless wife under Hammurabi's Code, 537.

Children of the devil, 73, 815.

China, Women of; foot-binding, 481; taught to procure concubines, 535n.

"Chora, choreo," their meaning, 699f.

Christ. See Jesus Christ.

Christians, early, refused to nent Ch. father, Greek, b. Antioch, Syria, A. D. 350 —d. 407 A. D. 94, 196, 241, 328, 642.

Church, silences women as it becomes paganized, 790.

Chrysostom, John, a promi-

Church, at Rome, in Paul's prison, 312; martyred, 314ff, 709.

"Church," a term which applies also to Israel, 780.

Circassian wedding described, 426.

Circumcision, its meaning, 531; entrance door for males into covenant, 532; not required of females, 531ff.

Clarke, Rev. Adam, LL. D., eminent Methodist minister and scholar, b. in Ireland—d. 1832; particularly distinguished as a Bible Commentator, 4n, 108, 188n, 234, 621, 713.

Clement of Alexandria, eminent ch. father, b. at Athens, A. D. 150 (?)—d. 220 (about). 251, 254, 257, 261.

Clement of Rome, bishop of Rome from A. D. 67. An Apostolic Father; some hold that Paul mentions him in Phil. 4:3, 144adn. 322.

Code of Hammurabi, See Hammurabi.

Collective nouns, why feminine, 64.

Paragraph

Coming, Second, of Christ, 50, 824.

Compromise, Ecclesiastical, under Constantine, 790.

Conception, Virginal, 506; Mary's testimony to, 747.

"Conception," of Gen. 3:16, a mistranslation, 120f.

Consonants, their value in Hebrew, 9ff, 120.

Constantine, the first professed Christian Emperor of Rome, b. 272 A. D.—d. 790.

Continence, Sophistical "gift of," for men, 702ff.

Conybeare, Rev. W. J., b. 1815—d. 1857. Principal of the Collegiate Institute, Liverpool, England, Joint author with Canon Howson of a valuable Life of St. Paul, 244, 312f, 328, 366.

Coptic Version, see Versions.

Corinth, doubtful teachings about Christian women of, 226ff; the real situation there, 192ff, 204, 266; very wicked city, 709.

Council of Laodicea, 244, 673.

Coverdale, Miles, English bishop; b. 1487; translated the Bible into English, published 1535; also edited the Cranmer, or "Great Bible," 143.

Cranmer, Thomas, whose name is given to the above-mentioned Bible, b. 1489: Archbishop of Canterfor his Protestant faith in 1556. 143.

Cross, Seven Words of, as tes-

Crucifixion, woman's testimony to events of, 749ff.

Cruden, Alexander, M. A., b. 1701 in Aberdeen, Scotland; author of Cruden's Concordance, 234.

Cruelty practiced to maintain male kinship, 483, 484, 489.

372

Paragraph

Crusades, The, 718.

"Curse" of Woman, its cruelty and source, 98ff, rabbinical, not Scriptural, 105f, 113, 723, 829.

Curulves explained, 676.

"Cush" same as Ethiopia, 468.

"Cutting instruments" made by Tubal-Cain, 55, 156, 439, 446.

Darwin, Charles, F. R. S., an eminent English naturalist and geologist, b. in Shrewsbury 1809—d. 1882; author of many books. From his name is derived the other title for evolution. — "Darwinism," but this theory is much more radical and extensive than were his teachings, 24adn, 55, 421.

"Daughter," sometimes used in Hebrew for town or city, 64, 468.

"Daughters of Joseph," 607ff.

"Daughters of men," 158ff.

Daughter of Caleb, her wealth, 613f.

Daughters of Zelophehad, 609f.

Dawson, Sir John William, LL. D., distinguished geologist and extensive writer; b. 1820 in Nova Scotia,—d. 1899; educated at Edinburgh, principal McGill University, Montreal, Canada, 158ff, 445n.

Days of Mingling. See "Mingling."

Deaconesses, 365f.

"Death" and **"Life,"** first use of terms spiritual, 97.

Deborah, 149, 199, 645ff, 773.

Deccan, capture of bride in, 428; symbolic capture, 432.

Deissmann, Adolph, Prof. N. T. Exegesis, University of Berlin, 5.

Paragraph

Delitzsch, Franz; b. 1813—d. 1890; Prof. Theology at Leipzig,—see Keil, 83, 108, 645.

"Desire," (Gen. 3:16),—a corrupt rendering, 102ff; correct sense demonstrated, 124-145.

Devil, children of the, 73, 815.

Dillmann, August, D. D., Prof. of Theology, Berlin, 108.

Dinah, a female judge, 61, 61n.

Dixon, Rev. A. C., D. D., an eminent American Baptist minister; b. N. Carolina 1854; pastor Metropolitan (Spurgeon's) Tabernacle, London, later, pastor of Univ. Bapt. Ch., Baltimore, Md. 56.

Dobschütz, Ernest Von, Prof. at Halle in N. T. Exegises; b. 1870, 226f, 266.

Driver, S. R., D. D., Regius Prof. Hebrew at Oxford; member of the O. T. Revision Company; joint editor with B r o w n and Briggs. See · F r a n c i s Brown. 108.

Duchess of Suffolk, declared no kin to her child, 63, 490.

"Duty of m a r r i a g e," — its meaning perverted, 603ff, 710.

Ecclesiasticus. See Ben Sira.

Edersheim, Rev. Alfred, D. D., lecturer on the Septuagint at Oxford; b. in Vienna, 1825—d. 1889; of Jewish extraction, converted in adult life; principal work, a life of Christ, 243, 335.

Edward VI, King of England. 1547-1553, 63, 490.
works. 53, 435.
tified by women, 750.

Egypt, Female kinship in, 62, 449, 615.

Eleazer, (see Rabbi), 202.

Elect of God, will be avenged, 404.

Paragraph

Eli, sons of, 654, 666ff.

Elisabeth, reason of her barrenness, 527.

Ellicott, Charles John, b. 1820, bishop of Gloucester and Bristol; chairman of Revision Company for N. T.; author of several commentaries; editor of Bible Commentaries bearing his name, 38, 237, 339, 365.

Endogamy described, 424ff.

Ephesus. Enmity against Christians in, 324.

Epiphanius, bishop of Constantia, Cyprus, 144adn.

"Episemos," how interpreted, 642.

Esau, 70, 411, 835f.

Eve, repents, 68ff; believes in coming Christ, 77ff; her traducers, 82ff; other references to her, 30, 34f, 37, 39ff, 90ff; no evidence of expulsion from the Garden, 95ff; God's warning to her, 124ff, 164; 489; her immaturity when she ate the forbidden fruit, 326, 338; first speaks the name "Jehovah," 79, 81; first woman to reverse God's marriage law, 123. her "turning," 124ff, 797; import of her name, 464; date of her day, 519; women not subordinate from her time, 456, 779; not subordinated by God to Adam, 418; matriarchate dates from her time, 456; first to discover kinship, 477; men her offspring too, 829; her sin atoned for, 241, 732ff, 830; women not fated to inherit her promise, 833f.

Evolution,—its theory of progress degrading to women, 422; contrasted with teaching of the Bible, 442ff; rejects early chapters of Genesis, 441.

Exogamy, described and defined by McLennan, 429, 430; his theory of its origin not accepted, 430; existence among many peoples, 431f; preceded by capture, 434; related to scarcity of women, 436; comments on by McLennan and Robertson Smith, and theory of origin by Plutarch, Tylor, Morgan, 435; its origin in polygyny, 436, 440, 445.

Farrar, Frederick William, Archdeacon, Dean of Canterbury; b. in Bombay 1831, d. 1903; voluminous writer, 86, 322, 374.

Faussett, A. R., A. M., b. 1821, in Ireland. See David Brown.

Female kinship, established by God's marriage law, 55; 156f, not derived from polyandry, 422; dates from creation, 439; advantages to human family, 45, 444; a primal Divine social law, 473; among Semities, 474, 474adn; protects woman's dignity, 473; sustained by birth of Christ, 491, 511; opposed by Satan, 497. See also Matriarchate.

"Final Authority," remarks on, 368 f.

Fissiparous reproduction, 40.

Flood, the, 465.

"Folk-lore," Genesis is not, 22.

Foreign women in Israel, 532.

"Formed" does not mean "created," 30, 338.

Frazer, James George; Folklore writer; b. 1854 in Glasgow; author several

French, early symbolic capture of bride among, 432.

Fronmüller quoted, 111.

Fuller, Nicholas, eminent Orientalist b. in England, 1557-d. 1622, 128.

Gabriel's appearance to Virgin Mary, 747.

Galilee, women of; names of some, 742; not self-interested disciples, 744;

A DICTIONARY-INDEX OF BIBLE LESSONS.
(Continued).

A DICTIONARY-INDEX OF BIBLE LESSONS.
(Continued)

A DICTIONARY-INDEX OF BIBLE LESSONS.
(Continued)

Irenaeus, a Greek ch. father, bishop of Lyons, France; b. about 130 A. D., pupil of Polycarp who knew St. John; his book on heresies highly valued, 88, 144adn, 252f, 256. 258ff.

Irish, ancient, symbolic capure among, 432.

Islands of Pacific, symbolic capture of brides in, 432.

Isaac's marriage, — traces of female k i n s h i p in arrangements for, 464, 553ff; idolatry prevents going to bride's family, 557; not consulted in choice of his wife, 556; takes Rebekah to his mother's tent, 560.

Jacob, his beena marriage, 462, 463.

Jael, 645, 649 ff.

Jair's inheritance, 611 f.

Jamieson, Robert, D. D., joint author with A. R. Faussett and David Brown of c o m m e n t a r i e s on the Bible, 148, 235.

Japhet, his home, 467.

"Jehovah," the name origimates with Eve, 77ff.

Jerome, a l e a r n e d Latin Father, b. in Dalmatia about 335; died at Bethlehem 420, A. D. A wealthy Roman l a d y and her daughter, Paula and Eustochia, went with him, and supported him out of their m e a n s while he translated the Scriptures into Latin. They were most impatient to have this done, for their own edification. He dedicated several of the books of O. T. to them, and in the Preface declared, "You are competent judges, in controversies as to texts, upon the original Hebrew; compare it with my translation, and see if I have risked a single word." His version is called the

Paragraph

Latin Vulgate, 135, 144 adn,— See also **Versions.**

Jerusalem taken by flying men, 718.

Jesus Christ: His virgin birth, 512ff; charter of rights of female kinship, 510 f; most certain personage of human history, 501 ff; His genealogy, 498; silence under t r i a l explained, 399 f; His demands higher than Moses', 588; causes women to speak in public, 723; ordination of a woman, 727; His atonement dishonoured, 732ff.

Joanna, 742.

Joseph the Blind, a rabbi who flourished about 400 A. B. A Targum is attributed to him, See Targum.

Joseph's s o n s adopted by Jacob, its meaning, 464; his "Daughters run over the wall," 607 ff.

Josephus, most celebrated of Jewish historians; b. at Jerusalem 37 A. D., governor of the two Galilees; active in the Jewish war, time of destruction of Jerusalem, A. D. 70; (gives striking historical testimony to the life of Jesus on earth,) 313, 503, 760.

Joshua, jealous for **Moses,** 212 f.

Joshua, Rabbi, his "rib" fable, 42 f.

"Jot" and **"tittle"** described, 4.

Judaizers, c e r t a i n Jewish teachers, professed Christians, who were bent upon h o l d i n g the early Christians to the observance of the Oral Law, or traditions of the Jews, and to a partial observance of the Mosaic Ritual. They appear first in Acts chs. 11 and 13. St. Paul was throughout his ministry i n conflict with them. T h e y persisted

Paragraph

long after Paul's day in the sects of the Ebionites and Nazarenes 193 f, 201, 203 f, 206 f, 212 f; 346, 352, 362.

Justice the basic principle of morality, 690.

Kaffirs, exogamy among, 431.

Kalisch, Marcus; b. in Pomerania 1828—d. 1885; English Biblical critic; tutor to the Rothschild family; his great work an uncompleted commentary on the Pentateuch, 153, 347.

Kames, Lord, Henry Home, a Scottish judge b. 1724—d. 1888, describes a Welsh wedding, 426.

Keil, Johann Karl F.; b. 1807 —d. 1 8 8 8; a Lutheran theologian; joint author with Franz Delitzsch of a c o m m e n t a r y, 108,—See Delitzsch.

"Kephale," head, its usage in Greek N. T. 282 ff.

Keturah, a second wife, not concubine, 548.

Khonds of Orissa, exogamy among, 431.

King, L. W., of British Museum; Prof. University of London; b. London, 1869, 457.

Kinship, Eve discovers it, 477; kinship always recognised by women, 475 ff; known to men only through women, 475 ff; female kinship in Arabia, 460 ff; female kinship God's ordinance, 445; transition to male kinship, 483ff, wh. injured Christ's genealogical record, 493 ff, 501.

Kling, Friedrich Christian, D. D., b, 1800; Prof. Theology at Marburg, then at Bonn; later, Dean of Marbach; wrote commentary on the Corinthian Epistles, 234.

"Kosmios," comment on its rendering, 644.

Knobel, Karl August. Hebrew scholar and Bible commentator b. 1807—d. 1863; Prof. Theology at Breslau, 108.

Lamech, began c a p t u r e of brides and polygamy, 55, 432, 438, 445.

Lange, John Peter, D. D. Prof. Theology at Bonn; b. 1802 in Prussia; editor and part author of a valuable series (24 large volumes) of commentaries on all the books of the Bible and the Apocrypha. "Dr. Lange is undoubtedly one of the ablest and purest divines that Germany ever produced," 36, 82, 158 n, 377, 400, 545, 576, 653, 659.

Language, the Greek, 17. See Hebrew language also.

Laodicean Church Council forbids ordination of women, 244; and approach to altar, 673.

Latin, Old Latin; Vulgate. See Versions.

Law, not an elevating, but restraining power, 565 ff Mosaic law not ideal, 562 ff; Oral of Jews,—see Talmud.

Law, William, b. 1686—d. 1761; educated at Cambridge; ordained ch. England clergyman; forfeited his position by refusing to take oath of allegiance to George I. Unsurpassed as an accomplished writer, his works made a profound impression; their influence remains to the present time, 32 f, 34, 35, 94, 168f, 171, 378, 384f.

"Laying on of hands" by Christ, 727, 795.

"Leaven," its symbolic meaning, 729 ff.

Lecky, W. E. H., a philosopher and writer, b. 1838 in Ireland—d. 1903, wrote valuable books. "History of Rationalism" and "History of European Morals," 317, 319 ff.

Paragraph

Levirate marriage: Described in Deut. 25:5; a custom peculiar to the Hebrews, —not polyandry, 487.

Lewis, Tayler, L. L. D., Prof. Greek Union College, Schenectady, New York; b. 1802—d. 1877; author many critical and theological works of high value, 82, 115, 128.

Lexicon, Gesenius' Hebrew. See Gesenius, 34; Brown, Briggs and Driver's. See Brown, 121; Schleusner's Greek-Latin to O. and N. T. See Schleusner, 201, 293.

Lias, Rev. J. J. Prof., St. David's College, Lampeter, Wales, 236.

Lidda, daughter of Sumerian king, 457.

Lightfoot, John, D. D., Master Catherine Hall, Cambridge, b. 1602—d. 1675; an excellent Hebrew scholar; in Rabbinical knowledge he has had few equals among Christians; author of extensive comments on N. T., 235, 237, 240, 243.

Lightfoot, J. B., bishop of Durham; b. 1828—d. 1889; wrote many valuable commentaries; Member Revision Company for N. T., 364.

Limboos, female kinship among, 473.

Lincoln, Abraham, President U. S. A., b. 1809—assassinated 1865. 503; quoted, 658.

Lordship of male over female, satanic in origin, 167.

Lowth, Robert. English bishop, b. 1710—d. 1787, a highly valued Biblical scholar,— see Patrick, 108.

Lubbock.—See Avebury.

Luther, Martin, great leader of the Protestant Reformation, b. 1483—d. 1546. His greatest literary work, a translation of the Bible.

Paragraph

His writings very extensive, 345, 619, 830f.

"Lying in wait," marginal reading of Gen. 3:15 accounted for, 116 ff.

Lycians, Mother - kinship among, 62, 472.

Macalister, Stewart, a noted archaeologist; findings at Gezer, 615.

Maine, Sir Henry, L. L. D., b. 1822—d. 1888. Prof. civil law, Cambridge; then Prof. jurisprudence, Oxford; next Master Trinity Hall, Oxford, 492.

Male kinship due to love of power, 555; cannot be maintained, but on woman's knowledge, 480 f.

Malignity, special, in persecution and martyrdom of women, 777.

Mammalia, parthenogenesis in, 509.

"Man child," the, of Rev. chap. 12, 311, 319 f.

Manipulation of Hebrew consonants unlawful, 9 ff.

Maoris of New Zealand, symbolic capture of bride among, 432.

Margoliouth, D. S., Prof. Arabic, Oxford, b. 1858, 139, 151, 654, 664 f.

Mark, his mother, 773.

Marriage, God's law of, and its benefits, 44 ff; the relation mutual 111, 302, 714; ceremony not prescribed in Bible, 590; beena and sadica marriage the same. 416, 417, 462; ba'al marriage, 416; war for marriage begun by Lamech, 432.

Martyrdom of women,—316 f, 321 ff.

Mary: Magdalene, 51, 74, 76, 81, 742 f, 749, 751, 754 ff, 761 ff, etc.; Mother of Jesus, 74, 76, 743, etc.; See Virgin Mary. Mother of James and Joses. 742ff, 749, 751, 754ff, 751ff.

A DICTIONARY-INDEX OF BIBLE LESSONS.
(Continued)

Paragraph

Massoretic text of O. T., 28.

Matriarch, the term an exaggeration, 53, 421, 458.

Matriarchate, matriarchy, 53ff, 194; described, 419f; dates from Eve, 456; in all regions settled by sons of Noah, 469; in Europe, 469; in the Bible, 553 ff; in See also Female Kinship.

Matthew's Bible. In 1537 an English Bible appeared, dedicated to the King, the author's name being given as Thomas Matthew, but no scholar by that name could be found. Undisputed tradition connects the. B i b l e. with John Rogers, the Smithfield martyr (see Rogers), who had reason to conceal his identity, 143 .

Maurice, John F. D., Anglican clergyman and author; Prof. Moral Philosophy at Cambridge, b. 1805 — d. 1882, 265.

McLennan, John Ferguson, Scottish social philosopher, b. Inverness, 1827—d. 1881. Principal works "Primitive Marriage," and "Studies in Ancient History." Cited, or quoted, 53 f, 57, 419, 425, 433 f, 444, 449, 460, 462, 471 f, 475. 483 f, 486 ff, 489, 491, 492.

"Mean" and "Great," mistranslations, 634 f.
Meekness, is not weakness, 396, 378; leads to tribulation, 398 f; no reward for it now, 398; a badge of royalty, 400; due to repose in God as King, 400; requires great balance of character, 402 f; a great revolutionary power, 403.

Mill, John Stuart, eminent English philosopher and economist, b. 1806.] Every woman should be well acquainted with his book, "The subjection of Women," 250, 307.

"Mingling, the days of." 86 ff, 118, 151, 154, 158.

Milton quoted 360.

Paragraph

Miriam, 153, 199, 280, 347, 773, 780.

Mishna,—see Talmud.

Mistranslations because o f sex-bias, 364, 367 ff, 616 ff.

Mistreatment of Roman female prisoners, 325.

Mitchell, H. G., Prof. of Hebrew and O. T. Exegesis, Tufts College; formerly at Boston University, b. 1846; author of many books; of late, rationalistic critic, 137.

Mizraim, 468.

Mongolians, symbolic capture of bride among, 432.

Monogamy, God's o r i g i n a l creation, 439; Bachofen's theory concerning, untenable, 420; the primitive form of marriage, 422.

Morgan, Rev. G. Campbell; Congregationalist minister; b. in England 1863, 20.

Mosaic laws not ideal 562 ff; about women, 563, 572 ff; suited to people emerging from slavery, 571 f.

Moses wrote the Pentateuch, 29; prophesied Pentecost, 213; veiled before the peopeople, 229; a p p o i n t s "heads" 280 f; his meekness, 400.

Mother, not a parent in British law, 490; of Samson, her barrenness, 526 f; of Mark, her house the first church, 773; of Zebedee's children—Salome, 742, 761.

Mother-kinship,. s e e Matriarchy and Female Kinship.

Moulton, J. H., M. A. D. Litt.,. Prof. Hellenistic Greek, Victoria University, Manchester, Eng. Author of valuable works on N. T. Greek; now deceased. 274, 374.

A DICTIONARY-INDEX OF BIBLE LESSONS.
(Continued)

Paragraph

Murray, Rev. Andrew, son of a Scotch minister who went to South Africa, and married. a. woman of Huguenot extraction. Andrew was the second son of a very large family, who have had an immense influence for good in that part of the world, and most gifted of them all; has written many religious books; d. 1917; quoted 380 f, 387.

Mutilation of Scripture because of sex bias, 674.

Mutterrecht, see Matriarchate.

Myer on the early dignity of Egyptian women, 453.

Nahor marries his niece, 474. Asia Minor, 419 ff, 459.

Nephilim, 158, 162.

Nero, Rome's most wicked and cruel Emperor, b. 37-d. 68 A. D., by his own hand, 310ff, 322ff, 777.

Neronian persecutions, 314ff, 321ff, 338, 790.

Neumann, Prof. Karl J., b. 1857, Prof., Ancient History at Strassburg, 325.

Nicon, a monk who preached in Armenia; d. about 998, A. D., 685.

Nineveh, interesting discoveries at, 448.

Noah, 448, 466.

Nosh-im, "exactors," rendered **na-shim,** "women," 621.

Object, of these Lessons, 1.

Old Latin Version. See Ver-

Old Testament text, 5ff. See Hebrew l a n g u a g e, and text.

'Onah,"—its meaning, 604.

Onkelos, a native of Babylon, contemporary with Gamaliel (Acts 5:34), author of the most highly esteemed of the Targum (see Tar-

Paragraph

gum), also c a l l e d the Chaldee Paraphrase, 134, 139.

Option affects t r a n s l a t i o n, 620ff.

Oral Law,— see Talmud, 201, 206, 208, 215, 243, 317.

Orestes, 491, 510.

Origen, a remarkable, learned, eloquent Ch. Father, son of the martyr Leonides of Alexandria, b. 186—d. 253 A. D., at Tyre. Lived after 231 at Caesarea, Palestine; most extensive work, his "Hexapla," (See par. 132), 16, 144adn, 196, 251, 257f, 261.

Orr, Prof. James, S c o t t i s h theologian, Prof. Apologetics and Theology, Glasgow College, b. 1844—d. 1913, 512ff, 662.

Pandora Myth, 85, 118.

Pagnino (Latin Pagninus), b. Italy 1470; Oriental Scholar; Dominican monk at Lyons, France; produced a Latin version of the Bible in 1528; a Hebrew-Latin Dictionary in 1529, 143f, 145.

Paraphrase, Chaldee, — See Onkelos.

Parent, Mother not a parent in British law, 490.

Patrick, Simon, bishop of Ely; b. 1626—d. 1707; wrote a paraphrase of Bible; several devotional w o r k s; began a commentary on O. T., which was finished by Lowth (see Lowth), to which Dr. Whitby's comments on the N. T. were added, and Arnald's on the Apocrypha, 108, 702.

Paul, the Apostle; at first Saul the persecutor. 189-250, 262,-271, 284, 291, 296ff, 304, 306-316, 320-362, 364-371, 417, 564f, 641, 708, 713, 721f, 723, 730f, 774, 777, 785, 791, 825, 832.

Paragraph

Payne-Smith, Robert; b. 1818—d. 1895, Regius Prof. Divinity of Oxford, Canon until Dean of Canterbury; member of O. T. Revision Company; his **greatest** work a very large Syriac Lexicon; author of Genesis in Ellicott's Commentaries (see Ellicott), 14, 38, 79, 82, 172f, 372, 500, 612, 614, 730, 782ff, 807.

Pelagia,—see St. Pelagia.

Pentecost, attendance of women at provided for, 789.

"Pericope de Adultera," treated of, 674ff.

Perversions of Scriptures by Gnostics,—see Gnostics.

Perils of beautiful maidens, 485.

Persis, a Christian woman of Rome, 297.

Peters, John P., D. D. American Episcopal clergyman; b. 1852; Babylonian explorer and Prof. Hebrew Univ. Pennsylvania, 57.

Peshitto, see Syriac Version.

Petrie, Wm. Matthew Flinders, D. C. L., English Egyptologist, b. 1853; founded British School of Archaeology in Egypt; Edwards Prof. Egyptology, University College, London; has made notable discoveries by his researches and excavations, 58-61.

Pharaoh, 59, 530n, 534, 542, 546, 615.

Phebe, deaconess of Ch. at Cenchrea, eastern harbor of Corinth, 364ff.

Philo Judaeus, a Greek philosopher, born at Alexandria, lived between 20 B. C. and 50 A. D. A highly allegorical interpreter of the O. T. Scriptures; believer in Platonism, 144adn.

Phoenicia, female kinship in, 62, 469.

Phrygia, dignity of woman in, 459.

Pierson, Arthur T., D. D., American Presbyterian minister; b. 1839—d. 1911; At different times pastor of Ch. in Philadelphia; of Metropolitan Tabernacle, London, and of Christ Church, London; extensive writer and preacher, 65.

Pliny the Younger, b. 62 A. D. In 103 he became governor of Bithynia, and wrote a famous letter to Trajan, the Emperor, which testified to the good character of Christians who were being persecuted, enquiring what sort of testimony should be received against them, 503.

Plutarch, an eminent Greek philosopher, and the greatest pagan biographer of antiquity, b. about 50 A. D. 320.

Polyandry, not the original social state, 422, 436, 442f, 486.

Polygamy 439; in the O. T., 589ff confused with remarriage of widowers, 595f; Moses could not exterminate it by law, 597.

Polygyny (plurality of wives), led to exogamy 436, 445; and then to male kinship, 443, 486.

Poole, Rev. Matthew, learned English non-conformist minister, b. about 1624,—d. 1679; wrote very valued critical notes and other works on the Bible, 108.

Pope, Alexander, poet, b. in London, 1688—d. 1744, 165.

"Power," — its misinterpretation to the opposite sense in I Cor. 11:10, 217ff, 248, 251, 641.

Prediction, Scriptural, 799.

Prejudice, sex, hinders Lord's second coming, 791.

Pride contrasted with humility, 384.

A DICTIONARY-INDEX OF BIBLE LESSONS.
(Continued)

Primal social law established female kinship, 464, 473.

Priscilla, P a u l's fellow-laborer, 192f, her ability, 195, an "official evangelist and teacher," 196, escapes martyrdom at Rome, 297, 323, 337.

Prisoners, female, under Rome, 325.

Pregnant nature of prophecy explained, 801.

Progeny a blessing or a curse according to quality, 523.

Promises a n d prophecies o f God not fate, 414, 833f.

Prophecy, its nature, 799ff.

Prophesy, w h a t the verb means, 778.

Psalms, two sung by women, 782.

Queen mothers, 62.

Rabbi and Rabbinism. Rabbi means "my teacher" (Matt. 23:8); Rabboni means the same, but is a more honorable title. None of the prophets or doctors of the law received this title until the time of Hillel and Shammai, leaders of the two rival branches of rabbinical teaching, Hillel b. at Babylon 110 B. C., died at the extreme age of 120 Allowing for variations in chronological reckoning, he might with bare possibility have been among the doctors who disputed with the c h i l d Jesus (Luke 2:41-47). Hillel was father to Simeon, with whom some identify Simeon of Luke 2:25. Gamaliel (Acts 5:34) was Simeon's son, and one of seven men only who bore the higher title, Rabban. The highest title among the Babylonian Jews was Rab or Rav. Abba Arika of Sura, highest of all, was known simply as Rab or Rav (see Rav). As he was head of rabbinism at Babylon, so was Rabbi Jehudah the Holy of Palestine. S o m e of these rabbis (or rabbins, as

the word is often written), led holy lives, and their teaching was exalted; others did not, and their teaching was corrupted,—especially as regards women. Rabbi Jehudah the Holy, publisher of the Mishna (see Talmud), was almost deified by his followers. Rabbis quoted or referred to.—8. 16, 18, 24, 42, 146, 151, 202, 208, 291, 300, 335, 346f, 352, 603, 606, 666, 668, 678. 735, and elsewhere.

Rachel, reason of her barren state, 525f.

Ramsay, Sir W. M., Prof. Univ. Aberdeen; b. in Glasgow 1851; widely known f o r researches in history of early Ch. in Asia Minor; extensive writer, especially about St. Paul, his Epistles and journeys, 62, 193f, 205, 220, 239, 315f, 321, 325, 328, 332, 350ff, 362, 458f.

Rationalism. Its inroads 739ff.

Rav, Head of the Babylonian rabbis (see Rabbi), 8.

Rebekah, 147; Not veiled (see also note on "Veil), 263, her barren state, 525; God's anointed, 530, 558ff.

Rebuke, a Christian duty, 386.

"Redeemed" persons in O. T., 57J.

Reproduction, fissiparous, 40.

Restraint in marriage, 576.

Resurrection, women important witnesses to events of, 754ff.

"Rib" (Gen. 2:21),—a mistranslation, 38ff.

Rogers, John; formerly a Catholic priest; later prebendary of St. Paul's, London; burned at the stake for his Protestant faith, at Smithfield 1555; see Matthew, 144.

Roman Church, T h e, — see Church at Rome.

A DICTIONARY-INDEX OF BIBLE LESSONS.
(Continued)

A DICTIONARY-INDEX OF BIBLE LESSONS.
(Continued)

A DICTIONARY-INDEX OF BIBLE LESSONS.
(Continued)

Paragraph

Solon, an illustrious Athenian legislator, b. about 638 B. C.—d. about 558; he was ranked among the Seven Sages of Greece, 471.

Song of Deborah, 645ff, 653.

"Sons," a geographical name sometimes, 467, 469.

"Sons of God," meaning of term in Gen. 6:2, 158ff, not all men are sons of God, 73, 815.

Sophistry about women veiling, 216ff.

'Sophrosune," meaning of it, 344, 640.

Spartans, mother-kinship among, 62, 472; capture of bride among, 427.

Speaker's Commentary, The, on the Bible. In ten vols., by Anglican bishops and clergy and edited by Canon Cook, M. A., 182, 185.

Spencer, Herbert, English philosopher and author on sociology, b. 1829—d. 1903. Denies a primal promiscuity in social life, 55(421; his theory of origin of exogamy, 435; suggests polygyny as cause of scarcity of women, 445; denies existence of polyandry among early Hebrews, 487. The **Targum of Jonathan**

Spirit of infirmity," The, must be expelled, 796f.

Spurrell, Rev. G. J., author of Notes on Genesis," cited, 121.|

Stanley, Rev. Arthur Penryn, Dean of Westminster, b. 1815—d. 1881, extensive writer and commentator; member of the Revision Committee of the R. V., 130, 158, 221, 234, 241, 248, 388, 390f.

Steele, Mrs. Flora Annie, English author, especially on India, b. 1847, gives light on Sarah, 535.

Paragraph

"Subjection," meaning of the Greek word, 292, 354ff; not of God, 450.

Subordination of women, not scriptural, 146ff; how brought about, 424ff; not of God, 450.

Suetonius, an eminent Latin historian, b. about 70 A. D., wrote of Jesus Christ, 503.

Suffolk, Duchess of, decreed no kin to her own son, 63, 490.

Sulpicius Severus lived 363-410 A. D., an Ecclesiastical historian, 315.

Sumer and Akkad, 62, 457.

Sumerian women, dignity of, 62, 455, 457.

Susanna, one of Christ's attendants, 742.

Symbolic capture of bride among various people, 432.

Symmachus, See versions.

Syriac, See Versions.

Tabernacle, Date of the, 657.

Tacitus, a celebrated Roman historian, b. abt. 50, A. D., 314f, 503.

Tallith, described, 240f; forbidden to male Christian worshipers, 241, 246.

Talmud, and Talmudic. The Talmud is the body of Jewish civil and canonical law. It is composed of two parts, the Mishna and the Gemara,—that is, Comments on the Mishna, The comments of the Babylonian Rabbis, added to the Mishna together make the Babylonian Talmud; the Mishna with the comments of Palestinian Rabbis make the Jerusalem Talmud. The latter is a much larger work than the Bible, and The Babylon Talmud is many times larger than the Jerusalem Talmud. The Talmud has more authority than the Bible, to the or-

A DICTIONARY-INDEX OF BIBLE LESSONS.
(Continued)

A DICTIONARY-INDEX OF BIBLE LESSONS.
(Continued)

CPSIA information can be obtained at www.ICGtesting.com
Printed in the USA
LVOW11s1055031015

456815LV00001B/1/P